A LEGACY OF LUXURY

CELEBRATING THE RREC'S DIAMOND JUBILEE

WWW.RREC-SHOWCASE.COM

CHAIRMAN'S WELCOME

Dear Enthusiasts,

With this being the RREC's diamond jubilee year, it would seem the perfect opportunity to reflect on matters past, present and future. It is often said that we should attract more youngsters to the Club because they are supposedly less interested in our cars. This may be so, but the fact is that a Rolls-Royce or Bentley motor car epitomises a way of life, something you grow into rather than have forced upon you. It happened to me – as you'll be able to read herein – and I am sure it happened to a number of you.

The great thing is that, once you're ready for it, you're ready for a great many other things that go with Rolls-Royce or Bentley ownership. Whether that is quality clothing, a unique watch or writing instrument, a beautifully crafted piece for your home, or simply the holiday experience of a lifetime, the pleasure derived from something rare and exceptional is quite unsurpassed and a natural fit for those who appreciate that "the quality will remain long after the price is forgotten" (FH Royce).

So, the Club's Publications Team, in collaboration with publisher St James's House, has endeavoured yet again to deliver precisely that. In the pages that follow, Roy Brooks chronicles his memories of the Club's first Section and Eliot Levin offers an insight into his write-up of our late President Eric Barrass's magnum opus *The Rolls-Royce Armoured Car* – a fitting tribute to 110 years of AX201, the car that transformed Rolls-Royce into a household name for excellence. In addition, David Towers sheds light on the remarkable engineer that was WO Bentley.

The past and the present come together in a comprehensive account of the RREC's 60 years, along with stories about significant cars of yesteryear, such as the Flying Spur (courtesy of Davide Bassoli), and insights into the motor car of the future in the shape of 103EX. Perhaps most surprising of all is John Fasal's contribution, which spans the realms of Indian royalty, cricket and Rolls-Royce.

But then, you don't just acquire a Rolls-Royce or Bentley, you buy into a hitherto undiscovered world of luxury and eccentricity. A world that will unfold before your eyes throughout this book, painstakingly put together by an editorial team that has managed to capture the experience of the marques that we all so admire. Experiences, after all, are like diamonds; they last forever.

Johan Vanden Bergh
Chairman

CONTENTS

THE ENTHUSIAST

A passion for motoring

SIXTY OF THE BEST

A history of the Club's first six decades by Lt Col Eric Barrass, Malcolm Tucker, Philip Hall, Jackie Robotham and Colin Hughes

ON 11 AUGUST 1957, 11 people assembled at Paternoster Farm, Yarnton, near Oxford, the home of Edward Harris. The gathering was the result of an advertisement that Edward had placed in *The Oxford Mail* proposing the formation of a club for the owners of pre-war Rolls-Royce cars.

Geoffrey Frank addressed the meeting and explained its objectives. It was unanimously decided that a club should be formed and that it should be called the Rolls-Royce Enthusiasts' Club (RREC). At this inaugural meeting, the Club's first officers were elected: Chairman, G Frank; Hon Secretary, RAH Woolley; and Hon Treasurer, F Bonham. The Club was born.

THE EARLY YEARS

The first Club event took place on 15 September 1957, incorporating a rally at the Royal Sun Inn, Begbroke, followed by a series of driving tests at Kidlington airfield near Oxford. The 14 cars entered included a 1921 Silver Ghost, three 20hps, three 20/25s and three early Phantoms.

In November of that year, around 80 Club members and friends gathered in the Royal British Legion Hall, Yarnton to see a one-act play by the local dramatic society. The occasion was used to present the first Club prizes and trophies to members. However, things quietened down over the following months and on 1 June 1958 an Extraordinary General Meeting was called at the Old Rectory, Woodeaton, Oxford, where the future viability of the Club was discussed. The EGM elected a new committee, whose officers were: Chairman, Surgeon Captain R Symmons; Hon

Secretary, F Bonham; and Hon Treasurer, Gladys M Harris (sister of Edward Harris). The new committee organised five Club events in 1958, including the first Concours d'Elegance, held at Weston Manor Hotel, Weston-on-the-Green, near Oxford.

During the late 1950s, the subscription was just 10 shillings (50 pence) per annum for full membership and five shillings (25 pence) for associates. In July 1959, the first Blenheim Concours was held, and by the following month, the Club's membership had reached 100.

THE 1960s

In early 1960, *The Bulletin* was established. It was in duplicated foolscap and provided good technical articles and offered items for sale. A note in the early editions read: "Enquiries for spare parts, service sheets, and general information should be addressed to the Assistant Secretary, Nigel H Hughes." At that time, a 1932 Phantom II was offered for £150 and a 1925 Phantom I by Hooper was offered for £130.

The Blenheim Concours in 1960 attracted 40 cars across five classes. The Chairman's Challenge Bowl was won by the best visitor's car, a 1933 Phantom II James Young tourer owned by CG Duce.

More and more technical articles appeared in *The Bulletin*, many written by Nigel Hughes and Ron Haynes. Nigel was an undergraduate at Oxford when the Club was started and, through the Oxford University Motor Drivers' Club, developed an interest in Rolls-Royce cars. Ron Haynes worked for Rolls-Royce at Hythe Road, North London. He was employed as a technical adviser and had

Opposite: Burghley House, the current venue for the Club's Annual Rally

Below: An RREC prize-giving during the Club's inaugural year, 1957

access to depot sheets and general arrangement drawings. He also had a phenomenal knowledge of pre-war cars.

By August 1960, Club membership had extended to Sweden and Denmark. At the AGM in 1960, the officers and members were re-elected en bloc and Eric Barrass joined the committee. The following year's AGM was held in the old tithe barn of Yarnton Manor. The Club accounts showed there was £50 in the current account, with £100 on deposit, and the chairman pointed out that this was not an excessive sum, in view of the Club's commitments for the following year.

At most early rallies, members of the 20 Ghost Club, VSCC Rolls-Royce Section and Bentley Drivers' Club were also invited. In 1960, first contact with the Rolls-Royce Owners Club (RROC) of America were made at a visit by a group of its members to the UK instigated by the 20 Ghost Club, but involving the other clubs. After being driven into London from Heathrow airport, they were taken to visit Stanley Sears' collection in Sussex the following day.

The Club's first annual dinner was held in February 1963 in the Oxford University Air Squadron's Mess. Bill Morton arrived in the 1906 three-cylinder car owned by Adam McGregor Dick, who accompanied him. Bill was the official Rolls-Royce historian of the time and also ran the Apprentices' School, and it was Bill and his team who had rebuilt the three-cylinder car.

In November 1963, *The Bulletin* became a litho production and sported a newly designed car badge. The first published list of members was added as an appendix.

In 1964 and 1967, pageants were held at Goodwood to celebrate 60 years since Rolls

met Royce and 60 years of "Silver Ghost" AX201, respectively. A large rally was held at Blenheim in 1968 when RROC members once again visited the UK. This rally was the first to be open to the trade. A 1935 20/25 Tickford coupé used during the war by Sir Winston Churchill and rebuilt by Rolls-Royce was offered for £500. Among the spares available were cylinder heads for all models at an average price of £200.

THE 1970s

By January 1970, 18 sections were operating. These were: Benelux, Central Southern, East Anglia, East Midlands, Eire, Essex, Europe, France, Gloucestershire, Middlesex, North Eastern, Northern, Oxford, Salisbury area, South Eastern, South Wales, South West and Switzerland.

On 1 May 1970, the annual Club Dinner was held at the Midland Hotel, Manchester, to celebrate the historic first meeting between Rolls and Royce in the same hotel in 1904. At the AGM of that same year, the chairman mentioned that the Club had enrolled 359 new members in the past 12 months. The membership stood at 1,500, of whom 307 were based overseas, in 37 countries. The Club subscription was set at £2.

At the end of May 1970, 47 RREC cars took part in the London to Vichy rally. Those who participated would never forget it: a motorcycle escort of Polices Routiers, including some from the French President's personal bodyguard swept other traffic from the path of the participating cars.

In 1973, the Club staged its legendary Great Alpine Rally. George Birrell and his committee of Andrew Beer, Michael Foster and Christopher Leefe all worked exceptionally hard to bring the event to life. That same year, RJ Gibbs, known as

"Gibby", was appointed Editor of *The Bulletin*, following Derek Randall. Gibby was a professional newspaperman and raised the publication to an even higher standard.

The Club's financial and public liability responsibilities continued to grow and it was decided that it should become a company limited by guarantee, to protect the committee and members. On 1 January 1974, RREC Ltd was registered. A fine company seal was commissioned and presented by Christopher Leefe.

In March 1974, having received microfilms of chassis sales cards for pre-war cars from Rolls-Royce, Gerry Jessop initiated a service to provide prints for members. The Club insurance scheme, run by Andrew Weir, passed to the Fenchurch Group and a much-improved package became available to members. In addition, Tony Donovan, a flamboyant and popular entrepreneur, laid the foundations of the successful Club Shop, which produced a profit of £300 in 1974.

The same year saw the production of the Club's first technical manuals, culled from articles in past issues of *The Bulletin*. A collection of workshop and special tools was also being assembled in answer to cries for help from members. The service was taken up by Philip Fulford and was successfully operated from his home in Surrey for many years. The need for supplying spares was another priority and with the help of the Essex Section, and Charles Tabor in particular, all spares were moved to the latter's home, Sutton Hall, from where a much-improved service was run.

The production of a Club membership list was (and still is) a bone of contention. However, the membership list of 1974, for all its faults, was very well received. It contained details of nearly 2,500

members in 42 countries and listed details of over 4,000 Rolls-Royce and Bentley cars.

Due in large part to the increasing number of historical articles in *The Bulletin* and the publication of some fine Rolls-Royce books, members were becoming more and more interested in the history of the marque, in which their own cars played an integral part. Henry Royce's extraordinary ability to breed dedicated disciples was reflected in ever-rising standards of restoration, maintenance and pride of ownership.

To assist with the ongoing escalation in Club activities, sub-committees covering events, technical matters and publications were set up. The corps of judges was formed for the annual rally and a number of apprentice judges recruited.

At the 1976 AGM, the momentous decision was made that the Club should acquire a building suitable for use as a headquarters. More than 50 locations were investigated and eventually The Hunt House at Paulerspury, near Milton Keynes, was found by Robert Brooks, a committee member and Oxford-based estate agent. It was purchased for £28,000 thanks to a loan from Charles Tabor, without whose generosity the Club would not have acquired the property. The site was in a semi-derelict and vandalised state, and work on its restoration commenced immediately.

The RREC's historic Silver Jubilee tribute to Her Majesty The Queen took place on 7 May 1977. At Her Majesty's invitation, the Club paraded 431 pre-war Rolls-Royce and Bentley cars before The Queen in the quadrangle of Windsor Castle. An unbroken chain of cars led from the castle to Ascot racecourse, where a further 600 post-war Club cars were assembled.

In the following September, the Sir Henry Royce Memorial Foundation (SHRMF) was granted charitable status and the fundraising appeal was officially launched. The turnover of the Club Shop reached £11,000 and plans were afoot to move it to The Hunt House.

At the 1978 AGM, Chairman John Schroder remarked that the subscription level should never be more than the cost of a tankful of petrol. Subscriptions were set at £10 for the UK and £8 for overseas members, and membership had reached 3,700.

THE 1980s

In February 1980, the first technical seminar was held at The Hunt House in the converted stable block. Over the next year more than 300 members attended these seminars. There was also a great upsurge in availability of technical information due to the facilities and records held at The Hunt House.

With the formation of Paulerspury, Swedish and Danish Sections that same year, the Club had 28 established sections, and post-1950 cars constituted 50 per cent of the membership.

Published in July 1981, *The Bulletin* 127 was the last to be produced by Gibby and the honour of life membership was conferred upon him. Peter Baines then took command. The Club's magazine had steadily grown, from its original size of 20 pages to 48 pages and, increasingly, sections were contributing their news.

At the 1983 annual conference, the need for major reconstruction at The Hunt House, to be funded by a direct appeal to members, was well received. The closure in 1983 of the School of Instruction at Hythe Road made many items

Previous pages, clockwise from top left: Tony Donovan (left) presents a retirement clock to Roy Brooks at the 1981 Annual Rally at Yarnton; the 1990 Annual Rally at Castle Ashby; Jack and Eric Sears in the 1905 Light 20 TT replica at the 1976 Isle of Man TT 70th anniversary rally

Opposite: Her Majesty The Queen looks on at the Club's Silver Jubilee parade at Windsor Castle, with Peter Baines (left) and John Schroder

Above: The Club takes to the roads of Windsor in 1977

Above: The Hunt House

Opposite, from top: Club stalwarts Peter Baines; and Philip Hall

Overleaf, from top: The Hunt House's precious and extensive archives; Club cars depart Windsor Castle via the Long Walk in 2002

available for the Club's workshop. These included a cutaway, but neglected, 1947 Silver Wraith engine that was meticulously restored to working order by members of the newly established Surrey Section. Subscriptions for 1983–4 were set at £20 for the UK and £15 for overseas.

In February 1985, the details of the Club's new archive building were published in *The Bulletin*. The concept was imaginative in architectural terms and trebled the space first anticipated, and work on the Eric Barrass Building, as it was to be called, commenced in July. The new tool-hire service also began, set up by Maurice Rixon and run by Tony James, who had computerised the whole operation.

The 1985 annual rally was held on the private estate of Sir Hereward Wake at Courteenhall, near Northampton. The Club Shop took a record £3,200 in one day, with umbrellas the best sellers! To fill a long-standing gap in Club activities in the West Country, a meeting was held in Bristol, out of which the Great Western Section was established to cover Bristol, Bath and the surrounding areas. The membership now exceeded 5,000 and spanned 57 countries.

The Club was positively thriving. Visitors were by now arriving at The Hunt House in increasing numbers, usually unheralded and often from overseas, but looking after and showing them round had become a real challenge. The first

visitors' book was already full and its donor, Stanley Sears, quickly produced a second. Requests for car histories were on the rise, especially from North America, and attendance figures for seminars climbed to over 1,500.

The official opening of the Eric Barrass Building was a huge success. Club members attended in force and the new development was deemed a triumph. Members had worked for days into the early hours, with displays moving in as workmen moved out. The day before the opening, much of the electrical work was still incomplete, but with great dedication the team prevailed.

The AGM was held at The Hunt House and it was agreed that it was the logical venue for all such future meetings. By now, the archives contained over 90,000 Rolls-Royce and Bentley car histories. More than 4,000 copies had already been supplied to owners and researchers all over the world.

The Club's first annual Euro (Continental) Rally, brilliantly organised by Eri Heilijgers, was held in Luxembourg. So successful was the first attempt that a second rally was agreed for 1988, to be held in Strasbourg.

The Bulletin of February 1988 listed no fewer than 126 Club events. The sections, of which there were by now 35 (including 16 overseas) provided, as they still do, the grassroots activities. The 1988 Welsh Weekend was held in April near Cardigan

Bay, and the annual rally was now officially a two-day event. More than 1,000 cars attended the Sunday rally against the magnificent backdrop of Castle Ashby in Northamptonshire.

At the Historical Weekend in October 1988, Alec Harvey-Bailey, the son of RW Harvey-Bailey "By", organised an excellent Spitfire event. Alec's contacts with retired Rolls-Royce staff and his own recollections of experimental cars brought home when he was a schoolboy were the basis of both Historic Weekend talks and publications.

The Club set up a scheme for recovering, through the DVLA, original or contemporary registration numbers for those cars carrying later numbers. Many hundreds of successes have been achieved since, especially on cars re-imported to the UK. In addition, the RREC's car insurance plan offered settlement for total loss at an agreed value. This required a valuation of realistic quality, and a valuer with knowledge and integrity – a role that was undertaken by one of the Club's great stalwarts, Brian Bilton-Sanderson. Brian's integrity was absolute. Indeed, he was so thorough in assessing cars that a number of well-advertised traders would not let him near their cars!

Since the Club's formation, a steady stream of complaints had reached the committee about restorers, repairers and the trade in general, and the subject was debated at the 1989 annual conference. Richard Shaw read a fine paper indicating the correct way of approaching traders, which was so well received that he was asked to run an "agony aunt" service. He agreed and became the Club's ombudsman.

The additional archive storage at The Hunt House was completed in August 1989 and rapidly filled to capacity. Proposals began for further development behind the workshop with a fundraising target of £150,000 to £200,000.

THE 1990s

The RREC's 20th Club Conference was held in March 1990. Delegates discussed a range of subjects including a proposed new building; Club Ombudsman; Club services; leaded petrol; and the production of membership lists. At the AGM the following month, the proposed new building at The Hunt House, which was to be called The CS Rolls Wing, was outlined and accepted wholeheartedly.

The Historical Series published an important book by Donald Bastow, who was for many years a member of Sir Henry Royce's design team at West Wittering. Entitled *Henry Royce, Mechanic* it is one of the most illuminating books ever written on the subject.

Mike Evans of Rolls-Royce Derby generously loaned the RREC, on a long-term basis, the only Myth engine extant – it now stands proudly in The

Hunt House in the Claude Johnson Link. The Club was also presented with a restored 20hp chassis, which has proved to be invaluable at technical seminars ever since. In addition, a large group of Charles Rolls's personal scrapbooks was purchased at auction by Rolls-Royce Motors and generously donated to the Foundation.

By 1990, the membership had topped 5,400 and the Club accounts showed a profit of £11,000. The 1991 Annual Rally attracted well over 1,000 Rolls-Royce and Bentley cars. Later that same year, one of the Club's finest driving events was organised in Norway – a week of perfect weather and the most stunning routes imaginable, alongside the vast, mirror-flat and scenic fjords, with colourful villages on the waterside. And in September, the fourth Euro Rally was based at Reims, France.

The SHRMF had designed a beautiful circular car badge with a navy enamel background, which prompted the production of a matching Club badge as an alternative to the old vertical radiator design. The new badge carried the Bentley logo in addition to the traditional Gothic elegance. As nearly 25 per cent of the Club members owned Bentley cars from Derby and Crewe, it seemed a most appropriate choice.

Subscriptions for July 1991 showed no increase, remaining at £30 for the UK, £25 for overseas and £5 for spouse members.

In early 1992, Philip Hall (later to become Chief Executive of SHRMF), in liaison with Richard Mann (who worked at Rolls-Royce's Hythe Road premises), collected 500 boxes containing 15,000 coachwork drawings: space at The Hunt House was shrinking rapidly. By March, membership had reached 7,600 and the New Members List continued to announce an influx of post-1965 cars.

In June 1992, an event for 20hps was run by the Central Southern and Oxford Sections at the traditional venues of Weston Manor Hotel and Blenheim Palace. It attracted a great turnout, which in turn led the General Secretary to suggest the formation of registers, for members who own particular models. The suggestion was accepted and registers continue to prove popular to this day.

A very successful Historic Weekend was held in November 1992. The subjects covered were the Schneider Trophy, the Experimental Cars (a brilliant presentation by Ian Rimmer), the Red Arrows RAF display team and an excellent dissertation by John Kennedy on the 1913 Alpine Rally. The General Secretary, Eric Barrass, talked at length on the Rolls-Royce armoured cars – a subject dear to his heart.

The opening of the CS Rolls Wing, which, along with the Barrass Building, was masterminded by local Club member Douglas Vaughan, took place on 5 September 1992. The size and splendour of the wing was hugely impressive: the magnificent blue velvet, electrically operated curtains covering the back wall, the cheering when the modern projection units lit the retractable screen and the applause when the recently installed electric hoist raised a bust of Sir Henry Royce into view. The considerable archive area above the lecture hall addressed the Club's problem of a shortage of space, at least for the time being.

The Euro Rally was held in Luxembourg. For the first time, the Continental members outnumbered those from the UK, with Sweden, the Netherlands, Denmark, Belgium, France, Switzerland and Germany all represented.

In 1993, new Chairman Brian Wiggins had plans drawn up and tenders sought for the proposed linking corridor between The Hunt House and the Barrass Building. The cost was £25,000 and in a short time this cloister, dedicated to Claude Johnson, was opened.

Due to the remarkable research carried out by John Kennedy, the Great Alpine Rally in June 1993, organised for both RREC and 20 Ghost Club members, covered much of the original route of 1913. John owns and restored 2260E, the car that Radley drove in the 1913 event, with meticulous detail. The 47 Silver Ghosts that took part all successfully completed the difficult 1,200-mile drive without casualties. The Loibl Pass was opened especially for the rally: 12 hairpins and an unmetalled road rising 900 feet in little more than a mile provided gradients of up to 29 per cent. The event started and finished in Vienna.

The archives at The Hunt House were attracting many researchers. The most ardent and dedicated was John Fasal, whose books on the 20hp and the Edwardian Rolls-Royce (with John Goodman) are both classics. Unless the RREC had acquired and developed The Hunt House complex and taken ownership of materials that otherwise faced destruction, such books could not have been produced.

HRH Prince Michael of Kent paid what was scheduled to be a short visit to The Hunt House and stayed for more than five hours. As President of the Institute of the Motor Industry, the Prince kindly presented the General Secretary with a framed citation from the institute in recognition of over 30 years of service.

Discussions took place with Michael Forrest, whose superb technical articles in *The Bulletin* were much enjoyed, on his idea of preserving originality by means of a Conservation Class for unrestored pre-war cars. This idea was adopted and a pre-Second World Car conservation class was added (and later a post-war one, too) to the concours classes at the Annual Rally at Althorp Park. The rally had 1,300 entries and the Rolls-Royce Company staged a large presence, with many cars and representatives from their dealer network.

In 1994, the SHRMF became the recipient of a magnificent gift from Dr Robin Barnard of a bound set of *The Autocar* magazines, complete with advertisements, running from 1904 to 1970 – an exceptional collection of great intrinsic and historic value. Appropriate glass-fronted mahogany bookcases were commissioned to house them in the Club library, and the resulting cases were so impressive that it was decided to replace the shelving throughout to a similar standard.

In May of that year, the RREC became affiliated to the RAC, which brought many advantages to members and, in September, the Round Britain Rally took place. It raised more than £20,000 for the Save the Children Fund, with the cheque handed over to Princess Anne in person. The rally was immensely successful, moving from town to town each day and attracting more than 800 cars. The subscription remained at £37, still less than the proverbial tankful of petrol.

By 1995, the number of Technical Seminars had reached 160 and almost 3,000 members had taken part. Several owners of pre-war cars indicated that their joining or rejoining of the Club was influenced by the introduction of the registers, and no fewer than 2,000 members had joined their appropriate register.

In September 1995, a well-attended Euro Rally took place in Sweden. That same year, a Blenheim gathering of Silver Shadows attracted 300 gleaming cars and led to the setting up of the RREC's post-1965 register.

In 1996, Philip Hall became the first full-time curator and chief executive of the SHRMF. The events list for that year covered more than 150 varied and imaginative Club events across the world, including a brilliant rally, commemorating the CS Rolls TT Victory Run in 1906, which was organised by the Isle of Man Section. By the end of 1996, membership had reached 8,500.

The 75th anniversary of the 20hp took place in 1997 and the 20hp Register held two wonderful events. The first was a trip to Normandy, on which the local reception was irreproachable, the driving magnificent and the record for the "most children in a 20hp" was established with 19! The second event was held at the Palace Hotel, Buxton, and included a visit to the historic Rolls-Royce factory at Nightingale Road, Derby. The internet was officially embraced by the Club that same year, as it was proudly announced that www.rrec.co.uk would be the portal to untold information.

By the autumn of 1997, it was common knowledge that Vickers had put the Rolls-Royce Motor Car division up for sale. The Club could only wait and hope that a British factory, if not a British-owned company, would take the marque into the future.

At the start of 1998, Rolls-Royce was still "in play" and one of the putative purchasers was a small group of Club members, who asked for official participation by the Club. However, the Management Committee thought it prudent to limit its involvement to an advisory capacity.

The SHRMF managed to acquire the complete post-war archive of James Young of Bromley.

Below: Former Club President Lt Col Eric Barrass

Opposite: The 2008 Annual Rally at Kelmarsh Hall

Overleaf: The Club celebrated The Duke of Edinburgh's 90th birthday in 2011 at Windsor Castle

Design sketches, full-scale drawings, costing sheets and correspondence with Rolls-Royce, their dealers and the customers were included.

Graham Morris, CEO of Rolls-Royce Motor Cars, spoke at the Club's Annual Dinner, reporting that Rolls-Royce's car-manufacturing operations had been bought by Volkswagen and that the deal suited both the Company and its employees. This, of course, was not the end of the story.

In June 1999, the Club hosted the inter-clubs meeting at The Hunt House. This long-established forum allows representatives from the manufacturer and key suppliers, as well as members of Rolls-Royce Clubs worldwide, to discuss their needs, hopes and fears.

Project Director Karl-Heinz Kalbfell and Powertrain Engineer Tim Leverton, whose work on Project Rolls-Royce would result in the creation of the new Phantom, visited The Hunt House to absorb the traditions and aspirations of generations of the many Rolls-Royce designers and engineers who had gone before.

A long-anticipated tour of Jordan took place in September. With 70 cars taking part and the full support of the Jordanian royal family and government, it was rally of a lifetime for those involved. Nights spent in five-star hotels and tents in the deserts, and days of driving on superhighways and sand tracks made this an event of remarkable contrasts.

THE 2000s

The 30th Club Conference, held in 2000, included discussions about the 15hp "Scottish car", the situation at Volkswagen and BMW, the RREC–

SHRMF relationship, the membership list and the Data Protection Act, the Club Shop, the RREC website, the election of Club officers, RREC investments, the make-up of the management committee, records and archives, section rally accounts and the future of the Club.

A long-planned Club event was the attempt to beat the Guinness World Record for "Most cars of the same make on the same road at the same time". On 28 May 2000, having assembled at Chester Racecourse, the Company's 10hp "Little Sue" and "Silver Ghost" AX201 led the cars out onto the public highway, to the applause of the people of Chester. The former record of 232 cars was soundly beaten by a total of 420 Rolls-Royce cars in an unbroken parade drive. That year's Annual Rally moved to Towcester Racecourse, which provided a vast area wholly suitable for the easy display of many cars.

In 2001, chairman Eri Heilijgers and vice-president Brian Bilton-Sanderson travelled to Munich to see the "new car" at the BMW development facility. Officially, neither could say much about the car; however, Eri summed things up well in The Bulletin: "I think that Chief Designer Ian Cameron and his team have created an excellent piece of engineering, of which Sir Henry would have approved."

The epic Malaysia Rally took place in 2002 and was celebrated in a special full-colour supplement to The Bulletin number 251. Not counting shipping, 1,000 miles were covered on the road, and the country's famed hospitality was extended by all, from the royal family to roadside well-wishers.

The star event of the year was the RREC's participation in Her Majesty The Queen's Golden Jubilee celebrations. Club cars paraded through Windsor town and the quadrangle of the castle, leaving via the Long Walk and parking at Smith's Lawn or Frogmore House. Some 550 cars took part and both Her Majesty and the Duke of Edinburgh enjoyed the day immensely. In terms of "holding an event" this was the Club's finest hour.

The sections and registers were busy in 2002. The 20hp Register celebrated the 80th year of the model at Leeds Castle and also recorded its inaugural rally in North-West Victoria, Australia. The Scottish Section held events at Balmoral and at the old Argyll motor works in Alexandria, the South-Eastern Section went to Ypres, the 25hp Register ventured to Prague and Central Southern members visited the Loire Valley.

During the summer months, the onerous task of copying all 54,193 pre-1939 drawings onto CDs was completed, thanks to the good offices of Roy Noble. This was a necessary task, as the originals could be destroyed by fire or flood and the ageing paper was slowly deteriorating.

At one minute past midnight on 1 January 2003 at a New Year's celebration, the Chairman of Rolls-Royce Motor Cars Ltd handed the keys of the first Phantom produced at Goodwood to its new owner, a member of the RREC.

That year's Club Conference delegates were treated to a new Phantom to peruse between meetings. Adrian Hallmark of Bentley Motors addressed the conference, as did Tim Leverton, Chief Engineer, and Mark Djordjevic, Exterior Designer on the Rolls-Royce Phantom project.

At the AGM in 2003, the Club elected its first lady-chairman, Jane Pedler.

The Bulletin 261 broke from tradition by not featuring a Rolls-Royce or Bentley motor car on the front cover. A Rolls-Royce-powered machine was shown, however: a Concorde taking off – a nod to the passing of this great aircraft from flying service.

The Annual Rally of 2004 was held at a new venue, Boughton House near Kettering, courtesy of The Duke of Buccleuch and Queensberry. The house, known as "the Versailles of England" was a splendid backdrop to the serried ranks of Rolls-Royces and Bentleys.

In October, the SHRMF announced that it had acquired a Vesta match case at auction. A presentation piece given to Henry Royce by Charles Rolls, it bore the inscription "From CSR to FHR, 4.5.04–4.5.09", putting to rest the long argument about the actual date on which the two first met.

To mark the centenary of Rolls-Royce, the Chairman of Rolls-Royce plc, Sir Ralph Robins, planted a "centenary" tree in The Hunt House garden. Further celebrations included an Around the World rally – a global joint effort for all organisations affiliated to Rolls-Royce. The RREC played its part and Club members participated in various legs of the tour.

By early 2005, there were 39 sections and seven registers within the Club and they planned to hold 137 events during the year. Perhaps the Club's most ambitious overseas rally was held in Borneo. Some 70 cars made the trip, which involved some serious driving, along with some super-luxury accommodation.

Early in the morning of 31 March 2005, the Club's General Secretary and *The Bulletin* Editor, Peter Baines, died. As well as coping with the shock of losing a good friend, the members of the Management Committee and The Hunt House staff had to do their best to make sure that the Club kept running with a minimum of disruption – a challenge they met admirably.

Attendees at the 2006 Historic Seminar were treated to a schedule of renowned speakers: Bernard King and Kris Sukhu on Sykes and the Spirit of Ecstasy; Ian Rimmer on 60 years of Crewe car development; Kris Sukhu on victory in the Schneider Trophy races; Simon Coss on 100 years of the Isle of Man TT; Reg Spencer's personal account of a Rolls-Royce career and Tom Clarke on 100 years of the Silver Ghost.

On 2 July 2006, Peter's widow, Jo, opened the Peter Baines Wing at The Hunt House. A large turnout of members attended to hear Jo thank all those who had given so generously to make the memorial a reality.

Many exceptional events were held in 2007 at section, register and national levels to mark the RREC's Golden Jubilee. Club members Peter Phillips and Chris Barrie, accompanied by John Pike, undertook a Silver Ghost centenary drive in Peter's car 6AD. Their destination was the Queen's Hotel, Penzance, originally chosen by Claude Johnson in 1906. Club cars also featured prominently in the Goodwood plant's Silver Ghost celebration, prior to the Silver Ghost centenary tour of Scotland.

The 2007 Annual Rally at Kelmarsh Hall was nearly cancelled due to torrential rainfall. However, good drainage, combined with the resilience of the British rally-goer, and the efforts of Trevor Baldwin and his team, made the weekend challenging but enjoyable. On the Sunday, a good turnout of cars, featuring the Silver Ghosts back from their tour, was crowned by a display of the Battle of Britain Memorial Flight.

The FBHVC Drive it Day events took place on 12 August and every section and register was invited to hold their own event – something they did with enthusiasm and imagination. The French Section even stopped the traffic on the Champs-Elysées to photograph their cars with l'Arc de Triomphe in the background!

The pinnacle of the jubilee year was a weekend rally at Walton Hall, Warwickshire – a three-day event that combined excellent dining, road runs, beautiful cars and easy camaraderie. Another highlight was the Club's participation for the first time at the Classic Motor Show at the NEC in Birmingham. This was a huge success for the Club: it won the Classic and Sports Car Award for the best club stand, and well over 100 new members were recruited.

In 2008, the Annual Rally was held at Kelmarsh Hall once again. It was a delight to see the oldest surviving Rolls-Royce, the 1904 10hp 2-cylinder car (chassis number 20154) on parade.

The Club again had a stand at the NEC Classic Motor Show, and that year it won the award for the Best and Most Informative Website. The Club has continued to exhibit at the show every year since. In December 2008, the first of the Club's yearbooks was published and distributed free to all Club members worldwide.

THE 2010s (so far ...)

In June 2010, an event was held at Dover to commemorate the centenary of Charles Rolls's historic two-way flight across the Channel. The Dover Museum held a special exhibition, for which the Club provided much assistance. That year's Annual Rally moved to Rockingham Castle, a location that proved very popular and would remain the rally's venue for five years.

In 2011, the Club celebrated the centenary of the Spirit of Ecstasy with a series of three lectures by Professor Ken Brittan, the first being at The Hunt House on 6 February – 100 years to the day of the official registration of the mascot. This was followed later in the year by events at Derby, at Beaulieu and at Rolls-Royce Motor Cars in Goodwood.

With the London Olympics and an extensive national tour to celebrate her Diamond Jubilee, Her Majesty The Queen did not have space in her calendar to receive a tribute from the RREC in 2012. Instead, the Palace suggested that the Club celebrate HRH The Duke of Edinburgh's 90th birthday in 2011. This took place on the evening of 15 April 2011 with a reception at Windsor Castle, at which Prince Philip mingled freely with Club members. The next day, the Duke witnessed a drive-past in the castle by members' cars.

In February 2012, the Club received the sad news of the death of its President, Lt Col Eric Barrass. In the early days of the Club, Eric had agreed to take over as secretary on a temporary basis; he remained General Secretary for the next 30 years. During his tenure, membership rose from a hundred or so around Oxford to some 8,000 worldwide. It was Eric's foresight and leadership that made the Club what it is today. A memorial service was held in Paulerspury's parish church in July.

At the 2012 Annual Rally, the Club and the Sir Henry Royce Memorial Foundation signed a

Annual Rally venues of recent years
include Rockingham Castle (top)
and the impressive Burghley House

new lease for The Hunt House. This followed several years of difficult, and sadly often acrimonious, negotiation. Happily, it paved the way for the restoration of a co-operative relationship between the Club and the Foundation.

The following year was the 80th anniversary of the Derby Bentley, which was celebrated by a display and parade of some 50 cars at the Annual Rally at Rockingham Castle. Derby expert Neill Fraser held a seminar about these highly desirable cars. Late in 2013, a new general manager, Jaclyn Smith was appointed, meaning that the Club was administered entirely by female staff. The Club was now running more efficiently and more professionally than ever before.

In 2015, the South of England Rally became the International Weekend. The brainchild of Ted Meachem, it was held near Folkestone, convenient for the Channel Tunnel. In addition, the Annual Rally moved to Burghley House near Stamford, where it continues to this day.

The Club celebrated two important marque anniversaries that year: 60 years of the Silver Cloud and S-Series, and 50 years of the Silver Shadow and T-Series. In addition to gatherings of these models at Burghley House, a Silver Cloud event took place at Bray, where the model was originally launched. The Silver Shadow anniversary was marked by a three-day event centred on Crewe Hall in October. The RREC also appointed a Publications Development Manager, Jackie Robotham – the first woman to be responsible for *The Bulletin* and other Club publications.

In 2016, the Silver Ghost Register celebrated 110 years since the announcement of the 40/50hp Rolls-Royce (aka the Silver Ghost) with a parade on the Saturday of the Annual Rally. The Post-War Six-Cylinder Register also celebrated 70 years since the introduction of the Silver Wraith and Bentley Mark VI.

The current Chairman, Johan Vanden Bergh, was appointed in April – one of the youngest and, coming from Belgium, the first overseas chairman the Club has ever had.

The inauguration of the Polish Section by Michael Moran brought the Club's tally of overseas sections to 22, in addition to its 18 UK sections. With the introduction of a Junior Members' page in *The Bulletin*, the Club now has more junior members than ever before and, thanks to recent promotions to encourage partners to join, the RREC now has the highest number of joint members in its eventful and hugely successful 60-year history.

RREC CHAIRMEN

1957	Geoffrey Frank
1958	Ralph Symmons
1967	Stuart Fortune
1975	George Birrell
1976	John Schroder
1978	Roy Brooks
1980	Tony Donovan
1981	Rob Emberson
1984	Brian Crookall
1985	Gordon Connelly
1987	Douglas Vaughan
1989	Malcolm Tucker
1991	Brian Bilton-Sanderson
1993	Brian Wiggins
1995	David Dudley
1997	David Evans
1999	John Clough
2001	Eri Heilijgers
2003	Jane Pedler
2005	Ian Rimmer
2007	Suzanne Finch
2009	Tony James
2011	Jim Fleming
2013	Trevor Baldwin
2014	Duncan Feetham
2016	Johan Vanden Bergh

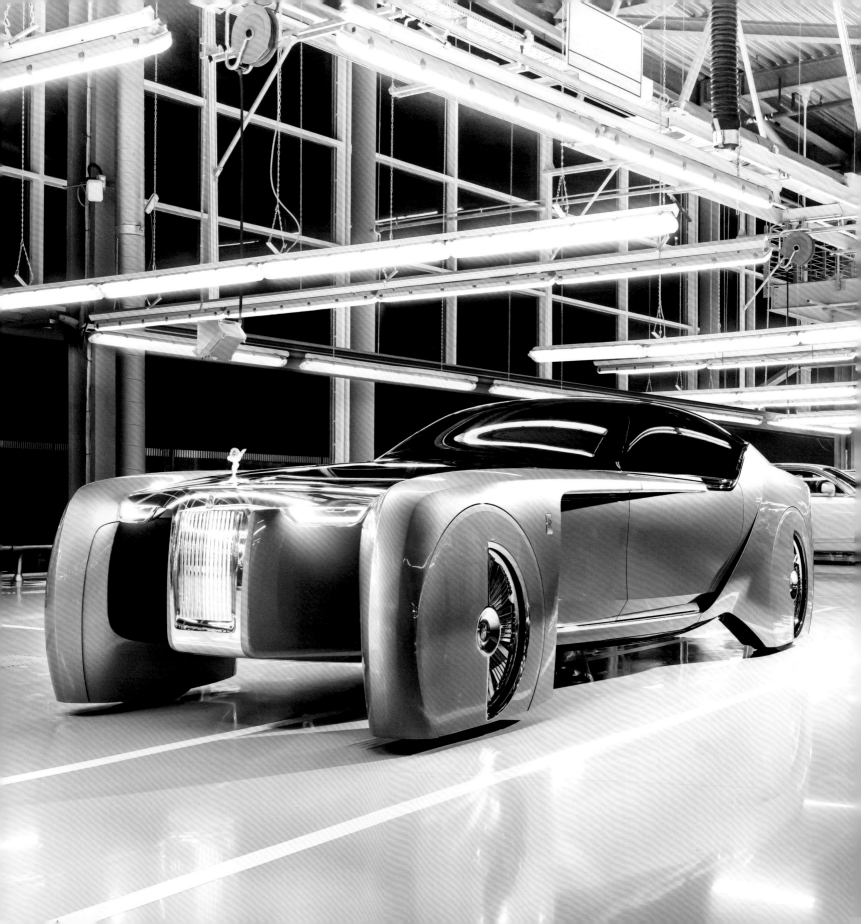

TOMORROW'S WORLD

Rolls-Royce's bold vision of the future

INNOVATION, ENCAPSULATED IN Sir Henry Royce's famous exhortation to "take the best that exists and make it better", has been at the heart of Rolls-Royce since day one. Every new model has represented a step forward in technology, performance and luxury. Few, however, have taken so big a leap – or made so bold a statement of intent – as 103EX, otherwise known as the Rolls-Royce VISION NEXT 100. This remarkable experimental Rolls-Royce sets out the company's vision of what luxury motoring will mean in the future.

MARKING A PIVOTAL YEAR

The year 2016 marked the centenary of the BMW Group. To celebrate this anniversary, Vision Vehicles were created by each of the group's brands – BMW, Mini, Motorrad and, of course, Rolls-Royce – to provide a tangible example of what we might expect from them in 100 years' time.

The year also marked a significant milestone for Rolls-Royce itself – the end of production of the seventh-generation Phantom. As well as being one of the marque's most important and successful model series, Phantom embodies the brand's renaissance under the stewardship of the BMW Group.

With Phantom's successor – due to arrive in 2018 – still shrouded in secrecy, the Vision Vehicle project provided the design team with the chance to show the world what might be coming out of Goodwood not just two years hence, but an entire century from now.

ADDRESSING THE BIG QUESTIONS

"In creating the Rolls-Royce VISION NEXT 100, we were mindful not to dwell on the past," says Director of Design Giles Taylor. "We wanted to be as innovative as possible and, at the same time, transcend the design history of the marque."

As the first step in the creative process, Giles and his team asked themselves: "How can we recast luxury for the next 100 years?" Almost immediately, this raised two further questions: "What will a Rolls-Royce owner expect of his or her car in the coming decades?" and "What can we envision today that will enable us to meet those future expectations?"

The answers lay in Rolls-Royce's deep understanding of its customers. As the sustained growth in bespoke requirements attests, they are highly individual. This led to a simple but crucial realisation: luxury means something different to everyone. The team's solution was to distil the concept of "luxury" down to four key tenets. Together, these not only underpin the car itself, but also help to define the future of luxury motoring at Rolls-Royce.

THE PERSONAL VISION

Most projections of the future address personal transport in purely functional terms: the current crop of driverless cars is a good example. The designers took the precisely opposite view: that Rolls-Royce owners want a personal, emotional connection with their car. 103EX, therefore, marks a return to the fully coachbuilt

103EX's numerous innovations include a reboot of the traditional luggage compartment; Eleanor, the virtual assistant and chauffeur; and the cabin's luxurious "floating" sofa

cars of the past. In a radical extension of the company's current bespoke offering, future customers will be closely involved in the design process, able to specify their car's shape, size and silhouette. Rolls-Royce will then design and manufacture the car for them, based on a chassis hand-built from the most sophisticated materials.

"103EX boldly points to a bright future for our marque," says Torsten Müller-Ötvös, Chief Executive Officer, Rolls-Royce Motor Cars. "One where our patrons' individual demands for complete and authentic personalisation will be met through an exquisite fusion of technology, design and hallmark Rolls-Royce craftsmanship."

The Effortless Journey Since 1911, the Spirit of Ecstasy, inspired by Eleanor Thornton, has been an elegant presence on Rolls-Royce cars. She has also been entirely silent – until now. In 103EX, "Eleanor" is the owner's virtual assistant and chauffeur, digitally connected to their life and surroundings.

Using the latest in intuitive artificial intelligence, Eleanor will make the car available when the owner is ready to travel. Once on the move, Eleanor advises on itineraries and schedules, provides reminders of tasks and appointments, and offers suggestions to make the journey truly effortless, for instance, assessing the destination to ensure a safe and timely arrival.

The other key part of the "Effortless Journey" is the hallmark Rolls-Royce "magic carpet ride",

delivered by a suspension system that allows the vehicle to almost skim across the road surface. The present V12 engine almost certainly won't exist in the future, so the design assumes that a suitable zero-emissions powertrain will power 103EX.

THE GRAND SANCTUARY

To step inside the car – which, thanks to the coach door and clamshell canopy, requires no bending or stooping – is to glimpse Rolls-Royce's vision of the future of luxury motoring. The centrepiece is a beautiful sofa, hand-upholstered in silk and lit to create the impression that it's "floating" within the cabin. The fact that Eleanor renders a cockpit or steering wheel (or, indeed, chauffeur) superfluous adds to the sense of space, providing passengers with an uninterrupted view.

103EX's cabin is encircled by handcrafted fine-line Macassar wood panelling, which sweeps from the coach door and up beside the second passenger to the side of the sofa, creating a clean, continuous and sculptural surface.

The front wall is dominated by the transparent OLED (organic light-emitting diode) screen, on which Eleanor provides passengers with visual information regarding the journey, destination and people awaiting them – or simply plays their favourite movie or TV show. The interior's simple elegance is completed by a deep-pile ivory wool carpet, woven exclusively for 103EX in London.

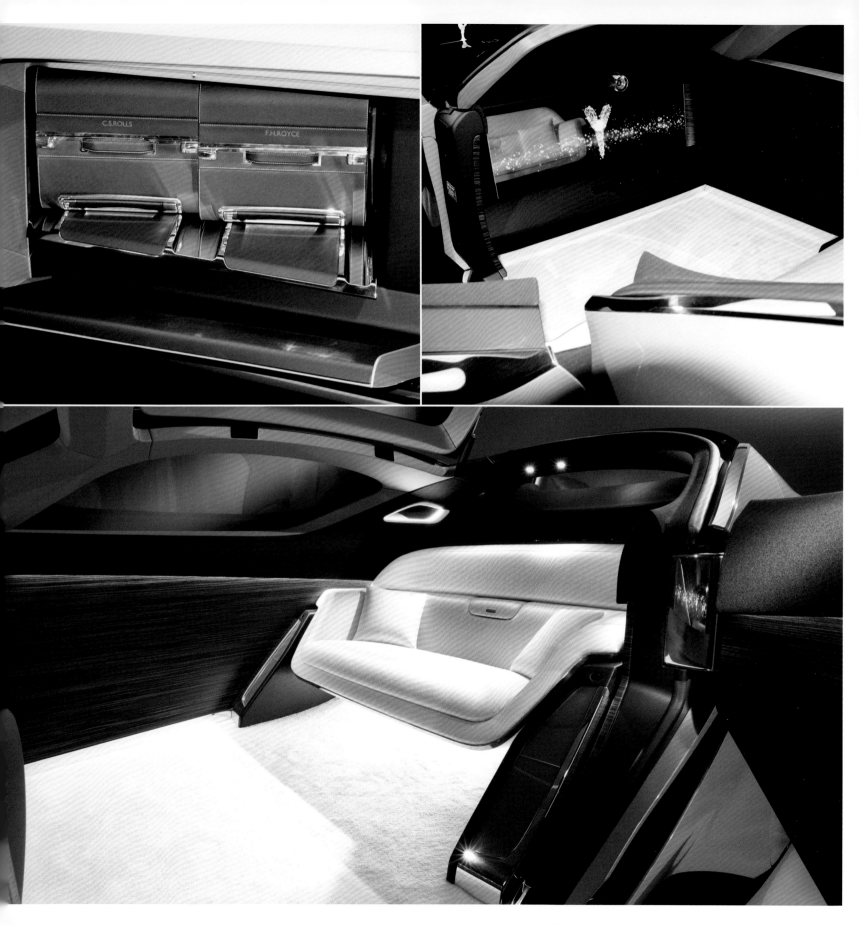

As with all Rolls-Royces, there are innumerable subtle details to take in and enjoy. Among the most pleasing is the finely crafted analogue clock, set centrally above the OLED screen, which serves as a reminder of Sir Henry Royce's humble beginnings making electric dynamos. "Rolls-Royce design today is the epitome of elegance," says Giles. "It's achieved through simplicity of design, under which lies the technology that makes our patrons' experience effortless."

THE GRAND ARRIVAL

It might seem a shame to leave such a sumptuous space, but 103EX makes even this a deeply pleasurable experience. As Giles explains: "The Grand Arrival creates a stage for our important passengers as they arrive at their ultimate destination."

The "Grand Arrival" begins with the theatre provided by the car's sheer scale. At 5.9 m long and 1.6 m high, it's the same size as the current Phantom Extended Wheelbase, and every bit as imposing. The narrow wheels, 28 inches tall, are hand-built from 65 individual pieces of aluminium and enclosed to create the impression of a futuristic catamaran.

Seen from the side, the coachwork rises elegantly over the shoulders at the rear of the car, providing privacy for the occupants. This line also imparts an air of powerful but graceful forward motion, accentuated by the rising beltline that ascends in a manner reminiscent of the great pre-war Rolls-Royces. This also contributes to an effortless, unruffled journey by improving airflow and reducing air resistance.

THE LIGHT FANTASTIC

103EX uses technology to deliver its Grand Arrival. As it comes into view, the illuminated Spirit of Ecstasy and Pantheon grille cast an otherworldly glow from the front of the car. As the car sweeps up to its destination, this glow spreads from the trailing edge of the front wheel arch to the rear of the single coach door.

When the car finally comes to a halt, the glass canopy, which is hinged on the left side of the vehicle, lifts up. The occupants are able to stand upright, while the canopy itself provides shelter from above and behind. Then, in one effortless movement, the single coach door opens and a step emerges from below the running board. As a final flourish, lights set in the underside of the step project a "red carpet" onto the ground to provide a suitably glamorous welcome.

MELDING THE PAST AND FUTURE

Within its highly futuristic lines, certain long-held Rolls-Royce design principles remain inviolate. The classic Pantheon grille, though daringly reimagined, is fundamentally as it's always been: the sharp-eyed will have spotted the red "RR" badge, signifying that this is an experimental Rolls-Royce. The grille forms the front of a fully

Left: 103EX's clamshell canopy and "red carpet" create an eye-catching sense of arrival

Overleaf: The car's illuminated, glass Spirit of Ecstasy

enclosed and smooth-bottomed hull, which contains the entire passenger area. Constructed from light yet incredibly strong materials, the hull is suspended from the wheels via exposed arms and struts, so it virtually "floats" above the road surface. Together with its "boat tail", it deliberately recalls the Rolls-Royces of the 1920s.

Even more iconic than the grille is the Spirit of Ecstasy. It's one of the world's most recognisable and desirable emblems, so changes are never undertaken lightly. The model fitted to 103EX is larger than today's and represents a respectful nod to the past, restoring her to the proportions she had on the regal Phantoms of the 1920s. For the first time in her 105-year history, she has been made from glass, handcrafted by Europe's finest artisan glassmakers.

The polished metal of the grille flows up over the car's nose, around the base of the Spirit of Ecstasy and along the top of the suspended laser-headlight hoops. It then narrows, shooting down the side of the long bonnet to create a dividing line between the car's upper and lower sections. This beautiful metal feature continues along the top edge of the coach door, describes a parabola up and over the rear shoulder, then encircles the rear of the glass canopy before flowing back down the other flank to create a "horseshoe" shape.

TWO-TONE PERFECTION

The car's two-tone design scheme is a feat of design and materials engineering. The upper section is entirely comprised of dark glass, flowing fluidly to create a seamless fastback canopy over the occupants. As well as providing privacy, the glass provides an amazing window on the world ahead before resolving itself into the bonnet of the car.

The lower section is even more dramatic in its design and execution. The silk-like "Crystal Water" colour scheme gives the surface a lightness that belies the vehicle's immense size. Whether at rest or in motion, and viewed from any angle, the car seems to simply float. This pared-back design shows what the design team felt able to do when freed from today's constraints by the coachbuilding and engine technologies of the future. For example, instead of the entire area under the bonnet being occupied by an engine, 103EX has a luggage compartment positioned just behind the front wheels. And, true to the principle of effortlessness, it opens automatically upon arrival, presenting two Grand Tourer cases.

As the first chapter in the story of Rolls-Royce at Goodwood ends with Phantom, 103EX provides a striking signpost for the next one. Above all, it is an unequivocal statement of Rolls-Royce's confidence in a future where autonomous cars need not be the anonymous, bland and utilitarian items some would have us believe. Instead, Rolls-Royce envisions a world of effortless, autonomous travel in spacious and beautiful luxury cars, each as personal as its individual owner.

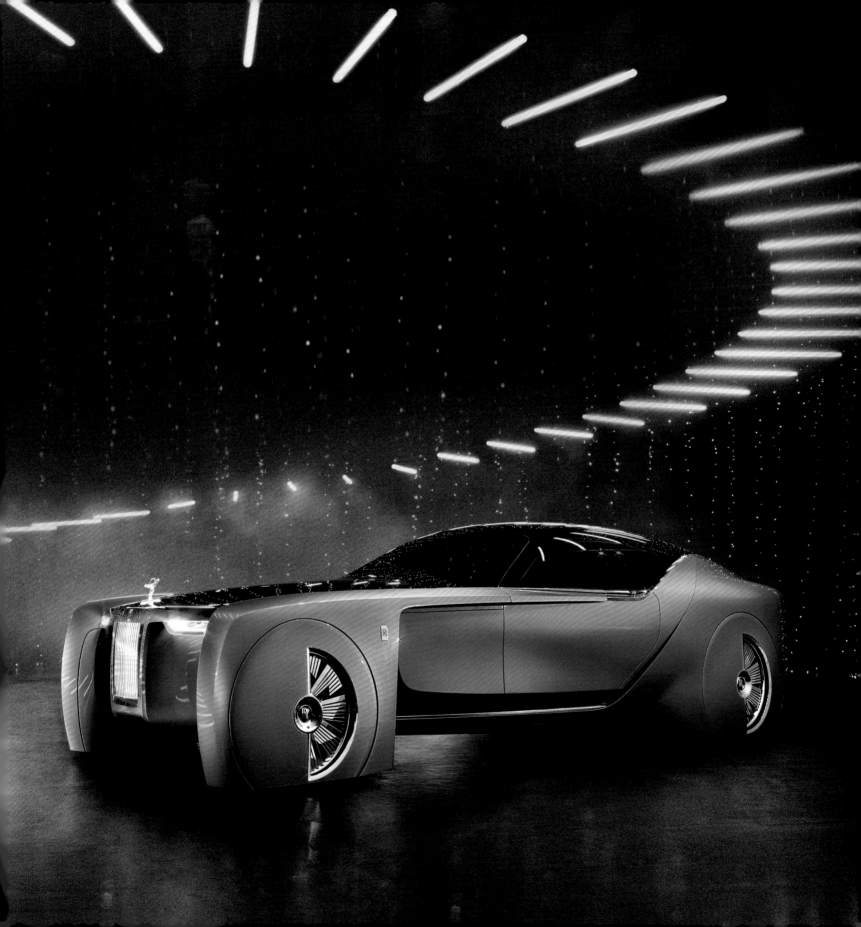

A FLIGHT OF INSPIRATION

Sixty years of the Flying Spur by Davide Bassoli

FOLLOWING THE SUCCESS of the R Type Continental, which was created in 1952, Rolls-Royce's directors decided to green-light a sporty Continental version of the Bentley S Series. The R Type Continental had been conceived as a completely new car, with its body design a collaborative effort between Ivan Evernden of the Experimental Department and HJ Mulliner's Technical Director Stanley Watts. By the end of its production, HJ Mulliner had dressed no fewer than 193 of the 208 cars built.

The S Type Continental was instead offered as a standard chassis only, with no specific body proposed. Compared to the standard S Series chassis, it had a higher rear axle ratio of 2.92:1, a higher engine compression ratio of 7.25:1 and a reduced frontal area, with the radiator grille 1.5 inches lower and the steering column more inclined. This allowed for a lower and more aerodynamic body, which enabled the cars to reach the then considerable potential maximum speed of 120 mph.

When first introduced, three different two-door body styles were offered: the HJ Mulliner saloon, also known as the "fastback", and the Park Ward two-door saloon and drophead. However, an increasing demand for high-speed saloons for family transport that could be used on the new motorways of the Continent prompted HJ Mulliner to consider a different body styling for the sporty Continental chassis.

BIRTH OF THE FLYING SPUR

The new concept, launched by HJ Mulliner as a four-door body style for the Continental chassis, was the news story of 1957. This new styling – Design no. 7443 – was officially known by the idyllic name "Flying Spur", which was derived from the Scottish family crest of the coachbuilder's Managing Director Harry T Johnstone.

Initially, the team at Crewe was reluctant to agree to this new body style, as the S Type Continental chassis was intended for two-door sports saloons and dropheads only. However, Johnstone was convinced of the new body style's potential – for HJ Mulliner it could open up a new niche in the market: the family car as fast transport – and he brought his influence to bear. He showed the beautiful design to Dr Frederick Llewellyn-Smith and the other members of the Rolls-Royce board, and was given the okay to proceed.

The new design's shape was an evolution of Design no. 7401, which was offered for the standard chassis, modified and resized to achieve the perfect proportions of the Flying Spur. The rear doors lost their rear-hinged opening, known as "suicide doors", and with its lower radiator grille and more inclined steering column, the layout of the car looked lower, giving it a more dynamic and sporty appearance. The Flying Spur's more sloped roof was in harmony with its more rounded pillars and boot, and to further enhance this sporty appearance, the rear wings were also more rounded in shape.

Previous pages: The first S1 Continental Flying Spur built, chassis BC90BG

Opposite, clockwise from top left: Rear view of BC90BG; the Flying Spur mascot; the rear doors on Design no. 7401 were rear facing, providing easier access to the rear compartment

Inside, the rounded dashboard was similar to that of the fastback, with all the dials, including the revolution counter, positioned in front of the driver. Restrained front seats contributed to the model's sporty appearance and were made with a lighter aluminium shell and Dunlopillo padding, which, together with the use of more aluminium in the floor area, meant that the Flying Spur was no heavier than the fastback. In the best of British tradition, all the interiors were upholstered with the finest-quality Connolly Vaumol hide.

HJ Mulliner ordered S1 Continental chassis BC90BG, which was fitted with the prototype body of the Flying Spur. Finished in Deep Grey over Clyde Grey with red hide, it was ready in April 1957 and registered 10LMK. Before BC90BG was used for trials, it was fitted with a Flying Spur mascot, instead of the usual winged "B", for the publicity photographs.

The prototype appeared in all of Bentley and HJ Mulliner's official documentation and advertising, and in addition to its distinctive mascot, BC90BG also had direction indicator lights on the front of its wings. It is not documented whether this was the case for any of the other cars from the first batch of 10 produced, but soon the indicators returned to their usual position in the fog lamps.

Following the production of this first batch, the Flying Spur was exhibited at the 1957 Earls Court Motor Show. The HJ Mulliner stand featured chassis BC45CH, finished in Regal Red with beige upholstery, which successfully caught the attention of the show's international attendees. The Flying Spur was also offered in two other very rare versions: as a four-light with a quarter-window fitted in the rear door, and as a six-light with a small quarter-window and a heavier rear pillar.

Many jet-setters were seen behind the wheel of one of these exclusive 120 mph, four-door cars. One such individual, who would be remembered for his geniality as well as his movies, was Alfred Hitchcock, who bought chassis BC34LEL, which was painted Tudor Grey with beige hide.

Over its eight years of production, the Flying Spur remained in great demand, becoming the most successful coachbuilt model on the Silver Cloud and S Type chassis. In total, 54 S1 Continental chassis were fitted with the standard six-light version (Design no. 7443), 14 with the four-light version (officially named 7443/B), and just two with the six-light, smaller rear quarter-light version (Design no. 7443/2/Mod. 2).

THE SECOND SERIES

The Continental version of the second Series (Design no. 7508) was launched at the 1959 Earls Court Motor Show, together with the standard steel saloon. The Continental chassis provided Rolls-Royce with the chance to offer its customers coachbuilt bodies and, with the company's recent

acquisition of the coachbuilder HJ Mulliner, to market the London firm's coachbuilt bodies.

In fact, considering that Freestone & Webb and Hooper had both ceased operating recently, and James Young was specialising increasingly in the long wheelbase and new Phantom V chassis, the Continental chassis was almost exclusively catered for by Rolls-Royce coachbuilders HJ Mulliner and Park Ward. At Pym's Lane it was decided that HJ Mulliner would produce the two-door and four-door sports saloon bodies, while Park Ward would produce those for the drophead.

Compared to the first Series body, the S2 Continental's radiator shell was like that on all the other Continental chassis – a little lower, more squared in proportion and inclined forward, giving a more racy appearance – while the larger boot lid now incorporated the rear number-plate. The big news, however, was hidden under the bonnet: the new V-8 engine.

This mechanical jewel, Crewe's new technological feat, featured an aluminium block and heads – a big step forward compared to the old, cast-iron straight-six. It was lighter but slightly noisier, calling for the introduction of hydraulic tappets, which were moved by a single camshaft fitted in the middle of the two banks. Crewe didn't normally release information concerning power and torque but, according to estimates, the new V-8 produced around 200 horsepower – nearly 20 per cent more than the straight-six.

In total, 113 S2 Continental chassis were fitted with the standard six-light saloon styling, six with the four-light styling (called 7508/B), and only three with the six-light, smaller rear quarter-light styling (Design no. 7508/D). The latter styling was also referred to as "Van Gerbig smaller quarter light", as handwritten on HJ Mulliner official drawings – taking its name from the customer who first requested this design. Interestingly, Van Gerbig, an American citizen with interests in Europe, having rejected both orders of this Flying Spur variant made for the S1 Continental, ordered S2 Continental chassis BC7CZ with the same configuration, but rejected that car as well before taking delivery, finally buying standard six-light chassis BC87LBY.

THE THIRD SERIES

As with the previous series, the S3 Continental versions were launched together with the standard models, this time at the 1962 Earls Court Motor Show. Substantially, the new models were the same as those offered on the S2 Continental chassis, with stylistic and mechanical updates.

Aesthetically, the main changes were to the front of the car, with the introduction of twin headlamps and new flashing side lamps, together with the different shape of the overriders. From a mechanical point of view, the engine's compression ratio was increased to 9.0:1 and it was fitted with bigger, two-inch S.U. HD8 carburettors and a new Lucas distributor. Like its predecessor, the S3 Continental maintained a rear axle ratio of 3.08:1, and featured front drum-brakes with four shoes and a lowered steering column.

Coachbuilders owned by Rolls-Royce offered the same body versions as on the S2, updated with the new frontal treatment. HJ Mulliner produced the revised versions of the Flying Spur and two-door sports saloon, which were very well harmonised with the new twin headlamps, now officially named Design no. 2011.

However, the real novelty was unveiled at the London Motor Show, with the introduction of coachbuilt bodies for the Silver Cloud III chassis, an option previously reserved for the Continental chassis only. The classical radiator grille, with its Greek-temple shape and proportions, elegantly matched the sporty lines produced by the coachbuilders, reviving a tradition that had begun with the Phantom II Continental in the 1930s.

This model proved to be so successful that it was decided to use the same name, Continental, for the more sporty Bentley models 20 years later. The 1963 model proved to be an extremely wise commercial decision, especially for the US market, where, traditionally, cars with the Bentley radiator grille fared less well. As with the Continental chassis, these new cars had a more inclined steering column compared to that of the standard Silver Cloud III.

So, the Mulliner Park Ward stand at the Earls Court Motor Show offered the Flying Spur saloon (Design no. 2042) for the Silver Cloud

III, although it was never named Flying Spur in the official documentation. Inside the car, the dashboard was similar to the Bentley version, except that the rev-counter was replaced by the four-in-one instrument fitted on the standard steel saloon Silver Cloud III.

In total, 83 S3 Continental chassis were fitted with the standard six-light saloon (Design no. 2011), five chassis with the six-light small rear quarter-light version, and only one with the four-light version. This latter motor car was built to the precise specifications of its first owner, with single headlamps as those fitted on the S2.

Of the Rolls-Royce versions, 52 chassis were fitted with the standard six-light saloon (officially named Design no. 2042), and just two with the six-light small rear quarter light version (Design no. 2042/A).

Following the success of these cars – true classics of their era – the name Flying Spur was used years later for a limited edition of the Silver Spirit III. Essentially, it was a Silver Spirit with a Bentley Turbo R drive train and engine, making it the first turbo-charged Rolls-Royce. Only 134 were produced.

The name didn't end there, however, and in 2005 Bentley Motors reintroduced the name Flying Spur, proposing a new generation of four-door saloons with the name. Based on the Continental GT platform, this remains to this day one of the most sought-after supercars available on the market – a fitting tribute to an iconic name.

POWER AND PURPOSE

The three incarnations of the new Bentley Mulsanne

HANDCRAFTED IN CREWE by a team of skilled artisans, the Mulsanne is the flagship of the Bentley range. As such, it represents everything the British brand knows about building one of the world's most powerful, luxurious cars.

As of last summer, the Mulsanne family comprises three distinct models, each with its own unique abilities and attributes. The Mulsanne, Mulsanne Speed and Mulsanne Extended Wheelbase all share Bentley's legendary levels of attention to detail and craftsmanship, while at the same time catering for their own distinct sector of the luxury-car market.

The new Mulsanne Extended Wheelbase, for example, has been designed with the rear-seat passenger in mind. An additional 250 mm of rear legroom, airline-style extending leg rests and a rear compartment sunroof combine to create one of the most relaxing automotive environments in the world. The Mulsanne Speed, on the other hand, is tailored for the driver, with 537 PS and 1,100 Nm of torque resulting in a 0–60 mph time of just 4.9 seconds and a top speed of 190 mph.

A suite of elegantly executed styling revisions mark the new Mulsanne out from its predecessor. The entire front-end style of the car (forward of the A pillar) has been completely redesigned. The fenders, bonnet, radiator shell, grilles, lights and bumpers, fore and aft, have all been updated, giving the car a more modern and integrated appearance.

On the inside, the new Mulsanne features exquisitely handcrafted wood, leather and metal fittings. It also boasts redesigned seats, new door trims and armrests, unique glass switchgear and a choice of 24 elegant hide colours. The new Mulsanne also features a suite of innovative, cutting-edge technologies, including a new touchscreen infotainment system, which has been developed especially for it.

The three distinct models each offer something different. The Mulsanne, with its understated elegance and sporting purpose, remains the consummate luxury limousine; the Mulsanne Speed is a masterpiece of luxury and performance thanks to its immense power, torque and refinement; and the Mulsanne Extended Wheelbase – with its extraordinary airline-style seats and rear-passenger bias – is the epitome of automotive comfort.

THE NEW MULSANNE

The new, imposing front end is dominated by a large stainless steel vertical-vane grille – 80 mm wider than before – which celebrates the great models of the past, such as the 8 Litre of 1930, Embiricos and R-Type Continental. Through these vertical vanes the Bentley matrix grille is visible.

Positioned either side of this are a pair of floating all-LED headlamps. These new units feature advanced adaptive technology and greatly increased night vision, with beam patterns that

Opposite: The new Mulsanne's redesign includes revamped tail lights and bumper

automatically adjust to suit the driving conditions. The LED lights sit flush within the seamless aluminium front fenders. Innovative design features, such as the discreet chrome-capped headlamp washers that sit within the adjacent outer lamps, demonstrate the marque's precise execution of detail. A new horizon line is also created across the front of the Mulsanne by raising the outer lamps so that their bases are in line with the main headlights.

The new one-piece bumper, radiator shell and bonnet integrate seamlessly with flush joins creating more visual width and presence. These features flow down to a lower vane-grille section, which is in turn flanked by "B" signature matrix elements – pushed further out to the corners by 53 mm either side – and finished in bright chrome. The brightware detailing continues on either side of the Mulsanne with a new B-shaped wing vent incorporated into the lower section of the fender.

At the rear, this more planted appearance continues with new tail lights and a redesigned bumper. The bumper, which has 26 mm wider lower corners and a strong light-catching feature line, creates a more purposeful appearance. The new tail lamps incorporate a "B" theme with light guides creating an instantly recognisable signature – particularly in the dark.

On the inside, the Bentley Mulsanne's reputation for impeccable interiors is further enhanced. It takes more than 150 hours to create the sumptuous soft-touch leather interior, which now features redesigned seats, armrests and door trims. The Mulsanne's seats are now available in two new styles: Fluted or Quilted. There is also a choice of 24 hide colours and single or duo-tone finishes.

Hand-selected veneers form pure and elegant surfaces throughout the cabin, and each of the 40 pieces is shaped by Bentley's artisans from a choice of 13 different veneers, and finished with trademark attention to detail. Elsewhere in the cabin, bright-polished stainless steel, unique glass switchgear, traditional knurled controls and deep-pile carpets enhance the luxury environment.

A suite of innovative and advanced technologies has been added, ensuring that the new Mulsanne is as technologically advanced as it is luxurious. These include a completely new infotainment system, which boasts cutting-edge navigation technology. At the core of the new system is an all-new touch-screen-based platform with additional haptic controls, classic analogue gauges and state-of-the-art rear-seat entertainment. The main eight-inch display touch screen is connected to a 60 GB solid-state hard drive for the storage of on-board media.

The new Mulsanne can be specified with one of the world's most powerful automotive OEM audio systems – Naim for Bentley Premium

The Mulsanne's distinctive grille and raised outer lamps as illustrated on an Extended Wheelbase model with duo-tone finish

Audio. This bespoke on-board audio system features 20 speakers, 20 channels, a 2,200 watt amplifier and Super Tweeters. And rear-seat passengers benefit from the introduction of the Bentley Entertainment Tablet – a pair of 10.2-inch Android devices (with 4G, Wi-Fi and Bluetooth) seamlessly integrated into the backs of the front seats. With typical attention to detail, a single touch of a button engages a beautifully weighted mechanism, smoothly deploying the screens from their stowed positions.

The Android-powered tablets, which feature a Bentley-specific interface, have access to over a million Android Apps – such as Skype, Google Play and Spotify – and can be used away from the car, in the office and at home. Each tablet has 32 GB of on-board storage (expandable to 128 GB via a Micro-SDXC card), USB ports and a front-facing camera. Audio can also be streamed through the vehicle speakers, and new destinations can be sent from the tablets to the Mulsanne's navigation system. Internet browsing is via the car's 4G Wi-Fi system, permitting access to internet radio and local or streamed video.

In the new Mulsanne, the 6¾-litre V8 develops 512 PS and 1,020 Nm of torque. This immense power – channelled through an eight-speed ZF automatic transmission – is available from just above idle right across the rev range, ensuring that with even the slightest input the driver is immediately rewarded with phenomenal acceleration.

The new model has a 0–60 mph time of just 5.1 seconds and a top speed of 184 mph. Its V8 engine features key technologies such as cylinder de-activation and variable cam phasing, which reduce both fuel consumption and CO_2 emissions.

The Mulsanne's prodigious power and torque are complemented by all-new chassis hardware including active engine mounts and suspension bushes. To further enhance the trademark "hushed ride", Bentley has integrated the latest noise absorption technology into the Mulsanne's tyres.

The Drive Dynamics Control system, operated by a rotary switch mounted next to the gearshift selector, can be used to choose from three standard modes – Bentley, Sport and Comfort – offering precise calibration of suspension and steering control systems. A fourth mode, Custom, allows the driver to select bespoke settings via the multimedia system to "tune" the Mulsanne to a preferred driving style.

The air suspension system with Continuous Damping Control creates a comfortable and refined ride at lower speeds, and lowers the Mulsanne's ride height automatically at high speeds to reduce lift and improve aerodynamics.

MULSANNE EXTENDED WHEELBASE

Designed for those with a preference for being driven, the Bentley Mulsanne Extended Wheelbase offers a first-class "air-travel" experience for the road.

The 250 mm extension of the Mulsanne's wheelbase is entirely to the benefit of rear-seat passenger legroom. This significant increase in interior space makes the Mulsanne Extended Wheelbase one of the most generously proportioned luxury limousines in the world. To make the best use of the additional rear legroom, Bentley has developed airline-style electronic leg rests, which are integrated into the bases of the two rear seats. These extend outward and pivot, affording rear-seat passengers the luxury of a choice between upright, relaxed and reclined seating positions.

A beautifully appointed console separates the two rear seats in the Mulsanne Extended Wheelbase. Ornate and functional, the console is appointed in handcrafted veneer, metal, glass and leather, and houses practical features such as USB ports, pen holders, cup holders and a glass-covered stowage area.

For passengers who wish to work on the move, both rear seats can also be specified with a deployable, folding table. And for privacy, electric curtains at the rear are standard and can be tailored with either a black or champagne coloured interior lining.

Rear-seat passengers also benefit from a large-format sunroof over the rear cabin. Controlled by the passengers or the driver, the tilting and sliding glass panel allows natural light to flood into the Mulsanne's beautifully appointed cabin, reinforcing the Extended Wheelbase's focus on the rear passenger.

MULSANNE SPEED

Featuring a more powerful version of Bentley's 6¾-litre twin-turbo V8 engine, the new Mulsanne Speed is truly tailored for the driver. With 537 PS, 1,100 Nm of torque and selectable sports suspension, the Speed combines outstanding driving satisfaction with supreme comfort.

The Speed has a 0–60 mph time of 4.8 seconds and has a top speed of 190 mph – exemplary figures in the ultra-luxury sector.

The connection between the car and driver is key, so the Speed's engine is paired with a recalibrated ZF 8-speed gearbox designed to enhance the driving experience. The gear strategy is optimised to make best use of the increased engine output, and is designed for instant delivery. "S" mode gives the driver even more control and maintains the engine speed above 2,000 rpm so that the turbochargers are always spooled and ready to deliver instantaneous performance.

To make the most of the Speed's power and acceleration, an even more driver-focused Sport suspension mode is included. While the Bentley and Comfort suspension modes provide a comfort-focused chassis set-up, the Sport mode stiffens the all-round air suspension for improved body control and adjusts the steering dynamics for greater feedback and accuracy.

Previous pages, clockwise from top left: The EWB's luxuriously appointed rear cabin; the Mulsanne's high-tech touchscreen; the Speed's full facia

Left: With its powerful V8 engine and top speed of 190 mph, the Mulsanne Speed is the range's impressive high-performance option

The Mulsanne Speed features a series of unique styling features that mark it out as the range's high-performance model. A dark tint finish is applied to the exterior brightware, giving the Speed a more menacing appearance. It also boasts 21-inch, hand-finished "Speed" alloys; dark tinted front and rear lamps; rifled sports exhausts; and Speed fender badging.

On the inside – in addition to the interior updates common across the Mulsanne range – the Speed also benefits from a number of new features that highlight its athletic, sporting abilities. For example, the Mulliner Driving Specification interior comes as standard, adding diamond-quilted seats, a knurled gear lever, drilled alloy sport pedals and optional carbon fibre waist rail inserts.

HANDCRAFTED IN CREWE

The Mulsanne is handcrafted in Crewe, with its 400-hour production journey beginning in the Body in White workshop. Working by hand and by eye, master metal workers expertly complete 5,800 individual welds.

Where the roof flows into the rear haunch through the deep D-pillar, a dedicated team brazes the joint by hand until it is totally imperceptible. It takes a human touch to achieve this, and once painted it is completely invisible to the eye – looking and feeling as though it were hewn from a solid piece of metal.

The sculpted nature of the Mulsanne's body means that the paint must be applied in different depths to appear even, which is why each one is hand-sprayed. After lacquering, each car is fine-sanded before being polished with lamb's wool for 12 hours to achieve an appearance so reflective it's termed the "Bentley Mirror Finish".

Opening the door of the Bentley flagship reveals a foundation of solid walnut, cherry or oak visibly running through the dashboard and overlaid with a choice of 13 different veneers.

After the root burl has been steamed and finely sliced into 0.6 mm-thick bundles of veneer, Bentley veneer experts travel to wherever it may be to analyse the results. The final selection process occurs at Crewe, where the veneer is chosen by the craftsperson who will ultimately bring it to life. Only the most highly "figured" sections – parts with naturally decorative marks – are chosen, before being mirror matched and applied to the solid wood substrate.

Of the 400 hours it takes to build a Mulsanne, around 150 are dedicated to creating the leather interior – before additional options are considered. Stitched, shaped and finished entirely by hand, the completed seats, doors and other leather accoutrements rival the quality of luxury domestic furniture, with the contrast stitching alone taking 37 hours to complete. But, then, you wouldn't expect anything less of Bentley's flagship model, would you?

FOR KING
AND COUNTRY

The origins of the Rolls-Royce
armoured car by Lt Col Eric Barrass

Taken from the RREC's latest Historical Series publication The Rolls-Royce Armoured Car, edited by Eliot Levin, the following extract tells the tale of one of the most formative and fascinating chapters in the history of Rolls-Royce armoured cars. It centres on the early wartime adventures of one Charles Rumney Samson – a Commander in the Royal Navy and a true pioneering spirit. Given command of a squadron of the Royal Naval Air Service, Samson personally recruited most of his men, including his brothers Felix and Bill. The squadron was equipped with a handful of "aged aeroplanes" and 10 touring cars, including at least two Rolls-Royce motor cars ...

25 AUGUST 1914 could be described as one of the most significant dates in this story, for on that day Samson was instructed by Commodore Murray Sueter, Director of Air Department Admiralty, to meet him urgently. Samson, with his brother Felix as driver, raced to the Admiralty.

Here Sueter gave him orders, emanating from Churchill, to take his squadron to Ostend without delay. Little detailed information was available. A force of Marines would be landed on 26 August but the exact location was not known. The squadron was to make its own way. No landing grounds were indicated. Samson must select his own from the air. He was to carry out independent reconnaissance missions, in particular keeping the channel under observation for enemy submarines during the passage of the British Expeditionary Force.

The aircraft were to fly from Eastchurch on the Isle of Sheppey, Kent. Men and transport were to travel in HMS *Empress*, a converted seaplane carrier, with a collier from Sheerness in attendance.

Samson, driven by Felix, raced back to Eastchurch, assembled his pilots and ground crews and issued his orders. The planes were to be overhauled and fuelled at once, working through the night. The earliest the squadron could be ready was 27 August.

Samson himself flew No. 50, an old BE2 biplane. The aircraft had no squadron signs or any distinguishing marks, so a Union Flag was tied to a strut on each plane. The pilots were each equipped with .45 automatic pistols. Two inflated cycle tubes were wound around each man to act as life belts.

The squadron took off successfully at noon. Formation flying proved almost impossible due to the wide differences in performance of the varied aircraft. A head wind gave no help. The estimated time of flight was one and a half hours. The actual time of over two hours so exhausted fuel that two aircraft turned away and landed on the beach at Dunkirk.

Miraculously, the remainder all arrived in Belgium, although several were damaged on landing. Samson circled Ostend looking for a suitable site and selected the racecourse. A camp was set up using tarpaulins borrowed from trucks in the nearby railway sidings. It would be an understatement to describe conditions as primitive.

The waterborne transport and backup arrived the following day, and a more permanent camp was quickly assembled. By 28 August, the aircraft that had landed at Dunkirk had

Previous pages: A first Admiralty Pattern AC Rolls-Royce, Dunkirk, circa October 1914

Above: Samson's party makes camp at Ostend, August 1914

Opposite, clockwise from top left: An armoured car nearing completion at the Clement-Talbot works; the same car showing the driver's compartment; a Silver Ghost chassis leaves Derby in 1914 en route to Erith, where its armoured body would be fitted

been refuelled and patched up to fly to join the squadron at Ostend. One pilot complained bitterly that at one time, in the teeth of a 50-knot wind, he was actually going backwards.

Samson then ordered reconnaissance flights over the area Bruges–Ghent–Ypres. These were carried out several times each day.

The promised Royal Marine Brigade turned out to consist of around 600 elderly reservists, hastily recalled to the colours. They had no artillery other than the guns of warships patrolling the coast. They were equipped with four early Maxim machine guns, which, like all their baggage, were transported on handcarts. They had no other transport on arrival.

The Brigade Commander, General Aston, with no means of reconnaissance except a few bicycles, asked Samson if he would organise a patrol to Thourout and Bruges. Felix Samson was told to take his Mercedes car and a Wolseley wagonette on which his Maxim (obtained by devious means from naval friends) was mounted. The cars were greeted with great enthusiasm by the inhabitants of both towns. They showed great relief and delight to see British "troops" in uniform. The Mayor of Thourout invited Felix to the Hotel de Ville for a glass of wine. He reported that a

German cyclist patrol had been seen approaching the town only an hour earlier. The cars patrolled the area but made no contact so returned via Bruges to Ostend to report.

The Brigade Commander valued this patrol so highly that he had discussions with Samson and his brother Felix on forming regular car patrols. Clearly old lessons were quickly being re-learned.

A number of personally owned cars, including the two Rolls-Royce tourers, were available and further patrolling was organised in conjunction with the continuing aircraft patrols. A few French Hotchkiss *mitrailleuses* [machine guns] were borrowed from a local French Territorial Infantry unit and mounted on tripods in the rear of several cars. Felix proposed removing all windscreen glass and substituting steel plates with slits. A few were so fitted, but so restricted the drivers' vision that they were quietly removed; their need not yet obvious. Just as a useful force was being established, orders were received from the Admiralty to move to Dunkirk en route to the UK, as they were considered too valuable to risk.

The French reacted strongly and the Area Commander, General Bidon, telegraphed the Admiralty and pleaded for their retention, vastly overrating their proven value, but realising their

potential. The Admiralty agreed, but insisted on the move to Dunkirk, considering Ostend to be too vulnerable.

At this time communications were poor, based almost entirely on the civilian telephone network, which was manually controlled and largely confined to official organisations and business houses, and the railway telegraph system using Morse code in French and Flemish. Rumour and scaremongering were rife and sifting for reliable information became extremely difficult.

The idea of having a British aero-cum-motorised ally at hand, backed by armed Marines, was worth pleading for.

Bearing in mind that the object of the meagre and mostly privately owned transport available was to seek landing grounds, recover pilots from crashed aircraft and, if possible, the aircraft themselves – in fact, generally to serve the RNAS squadron – Samson showed immense initiative in using these cars for military reconnaissance as the situation appeared to require.

The move to Dunkirk was successfully concluded in three days. The aircraft flew to the aerodrome and the transport followed. The Marines travelled in local buses and three London General Omnibus Company bus chassis now fitted with charabanc-like bodies.

Samson constantly moved around, liaising with the local civic dignitaries and troops. The latter were almost all reservists and territorials, hastily mobilised and armed with little but rifles and tremendous zeal. Their artillery pieces were French 75s and at least two armoured Minerva cars carried Lewis guns. These vehicles were basic in design, but were not unnoticed by Samson. Later during 1914, the Belgians made great efforts to produce armoured vehicles and Mors, Minerva

and SAVA (Société Anversoise pour la Fabrication de Voitures Automobiles – if you must know) from their Antwerp factories. These were all of crude design: boilerplate-clad and open-topped, and armed with French Hotchkiss machine guns.

Samson also kept close contact with his naval friends serving on ships based in Dunkirk. It was due to his pleadings that a number of Maxim guns were removed from warships, where their use was limited, and handed over to arm his cars.

On 2 September, Mr PC Sarell, British Consul in Dunkirk, asked Samson for transport to Lille as he urgently needed to talk to the Vice-Consul there. In his peregrinations, Samson had been introduced to Cavrois O'Caffrey, a Jesuit priest of Irish origin and a fluent speaker of German and French, who owned a bicycle. His knowledge of the area and local population was vast and he quickly became Samson's "agent". O'Caffrey had introduced Samson to Mr Sarell, who became totally involved and his office became an intelligence centre. The Revd O'Caffrey, always on the alert for a free ride and to be helpful as an interpreter, volunteered to join them. In Lille, O'Caffrey telephoned the Chief of Police who told him that a patrol of around 40 German cavalry were in fact at police HQ and two officers were "bullying" the Préfet du Nord.

The redoubtable reverend then boarded a tram car into central Lille and returned by the same means to say that he had counted a column of 1,000 German infantry in the main square with cyclist patrols active all over the city.

Over the telephone, O'Caffrey arranged with a lawyer of his acquaintance that he would come out to Lille between 10 am and 3 pm daily with news of German movements. The lawyer, to help

Opposite: Following the bombardment from the sea of east coast towns in 1914, Rolls-Royce armoured cars were sent to act as Coast Defence Vessels, here pictured in Southwold, Suffolk, March 1915

identification, would wear a white waistcoat! By such means was intelligence gained.

Churchill pressed for attacks on the Zeppelin sheds at Düsseldorf and Cologne. To this end he ordered an air detachment to proceed to Antwerp. Samson carried out the order, leaving him with just five aircraft to pursue the formidable recce flights he had been ordered to do.

On 4 September the first "motor" fight took place. A patrol set out, consisting of Felix in his armed Mercedes and an unidentified and unarmed Rolls-Royce tourer. Ten Marines, armed with rifles, were squeezed aboard the two cars. At Cassel gendarmes hailed them to tell them of telegraphed reports that German motor patrols had passed through Armentières in the direction of Cassel. A telephonist at the local post offices confirmed the report that at least five cars had been seen. Samson immediately set out to intercept them.

Samson in the leading car encountered the German patrol a couple of miles out of Cassel. He skidded to a halt with something of a "handbrake turn", which enabled him to bring the Maxim gun mounted in the rear of the car to bear. The marines were quick to add their rifle power. The Germans jumped into a ditch beside their car and fired in response. At this point the firing pin of the Maxim sheared and the Germans were able to escape, their car undamaged. The point was underlined that a machine gun mounted in the back of a touring car could only fire in one direction – backwards.

The Rolls-Royce car was hit by rifle fire in many places but was not disabled. The patrol then returned to its base in Cassel.

On 5 September, General Bidon, under whose command Samson was operating, then asked for cars to cover the withdrawal of his men from Lille who were under heavy enemy pressure. Only Samson's car carried a machine gun, so he persuaded the French to lend him two *mitrailleuses* with four *poilus* [French infantrymen] to man them.

Samson had already devised a drill for the tactical use of the cars, which moved about 70 ft apart. They halted with each following car on the opposite side of the road. A keen eye for easy turning places was constantly in mind. When entering the usual sprawling villages, the leading car reversed in, so that his gun could bear, and stopped and covered the next car, which then passed and took the same action so that covering firepower was always available.

In towns or heavily built-up areas the policy was to close up, to be certain of retaining visual contact and to be able to move as rapidly as possible. The cars were at greater risk when moving through woods and descending steep hills. The method adopted in the first instance was for the leading car to drive flat out through wooded areas or up the hill, stopping only at the end of such obstacles to give cover to the remaining cars, thus precluding possible ambush. When halted, cars always took up positions enabling the machine gun to bear. The cars themselves, of course, had no armour plating.

Air and ground co-operation in this open warfare was in its infancy. Aero escorts invariably flew ahead at low-level as "spotters", firing Verey lights to indicate a "find". Samson was quick to realise and exploit the vital potential of such tactics.

The small convoy entered Lille with tactical care to find no trace of Germans, so Samson paraded his cars in the town square to create the illusion of a British presence. The inhabitants cheered themselves hoarse.

Previous pages: A Rolls-Royce armoured car training and "showing the flag", March 1915

Above: Winston Churchill, possibly visiting British troops in northern France, October 1915

Opposite: The driver's accommodation was primitive and his view very limited

Samson discussed the situation with the town *préfet*. Following the meeting, Samson signed a certificate reading: "I have today occupied Lille with an armed force of English and French troops." Sadly, one French element failed to follow up Samson's initiative and, being too vulnerable to remain, he withdrew on the orders of the French commandant to Dunkirk.

Samson received his first wound at this point, gashed by a shard of windscreen glass shattered by a bottle of beer, thrown as a welcoming gesture by a patriotic Frenchman. Samson's answer was to order the removal of glass from the windscreens of all his cars.

This affray led to discussions on how the cars might be better protected. He contacted the Director of the Air Department of the Admiralty, Commodore Murray Sueter, with proposals put forward by Felix, who had already visited the Forges et Chantiers de France at Dunkirk to discuss the possibility of fitting plating of his own design to his Mercedes. The design included hinged flaps covering the radiator, manually operated to be used when under fire.

Only boilerplate was available. Under test this was found to stop penetration of a British .303 rifle bullet only at 500-ft range and beyond. The German Mauser rifle at that range was

straight through the plating, leaving a clean hole. The weight of the metal cladding caused the springs of the cars to compress alarmingly and tyre pressures of over 60 psi were necessary.

Felix's initial design was improved upon in a number of ways. The windscreen was replaced by steel plating with a vision slit for the driver, much restricting his vision, but giving him vital protection. The armoured body was open, the sides made up of flat plates with a raised "pulpit" at the rear with a tripod mounting for a Maxim gun. The car was christened "Iron Duke". This was the first Royal Naval Air Service pattern. The Rolls-Royce chassis was of the Alpine specification to which all Silver Ghosts in contemporary production were built.

Samson prevailed on the Admiralty to send out real armour-plating sheets cut to the pattern, which were bolted, riveted or welded onto the chassis at Dunkirk. Churchill was quick to hurry production forward and set up a committee chaired by Lord Wimborne with the task of agreeing a final design and putting early production into being.

Meanwhile, still at Dunkirk, a second design, this time by the Admiralty as opposed to the RNAS, was built. This gave far better protection and had overhead cover and a revolving turret carrying a Maxim and later a Vickers machine gun.

Opposite: A Rolls-Royce 1920 Pattern Mark I armoured car passes Her Majesty The Queen in May 1977

Right: Captain FM Boothby, first Commander Royal Naval armoured cars

Air and ground patrols continued. A combination of Lt Dalrymple Clark flying a Short Brothers biplane with an 80 hp engine and Samson in his 40/50 Rolls-Royce touring car, carrying a Maxim gun mounted in the rear compartment, patrolled the Cassel-Bailleul road and surrounding area. In Bailleul, Samson contacted our friend the advocate (in his white waistcoat), who reported 2,000 Germans marching from Lille on the road to Douai. Who actually did the counting is not known.

It was quickly established that motorcars, given reasonable road or track conditions, were faster, quieter and more easily adapted to ground-air co-operation than cavalry. Samson was aware of the insecurity of his base and sent Sueter, the DAD, an urgent request for 50 Royal Marines. Churchill intervened and agreed to send a "large force" and ordered "many cars" to be armoured.

With a severe shortage of motor drivers and mechanics, it was decided to establish an armoured car division. Enlistment was opened and given much publicity, resulting in brisk recruitment, which included a number of fitters and mechanics from the Derby factory, no doubt

egged on by Claude Johnson, still concerned that the war would kill the luxury car trade.

Of all the motor chassis used so far, the Rolls-Royce emerged as outstandingly the best. Its reliability, power and capacity to absorb punishment had already become legendary. Thus the famous Admiralty Pattern 1914 Mark 1 Rolls-Royce armoured car came into being – one of the most successful and long-lived armoured fighting vehicles in history.

The Admiralty ordered the formation of the Royal Naval Air Service Armoured Car Division. Its depot was at the Clement-Talbot motor car works near Wormwood Scrubs in West London. Its commander was a talented pioneer naval airman, Commander Boothby, whose task was to turn the ad hoc organisation of Samson's Dunkirk force into a more established formation for future operations.

Lord Northcliffe handed over the Daily Mail airship sheds at Wormwood Scrubs as additional accommodation. Recruiting was handled from the RNAS headquarters at Crystal Palace. The first car register and squadron make-up show an establishment of 20 squadrons plus a small reserve squadron.

Of these, Numbers I, II, III, IV, VII and VIII were each based on 12 Rolls-Royce armoured cars plus armoured lorries, wagons, wireless vehicles and ambulances. Recruiting centres at London, Liverpool, Derby and Glasgow sought motor mechanics and drivers. Rolls-Royce, Derby, lost many valuable workers, inspired by the white-hot patriotism of the day to join this new branch of the services. Courses were set up at Whale Island, Portsmouth for gunnery and at the Small Arms School at Hythe in Kent for machine gun training.

The first contract with Rolls-Royce was for 77 chassis. It was met from production and by recalling unsold chassis from dealers and coach makers throughout the country. The guarantee books mention Barker, Cockshoot, Connaught, Jarrott, Labourdette, HJ Mulliner, Radley and Vanden Plas. There is no evidence that privately owned cars were given or loaned for this contract.

The chassis are all fully recorded in detail in the archives of the Sir Henry Royce Memorial Foundation at Paulerspury in Northamptonshire. The 40/50 chassis – designed in 1906 – had, by 1914, undergone many changes and most of those prepared for armoured bodies were of the Continental or Alpine specification.

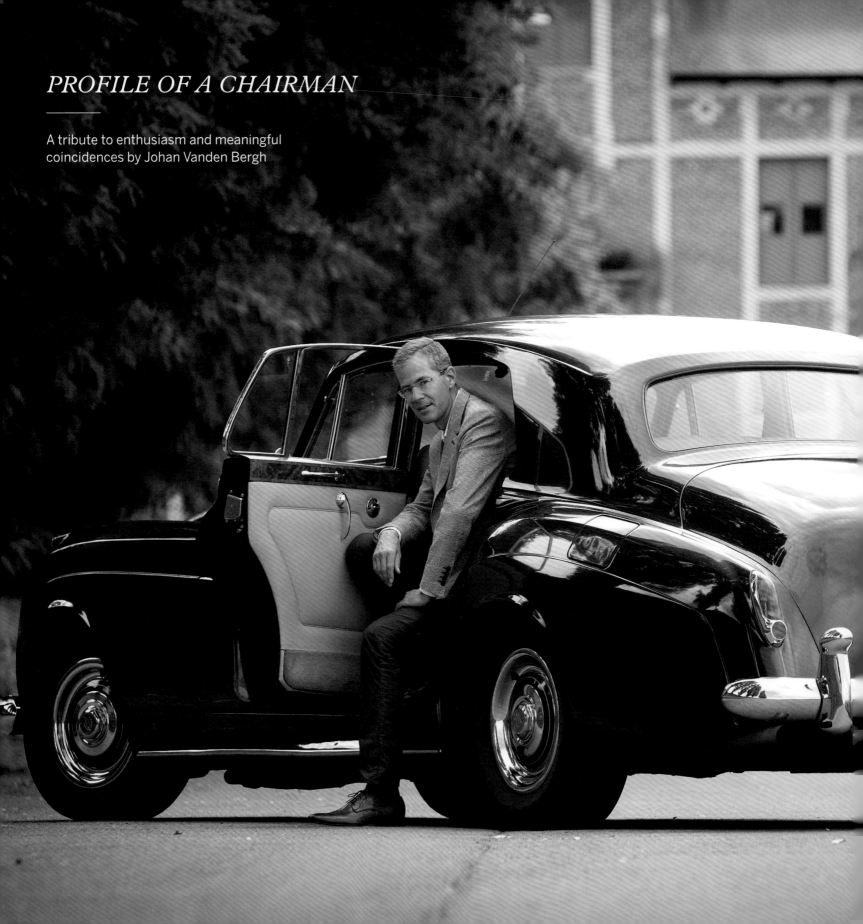

PROFILE OF A CHAIRMAN

A tribute to enthusiasm and meaningful
coincidences by Johan Vanden Bergh

ALTHOUGH VERY MUCH a personal story, this article could be about anyone – and certainly any member of the RREC – for it is, first and foremost, a story of enthusiasm, some perseverance and a lot of patience.

I have always been fascinated by cars, and British ones in particular. I still remember wondering as a child which was the more expensive – a Rolls-Royce/Bentley or a Jaguar/Daimler? Over the years, things became clearer, however. It is difficult to say what sparked my Rolls-Royce enthusiasm exactly, but one childhood memory stands out.

My parents were living in a closed estate, meaning that the road that encircled it was visible from both sides of the house. On one occasion, a Silver Cloud (or S Type) passed by when I was in my room, so I made a run to the other side of the house to see it passing again. All I could hear was that typical sound of a large amount of air being displaced. There was no engine sound or any sort of mechanical noise.

The years passed by and when my brother got married, the wedding car was a beautiful dark blue Silver Shadow. The chauffeur wore a cap and gloves, as one might expect, and I was allowed to sit next to him – what an experience! It left a lasting impression, and it wasn't long before I realised I wanted to drive a Rolls-Royce myself.

By the time the news was announced that the company was up for sale in 1998, I had become pretty desperate. I was working in the car industry by then and, having done lots of "mystery shopping" (whereby I covertly assessed the customer experience), I decided to pose as an interested buyer of a second-hand Silver Shadow LWB and had a test drive.

Once bitten, forever smitten ... I was addicted and a year later, in June 1999, I borrowed an XKR from the Jaguar importer (I was working for Lexus then, so this wasn't an unusual thing to do) and went "mystery shopping" at the official distributor for Rolls-Royce and Bentley in Belgium. No need to explain my hidden agenda – the chance to drive the then brand-new Arnage, which was renamed the Green Label retrospectively.

GHOST OF A CHANCE

But I'm getting ahead of myself – other events had occurred parallel to these. I never failed an exam as a student, except for one time. Bad news rarely comes alone and it so happened that the day after I was due to retake the test, the Rally of Brussels – organised by the leading car magazine of Belgium – was being held, and it had been made public that AX201 would be attending. I was excited and depressed at the same time. My education took priority and I studied and left the rally to its own devices.

I graduated with flying colours the following year and was determined to start my career in the car industry with a particular brand – one that was to become a market leader for many years to come. Toyota was a force in rally championships at the time, and on one occasion we took a truck with a rally simulator along to the Ypres Rally. The truck's drivers came from the town of Crewe and I knew that AX201 was resident in the Crewe factory's own museum (the Lineage Exhibition) at the time. This was before the age of the email, so on his return home one of the drivers faxed me and told me to get in touch with Mrs Mulatero, who organised factory tours. A Crewe Experience was duly booked for September 1998.

Lightning never strikes twice, but it did for me. AX201 was out. Undeterred, I arranged to visit again in June 1999, but one week before I was due to set off the depressing phone call came – AX201 would be out again. Never mind, I thought, and went along anyway, also visiting the Jaguar factory in Browns Lane, Coventry.

Fate clearly had it in for me, so I decided to make my own luck. On a raining weekday, with nothing to do, I decided to make a call. "Yes sir, AX201 is here," replied the voice down the phone. "No sir, she won't be leaving this week." Right, I told myself, it's now or never. So I jumped on a plane, destination Manchester Airport. A short train ride later I was being made very welcome by tour guide Rod Tilley and was soon introduced to Michael Edge, Custodian of Historic Motor Vehicles, Rolls-Royce and Bentley Motor Cars.

I was soon to find out what that meant precisely. Michael excused himself and I was left alone in the Lineage for a few moments. When he re-emerged, he spoke words that are ingrained on my brain forever: "I had a word with my boss – we are going to take AX201 for a ride." Before I realised what was happening, we were pushing a Derby Bentley out of the way, AX201 burst into life and we were off.

The emotions that stormed through my head in that moment are almost impossible to describe. You try desperately to grasp, to savour the moment, knowing that it will never happen again while at the same time trying to come to terms with the myth. Or was it a reality?

The Silver Ghost is said to do everything in top gear, and by the time we got to the factory gates she was in fourth gear and the driver never changed down again. The Silver Ghost is also supposed to whisper like a ghost, and indeed she did. Even the silver plating had something unreal about it. England being England, it had started to drizzle, but once back in the Lineage, it took her 15 minutes to shine like new again. As if the wet had vaporised into thin air.

To round things off I was treated to another factory tour, but I don't think I noticed very much – I was still recovering from the ride. Rod then kindly drove me back to the station in an Arnage. Before letting me out of the car, he said: "You're clearly an enthusiast. If you ever come back to Crewe, you have to follow the Chauffeur's Course."

A MATTER OF COURSE

No prizes for guessing what I did next – I signed up for the following year. Another Rolls-Royce holiday! In the meantime, I gave the secretary of the Belgium Flemish Section of the RREC a call, but truth be told I didn't dare join, such was the image of the marque.

Come Spring 2000, I was sent the Highway Code accompanied by a nice letter setting out in clear terms that students must pass their Highway Code test before being allowed out on the road. A fresh wave of exam stress engulfed me, but I studied like hell and all went well.

The first time I drove on the left was in a new Silver Seraph. The subsequent test on the road took place in a Red Label Arnage and earned me a Certificate of the Rolls-Royce & Bentley Motor Cars School of Instruction. Theoretically, I was now supposed to know how to behave on the road, clean the car, do

Left: Johan's beloved Silver Cloud II SAE335

Opposite: A "marriage" made in heaven?

Overleaf: Johan takes to the wheel of AX201, fulfilling the ambition of a lifetime

basic maintenance and change a tyre in two minutes flat (including opening up umbrellas for the passengers in case it rained).

Something else happened during that week of training – I learnt about the Mobile Security Course. No need to guess what was on the agenda for 2001! By then, however, I'd been given the confidence boost I so badly needed and applied to join the RRFC through the Belgian Flemish Section, assuming it would be pretty rare for any of the members to have taken the Chauffeur's Course. It turned out I was the only one to have ever done it. This, of course, was brilliant because I ended up driving various models of Rolls-Royce and Bentley – my certificate inspiring confidence in the owners that this twenty-something-year-old (I was 27 by then) was not going to brutalise their precious motor car.

Still, I did the Mobile Security Course and soon knew everything about declaring a car bomb-free, route planning, reversing out of shooting range at close to 60 mph and swinging the car round with and without braking. All good fun, but it was the driver-awareness training that probably proved most useful – quite by coincidence it served me well only a few weeks later when I avoided getting sucked into a game of road rage with another driver on the motorway.

Three months passed and I got the chance to drive SAE335 – a 1962 Silver Cloud II – for the first time, courtesy of Robert Lambrichts, Treasurer of the Belgium Flemish Section. Come to think of it, treasurers seem to have very good taste in cars. One of the highlights of my life was when South Eastern Section Treasurer Martin Coomber let me drive his

magnificent Phantom III, 3AX65, which boasted Belgian coachwork by Vanden Plas and was "born" in the same year as my late mother. It was, and still is, fitted with arguably the best Phantom III engine around – it certainly produced a majestic sound that could not be bettered by any other motoring machine.

A SILVER LINING

In 2004, I was talked into becoming the Editor of the Belgium Flemish Section's magazine. Before I realised what I had got myself into, I was despatched to the yearly Club conference. In 2012 and 2013, I chaired the Continental Sections Conference, and then something else happened. Well, two things really. Firstly, I realised that my 40-year mark was coming up, and secondly I noticed that the costs of my house had settled down. A rather daft idea crossed my mind – another of those "now or never" moments.

Possibly fuelled by my urge to have a proper car again (I had left Lexus by then, so was having to make do with fewer cylinders under the bonnet), I called Robert and asked whether SAE335 was for sale (having mentioned previously to him that I would like to be considered if he ever decided to sell her). We agreed to meet at the British Classic Car Meeting and, in glorious sunshine, a deal was struck.

The car was in my garage by 1 August 2013, suitably christened with Champagne. On my birthday, I collected my girlfriend (who had been kept blissfully unaware of proceedings) in a Rolls-Royce, having explained to the restaurant we were going to that it is customary for Rolls-Royce motor cars to pull up at the entrance of a

restaurant and stay there. Parking is an inferior act best left to lesser motor cars.

The following day, I drove SAE335 to The Hunt House, her maiden trip to home turf following years of use on the Continent. The "marriage" of SAE335 and me was seemingly inevitable since the day I'd first set eyes on her. When my mother died in 2011, I had asked Robert to come in his Silver Cloud and he had obliged. Unbeknown to me then, the car was already becoming part of my history or rather, perhaps, I was becoming part of its.

I was co-opted onto the RREC Board of Directors on 7 May 2013, and was appointed Deputy Chairman the following April. The rest is history ... well, not quite. In 2014, I lined up for a drive in Mermie Karger's 1913 Silver Ghost Saoutchik Tourer, 2442. It was an unbelievable experience. At more than 100 years of age, this car still felt so capable, so brilliant, so ... modern. There really isn't much that a modern car can hope to do better than a Silver Ghost.

So, that was it as far as motoring highlights go, or was it? One of the duties of the Chairman is to represent the RREC, and to be seen doing so. It involves (a lot of) handshaking and touring around. Courtesy of P&A Wood and Bentley Motors Limited, the Club still has exclusive use of SU13 and AX201 at its flagship events. This includes, first and foremost, the Annual Rally. Both cars remained with the factory when it was sold in 1998 and are therefore now the property of Bentley Motors Limited, which kindly allows P&A Wood to take them to important RREC events. The more so in 2016, of course, as it was the 110th anniversary of the 40/50 hp that was subsequently to be known as the Silver Ghost.

DRIVE OF A LIFETIME

And so it happened that barely two years after driving 2442, I found myself again at the wheel of a Silver Ghost, or rather *the* Silver Ghost. The experience was the same as that of 1999, apart from the fact that I'd moved diagonally from the VIP seat in the back to the driver's seat in the front. It felt like touching a holy shrine and handling a baby at the same time, very smooth and tender, obeying its chauffeur's every wish with a smooth and surprisingly rapid response. You don't put AX201 into gear, you gently convince her to slide into gear, and everything that follows thereafter is a pure delight.

Meaningful coincidences – it is a somewhat philosophical term that I picked up from a book many years ago. A lot of things happen to all of us in life, seemingly unrelated, coincidental. Yet, with the benefit of hindsight, were they really? Why did I fail that one exam? Why did I choose to work for Toyota? Why did those lorry drivers live in Crewe? Why did they get AX201 out for me? Why did I take these courses in Crewe? Why was one of the first Club cars I drove SAE335? Why was I co-opted?

Unlike the many people who from early on in life seem to know what they want from it, I never told my parents that one day I would own a Rolls-Royce (although I came very close when I brought home a brand new Silver Seraph Last of Line one day and gave my parents the ride of a lifetime). Yet that is exactly what was meant to be. A coincidence, yes, but a meaningful one.

This article is dedicated to the memory of Celia Fitzhugh, Special Advisor to the RREC Board, who prompted me for more than a year to commit this story to paper.

FIRST AMONG EQUALS

The origins and outstanding success of the Club's
Northern Section by Professor Roy Brooks

Members of the Rolls-Royce Owner Drivers'
Course outside Bolton Technical College (including
Roy Brooks standing nearest to the steering wheel
of a 1931 Hooper bodied 20/25) in April 1966

TODAY, THE ROLLS-ROYCE Enthusiasts' Club (RREC) can proudly boast of almost 10,000 members in 40 geographically based sections scattered throughout the world. It was by no means always thus, as I soon discovered when I joined the Club way back in 1964 and when I formed the Club's very first section, almost by subterfuge.

It's worth recording how I actually became a member, since I hadn't even heard of the RREC when I bought my first Rolls-Royce two years earlier. Knowing little more of the marque than its reputation of being the "Best Car in the World", I found Rolls-Royce motoring decidedly different to running an "ordinary" car. So much so that I wrote an article about my experiences; this appeared in *The Autocar* magazine 9 January 1964.

Within a very few days an unexpected handwritten letter arrived from one Lt Col EB Barrass, OBE, TD, inviting me to join the RREC. "I have just read your excellent article on the ownership of a pre-war Rolls-Royce," he wrote. "One point you did not mention is the great advantage of joining a club like this. We have 550 odd members, a great source of help to the chap who likes to do his own work. Through pooling the knowledge and experience of our members, there are now few problems we either cannot solve or prevent." I could not wait to join and immediately sent off my bankers order to cover the annual membership fee, then the princely sum of £1.

DISTANCE LEARNING

It felt great to be a member of a Rolls-Royce club and I avidly perused the bi-monthly *Bulletin*. It contained lots of helpful technical information, but the club activities listed were relatively few and centred primarily around the Oxford area, where the club had started seven years earlier.

Living in Lancashire, almost 200 miles away, was something of a deterrent, although well worth the effort for such events as the annual rally at Blenheim and the annual dinner at Weston Manor. My suggestion to Eric Barrass (now on first-name terms) that maybe I could organise a Club event in the north met with a distinctly cool reaction. "We like to have the events fairly close by so we can ensure their proper running!" he replied.

While only having the title of club secretary, Eric actually ran the RREC – extremely effectively – almost as if it was his regiment, with himself as its benign colonel in chief. He and I, along with our families, became great friends.

Feeling, in Rolls-Royce terms, something of an outcast, I decided that there was something I could do by way of a Rolls-Royce event near home to which the club could not object. At that time I was the head of motor vehicle work at the Bolton Technical College and had access to a large motor vehicle workshop and support staff.

During the summer term, as students entered for examinations, work became very light, especially in the evenings. We regularly put on owner-driver maintenance classes during such times and they were very popular. Why not do something to which the Club could not object and put on a Rolls-Royce Owner Drivers' Course, operated by the local authority, not the RREC? The college principal, Dr AG Peace, himself a keen motorist, agreed and the course was duly scheduled to start 26 April 1966.

In spite of some reluctance, Eric Barrass was persuaded to let me have a list (handwritten again) of all the RREC members within a 100-mile radius of Bolton, and I contacted every one. The 30-shilling (£1.50) fee for the eight-week course seems ridiculously cheap by today's standards. Understandably, almost everyone joining the course was an RREC member.

A CLASS ACT

There was just one major snag: I had great difficulty in finding a suitable lecturer. All the likely sources were tried, including the factory at Crewe and all the local dealers. No success. Even Mr FA Hutton, the principal of the Rolls-Royce School of Instruction in London, wrote to say that he himself would "enjoy doing the carburetion lectures", but felt the distance involved too great.

I decided to approach the press regarding the course and lack of a lecturer. Somewhat to my surprise, newspapers – national and local – were decidedly interested. In retrospect, I realised that here was a world first of its kind. "Ordinary" folk being taught how to maintain their own Rolls-Royce was unheard of. This was really the province of liveried chauffeurs and highly skilled mechanics.

The *Sunday Express* 5 March 1966 ran a piece headed, "Entrance to this school is only by Rolls", which ended with an interview with Dr F Llewellyn Smith, Managing Director of Rolls-Royce Motor Car Division. "This sounds like a very good idea," he said of the proposed course, "and I admire Mr Brooks for his enterprise." On the previous day, the *Manchester Evening*

News had printed a large illustrated article, ending up with the comment: "The pay is not quite in the Rolls-Royce class – £1 an hour", while *The Guardian* reported the course as being on "How to look after your Rolls-Royce".

With the deadline date fast approaching, a would-be course member, Brian Pollard, suggested that I contact Maurice Booth, then foreman mechanic of Rippon Bros Ltd, long-established Rolls-Royce agents in Huddersfield. This I duly did. After a considerable amount of coaxing, Maurice, who had never done this sort of thing before, agree to undertake the job, but only if he did the actual practical work and I did the talking. He was so nervous about the idea that he would not let me release his name or where he worked before the course started.

MEDIA ATTENTION

BBC Television asked me if it could do some filming at the college on the day prior to the course starting. A selection of cars was quickly arranged via their remarkably willing owners and filming went without a hitch. The report was a news feature the next evening. I was too busy to see it, but clearly a lot of people did and the college switchboard was jammed by callers wanting details.

On the evening of the course, I arrived early for the class, only to be met by considerably more photographers and reporters than the 19 members of the class. I was obliged to pack the news hounds into a classroom and give my

first and totally impromptu press conference. Press coverage was worldwide. Over time, press cuttings came in from as far away as New Zealand and the US. The various reports of what I had said and their descriptions of the course differed so much that I seriously wondered if they had been at the same event as me!

Among the best was the maybe slightly creative interpretation by Michael Gagie in the *Daily Mirror*, under the headline, "They've joined the Rolls set, for only 30 bob".

The first paragraph set the tone: "The emotion was almost a tangible thing. It was coming across 200 miles of telephone wire. And it was simply an outrage. 'But you CAN'T have amateurs messing about with our cars', the man from Rolls-Royce spluttered, 'It's asking for trouble'. There WASN'T any mistake. Rolls-Royce maintenance has become a subject on a night-school timetable at a technical college in Bolton."

In the tail of the piece the author does say: "I told the man at Rolls that they were really a decent bunch, not trying to meddle too much in things that don't concern them." It might seem that the anonymous Rolls-Royce spokesman was not quite singing from the same hymn sheet as his managing director who earlier had stated his admiration of the enterprise. But it made good copy for the *Daily Mirror*!

Local opinions were generally favourable, but one Bolton alderman, J Vickers – referring to the course in a town council meeting a few days

Clockwise from top left: The Northern Section's first rally, held at Lymm Park in 1967; BBC cameras set up outside Bolton Technical College; cars line up outside the college to be filmed

Below: (left to right) Roy Brooks, George Fenn (Managing Director of Rolls-Royce) and Trevor Chinn (Chairman of Lex Mead) cut a radiator-shaped cake at the Midland Hotel in 1979 in celebration of the first meeting of CS Rolls and FH Royce

Opposite: The Midland Hotel – one of the Northern Section's many prized local landmarks

Overleaf, clockwise from top: The first RREC National Spares Sale at the Territorial Drill Hall in Bolton; marking 50 years of the Silver Shadow at the site of its launch, the Wild Boar Hotel near Tarporley; the Vintage Rolls-Royce Exhibition in Blackpool's Winter Gardens, 1976

later – was far from approving. "If they had been seeking an engineering course with more limited appeal in Bolton they would have had to make a tremendous search." He suggested that the only subject that might have qualified was, "the history of the ducking stool!"

Our instructor, Maurice Booth, who had worked on Rolls-Royce cars since joining Rippon Bros on the day before his 14th birthday, proved to have an unrivalled knowledge of our cars. He and I worked well together, him with the technical skill and me helping him to overcome his initial shyness. Maurice became one of my closest friends until sadly he died prematurely, aged 45, in July 1970. The Maurice Booth Memorial Library was subsequently set up by the Northern Section in his honour via donations from section members; it is now located in the Hunt House and has become arguably the finest library of Rolls-Royce material in the world.

The course was immensely popular with the participants, some making considerable efforts to attend. Dr Eric Wraith (who, rather appropriately, owned a Silver Wraith) paid a locum to take his Monday evening surgeries; David Mitchell who kept the same 20hp Shooting Brake until he died only last year, made the round trip of some 150 miles each time; and one member had his brother attend when he had to go in hospital. Each session lasted well over the scheduled two hours; often I was getting home near midnight.

SECTIONAL INTERESTS

It is apposite to mention that there was no declared formal start to the Northern Section. Indeed, the title "section" was not yet used within

the RREC. I decided on the "Northern Section" simply to distinguish it from the "Southerners". As organiser, I had acted as chairman from the beginning and simply assumed the title, the de facto start of the section being the first meeting of the course, 25 April 1966. Towards the end of the eight weeks we formed a small committee and each one of us put 10 shillings in a tin box to start off section funds. The section has never since been out of funds. My late wife Rita became the treasurer, who carefully guarded the section's finances for the first nine years and hosted the committee meeting at our home for even longer.

With the addition of trimming and bodywork courses, the maintenance classes continued very successfully for some years at the technical college until I left there and moved into training teachers of automobile engineering. However, the courses continued in a variety of locations and the section still follows the tradition with specialised courses for the pre-war and more modern machines. Recently, we have started monthly "Tea & Tech" evenings; essentially a simple technical chat time with tea and biscuits by way of refreshments, which has proved very popular.

Maybe reflecting the section's technical origins, our first rally in April 1967 at Lymm Park near Stockport was not simply a concours, but included practical competitions. One of which was to be the quickest to change a spark plug; another was a Le Mans-type start. From a given line, drivers had to race to their cars, start them using the handle and drive back to the start line. Not today!

As well as being the Club's very first section, we can also claim quite a few other firsts. One of which being the regular appearance of "Northern

Notes" in *The Bulletin*, starting in November 1966, well before any other section news. Ours was the first Section Newsletter, free to all section members and with its masthead designed by the Rolls-Royce factory artist.

NORTHERN SOUL

The Northern Section has always had one major permanently unbeatable advantage over other sections – geography. Within our boundaries are such landmarks as the location of the original Rolls-Royce factory in Manchester; Royce's home, Brae Cottage in Knutsford; the Midland Hotel where Rolls and Royce first met; and the Crewe factory where all the post-war Rolls-Royce and Bentley cars were made until the end of 2002. The first Rolls-Royce car under BMW ownership was delivered on 1 January 2003. Bentley production at Crewe has continued unabated after Volkswagen purchased the company from Vickers in 1998.

The section has taken care to appreciate its geographical good fortune by, for instance, holding events in the Midland Hotel, being privileged to visit Brae Cottage numerous times and maintaining cordial relations with Crewe. One small example of our interest in local Royce matters occurred when it came to our attention that the grave of Henry Royce's mother, Mary, in the Tabley Hill Cemetery near Knutsford had seriously deteriorated. Some 30 section members contributed the cost of restoration and the work was dedicated at the graveside, exactly 105 years to the day of when she died, just four months before the first Royce car took to the road.

Being canny Northerners, we decided very early on that we should aim to make a profit on every event. Initially, such an attitude was somewhat frowned on by the main RREC, but it didn't take long to catch on.

Another first was the Spares Sale at the 1969 annual rally. Rippon Bros decided to clear out much of its substantial stock of mainly second-hand pre-war Rolls-Royce parts and coachbuilding items. They asked me if we would like them. Can a duck swim?! We sent a lorry over to Huddersfield and returned with a treasure trove of material. Today, it would make a retirement fund. Most of it we sold at the annual rally at Blenheim.

Prices were ridiculously cheap. Outstanding, I remember, were the cylinder blocks and crankcases at ten shillings (50p) each – providing you took a front axle at the same time! The section continued to organise and staff the Spares Sale for several years. It has now become an essential and valued feature of every annual rally.

In 1974, the section organised the first RREC National Spares and Vehicle Sale, taking over the huge Territorial Army Drill Hall in Bolton for the purpose. The late Peter Harper – whose full-page, back-cover advertisement was a feature of the Club *Advertiser* for many years – was the auctioneer and presided over the dozen or so cars that had

been entered. These included a very presentable Silver Cloud III selling for £3,600 and a complete Phantom II chassis reaching £100. Spares on the 28 stalls were incredibly cheap: for example, a brand new pair of P100 headlamps cost only £50. We were very modest with our charges. Auctioned vehicles were 5 per cent for the first £1,000 and 2.5 per cent thereafter, maximum commission £100; spares were 5 per cent of sale price. We still made a decent profit.

Always looking for new ideas, in 1976 the section organised a Vintage Rolls-Royce Exhibition in Blackpool's Winter Gardens, spanning the Bank Holiday weekend and masterminded by the late Matt Wright. It was absolutely untried and possibly the most ambitious event of its kind the Club had ever undertaken, and we fervently hoped it would succeed – particularly for those members who had generously put up financial sureties. Granada TV ran a piece about the exhibition during its evening news and the *Blackpool Gazette* gave the show editorial coverage. Holidaymakers loved it, with some 8,000 visitors queuing up to pay the 25p entrance fee. After all expenses, we made a jolly good profit.

A THRIVING ENTERPRISE

During the late 1970s, we went into republishing the 20hp Parts Catalogues. I can recall personally slaving over an old Xerox copier to produce 10,000 copy pages to be collated and bound for sale. That was another decent money earner; equally so the 20hp Instruction Book in 1980.

Over the years, under a succession of excellent chairmen, willing committee members

and a splendid lot of members, spouses and families, the section continued to thrive. With no set boundaries, initially, our area comprised virtually everywhere "North of The Wash". Indeed, a member in Edinburgh once took me to task for not organising events near to him.

Currently with some 600 members, we still have a larger membership than any other section. What is more, we offer a huge range of Club activities. Over the past 12 months there have been some 110 events arranged for member participation. You could have tried your hand at most things, from clay-pigeon shooting to crown green bowling; from a Valentine's Day lunch to repairing a Rolls-Royce; or a simple Noggin & Natter evening (five venues each month) to watching the Gold Cup Race at Oulton Park. These are in addition to all the usual dinners, section weekends away and the like.

Maybe more unusual than most events is something that has been brilliantly organised for the past three years by our indefatigable Events Officer, Elizabeth Earp and husband Andy. This is where we are entirely devoid of our cars, during week-long holidays in Madeira.

Based at the Royal Savoy Hotel, where the manager just happens to be an Honorary Member of the Northern Section, these holidays are well above the ordinary. We are also fortunate to have a close relationship with the island's splendid Clube de Automóveis Clássicos da Madeira and are inevitably invited to at least one of its classic car events during each stay. Another such holiday is planned for 2017.

THE GOLDEN SECTION

In April 2016, with me now "promoted" to President Emeritus, we celebrated our 50th anniversary in style, although not at the old technical college in Bolton where it all began, which sadly has been demolished. We were privileged to use what may now be regarded as our new spiritual home, the University of Bolton, which effectively "grew" out of the old college. On a lovely sunny day it provided a superb setting for our 50th Celebration Rally and the 59 cars, bringing almost 250 members and guests. Luncheon was provided in the magnificent Assembly Hall at the nearby Bolton School, a prestigious independent grammar school that can trace its origins back to 1516. Additional celebrations were arranged by way of four garden parties in different parts of the region.

Admittedly I am biased, but it's fair to say that the Northern Section has done well for more than half a century and "used its talents wisely". Even so, we are conscious that there can be no resting on our laurels and constantly strive to do even better. Interestingly, although the section can justly claim a lot of firsts, we are as certain as anyone ever can be of at least one more when, in 2026, we will be the first section to reach its Diamond Jubilee.

Undoubtedly, there are many other people and significant events that have contributed mightily to our success and have not been mentioned. However, please allow me to plead lack of space compounded by an imperfect and ever-fading memory; nonetheless, everyone who has helped along the way is appreciated. After all, "The cars may be the catalyst, but it is the people that matter."

WO in a 1928 4½ litre Bentley

Overleaf, left to right: The camshaft
drive on the 6½ litre Bentley; the
Bentley 3 litre engine with bevel
camshaft drive

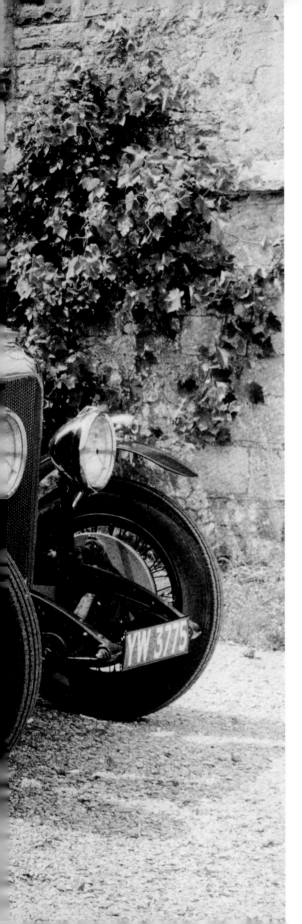

AN ENGINE OF INNOVATION

WO Bentley and his engineering
masterpieces by David Towers

BORN IN 1888, WO Bentley went on to guide
the creation of Bentley's classic models until
the early 1930s, designing some of the marque's
most iconic engines.

The name "Bentley" might not be mentioned
in the RREC's full title, although it does appear in
the subtitle – "the Club for Rolls-Royce and Bentley
Enthusiasts". And Bentley cars, which share a long,
entwined history with the Rolls-Royce marque,
are an important part of the RREC.

The man behind the Bentley name was Walter
Owen Bentley, or "WO" as he was often called.
He was born to a wealthy family in Hampstead,
north London on 16 September 1888, the youngest
of nine children. In 1902, aged 13, he was sent to
Clifton College, a prestigious boarding school in
Bristol, leaving at the age of 16 to start work as an
apprentice engineer at the Great Northern Railway
in Doncaster.

In 1912 he joined his brother, Horace –
also known as HM – to sell cars made by the
French manufacturer Doriot, Flandrin & Parant
(DFP). He made the engines more powerful by
incorporating aluminium pistons and a revised
camshaft. The lighter aluminium pistons allowed
the engine to operate at higher revs and at a higher
compression ratio, thus increasing its power.

PISTON POWER

During World War I, his aluminium pistons were
incorporated into Rolls-Royce Eagle engines
and used by the Sunbeam motor car company.
WO also developed the BR1 rotary aero engine
(used by the RAF in the Sopwith Camel) and the
bigger BR2 (used in the Sopwith Snipe). He was
awarded an MBE for his contributions to the war
effort, and, in 1920, he received £8,000 from the
UK government's Royal Commission on Awards
to Inventors for the invention of aluminium pistons.

Early in 1919, WO joined his brother HM in
Cricklewood, north-west London, to form the
company Bentley & Bentley to produce a three-
litre motor car. The first road test was in January
1920 and the first delivery in September 1921.
For 10 years, until mid 1931, Bentley produced
3,061 chassis and engines, 53 per cent of which
were with the three-litre four-cylinder engine.
The engines were both very advanced and very
interesting. The five types of engine produced
by the WO Bentley company, in chronological
order, can be found overleaf.

Essentially, the first four engines were
designed by WO Bentley and are of a similar
design. With the four-litre engine, the Bentley
board of directors decided they wanted a simpler
and cheaper engine. WO objected to this, and
was not involved in its design.

THREE-LITRE ENGINE

Over half of the WO Bentley cars incorporate
this engine. Like the subsequent WO engines, it
had a single overhead camshaft and four valves
per cylinder. Four valves/cylinder gives better
"breathing" than two valves, so it produces more
power. Most modern cars have four valves/
cylinder, although this didn't become common

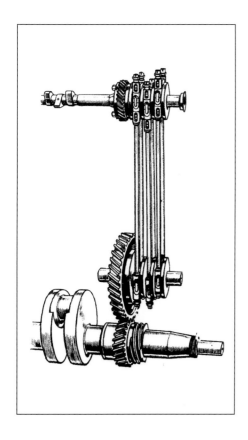

until the 1980s. Rolls-Royce cars didn't have four valves/cylinder until the Goodwood models produced under BMW from 2003. Most Rolls-Royce aero engines, including the Merlin (in the Spitfire) had four valves/cylinder.

Also, it had an overhead camshaft (rather than side camshaft and pushrods), which gives better control over opening the inlet and exhaust valves. One cam and rocker operated the two inlet valves, while the exhaust valves were operated by individual cams. As the camshaft was over the centre of the engine, the two sparking plugs were on either side of the cylinder head. At that time, there were problems of sealing the cylinder block to the head, so the engine had an integral block and head (with no joint), like the Rolls-Royce Silver Ghost engine.

Both WO Bentley and Henry Royce (of Rolls-Royce) disliked driving the camshaft by a chain. At the front of the engine, the three litre used a bevel gear driven directly from the crankshaft, a vertical shaft and a bevel gear to drive the camshaft. Rolls-Royce had a side camshaft, as it would have taken too many gears to reach an overhead camshaft, with associated backlash and timing problems.

This was a sporting engine, which won the Le Mans 24-hour race in 1924 and 1927. Many of the original bodies were saloons and limousines, rather than the current more sporting "tourers" (convertibles). These cars were competitors to the 20hp Rolls-Royce car with its 3.1 litre six-cylinder engine. The Bentley engine would be more powerful than the 20hp Rolls-Royce, but not as smooth, with the Bentley having only four cylinders against the Rolls-Royce's six cylinders.

Like many British car engines, the Bentley had a long stroke of 149 mm. Today, a stroke of over 100 mm would be considered "long". At the time, the UK motor taxation system encouraged engines with a long stroke, as the "RAC horse power" was a function of the bore of the engine, with no account of its stroke. RAC horse power determined the cost of the annual road fund licence. So, UK cars tended to have engines with a narrow bore and long stroke. The longer stroke

Engine	Cylinders	Capacity (cc)	Bore (mm)	Stroke (mm)	Valves/Cylinder	Camshaft	Power (bhp)	Production (years)	Sales
3 litre	4	2,996	80	149	4	Overhead	71–87	1922–31	1,639
6½ litre	6	6,597	100	140	4	Overhead	110–130	1926–30	539
4½ litre	4	4,398	100	140	4	Overhead	100–130	1928–31	733
8 litre	6	7,983	110	140	4	Overhead	200–230	1931	100
4 litre	6	3,915	85	115	2	Side	120	1931	50

would increase the capacity of the engine and its power, but it also tends to limit the maximum revs of the engine, thus limiting power. Also, a small bore means relatively small valves, which limits the "breathing" of the engine – the more air you put into an engine, the more power it produces. However, long-stroke engines tend to give high torque at low engine speeds, which makes the car feel more relaxed – which was good for a Rolls-Royce.

All the WO Bentley engines have a long stroke, making them flexible with high torque at low engines speeds. This arrangement is not ideal for sporting engines, but Bentley engines were still very successful in motor sport, winning the Le Mans 24-hour race in 1924 and 1927.

SIX-AND-A-HALF-LITRE ENGINE

WO explained: "the noise level and impulses of a four-cylinder engine were always unsuitable for the closed coachwork we were obliged by public demand to offer on our chassis." So, a six-cylinder engine was required.

This engine started from a six-cylinder variant of the three-litre four-cylinder engine, but with a slightly reduced stroke of 140 mm, giving 4,224 cc. It was Bentley's first six-cylinder engine, and competed with the Rolls-Royce Phantom I (the large Rolls-Royce), with its enormous 7,668 cc engine. By chance, the prototype Phantom I 11EX and the prototype Bentley met in France in 1924. A race showed that the cars were equally matched, with both engines producing about 100 bhp. The race stopped when the Rolls-Royce driver's hat blew off! From this, WO decided to increase the engine's size by increasing the bore to 100 mm. This gave 6,597 cc and 140 bhp.

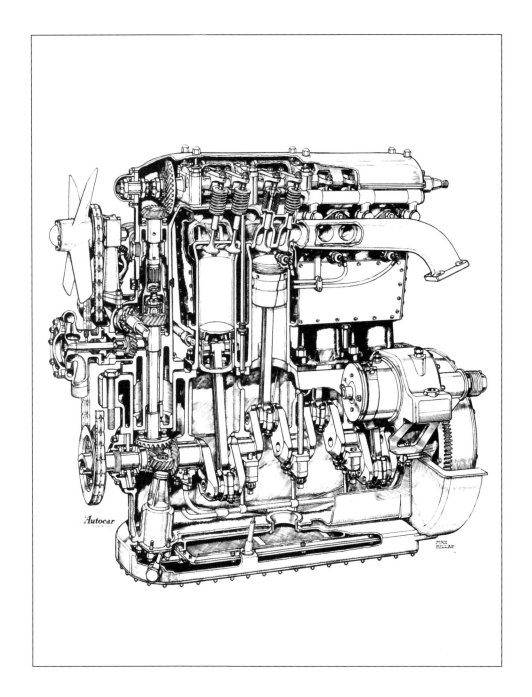

WO with a 1928 4½ litre Bentley and
a 1913 DFP 10/12 hp Special Sports

In many ways, the engine was similar to the three litre, but with two more cylinders, making it smoother. The increased bore allowed larger inlet and exhaust valves. There was the familiar four valves per cylinder and an overhead camshaft. One would have expected this engine to have a similar bevel camshaft drive to the three litre. However, it was quite different and very unusual.

At the back of the engine, the crankshaft incorporated a gear to drive another shaft that went at half the crankshaft speed, which was required by the camshaft. Then, there were three connecting rods between the crankshaft driven shaft and the camshaft, offset by 120 degrees to each other. It is most surprising that such a system works, as it could be difficult to make the timing of the camshaft, relative to the crankshaft, both accurate and consistent. However, the system worked and it was quieter than the bevel gear on the three litre.

Like a "good" modern engine, there were seven bearings from the block to the crankshaft, with one of these either side of the connecting rod bearing on the crankshaft. And there was an additional bearing on the crankshaft to support the drive to the camshaft (i.e. the three connecting rods). WO may have devised this camshaft drive from his apprenticeship on steam engines. With this engine, Bentley had engines that were competitive with the equivalent Rolls-Royce 20hp and Phantom I models.

A more powerful, "Speed Six" version of the six-and-a-half-litre was unveiled at the Olympia Show in October 1928. It proved popular with 177 sales in 1929–30, almost taking over from the standard six-and-a-half-litre in 1930. The Speed Six engine won the Le Mans 24-hour race in 1929 and 1930. Sadly, in 1930 the Bentley board decided to discontinue production of the six-and-a-half to concentrate on sales of chassis with four- and eight-litre engines.

FOUR-AND-A-HALF-LITRE ENGINE

One would expect the four-and-a-half-litre engine of 1928 to be a six-cylinder version of the three-litre engine, and to have been Bentley's second engine, after the three-litre four-cylinder engine (as has been described in the introduction to the six-and-a-half-litre engine)

However, the four-and-a-half-litre engine was a four-cylinder version of the six-and-a-half-litre six-cylinder engine. Thus, it was designed to be the successor of the three-litre engine – a larger and more powerful engine for the three-litre cars.

As it was derived from the six-and-a-half-litre engine, one would have expected the camshaft drive to be similar to the six-cylinder engine with its sophisticated three connecting rods. However, the four-and-a-half-litre engine reverted to the bevel drive of the three-litre engine, probably because it was cheaper and less time-consuming to set up.

This engine was very successful and won the Le Mans 24-hour race in 1928. The famous "blower Bentley" used this engine. It was proposed by Tim Birkin and funded by Dorothy Paget. The Villiers supercharger was at the front of the engine, driven directly by the crankshaft. In race form, the engine produced 240 bhp with a boost pressure of 11 pounds per square inch, compared with 130 bhp of the unblown engine. WO Bentley did not approve of this engine, as he felt the supercharger would over-stress the engine and lead to its failure. This proved to be the case, as it never won a race. Nevertheless, it is a very famous engine, and 55 were produced.

EIGHT-LITRE ENGINE

In 1931, the eight-litre six-cylinder engine replaced the six-and-a-half-litre engine. It is very similar to the six-and-a-half-litre but with its bore increased from 100 mm to 110 mm. The capacity of the engine was 7,983 cc, which was more than the 7,668 cc Rolls-Royce Phantom II engine. And, it was one or two cc more than the Hispano-Suiza H6C engine, even though the Hispano-Suiza engine had the same bore and stroke as the Bentley eight litre!

With the eight litre, Bentley took the opportunity to design a new chassis that had deeper side members, which made it stiffer. However, the eight-litre chassis was very heavy at 37 cwt (1,880 kg), as much as a four-and-a-half-litre Bentley with closed coachwork. Only 100 eight-litre Bentleys were produced. It is probable that only half of these were delivered before the company went into receivership in July 1931. The last one was delivered in December 1932.

The common factors of these WO Bentley engines are aluminium pistons, four valves/cylinder, a central overhead camshaft, unusual drives from the crankshaft to the camshaft and a similar stroke. They were sporting engines.

FOUR-LITRE ENGINE

The Bentley Board decided that the company needed to have a model that competed with the Rolls-Royce 20/25. With the recession, sales of the eight litre were slow. Thus, a smaller and cheaper engine was required.

The previous Bentley engines were expensive to produce, with their four valves per cylinder and overhead camshaft. A simpler and cheaper engine was required, slightly larger than the 3.7 litres of the Rolls-Royce 20/25hp. WO Bentley was not involved in the design of the engine, and didn't approve of the result.

The principal designer was Harry Ricardo, assisted by Wilfred Whatmough (later involved with the forklift truck and speciality engine makers Coventry Climax) and Harry Weslake – all very accomplished engine designers. It was a six-cylinder engine with an overhead inlet and side exhaust valve per cylinder, driven through a side camshaft and pushrods, with twin SU carburettors. The post-Second World War Rolls-Royce 4.25 litre to 4.9 litre engines (1946–59) were very similar.

Time was tight, as the company's financial position was dire. So, for the chassis, a lightly modified eight-litre chassis was used. This chassis was too large and too heavy. The four-litre engine was significantly shorter than the eight litre and lower. This could have allowed a shorter chassis and lower bonnet line, thus saving weight.

The first batch of 25 cars had not all been completed when Bentley went into receivership in July 1931. There was a second batch of 25 cars, many of which were snapped up by the London motor dealers, Jack Barclay. The last one was registered in June 1933, two years after the collapse of Bentley.

Bentley Motors' receiver was appointed on 10 July, 1931, and the liquidator was appointed in September. Bids had to be received by November. It was expected that Napier would acquire Bentley Motors, and WO was planning to move to Napier.

However, The British Equitable Central Trust made a bid of £125,000, slightly more than Napier. Behind this company was Rolls-Royce, who acquired Bentley Motors. The remaining batches of 100 eight-litre and 50 four-litre chassis and engines were produced at Cricklewood. Bentley cars under Rolls-Royce were completely new, essentially sporting versions of the 20/25hp and 25/30hp, now called three-and-a-half and four-and-a-quarter-litre Derby Bentleys. It is clear that Rolls-Royce acquired Bentley to eliminate a competitor and add a sporting car to their range.

Under Bentley Motors, WO was employed "for life". This was reduced to three years when Rolls-Royce acquired the assets of Bentley Motors, and traded under the name Bentley Motors (1931) Ltd. WO had a minor role in this company, and was probably unhappy and frustrated.

MOVING ON

In 1935, a four-and-a-half-litre Meadows-engined Lagonda won the Le Mans 24-hour race. A week later the Lagonda car company was acquired by AP Good, and WO left Rolls-Royce to became technical director of Lagonda, based in Staines. He was joined by most of Rolls-Royce's racing department. The existing Meadows engine was uprated by Harry Westlake.

To compete with the V12 Rolls-Royce Phantom III of 7,338 cc, WO designed a 4,485 cc V12 engine with a single overhead camshaft to each bank operating directly on two valves per cylinder (in line). The engine produced 170 bhp at 5,500 rpm, and 220 bhp in racing form. The V12 and six cylinder LG6 had independent front suspension. 185 V12 Lagondas were produced from 1938 to 1940.

Following the Second World War, WO designed a 2.6-litre six-cylinder twin overhead camshaft engine for Lagonda. Lagonda was purchased by David Brown in 1947 together with Aston Martin. This engine was used in several Aston Martin cars until 1958, and was uprated to three litres in 1953.

In 1949, WO became a consultant to Armstrong Siddeley, and designed a three-litre six-cylinder engine. However, Armstrong Siddeley concluded that the engine was too expensive and used a simpler 3.4-litre six-cylinder engine in their Sapphire 346 of 1952.

Thus ended WO's career. He was Patron of the Bentley Drivers' Club from 1947 to his death on 13 August 1971 at Woking, aged 82. Writing in *The Times* after WO's death, one friend commented that, "in the eyes of those who own, have owned, or aspire to own one of the Bentley cars he created, he was admired and respected – indeed, I think, loved is not too strong a word – for to know his cars was to know him. Seeing the loving care bestowed upon his cars has more than compensated for all his earlier disappointments."

A 1961 Park Ward Continental
Drophead Coupé

COACH CLASS

Park Ward, the innovative coachbuilder
by Malcolm Tucker

OLD CARS, VINTAGE cars, classic cars, call them what you will, but all cars of a certain age make most people smile. They encapsulate nostalgia like no other artefact, for they can transport us, in reality and in reminisces, to a time gone by. A time that we may remember or may wish we'd experienced.

The charm of an old Rolls-Royce or Bentley is sustained by the engineering merit of its design and construction, which, even when tired and ill-maintained, gives driver and passengers a feeling of cosseted pleasure. Today, most likely the cars we experience will be in good condition – restored or in well-kept, original order – the senses of hearing, touch and smell well catered for by smooth and near-silent engines, and beautifully crafted controls and interiors, all enhanced by the scent of supple leather and warm oil.

The most important sense for enjoying an older car, however, is surely sight, for the lines of the coachwork and its many details tip us off to a vehicle's desirability like no other sensation. With a car built on a separate chassis, the coachwork could be of any design the customer desired, and of the many London-based coachbuilders who plied their trade in the 20th century, one of the most stylish and innovative was Park Ward & Co. Ltd.

The company was prolific in the furnishing of coachwork to Rolls-Royce and Bentley, eventually supplying more bodies to these companies than any other. The majority of bodies were of standard designs, which were functional and supremely fit for purpose, but by no means as exotic as they might have been. However, when the designers were unfettered by financial restraints, and the customers appreciated flair and panache, Park Ward produced some of the most attractive, stylish and exotic bodies ever to grace the two marques. Whatever the individual design, the transition from drawing to engineered materials often called for innovative design solutions, and it was in this aspect of coachbuilding that Park Ward excelled.

STARTING OUT

William McDonald Park and Charles William Ward first met when they worked for FW Berwick Ltd: Park as manager – coachworks, and Ward as manager – engineering. The company imported French-built Sizaire-Berwick chassis and bodied them in London's Park Royal district. By chance, the radiators were very similar in form to the Rolls-Royce design, but after some legal sabre-rattling, an amicable agreement was reached and the French car's radiator was redesigned in a V shape.

In 1919, the two managers decided to set up on their own and took premises on the corner of Willesden High Road and Cobbold Road, North London. An early client was Fiat, possibly because Ward had worked for the company previously and was on friendly terms. WO Bentley became a customer and 217 of his cars went on to carry Park Ward coachwork.

The first Rolls-Royce to do so was Silver Ghost chassis number 49TW (Park Ward body number 570), which left the works on 25 February 1920. The coachwork was a two-door, four-seater tourer with a fully concealed hood when open. This clever set-up was achieved by having a hood that would lie lower than the body's sides and be concealed by a metal cover shaped to blend with the body.

In 1933, the first Bentley produced under Rolls-Royce ownership was launched as the 3½

Below: The Park Ward all-metal body frame for the Derby Bentley

Opposite, clockwise from top left: The first Derby Bentley, B15AE; and Derby Bentleys B137MX; and B125MX

Overleaf, clockwise from top left: Rolls-Royce Phantom II chassis number 86SK; 1925 Rolls-Royce Phantom I, with a similar body to the first Rolls-Royce with a Park Ward body, Silver Ghost chassis number 49TW: a publicity shot of the Wentworth limousine

Litre model, and the first production four-door saloon, chassis number B15AE, carried a Park Ward body. This model, now known as the Derby Bentley, proved hugely popular with those who wanted a car of Rolls-Royce quality but faster, more nimble and better suited to being driven by its owner rather than a chauffeur. Park Ward worked closely with Rolls-Royce in developing bodies that were light, strong and, as many were ordered for "stock" by the dealerships, competitively priced.

A BREAK WITH TRADITION

Over the eight years that Derby Bentleys were produced, and alongside the "one-off" creations, there were several examples of relatively long production runs; up to 10 a week. The evolution of these body styles had three major designs, and it was the last, which appeared in 1936, that was the innovative break with coachbuilding traditions in terms of construction.

The 16 September 1936 edition of *The Motor Trader* described the new structure: "Something new in all-metal bodywork construction has recently been evolved by Park Ward & Co. Ltd, the coachbuilders of Willesden, NW10. It is a new system of steel construction, quite different from the pressed steel idea because it involves the use of a complete metal frame, and it has already passed the experimental stage. Extensive tests in

this country and on the Continent were carried out many months ago, and Bentley cars with all-metal bodies of this new type have been in service in the hands of private owners for two or three months.

"In this new construction a steel framework takes the place of a wooden framework and metal panels are used, the frame members being built up of sheet-steel bent, wrapped and welded to form a box section. It is on this method that Park Ward has taken out a patent. With this type of member a reasonable strength, combined with lightness, has been achieved. As experiments were continued many interesting facts about metal bodywork construction came to light, and the designers were able to incorporate improvements from time to time.

"The cross-bracing is welded into the box section, and all members are assembled in jigs. The joints are then welded, the body frame looking very similar to one in which timber is employed. Sheet-steel panels are used and are attached to the frame by turning over the edges to clinch them on the frame and by spot welding them to prevent any possible movement. The frame is attached to the chassis by sheet-steel sills built into the box section, which are exactly the same as wooden sills.

"In appearance, the all-metal bodies are almost exactly similar to the normal type. In fact, at the Ramsgate Concours where Sir Malcolm Campbell showed his Bentley with all-metal body,

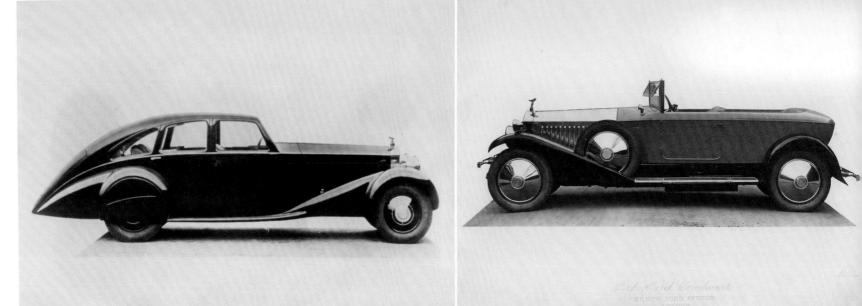

it was almost impossible to tell without very close examination the difference between it and the standard body."

At about the same time as the "all-steel" bodies were being developed for the Bentley chassis, Park Ward addressed another problem, this time for the more formal Rolls-Royce cars. This was how to allow more legroom for rear-seat passengers when a short wheelbase car was ordered with a retractable glass division between the front and rear compartments. When driven by the owner, there was no need for confidentiality but the retractable division ensured that when piloted by a chauffeur, privacy could be maintained. The well-established method for opening the division was by handle or electric motor, which would lower the glass into the backrest of the front seats, in front of any furnishings that would enhance the rear compartment, such as picnic tables or a cocktail cabinet.

Park Ward's solution was an arrangement that raised the glass up and back above the rear compartment headlining. This meant that the front-bench seat backs could be designed at an angle, enabling rear passengers to partly place their feet under the front seats, and even more intricate furnishings could be attached to the backs of the front seats. To close the division, one would wind the crank handle, which opened the headlining flap; the glass then slid forwards in a descending arc, until the lower edge met the woodwork of the seat division, and stopped in the vertical position. It could be lowered a further inch so that the chauffeur could receive his instructions. It is unclear exactly how many of these "disappearing" divisions were fitted, but it was probably around 43 or so.

AIRFLOW INNOVATION

Park Ward's innovation was not restricted to components alone, and while is it true that a good few coachbuilders were building bodies that reduced wind resistance, Park Ward had built two such bodies on Derby Bentley chassis, the designs of which were adapted in the final form for a 1934 Rolls-Royce Phantom II, chassis number 86SK.

In 1952, Charles Ward described the car in an illustrated talk given to the Worshipful Company of Coachmakers and Harness Makers: "1934 40/50 Rolls-Royce six-light Airflow saloon; this is the third development stage from the original experimental Airflow Bentley, where we were challenged to build an Airflow body on a Rolls-Royce chassis and here you can see our interpretation of this design. You have already seen three stages of development, i.e. Bentley number one was a two-door, four-light Saloon, number two was a four-door, four-light Saloon and number three, portrayed here, is a four door, six-light Saloon. If you will look at the wings of this car you will see that we have modified the cycle-type of wings and are now producing on this body one which is faired, with a sham cycle type front wing. In other words, this cycle wing was mounted on the body and not directly to the wheel.

"You will further see how we have faired the rear portion of both the front and rear wings; further I want you to look at the enclosed rear wheel, which we have designed by fitting the first full-length panelled spat, and it is interesting to note how the running boards run into the fairing of the front wing. The very long overhang of the rear of this body carried a tremendous luggage boot, and housed in this boot were four sets of golf clubs, in addition to this was luggage for four people for three weeks' Continental holiday. You can see that in the rear doors we have fitted quarter ventilator windows, and if my memory is correct this was the first car to have this type of vent window in both front and rear doors. This body gave rise to great controversy in the higher-up design personnel in general, and one very important person in the motor industry stated that the car would go faster backward than forward. This latter point I believe is technically correct."

What Charles Ward did not mention was that in the form described, the tail was so heavy that the car was highly dangerous when driven in the wet at over 40 mph. So the tail was shortened and, with reduced weight capacity, the rear end stayed where it should while cornering at speed.

When car body production restarted after the end of the Second World War, British car design picked up where it had been left off in 1939, but it was not long before Park Ward was again at the forefront of innovative design. A good example was instigated by "Doc" Llewellyn-Smith, who was on the boards of both Rolls-Royce and Park Ward Ltd, the company having been bought by Rolls-Royce in 1939. He was concerned that British coachbuilders were lagging behind the latest US designs and would suffer in the post-war world market. Park Ward rose to the challenge and the Wentworth coachwork on a Silver Wraith, chassis number WGC47, was designed for the 1948 London Motor Show. The style known throughout the trade as "the New Look" was not successful and customers continued to appreciate the traditional approach of British coachbuilders.

The Wentworth's straight line at waist height from front to rear wing was too advanced for its day, but Park Ward would try again some 10 years later, and this time they were to set the trend for many years to come. Rolls-Royce's executive vice-chairman in 1957, the American Whitney Straight, was a racing driver, ace pilot, war hero and canny business man. In that year, he attended an exhibition by the Norwegian industrial designer Vilhelm Koren at the Royal College of Art, London. He was so impressed that he persuaded "Doc" Llewellyn-Smith to view Koren's exhibition. Llewellyn-Smith was also impressed with the Norwegian's approach to modern design and offered him a job in the Rolls-Royce styling department. Remember, it was Llewellyn-Smith who was so concerned with the reliance on traditional styling that Park Ward produced the Wentworth Silver Wraith.

KOREN'S MODERN STYLING

Koren's first job was to come up with a radically new alternative style for the Bentley Continental, based on the S series chassis. He worked quickly, producing only one quarter-scale clay model. So close to the design chosen for production was this singular model that only minor alterations were necessary to obtain the green light from the Rolls-Royce directors.

Park Ward, being a division of Rolls-Royce since 1939, undertook the work of producing the actual bodies, which meant that Koren spent more time in Willesden than in Crewe. It was not long before the car, which was to be known formally as the Bentley S2 Continental Park Ward Fixed Head Saloon or Drophead Coupé, was nicknamed the "Korenental". As things turned out, only the open version was produced. The innovative break with tradition was, again,

the straight waistline running the full length of the car. This time the motoring public liked it and the car stayed in production throughout the rest of the S series cars' life. With the launch of the S3 iteration in 1963, saloon and drophead versions were produced in Bentley and Rolls-Royce guises. These versions sported a revised frontal aspect with twin headlights and altered front wings to accommodate them, but by then Vilhelm Koren had left Park Ward and Rolls-Royce.

By 1958, the replacement model for the S series was well underway, and there were two major changes to be seen. Most importantly, the car was to be of semi-monocoque construction wherein the body shell itself gave overall rigidity, strength and locations for the major components. The days of separate chassis cars would soon be over, and with them those of the coachbuilt car, as little could be altered on a semi-monocoque body. But Park Ward's bold new styling by Koren lived on in essence in stylist John Blatchley's Rolls-Royce Silver Shadow and T Type Bentley.

Park Ward continued as a separate division of Rolls-Royce at its Willesden address until 1981, having been merged with HJ Mulliner in 1961, following the latter's acquisition by Rolls-Royce in 1959. The company continued producing bodies for Rolls-Royce Phantom limousines and the Silver Shadow-based Corniche cars until the models' demise. The trade name Park Ward is now owned by Bentley Motors.

Dalton Watson Fine Books will be publishing a two-volume book on the History of Park Ward & Co. Ltd by author Malcolm Tucker in 2017.

Park Ward fixed head coupé
coachwork on a Rolls-Royce
Silver Cloud III chassis

A REGAL RETURN

The rise of the Silver Wraith II by Tony Flood

THE YEAR 1977 was significant for the country in general and for Rolls-Royce in particular. As Britain and the Commonwealth prepared to celebrate the Silver Jubilee of Her Majesty The Queen, Rolls-Royce unveiled what would prove to be a memorable facelift to its Silver Shadow range. Forty years on, it's time to commemorate the introduction of a very special car.

This greatly refreshed range was introduced in February 1977 as the Silver Shadow II, while its long wheelbase (LWB) equivalent was announced to the world at the Geneva Motor Show the following month. The company decided, however, that the LWB would not simply be marketed as a variant of the Silver Shadow II, but that it would be prudent to reintroduce an old Rolls-Royce name. The name "Silver Wraith" was initially used on the very first Rolls-Royce model built at Crewe in 1946 and had not been used since 1958. The revised Silver Shadow LWB version was therefore named Silver Wraith II – as the marketing department stated at its launch, "We are tidying up the model range."

This was the first time that Crewe had made a decision concerning using a previous Rolls-Royce model name. Once this policy was accepted by loyal customers, future LWB model variants would also be given their own unique names and equally accepted in the worldwide marketplace.

The Rolls-Royce Silver Wraith II had a unique production sequence and engineering specification. The majority of the body-shell construction was produced by Pressed Steel

Fisher, a company based in Cowley, near Oxford, and started its production sequence as any other Silver Shadow, but with obvious differences. As the finished shell was designated to be an LWB, Pressed Steel Fisher purposely omitted the roof assembly and also the rear doors. Once completed to this stage, the shell was despatched to the Mulliner Park Ward factory at Hythe Road in Willesden, north-west London. There, modifications would be carried out so that the finished body shell would be ready for main production as a Silver Wraith II.

WILLESDEN FUNCTION

The first operation carried out at Mulliner Park Ward was to place the shell in a jig and literally cut the body in half just rear of the centre door pillar, or – in body engineering parlance – "the BC post". With the body shell now in two parts the jig used for the cutting operation moved the two displaced body-shell parts 4 inches (101 mm) apart and a prefabricated floor section was welded to join both displaced body sections together, which resulted in a revised and lengthened shell. The roof was manufactured as a one-piece pressing and subsequently welded into position. This also included whether or not the rear window would be of the smaller or larger specification. Revised rear doors were produced and fitted to suit the now enlarged aperture.

A second variant body shell was produced solely for the North American market and was clearly recognisable as having the fuel filler located in the left-hand, rear-door pillar. The reason for this change, which came into effect from September 1976, was termed "the fuel integrity package", by which it was deemed that, upon an impact or a "rollover" condition, no rupturing of the fuel tank in particular should occur, and any leakage or damage to the fuel system in general should be prevented. This necessitated not only the introduction of a revised fuel tank but also its relocation from the boot (trunk) floor to directly behind the rear seats.

The third variant body shell to be produced was for those vehicles ordered with a centre division. Extra work would be carried out to the internal centre of the body shell in order that the division could be installed. Significant reworking was also required to the boot area to ensure that the rear air-conditioning unit could be installed. Reworking was also required of the area directly below the rear window to install the rear air-intake system.

Once all of this work was completed, the finished body shell was sent to Crewe for building just like most cars – namely painting, assembly, road testing and finishing. However, in the event of a centre division having to be installed, once the normal assembly work was done, the car was sent to a dedicated area of the factory for division. Only then was it allowed to proceed to normal road testing.

CAR SPECIFICATIONS

The Silver Wraith II was defined by several key specifications. Rack-and-pinion steering allowed the driver improved handling, while the model's split-level automatic air conditioning was identical to the specifications on both the Corniche and the Camargue. A totally revised instrument board was less cluttered than the previous configuration and also included an electronic speedometer, which eliminated the use of a cable. In addition, a redesigned steering wheel incorporated improved impact features.

Improved engine cooling was achieved with the introduction of a new seven-bladed fan and an auxiliary electric fan. To improve fuel efficiency, revised carburettors were fitted, while cars destined for Japan and North America were installed with a fuel recirculation system whereby the fuel was constantly pumped around the vehicle to keep it cool from the underside airflow, and any unused fuel was returned to the tank. For certain states – particularly California – a fuel cooler was fitted. A twin exhaust system was another obvious and significant change, and updated driver's door and interior mirrors were also incorporated.

However, it was the new external features that made this particular model so easily recognisable. The car's front and rear appearance was enhanced, with the bumpers now displaying polyurethane mouldings fitted to thick aluminium beams, very similar in appearance to the energy-absorbing type that had been used on cars built for North American since September 1973. For markets other than North America, however, the collision features were not part of their function and they were of a rigid construction.

A front air dam was introduced and was fitted directly below the front bumper, which gave greater vehicle stability at high speeds. However, this feature was omitted from cars built for North America because it would have

The Silver Wraith II
centre division variant

interfered with the performance of the energy-absorbing front bumper in a collision.

New door handles were introduced and, after around 200 cars had been built, a redesigned boot handle formed a revised part of the external appearance. A slightly deeper radiator grille became a distinguishing feature, while a nameplate that read "Silver Wraith II" was fitted to the right-hand side of the boot lid. It was also decided that this particular model should look different to its smaller stable mate, the Silver Shadow II. So, in addition to having different wheel-trim assemblies that it "borrowed" from the Corniche and Camargue models, in an attempt to give the impression that the car had a "lower standing" appearance, stainless steel trims were fitted to the external top of all four doors. Further stainless steel fittings were considered, including trimmings around the body-shell door apertures, but this was rejected as it would have severely compromise door-opening clearances.

The first standard non-division and North American specification cars commenced production in November 1976 and were completed in early February 1977. However, production of the division variant for those discerning owners who wished for the total privacy and luxury that a centre partition between themselves and their chauffeur provided did not commence until late February, with the first car being completed in July.

A FIRST-CLASS DIVISION

The division installation was initially completed at Crewe but, during 1978, this task was entrusted to Mulliner Park Ward in Willesden. This was because Crewe required extra space to complete the building of the Camargue, which had moved from London to Crewe at that time.

Once introduced, division cars were not made available for the North American market. The popular myth is that the division glass did not meet the federal regulations, but this is not the case. In fact, as mentioned earlier, the fuel tank had been relocated behind the rear seats, which made it impossible to install the rear air-conditioning unit in the same boot area space.

During 1978, further improvements were made to the Silver Wraith II. Firstly, a headlamp wash/wipe facility was introduced. This feature had been part of the original specifications for the car at launch but was delayed and become a significantly noticeable change once the car was firmly established. This was not an entirely new feature, as it had been a legal requirement in Sweden since 1973. Owing to weight requirements the wash/wipe facility was not fitted to those cars destined for North America as they were already very close to their federal certification weight limit and the inclusion of this feature would have put them in a higher taxation class.

A significant improvement was also made to the air-conditioning system. Drivers and passengers of the early Silver Wraith II cars did not always welcome air blowing through the instrument-board vents directly into their faces. As there was no override other than switching the system off, an improvement was incorporated whereby the driver or passenger could operate an switch installed on the instrument board that redirected unwanted air from the facia vents to the windscreen vents.

END OF AN ERA

Nineteen seventy nine was a significant year in Rolls-Royce's history as it marked the company's 75th anniversary. To commemorate this milestone the company decided to build a limited number of models with red interlocking Rolls-Royce badges on both the radiator grille and the boot lid. Only one Silver Wraith II was so built, with the car in question being passed to Crewe's sales department on 31 October 1979. Today, this unique vehicle would surely be a treasured acquisition.

In the final year of Silver Wraith II production, those cars destined for California underwent a considerable engineering change. In order to meet with the strict federal exhaust emissions standards set by the US state in 1980, a sophisticated fuel-injection system was introduced.

The last Silver Wraith II motor cars were built in the autumn of 1980. A small number had their coach work, finishing and road testing carried out at the Hythe Road factory in Willesden, as the priority at Crewe was to ensure the completion of the first Silver Spirit range to a very tight time scale stipulated for December 1980.

The final car – chassis number LRL 41619C – was assembled on 3 November 1980 and destined for California. It may be of interest to note, however, that this chassis number was not the last one for this model. In fact, 29 chassis numbers were allocated after it – for a number of reasons, the company did not always build cars in number order.

THE BENTLEY CONNECTION

It would be an oversight not to mention the Silver Wraith II's "sister car" – the Bentley T2 long wheelbase. Very few of this particular model were ever built and only to special order. It was not actively marketed and never appeared in any of the company's official brochures or price lists.

The very first one built was ordered by a Mr (later Sir) Horace Kadoorie, who was the joint owner of the famous Peninsula Hotel in Hong Kong and an ardent Bentley enthusiast. This car was not only a rare Bentley at the time, but also the owner insisted that it must have no Rolls-Royce markings on it whatsoever.

The reason for this request was that, during the early to late 1970s, Bentley markings were disappearing, owing to cost, and being replaced by Rolls-Royce motifs – for instance the engine rocker covers, speedometers and brake pedal. Failure to comply with Kadoorie's wishes would not have been in the company's best interest. Not only had he ordered this particular car but also, only a few months earlier in the summer of 1976, he had taken delivery of eight Silver Shadow cars for hotel use which, of course, was a very useful publicity tool for Rolls-Royce.

This very special Bentley was handed over to Kadoorie at the London showroom offices at Conduit Street, and was then driven by its owner in the UK for a few weeks until he shipped it to Hong Kong in September 1977. It would be interesting to know the car's current owner and location, as its rarity value would be hard to estimate.

In conclusion, the Silver Wraith II should not be seen as a "stop gap" model, but as a very important model – a significant chapter from Crewe's great heritage.

A STAR OF INDIA

The life and passions of His Highness
Sir Ranjitsinhji Vibhaji by John Fasal

KUMAR SHRI RANJITSINHJI was born on 10 September 1872 in Kathiawar – the region that now constitutes part of modern-day Gujarat and lies on the Western coastal side of India. At that time, Kathiawar comprised several hundred princely states, and Ranji (as he was known) was adopted by his father's cousin, the ruling and then childless Jam Saheb Sir Vibhaji of Nawanagar. The subject of this feature, Ranji would go on to become one of the most celebrated and enlightened rulers of the 3,721 sq mile state of Nawanagar.

The majority of the princes from Kathiawar and the province of Bombay Presidency sent their sons to the Chiefs' College, or the Rajkumar College, in Rajkot, and Ranji was no exception. The college's principal was the highly regarded Chester Macnaghten, and he was to have a considerable influence on Ranji, who entered the college of just 37 boys at the age of eight in June 1880.

The headmaster became aware of the potential of this outstanding natural athlete and arranged for him to travel to England in 1888 with two other students to meet the right people and go to the right places. Ranji entered Trinity College, Cambridge University (completing his studies in 1894). Cricket became his passion at Cambridge – a passion that brought honour on himself and his alma mater.

SPORTING PROWESS

In 1895, he made his first appearance for Sussex County Cricket Club and went on to lead the club's batting averages every year until 1902. He was champion batsman for All England in 1896 (a feat he repeated in 1900), scoring 2,780 runs – the highest total made in one summer by any cricketer. He made 10 centuries and was described as "the finest living batsman".

While convalescing from congestion of the lungs during the cold winter of 1896–97, he wrote *The Jubilee Book of Cricket* with the help of CB Fry and others. The following August, *Vanity Fair* issued its famous "Spy" cartoon, titled "Ranji" in honour of this remarkable sportsman.

Ranji went on to tour with Andrew Stoddart's All England XI to Australia during the winter of 1897–98. A writer of the day described him as a slight man who had "the eye of the hawk and wrists like Toledo steel" and "a wonderful art of timing the ball". He played so well for England against Australia in 1899, when the rest of the team failed, that the newspapers proclaimed, "Ranji saves England!"

Tragedy struck in the summer of 1915 while on sick leave from France on a grouse shoot near Filey in Yorkshire. A neighbour in the butts was shooting down the line of participants and Ranji received pellets in his face. He was rushed to Leeds Infirmary, where doctors removed his right eye. Ranji took this setback with great stoicism but it put paid to any future in his favourite game of cricket. Even King George V wrote to his "Dear Friend" to express his sympathy.

Ranji excelled in other sports, being a very fine shot with shotgun and rifle. After his accident, gunmaker Purdey built a special cast-off stock for him, in order that he could bring it to his right shoulder and use his left eye. He was also an accomplished fly-fisher and a very skilful tennis and billiard player.

ACCESSION AND WAR

With the demise of the Maharaja Jam Saheb of Nawanagar in August 1906, His Highness Ranjitsinhji was installed on this ancestral *Gadi*, or throne, on 11 March 1907 by the Agent to the Governor. He inherited the "disease-ridden, squalid and dusty city of Jamnagar" and began to transform it into "a model city of lakes and gardens, of flowering trees and waterways".

On accession, he found the state finances in a very sorry state and was obliged to take out loans from the government and from the Maharaja of Baroda. He stimulated the local economy by building the deep-water harbour of Bedi, which was to pay huge dividends. A benevolent ruler, he would go unattended into the villages to hear his people's complaints and devoted much effort to improving their welfare.

At the outbreak of the First World War in August 1914, Ranji offered the Viceroy, Lord Hardinge, the full resources of his state and proved to be one of the most loyal rulers when it came to supporting the call of the King Emperor, George V. Significant contributions of men, materials and financial donations included 14 motor cars, fully equipped with eight Indian and two European chauffeurs; one ambulance with driver for use in Bombay; six large, double-poled tents for field hospitals; the use of Jamnagar House in Staines, Middlesex, furnished with 45 beds as a hospital for wounded soldiers; 48 horses; 50 ponies; and a share in a fleet of ambulances presented by the states of Kathiawar.

Ranji left India on 16 November 1914 for the Western Front and took up an appointment as aide-de-camp to Field Marshal Sir John French. The authorities would not permit the princely order to fight on the front line, much to their regret and against their warrior tradition. Three of Ranji's nephews served in the war, including Lieutenant Kumar Shri Dajiraj, who served in France for a year and a half and was killed in action in September 1917.

The Nawanagar Imperial Service Lancers performed garrison duty at Karachi throughout the war. Half of the squadron was sent to Jacobabad on military duties, and a signalling party of the Imperial Service Lancers was in Egypt with the Expeditionary Force. The Indian government expressed a wish to bear the extra charges over and above the normal expenses, but with characteristic generosity and loyalty, Ranji proposed that the monies be found from the funds connected with the war effort.

In the 1919 New Year's Honours, Ranji was promoted to Lieutenant-Colonel, awarded the Insignia of a Knight Grand Commander of the British Empire (GBE) and granted a salute of 15 guns. He was also made President of the Princes' Committee, campaigning on behalf of Indian troops overseas. The following year, Ranji became one of India's three representatives at the League of Nations in Geneva. He took his lifelong friend CB Fry – another outstanding cricketer, as well as a politician, diplomat and writer – with him as his assistant.

Ranji was almost solely responsible for obtaining India's place on the governing body of the International Labour Bureau in 1922, and in 1923, he was awarded the highest Order of Chivalry bestowed on the ruling princes and chiefs of India, that of a Knight Grand Commander of the Most Exalted Order of the Star of India (GCSI). The insignia of this order is more beautiful and certainly more valuable than that of any other order, as it is ornamented with a considerable number of diamonds. In 1931, he was appointed Chancellor of The Chamber of Princes – the

position also carried out by his successor, the Maharaja Sir Digvijay Sinhji of Nawanagar.

A LOVE OF LUXURY

With the huge growth in the State Treasury during the Edwardian era, Ranji indulged in his passion for jewels. He had met Jacques Cartier (who had been running the London branch of the famous Parisian jewellers since 1909) at the 1911 Delhi Durbar. One of his last commissions was for an exceptional ceremonial necklace set with the Queen of Holland diamond. Described as internally flawless and having a definite blue tint, this one gemstone had a weight of 135.92 carats and was valued at approximately £250,000 – although the gemologist admitted at that time that no true market price could be given for such a stone. Cartier (the company) eventually bought the stone back and in 1978 it was sold by an American for $7 million.

Sailing was another passion of Ranji's. It was reported in the *Indian & Eastern Motors' Journal* of 1923 that "the Maharaja had just received delivery of four launches from Thorneycrofts. Further, the Maharaja, has at present under construction at Messrs Thorneycroft's yard at Hampton-on-Thames, a substantial sailing yacht of some fifty-eight tons, in addition to a seventy-four foot motor launch, both of which, after completion, will be subsequently dispatched to his State in India". He also owned the magnificent yacht *Star of India*. The 234-ft, 735-ton steam yacht was built in 1888 by the Fairfield Shipbuilding & Engineering Company of Glasgow and in the autumn of 1927, Ranji spent more than £30,000 on putting the vessel in perfect order, regardless of expense, including the installation of two large state rooms.

Previous pages: Ranji sitting in the front of a Napier 24hp

Opposite: Spy's cartoon of the great batsman from the August 1897 issue of *Vanity Fair*

Above: Ranji in his 1907 28hp Lanchester, pictured outside Pratap Vilas Palace in Jamnagar in 1911

Above: His Highness Ranjitsinhji's coronation in Delhi, 1907

Opposite, clockwise from top left: Ranji's 1921 40/50hp tourer; a line of his Rolls-Royce cars, November 1927; six of Ranji's Lanchester cars, and a Silver Ghost from the neighbouring state of Rajkot, pictured outside his impressive palace garages

Overleaf: Ranji's successor the Maharaja Sir Digvijay Sinhji of Nawanagar at Jamanagar House in Staines with his 1937 Humber Pullman Limousine

In 1924, Ranji purchased Ballynahinch Castle in Connemara, Ireland from the Berridge family, who had restored and enlarged the castle to its latter-day condition. The lakes of Upper and Lower Ballynahinch, Derryclare and Lough Inagh were all part of the vast estate, and the property was famed for its fisheries. Indeed, it was a wonderful retreat for Ranji to visit every summer around June. When he did so, he would buy five motor cars – two limousines and three smaller cars – in Galway before arriving and, when leaving to return to India in October, he would give the cars to the locals as gifts; one to the parish priest, perhaps, one to the local vicar and so on – each and every year! He even had his own train carriage on the line from Galway to Clifden, which stopped off at Ballynahinch railway station (this closed down eventually in 1936).

A MOTORING CONNOISSEUR

Another activity that Ranji enjoyed was cycling. In 1894, a young student attended a crammer in Cambridge, which helped him gain entry to Trinity College, and he too was a keen cyclist. His name was Charles Stewart Rolls. It's quite possible that the pair crossed paths, and many years later, Ranji was to own eight Rolls-Royce cars.

In the *Cycle and Motor World* dated 10 February 1897, the front cover pictured Ranji seated in his Daimler. Reference was made to the fact that in Cambridge, he acquired "the first motor car ever to be observed coughing its way along the streets of the city". His early passion for motor cars was never to diminish.

Ranji befriended the Lanchester brothers, Frederick and George, makers of a remarkable car that became a serious competitor to the Rolls-Royce marque. Their eldest brother was the distinguished architect Henry Vaughan Lanchester, who built the magnificent Umaid Bhavan Palace for the Maharaja of Jodhpur between 1929 and 1943. Ranji and his nephew, Digvijay Sinhji, became their best customers, buying more than 40 Lanchester cars.

The first was a 1904 12hp two-cylinder, which Ranji drove in the Delhi to Bombay trials, a distance of nearly 900 miles. Its performance was remarkable – not a single breakdown, an average speed of 30 mph and a deduction of only 1½ marks over the eight-day trial. Further orders

were placed and in 1907, two 28hp Lanchesters arrived – one a formal limousine with a ventilated roof and the other a detachable top tourer. By 1912, Ranji's motor house counted 12 Lanchesters, and by 1925 the superintendent of the palace garages, JH Manning, informed the press that he had three 40hp Lanchesters in his care and over 60 quality cars to maintain.

No doubt Ranji influenced his neighbour, the Thakore Saheb of Rajkot, into buying a 1910 28hp six-cylinder Napier. Other keen followers of these marques were the Maharajas of Alwar and Rewa. Ranji's successor shared his love of Lanchester cars and the present Jam Saheb Shri Sataji, born in February 1939, mentioned to the author during his visit in December 1980 that Mr Lanchester made the family a small car – the most expensive car in the world! When asked why it was the most expensive, he replied, "I used to drive down the corridors of the Pratap Vilas Palace smashing into the priceless Chinese vases."

Always keen to research new cars, Ranji had trials in many other makes. His good friends the Maharajas of Gondal and Bhavnagar were both enthusiastic motorists and there is a fine photograph of Ranji in the front of a c. 1909 24hp Napier with the Bhavnagar coat-of-arms emblazoned on the rear doors.

It was only in the 1920s that Ranji took to the ownership of Rolls-Royce cars, and his earliest model was a 1920 40/50hp Ferguson tourer (chassis number 98AE), originally supplied to JI Morgan of Dublin. The firm of JB Ferguson of Chichester Street, Belfast was a prominent coachbuilder in Northern Ireland from 1907 that supplied quality coachwork on pre-war Silver Ghosts to clients who included the Duke of

Westminster, Sir Stanley Cochrane and Sir Otto Jaffe, among others. No doubt Ranji appreciated the supremacy of the Rolls-Royce Alpine Eagle chassis, often referred to by the Company as their "high speed" model, which met his touring needs in Ireland. This car was acquired in October 1929 but it is not known if it returned with him to India.

An order was received from Rolls-Royce Limited (Bombay) on 20 October 1920 for two Silver Ghosts for the Jam Saheb of Nawanagar, Jamnagar House, Penton Road, Staines. Chassis numbers 171LG and 180LG were delivered in the early months of 1922 to Hammersmith coachbuilding firm William Cole and Sons for a saloon and tourer respectively, both to be finished in polished aluminium throughout.

The 1921 40/50hp saloon 171LG was fitted with smoked glass windows with additional wind-up gauze windows to prevent mosquitoes from entering the compartment. It was featured in *The Autocar* of 16 March 1923. The 1921 40/50hp tourer 180LG was first registered by Middlesex County Council as ME5831, which it continued to bear in India until it was designated the red state number Nawanagar No.2. The US car collector Lars de Jounge, who lived in India for six years during the 1960s, acquired the car in 1965 and had it partially restored in Poona before shipping it back to California. This car is presently on view in the impressive Auto & Technik Museum Sinsheim in Germany.

The 1922 40/50hp Hooper landaulette 69ZG, originally supplied to Sir Abe Bailey, replaced Ranji's earlier 1911 40/50hp HJ Mulliner landaulette. Sir Abe was the South African diamond tycoon, politician, financier and cricketer. Ranji acquired 69ZG via Messrs Hall Lewis & Co.

of Park Royal in October 1929 for £575. Among the many listed specifications, provision was made to fit a Lucas hydraulic jack under the front seat. The booklet of Rolls-Royce accessories quotes a price of £4.17.6d for this double-action jack, a considerable sum in 1922.

In 1931, Ranji became the fourth owner (following renowned author Edgar Wallace) of a 1925 New Phantom, later known as the Phantom I. This car was fitted with limousine coachwork by Joseph Cockshoot & Co. of Manchester, the city remembered as the birthplace of the Rolls-Royce factory. It was followed by another Phantom I – 1926 chassis number 46SC, which was fitted with a cabriolet body by Windovers. Ranji acquired this in 1932 from the estate of the late Sir William Waterlow, the former Lord Mayor of London. In October 1934, this car passed to the State of Junagadh and its colourful ruler, who was obsessed with dogs – but that is another story!

After a very full and colourful life, Lieutenant-Colonel His Highness the Maharaja Sir Ranjitsinhji Vibhaji, Jam Saheb of Nawanagar, GCSI, GBE passed away in his ornate Bhavindra Vilas Palace in Jamnagar on 2 April 1933 – the same month and year as an engineer he greatly admired, Sir Henry Royce.

The last tribute goes to Ranji and Royce's mutual friend, the sculptor Eric Gill, who wrote in his autobiography, published seven years after Ranji's death: "Even now, when I want to think of something wholly delightful and perfect, I think of Ranji on the county ground at Hove. There were many minor stars, each with his special and beloved technique, but nothing on earth could approach the special quality of Ranji's batting or fielding … such craftsmanship and grace entered into my very soul."

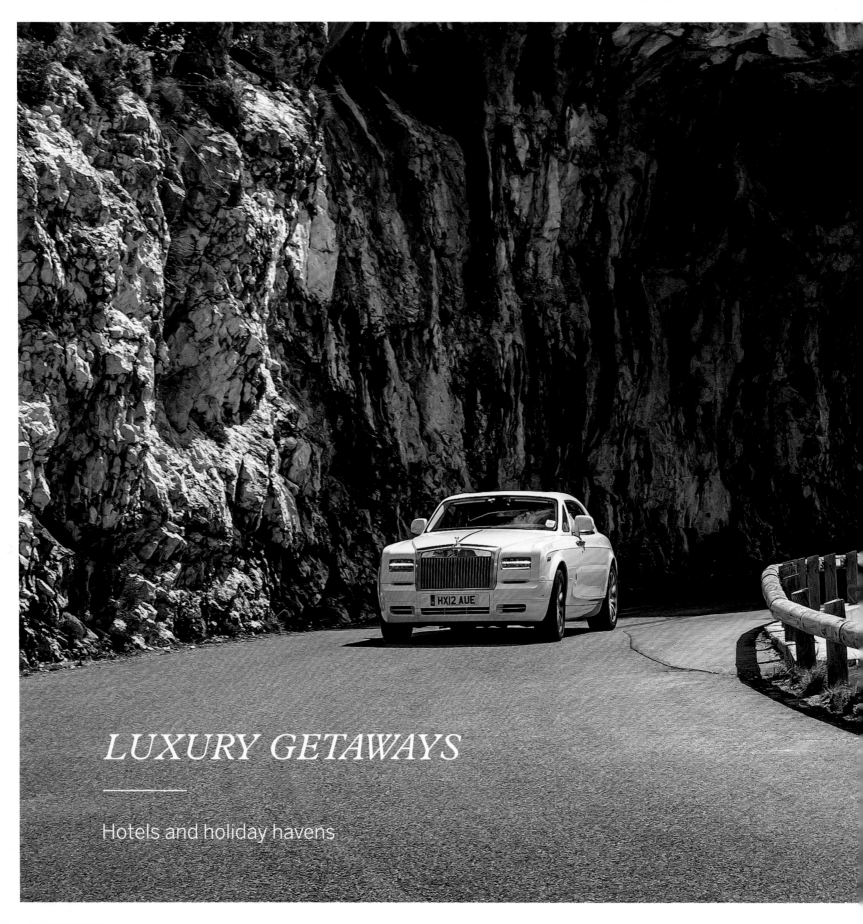

LUXURY GETAWAYS

Hotels and holiday havens

BAREFOOT ELEGANCE

Perivolas, Santorini, Greece

"THIS IS A magical place," smiles Costis Psychas, owner of the Perivolas, a family-run luxury hotel and villa located high on a cliff on the dramatic, romantic Greek island of Santorini. "We're literally within the crater of a volcano here, and you can feel the omnipotence of the landscape reconnecting you with nature and with your true self. That, to us, is what luxury is all about."

In the daily rush to meet deadlines and make arrangements, it's easy to lose touch with these important aspects of life. Spending time on a volcanic island can bring them back into focus. Perivolas Hotel's network of 300-year-old caves provides the perfect backdrop. It transforms humble fishermen's cottages, stables and quays into 20 bright, airy rooms and suites with expansive terraces overlooking the crater lake.

"Perivolas offers contemporary amenities while maintaining the ergonomic function of the old days," says Costis. "And air conditioning isn't required. The caves work with nature, keeping cool in the summer and warm in the winter."

Some rooms have their own outdoor Jacuzzi or plunge pool, and the renowned Perivolas Suite boasts its own steam room, hot tub and private pool. There's a large gym and a spa carved into the cliffside, which uses local products and offers tailor-made holistic treatments. The resort's infinity pool cascades over the cliff into the glassy blue Aegean sea.

And then, of course, there is the cuisine. "For us, it's not about complicated gourmet food," says Costis. "It's about simple, local ingredients prepared with a lot of love. We want our guests to enjoy the flavour of locally grown tomatoes; to really notice the taste of the capers."

The jewel in Perivolas's understated crown, however, is The Hideaway – a villa located directly on the seafront on the tiny neighbouring island of Therasia. Recently added to the hotel's portfolio, this refurbished pumice mine dates back to 1850, and today it houses four bedrooms, a heated swimming pool, a wellness area, a private beach and dock, two boats, a fully equipped watersports centre, a heliport and staff including a captain and a chef. Unsurprisingly, it draws an influential and discerning clientele, including television and film stars, internationally renowned athletes, leading fund managers and others.

"Our guests are completely free to do what they want," says Costis. "There are no paparazzi – it's almost like a private island. That means people can arrive by private helicopter, so no one needs to know they're here. The villa is five minutes away from everything they might need, but on its own, completely isolated from the crowds. I think that's why those who come to The Hideaway are often high-profile people who want to get away from their normal life where there's always someone watching, always someone needing something from them."

Reborn as a luxury destination, the Perivolas paradise was originally the dream of Costis's parents when they bought the plot in 1969. "They started with the family home," today's owner recalls, "gradually adding units over a 20-year period." Then Costis took the mantle, reimagining the caves as an exclusive luxury retreat and painstakingly rebuilding The Hideaway into a villa deemed worthy of a Philippe Rotthier European Prize for Architecture.

Today, the Zen concept at Perivolas reflects the lifestyle of the owner. "Costis is a sailor, a dreamer, an eternal optimist and a seeker of harmony and solitude," says Vanda Cordeiro, Manager of Perivolas. "He is very much in tune with the sea, keen to share that energy and spirit." He's hands-on too. "He likes to build things – and The Hideaway, in particular, was his vision, and that comes through in the simplicity of the lines and the colours. Costis's philosophy is at the heart of everything we do at Perivolas."

Costis describes this brand of luxury as "barefoot elegance". There is no ostentation and no stress. "This is not the place for people who want gilded mirrors," says Vanda. "Perivolas is for those who want to get away from it all and reconnect. Everything is simple and minimal, harmonising with the traditions of the island and with nature while still existing in the modern world.

"We don't have TVs – that little box that pulls you in; we don't have big mirrors – so guests can't judge themselves, agonise over whether their hips are too small or too big. We just enjoy the rhythm of the sea, the energy from the sun. There's no pressure. You can't see what's on the news, you don't have to make telephone calls, you don't have to care what other people are doing. We believe this makes people happier, enabling them to focus on *feeling* and *being*. That's very liberating. It differentiates us from other places. It's a simple elegance that captures the magnificent essence of island living."

Everything at Perivolas is customised to each guest, from unique spa treatments and menus to thoughtfully curated excursions – whether a private jaunt to a nearby island or a walk to a local farm to collect fresh eggs. "Most people don't have access to that purity any more, where nothing is processed," says Costis. "We know that what really matters is the essence of things. It's not about products that carry a name and a brand; it's about things that are unique, made with care and love. When you come to Perivolas, you can feel that. And, because Perivolas is only accessible by sea or air, it's the perfect escape geographically as well as mentally. Guests are completely free to be what they want."

Making the *Condé Nast Traveler* Gold List of the world's best hotels every year since 2011, Perivolas offers both the simplest and the finest things in life. It's a place where the stress of daily life vanishes, replaced by the warmth of the sun on your back and the calm blue of the Aegean.

— www.perivolas.gr

HEAVENLY HOST

———————

Tintswalo Atlantic, South Africa

BEHIND YOU RISE the muscular bluffs of the Table Mountain National Park. Ahead, the shark's fin promontory of the Sentinel stands guard over the turquoise waters of Hout's Bay. Beyond lie 3,000 miles of ocean, then Uruguay. This is South Africa's gem of a boutique hotel, Tintswalo Atlantic. "It's as close to paradise as you can get on Earth," says owner Gaye Corbett of her family-run Cape hideaway.

Yet in March 2015, the lodge suffered an infernal fate. A wildfire swept over the mountain, engulfing the entire hillside below Chapman's Peak. Staff and guests were evacuated safely but the hotel site was left a smouldering ruin. "We cried our eyes out," Gaye recalls. "But you never lose anything that you can't recreate. Within a month we had plans drawn for the rebuild."

Within seven, Tintswalo Atlantic was operational again. "And it's better than ever," Gaye adds, proudly. But don't take her word for it. The reborn lodge has already won a TripAdvisor Travellers' Choice award for 2016, while the *Daily Telegraph* hails its "sublime views, excellent food and warm service".

The origins of Tintswalo lie further north, in the Corbett family's Johannesburg business – initially shopping centres but, through their development, branching out into community outreach and education programmes. These community links gave them the chance to tender for a lodge on the Manyeleti Game Reserve, adjacent to the Kruger National Park. It was a leap of faith.

"We were camping people," says Gaye. "We had no clue how to run a five-star lodge but we love the bush. So we built it."

The Corbetts' philanthropic entwinement with the local tribe begat the name. "Tintswalo" translates as "the intangible feeling of love, gratitude and peace bestowed upon someone offering you a meaningful and worthy gift". The "gift" was such a success that an equestrian estate in Johannesburg followed and then Tintswalo Atlantic – "the third leg of the tour".

You sense that the trauma of the fire – and swift recovery – makes the lodge even more special now for Gaye and her family. "It feels like my own home," she says. "We're a tight-knit family and do a lot of the hosting ourselves because I want it to feel like I'm entertaining guests." From the ashes, a heavenly welcome awaits.

— www.tintswalo.com

AN ADRIATIC IDYLL

Adriatic Luxury Hotels, Dubrovnik, Croatia

"THOSE WHO SEEK paradise on earth should come to Dubrovnik," George Bernard Shaw once said. With sumptuous accommodation and first-class service, Adriatic Luxury Hotels (ALH) ensures that its guests in this beautiful Croatian city are certain to agree.

ALH operates some of Croatia's finest hotels and villas, set in Dubrovnik's most stunning locations and offering glorious views of the Adriatic Sea as standard. The most luxurious properties in ALH's extensive portfolio feature in its Dream Collection. It includes Hotel Excelsior, a Dubrovnik landmark for more than 100 years.

"It is where the discerning visitor travelling to Dubrovnik has always chosen to stay," says an ALH spokesperson. Guests have included Roger Moore, Francis Ford Coppola and even Queen Elizabeth II, drawn by the flawless service and luxury facilities. After extensive refurbishment in 2016, the hotel unveils its new look in the summer of 2017. For an even more exclusive experience, Hotel Excelsior also includes a private residence, Villa Agave – once owned by famed British archaeologist Sir Arthur Evans and providing a luxury bolthole along with all the services of the hotel.

The sleek and stylish Hotel Bellevue is another gem in the Dream Collection. Carved into a cliff overlooking the Adriatic, it boasts two restaurants and a spa, and has been named one of "Europe's coolest new hotels" by *The Sunday Times*. And, in 2012, ALH opened the five-star Villa Orsula. Built in 1939 as a private residence, it combines classic Mediterranean design, luxurious accommodation and personalised service to create a superb holiday experience in the heart of Dubrovnik. Finally, the striking Villa Sheherezade is a vision of white and turquoise amid vast terraces and lush gardens, described as "a palace in which legends have been born and epic romances played out". Elizabeth Taylor and Richard Burton stayed here and it is a popular setting for films.

Set against sea views and the beauty of Dubrovnik's Old City (a Unesco World Heritage Site), each Dream Collection property makes the most of the city's charms, and offers a range of activities from art tours to yachting. With all this and ALH's renowned service and facilities, every guest is certain to conclude that this really is "paradise on earth".
— www.adriaticluxuryhotels.com

DISCRETION ASSURED

Velaa Private Island, Maldives

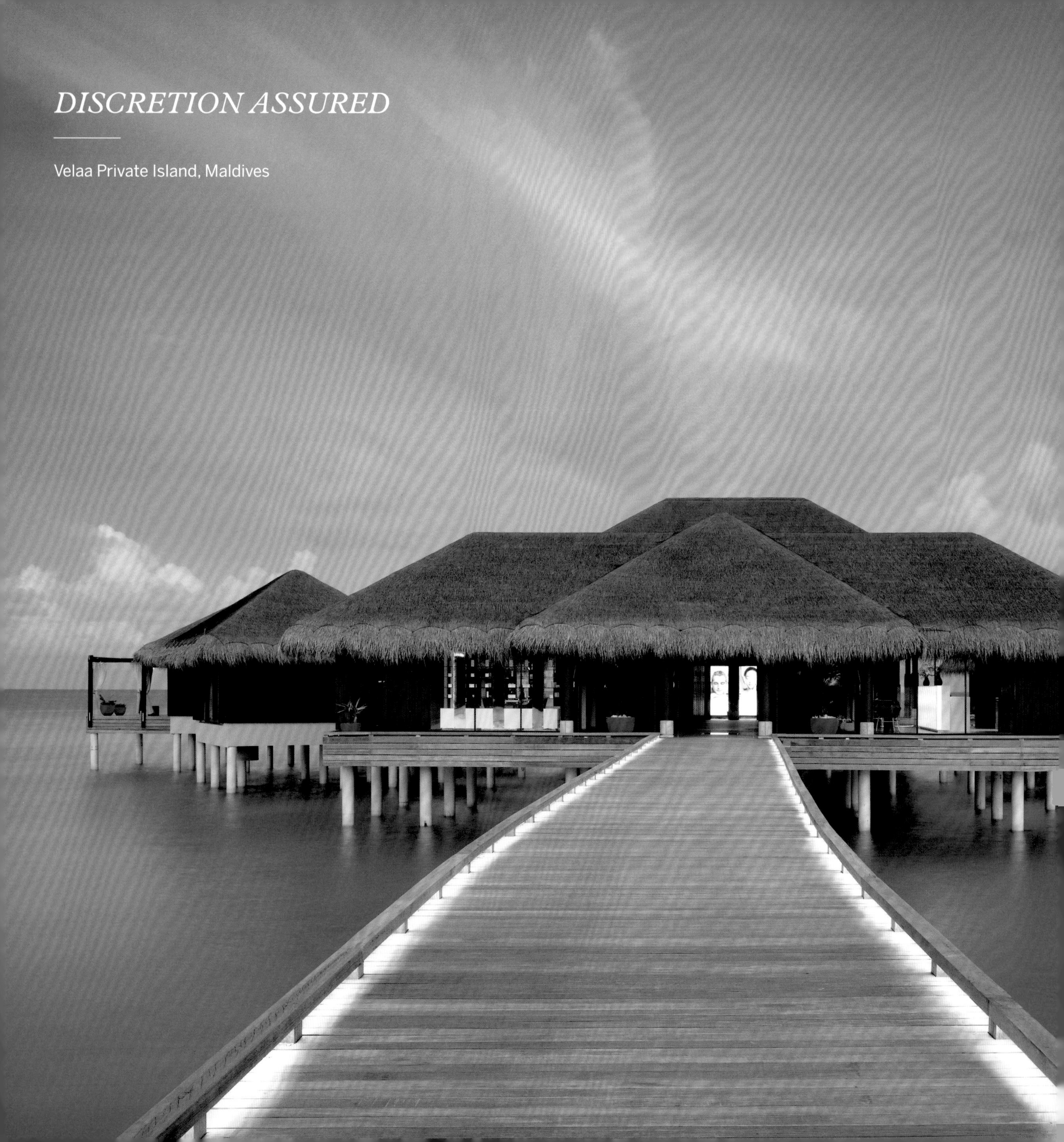

VELAA PRIVATE ISLAND has a guest list that includes Hollywood celebrities, sports stars and business elites. But, as the resort's Director of Sales and Marketing Gabriela Markova says, "This is a place where people come not to be seen or heard". Velaa is a palm-fringed atoll in the Indian Ocean, 187 km north of the Maldives capital, Malé. "The concept of the resort is a home away from home," she continues, "where you can do as little or as much as you like, all arranged by your own butler."

The epithet "private" is overused in luxury travel, but Velaa is the genuine article. Czech investor Jirí Smejc, a longtime devotee of the Maldives, acquired Velaa in order to create his ideal of barefoot luxury and complete privacy (Velaa is the only island in the Maldives with a no-drone policy). After considerable investment, the architect-designed haven opened in December 2013, boasting gourmet restaurants, a Champagne bar, a Clarins spa, a 500-bin wine cellar and its own nine-tee golf course created by José Maria Olazabal.

There are 47 villas in the resort, some dotted along the beach, others, such as the Sunset Deluxe Water Pool Villas, suspended over the turquoise ocean. The Romantic Pool Residence is only accessible by boat. "Even when we are full, there are only 147 guests," says Gabriela. "And we have a very high staff ratio per villa."

Czech architect Petr Kolár designed the entire island complex, giving continuity to the villas and their interiors. "It allowed more space for creativity than our urban commissions," says Kolár, "but it was challenging to find natural materials that were also durable. For the interiors, we chose colours and tones that provide a relaxing, cosy atmosphere."

Villas and their outdoor bathrooms feature bamboo and rattan, along with wood-panelling from Borneo and stone paving from Jordan.

Petr Kolár's most striking design is the 23m-high Tavaru tower, inspired by the shape of a cocoon and clad in undulating, perforated canvas. It houses the wine cellar, which resembles a tall, wood-panelled library, where guests can sample Old World classics including the largest collection of Romanée-Conti in the Maldives, as well as wines from boutique wineries around the world. The sommelier hosts weekly tastings as well as private wine degustation dinners.

Perhaps to offset the temptations of Velaa's restaurants and bars, the island caters for most sporting tastes, with its golf academy, squash and tennis courts, and a football pitch. "If we have footballers staying," says Gabriela, "we sometimes host informal matches between staff and clients!"

The resort operates a PADI-certified diving centre and its resident marine biologist offers guided snorkelling safaris. Water sports on Velaa range from wake-boarding, kite-surfing and kayaking, to the wonderfully James Bond-style two-man submarine and sea bob. "We are always looking for the newest water toys to add to our list, jetpack being our latest addition," says Gabriela. "This really sets us apart." Toys aren't provided exclusively for adults on the island, however. Velaa welcomes families and provides a nanny for each child, a dynamic water-play area and activities for all ages, from pizza-making to a console-packed gaming room.

Velaa Private Island offers an idyllic mixture of seclusion and seduction and conviviality – a home from home in private luxury.
— www.velaaprivateisland.com

ANCIENT WONDERS

argos in Cappadocia, Turkey

"WE CALL OURSELVES an ancient village with a reception desk," says Asli Ozbay, architect at the argos in Cappadocia hotel. "Visitors can to stroll through the streets within the hotel, while other guests are enjoying their rooms."

Cappadocia, the high rocky plateau of Anatolia in central Turkey, is one of the most popular destinations for world travellers. A mysterious, even unearthly expanse of ravines, canyons, mountains and valleys, it was formed by millions of years of soft volcanic lava and ash. Wind and water have left tall, oddly shaped pillars of lava, the so-called "fairy chimneys".

However, what really sets Cappadocia apart from virtually every other place in the world is its history of human habitation. Life underground is known to date back to Hittites, but Cappadocians were mentioned in the Bible and by the Greek historian Herodotus in the fifth century BC.

Located at the top of this land of splendour, argos in Cappadocia is unlike any other luxury hotel. The unique getaway is a restored village built around an ancient monastery, with "mansions" connected by 1,200-year-old underground tunnels. Using traditional techniques of regional architecture, it took 19 years of excavation and restoration to create the hotel, and archaeologists continue to work on the restoration of the surrounding village.

"All 51 of the guest rooms and suites of the hotel are different from one another," says Asli. "Some are hidden within caves, others have windows, some are suites with private pools, and all have terraces or balconies that look towards mesmerising views." Numerous antiques provide eccentric examples of 3,000 years of Cappadocian history. Unusually, there are no televisions, just iPods so that people can relax and enjoy a world

of timeless eternity. "We want to preserve the sense that you are in a modest Anatolian village," says Asli, "but with all modern conveniences."

Guests can dine at the Seki Restaurant, which offers Turkish and international dishes made with local ingredients and herbs from the garden. The ancient wine cellar – which has an ancient winery and a chapel for private tastings and parties – holds 22,000 bottles, including award-winning wines from the hotel's own Syrah and Pinot Noir-like Kalecik Karasi grapes.

Concerts of Sufi, jazz and classical music are held in the Bezirhane hall, a domed space that was once a monastery, a resting place for Silk Road camels and a linseed oil press. The concierge can organise excursions to local attractions such as the Goreme Open Air Museum, with its chapels and frescoes dating back to the ninth century, to Uchisar Castle, or to nearby volcanoes and valleys. Visitors can also soar above the amazing rocky landscape in a hot-air balloon or go hiking and horse-riding. A luxury spa will soon be added to the hotel's list of attractions.

Named by *Condé Nast* Johansens as one of the most romantic hotels in the world, argos has won a plethora of awards. In 2015 alone, it was one of *National Geographic*'s Top 10 Magnificent Hotels, the World Luxury Hotel Awards named it Europe's Best Scenic Environment and the Seki Restaurant received a *Wine Spectator* Award of Excellence.

There is something mystical about the Cappadocian landscape. "It's not surprising that so many branches of religion derived from Cappadocia," says Asli. "It is fascinating and almost miraculous in its beauty, in a way that can't be defined. There are no cars or highway noises, making it the perfect place to relax, to meditate or just be with the one you love."
— www.argosincappadocia.com

THE ROYAL TREATMENT

___

Maikhao Dream Villa Resort & Spa, Phuket, Thailand

THE THAI WORD "maikhao" translates as "white silk", and connotes luxury that is fit for a king. It is an apt name for the luxury beachfront resorts owned and operated by Maikhao Dream Hotel & Resorts.

The company provides a deluxe and sophisticated five-star service, featuring classic Thai hospitality. "Our resorts are designed to make guests feel like royalty," says Vivian Ng, Group Director of Sales & Marketing. "There are authentic Thai touches that evoke grandeur, like the elegantly hand-painted scenes of Thai folklore on the feature walls in the villa and on glass panels, or the fine Thai silks."

Maikhao Dream Villa Resort & Spa is a collection of 22 private pool villas situated on the northwest coast of Phuket, amid the tranquil surroundings of the pristine Maikhao beach. Guests can elude the hustle and bustle of the island, yet popular attractions and nightlife can be easily accessed by the resort's convenient chauffeur services. It is the holiday island's only direct-access beachfront private pool resort, and attracts those looking for a peaceful setting in which to completely unwind. Each villa features its own private swimming pool, jet pool, outdoor

pavilion, well-equipped kitchen and home entertainment. The signature three-bedroom pool villa contains 650 sq m of luxury space and a rooftop sun terrace.

Authentic Thai cuisine and mouth-watering coastal favourites are available at the all-day fine-dining Dokbua Restaurant, or can be served to the six-seat dining table of a guest's villa. The Maikhao Dream Spa offers pampering and indulgent treatments as well as a unique concept of wellness and healing, with three customised programmes: detox, anti-stress and weight management.

"Each programme can be followed for between five and 21 days," says Vivian, "and contains three main elements: Traditional Thai, Ayurverdic and Eco." Each begins with an in-depth consultation: 80 per cent of the programme is based on nutrition and 20 per cent on activities and exercise.

"Guests are often mesmerised by the size of their beach-front villa," concludes Vivian. "They indulge in pampering spa treatments and bring home memories of private Thai cooking or massage lessons, among other bespoke experiences."
— www.maikhaodream.com

HERITAGE MEETS SPLENDOUR

The Royal Crescent Hotel & Spa, Bath

IN THE 18TH century, Bath was Europe's most fashionable city – the place where society people from all over the continent travelled to take the waters in the Roman spa. The city also offered plenty in the way of amusement, including scandal, intrigue, elopement and duelling.

Of all Bath's many neo-classical Georgian masterpieces, the famous Royal Crescent, designed in the 1760s by John Wood the Younger, is unmatched in splendour and magnificence. In the middle of the terrace, occupying a pair of spacious conjoined mansion houses, is The Royal Crescent Hotel & Spa which, in 2017, celebrates two and a half centuries since the laying of its first stone.

The hotel comprises 45 suites and rooms, shared between the mansions and its coaching houses, which are accessed via an acre of tranquil gardens to the rear of the building. "Although we are a five-star hotel, we aim to create a feeling of relaxed luxury, free of any stuffy formality," says General Manager Jonathan Stapleton. "Being an independent establishment, not part of a chain, enabled us to give our designers a special freedom." The result mixes classic Georgian luxury with elegant contemporary style.

Contained within the coaching houses is the sumptuous Dower House Restaurant, as well as The Garden Villa, which can be used as a private residence for up to 10 guests. "The newly refurbished Spa & Bath House offers a range of treatments, and all of our guests have unlimited use of the facilities," says Jonathan. "We're confident that they will come away feeling they've had the ultimate treat."

Non-resident visitors are also welcome. A range of lavish teas can be taken in the gardens and The Wedding Garden can accommodate every kind of celebration. The Royal Crescent Hotel & Spa is also a favourite with corporate clients, who can attend luxury board meetings before enjoying the facilities during their down time.

Concierge services with a special personal touch are available to all residents, and – rarely for an establishment outside London – the head and deputy concierges are members of the prestigious Golden Keys Concierge Society. "Some of our guests have described this hotel as a kind of Narnia," says Jonathan. "You walk through the front door from the bustle of Bath, and a moment later you can be in the stunning, large, tranquil gardens – it is relaxed luxury at its very best."
— www.royalcrescent.co.uk

A BOUTIQUE TRAILBLAZER

Blakes Hotel, London

BACK IN 1978, the celebrated designer, restaurateur and actress Anouska Hempel created a small hotel. All 45 rooms were created with an individual style that exuded her personal aesthetic; indeed, many of the pictures and furnishings originated from her own personal belongings. Nearly 40 years on, this inaugural luxury boutique hotel, Blakes, boasts many imitators but few equals. Each room has a lavish, almost startling personality, from the colours to the geometry to the pictures on the walls.

"Our rooms are not for everybody," says Ian Telford, General Manager. "They are for people with a sense of adventure, who are not afraid to be different."

Now owned by a group of private investors who plan to expand the brand – first in London, then internationally – Blakes remains as wonderfully unique as ever. "Every room tells a different story," says Ian. "Each gives our guests the possibility of being transported to another land."

Prior to designing Blakes, Anouska travelled across Asia and gained a rich appreciation for eastern ideas of opulence. Under her watchful eye, she has overseen additional design renovations in a few rooms, maintaining her strong sense of style. In addition to aesthetics, practicality is key; absolute privacy is a standard, which is why generations of travelling celebrities have chosen to call the hotel home.

Blakes is, however, moving with the times, but not forgetting its past. Its eponymous restaurant, a much-loved basement hangout, has been moved to the ground floor. The relocation offers natural daylight to enhance the stunning architecture and design. Anoushka felt inspired by a trip up the Bosphorus, and Blakes' restaurant is intended to reflect the inside of a luxurious steamboat. The food is Mediterranean with a touch of Asian fusion, with a menu based around the freshest organic ingredients. Perhaps not the standard meal for a steamboat passenger, but then Blakes only evokes the most pleasing elements of the past.

The garden has been reconfigured by British fashion designer Matthew Williamson, following a successful pop-up event in the summer of 2015. With his love of colour and geometry, he suits Anouska's style seamlessly. "Matthew is another designer with an extravagant sense of drama," says Ian. "We wanted something new, bold and unpredictable and we got it. He's taken the Mediterranean and the Bohemian foundation as inspiration and used various patterns and colours to create something truly unique, bringing Blakes into the 21st century without compromising its history."

Daylight is all very well for plants and early risers but, in the old basement restaurant, a lounge bar called Blakes Below caters to those who prefer twilight at all times. This redesign also offers more room for cultural events and social gatherings, from live gigs to London Fashion Week events, while maintaining the discretion and neighbourhood feel that South Kensington's residents value so much.

"Our hotel residents, and patrons that use the restaurant, bar and garden are at the centre of everything we do," says Ian. "We want everyone to leave Blakes with a fond memory that they will carry with them until they return." Blakes is a glamorous place to stay, eat, drink and hang out, but with a cosy neighbourhood feel. It's not easy to combine such things smoothly – but then Blakes has made its name from the alliance of the unexpected.
— www.blakeshotels.com

EASY LUXURY

Awarta Nusa Dua Luxury Villas & Spa, Bali

INSPIRED BY THE legendary 12th-century Balinese romance between a Chinese princess and a Balinese king, the resort of Awarta Nusa Dua Luxury Villas & Spa fuses Indonesian and Chinese culture to create a memorable holiday experience.

"Bali has an enchanting and intriguing history," says Director Naomi Siawarta. "We have tried to reflect this, together with the oriental influence of the Chinese heritage, throughout the resort in its architecture and décor. We have also combined luxurious facilities, inspired by Indonesian, Malaysian and Chinese culture, with home comforts that will be familiar to all. That means people can come from all over the world and still feel at home. But a home that is more luxurious, more peaceful and on a truly beautiful island. Bali is a magical place and Awarta is like being in a dream."

The complex of 14 villas is clustered around two restaurants, a bar and an award-winning spa. The services on offer are exceptional, from the welcome drink and foot bath that visitors receive upon arrival to the exclusive 24-hour butler service. Each villa has a private pool, as well as access to a private beach club and gym, private transport and excellent security. Bali is a special place, with incredible weather and scenery, and a fascinating local culture to explore. The season is best from May to October, when the tropical climate experiences cooling winds.

The resort's two restaurants are Ru Yi, which serves Chinese fine dining, such as sea cucumber and abalone, and The Long Table, which serves local delicacies, as well as international classics. "People like to try local food but they also want comfort food, something like what they have at home," says Naomi. "We also have the Eight Degrees bar, which is more sophisticated that most bars in Bali, modelled on a British club."

The award-winning Thevana Spa is another special place for guests, bringing tranquillity through traditional Balinese treatments. "It's very different to other spas," says Naomi. "We begin by taking people into a relaxation room where they can have a welcome drink and listen to soft Balinese instrumental music to help them relax. People travel from across the world and when they reach us they are often exhausted, so we just want to put our guests at ease and rejuvenate them."

The satisfaction of its guests is at the heart of everything that Awarta offers. Before arrival, they are asked if there are any sites they wish to visit – such as the famous sacred monkey forest, or the stunning Tanah Lot temple – as well as any dietary requirements they may have or even whether they will be celebrating any special occasions during their stay. The resort will make any necessary arrangements, offer suggestions and advice, and provide a private car for excursions. A car is also available for any trips to the nearby private beach.

"Balinese culture has a special way of greeting people with our hands closed together, and all the time they are with us, we ensure that we take close care of our guests," says Naomi. "It's all about service: the knowledge that, wherever you are on the resort, guests will be safe and happy. They can enjoy their holiday with complete peace of mind."
— www.awartaresorts.com

PRIVATE PARADISE

Coco Privé Kuda Hithi Island, Maldives

Few properties can claim to be unique, but Coco Privé Kuda Hithi Island actually is. With 1.4 hectares (3.5 acres) of lush, tropical greenery embraced by white sand beaches and the gloriously clear, warm waters of the Indian Ocean, it is a private island in the Maldives with a difference.

"Coco Privé is available only for exclusive hire," says Marketing Director Shafa Shabeer. "You and your friends and family have the entire island to yourselves. It's very much an intimate home, not a resort."

Remarkably, Coco Privé is owned and managed by a local family. It features six beautifully designed villas, standing among the coconut palms: four in the master residence (including a smaller one, ideal for personal or security staff); and two set apart, for those who might want more privacy. Facilities include a cocktail bar, a generous wine cellar, dining room, kitchen, library, gym and swimming pool. A personal spa therapist is also available whenever guests want. It goes without saying that guests will enjoy a luxurious experience with exemplary service, as the island comes with a team of 30 dedicated staff including butlers and a private chef. "We focus on the intangible," says Shafa. "It's your time, your space; it's all about you. Every stay is completely tailored around a guest's individual needs. We get to know their tastes and preferences before they arrive – food, drink, on- or off-island activities they love, and so on, which allows us to create a highly bespoke experience."

With past visitors including royalty, celebrities and high-flying international business people, client confidentiality is absolutely essential, so Shafa is unable to provide details of the various experiences guests have enjoyed here. "It depends on how a guest wishes to be entertained," she says. "We can arrange simple pleasures, such as a snorkelling excursion with a marine biologist to go spot turtles. Or it can be something completely grand, such as flying in a Michelin-starred chef for a seven-course BBQ dinner on the beach, complete with a music band. We can arrange almost anything!"

— www.cocoprive.com

CLUB CLASS

St James's Hotel and Club, London

THERE ARE FEW institutions that can claim to have had Winston Churchill, Henry James and Ian Fleming as members. But St James's Hotel and Club in Mayfair, London has been attracting such luminaries for more than 150 years, first as a gentlemen's club and now as a five-star hotel for those in search of a luxurious, discreet bolt-hole in one of the city's most desirable areas.

A stone's throw from Buckingham Palace, St James's has an enviable history to match its geography. It was founded in 1857 by British aristocrat Earl Granville as a home for travelling diplomats. In the 1940s, it was briefly the home of Bond creator Ian Fleming, who no doubt found inspiration over a martini at the bar. And in the 1980s, Michael Caine, Roger Moore and Liza Minnelli were all regulars.

The Victorian townhouse was closed in 2006 for a multimillion-pound refurbishment by the German designer Anne Maria Jagdfeld and re-opened in 2008 as a hotel with 60 guest rooms and suites. But the intimate atmosphere remains. "It's a warm and friendly place," says General Manager Anjana Pandya. "You don't have to be suited and booted. We want our guests to feel relaxed."

St James's offers highly personal service alongside modern comforts. Cashmere wallpaper and Murano glass chandeliers provide handsome design touches, and the building's artistic heritage is celebrated in an art collection that includes Impressionist, Expressionist and Cubist works from all over Europe.

The National Gallery is a few minutes' walk away, and Mayfair and the West End are on its doorstep. "Fortnum & Mason and many shops on Bond Street and Regent Street offer discounts to our guests," says Anjana. There's even a secret passageway into Green Park.

The hotel's Executive Chef William Drabble has held a Michelin star since 2010, and oversees the room service and William's Bar & Bistro, as well as St James's destination restaurant, Seven Park Place. With just nine tables, the latter is one of the world's smallest Michelin-starred restaurants and serves seasonal French dishes using the very best British produce in a truly intimate setting. "We wanted to make the hotel a destination for gastronomes," says Anjana. Mission accomplished. — www.stjameshotelandclub.com

STROKE OF GENIUS

Monte Rei Golf and Country Club, Portugal

MONTE REI GOLF and Country Club might have won accolades as the number-one golf course in Portugal for its Jack Nicklaus signature course, but it offers far more than just a golfing experience. According to General Manager Salvador Lucena, some of its visitors, who include a mix of families, friends and small corporate groups, have no interest in the sport at all. "In the summer months," says Salvador, "many people come for a family holiday, to enjoy the sun, the sea and the landscape, and very few of them play golf. However," he adds knowingly, "occasionally a father and son will sneak out for a game."

Set in more than 1,000 acres of unspoiled countryside, Monte Rei enjoys views that are unparalleled in the whole of the eastern Algarve. Situated between the towns of Vila Real de Santo António and Tavira, it is just a short drive away from the golden beaches of the Atlantic coast. To the north, it is dramatically framed by the Serra do Caldeirão mountains.

For keen golfers, Monte Rei provides a top-notch experience. The course, which was first opened in 2007, was personally designed and supervised by champion golfer Nicklaus to be in harmony with its environment; and to be used by both the seasoned and the amateur player. A par 72 Championship golf course, it features an enjoyable series of eight par-4s, five par-3s and five par-5s in a challenging and distinctive layout. With water coming into play at the 11th and 18th, each hole blends effortlessly into the natural canvas of the course, which was named Portugal's number-one golfing destination by *Golf Digest* magazine in 2016.

"The course is the anchor of the resort," says Salvador. "We welcome golfers, valet park for them, unload their clubs from their car, have buggies prepared, offer water and towels, clean the clubs – we do everything a professional golfer would expect and offer the highest level of service, which includes a large clubhouse with two restaurants.

"In fact, gastronomy is something we take very seriously," he adds. "The resort's food and beverage operation is overseen by Michelin-starred chef Albano Lourenço, who is one of the most respected chefs on the Portuguese culinary scene. Vistas, the resort's signature restaurant, offers a complete gourmet experience, providing the ultimate in gastronomic delights with a unique ambiance and uncompromising standard of service." This fine-dining restaurant not only serves up impeccable cuisine, it also delivers stunning views out across the manicured fairways and lake to the Atlantic Ocean beyond.

The second of the clubhouse's culinary offerings, Monte Rei Grill, is a less formal affair. Serving a range of light dishes from breakfast through to the early evening, Chef Lourenço's menu makes use of the best regional products to create a selection of enticing local and international delicacies.

At present, the resort comprises a village of residences from one to four bedrooms, fully serviced like a luxury hotel. The village's social point is Veranda, which features an additional restaurant and bar, tennis courts, swimming pools, gym and spa facilities, along with a new Kids Villa dedicated to younger guests. Some of the villas have private pools and gardens, and all are built in traditional Portuguese style and spaced well apart to provide privacy and enable everyone to enjoy the views. "Each bedroom is like a five-star en-suite hotel room," says Salvador. "It's like a home away from home with full hotel services and security."

The construction of a set of luxury apartments called The Clubhouse Residences commences in early 2017. Made up of two-bedroom apartments and three-bedroom penthouses, these are designed in a refined, contemporary style, featuring generously sized terraces, and all finished to the highest of specifications. Just a few steps from the iconic Monte Rei Clubhouse, residents will benefit from convenient access to the spectacular North Course, to world-class dining options and to their own private swimming pool, gym and spa facilities.

"The Clubhouse Residences invite you to enjoy an exclusive, contemporary lifestyle," says Salvador, "and will make the ideal vacation home, primary home or rental income opportunity." In addition, to

further enhance the resort's golf offering, a second Jack Nicklaus signature course is in development.

Green fees start at €150 per day in low season, with a one-bedroom villa starting at €200 per night, including breakfast. The business has been growing at a rapid pace for the past three years and is continuing to expand. Monte Rei has become a very desirable destination for weddings and parties, which can take place in the clubhouse or the gardens. The resort also provides the services of a dedicated event planner to assist at every stage, from venue selection and set up to menu selection.

Out of season it hosts exclusive events, particularly golf tournaments, although for those whose enthusiasm surpasses their playing ability, the Monte Rei Golf Academy's PGA Professionals are always on hand to help guests improve their game with a spot of one-to-one attention.

The key to Monte Rei's success is providing something for everyone, all within a beautiful setting. "If guests want, we can arrange activities for them," says Salvador. "We offer tennis lessons, personal training sessions, cooking lessons with our acclaimed chef and wine tastings. We can organise excursions to nearby towns or to the Ria Formosa natural park, a natural strip of protected small islands in a lagoon."

Something for everyone, then – there's no need to be a devout golfer to love this particular resort.
— www.monte-rei.com

THE GREAT ESCAPE

———

Puente Romano Beach Resort & Spa, Spain

"WE'RE LIKE A tranquil Andalusian village in front of the sea," says Jorge Manzur, General Manager of Marbella's Puente Romano Beach Resort and Spa. "It's all about location and quality – the low-rise white buildings and paved streets make it feel like a beach-side Andalusian village, surrounded by sub-tropical gardens. So even when we're full it doesn't feel like it."

Its appeal also lies in the fact that this 255-room luxury southern Spanish resort caters to all tastes. The shaded Plaza Village square is Marbella's top culinary destination, with six settings including Nikkei (Japanese-Peruvian fusion) and Thai eateries and the two Michelin-starred Dani Garcia Restaurant, where guests can sample the acclaimed Malaga chef's daring take on Andalusian cuisine. The square and the restaurants are always lively with music. "The music is part of each restaurant's personality," says Jorge. "They all have their own tracklists and there's always a jazz band playing on the waterfront." Music is also the draw every weekend at La Suite, the resort's new nightclub with resident DJs.

Key to Puente Romano's success is the professionalism of the staff, numbering 600 in high season. "It's just as important for us to invest in staff as well as in the hotel," says Jorge. Every employee is trained monthly, and representatives from the hospitality consortium Leading Hotels of the World attend the resort twice a year to help the staff perfect their skills.

The resort is constantly improving, opening a set of four- and five-bedroom villas with sea views in 2016. These are targeted at families and come with butler service and a chauffeur on call. Another recent addition is the Six Senses Spa, the only one in Spain, which features Yogic and Integrated Wellness programmes to provide personalised solutions such as sleep improvement or detox.

"We want to be the best hotel in Europe," says Jorge, after being awarded Best Resort in Spain by *Condé Nast Traveler*. This luxury Andalusian resort has an intimate appeal, but its ambitions are anything but modest.
— www.puenteromano.com

SET TO STUN

Park Weggis, Switzerland

MARK TWAIN ONCE sought inspiration and peace in the hills of Weggis, Switzerland, as did Queen Victoria. And, with its stunning lake and mountain scenery, it's not hard to see why. The historic Weggis has always drawn royalty – literary and otherwise – to its idyllic location. Park Weggis is a hotel that has been offering guests adventure and relaxation since 1875. Set on the shores of Lake Lucerne and overlooking famous alpine peaks such as Pilatus, it's a luxurious escape that's around 30 minutes' drive from the cities of Lucerne and Zurich.

This five-star superior resort is now part of the Relais & Châteaux and Swiss Deluxe Hotels groups. "Today's typical guest likes to enjoy life, to discover something new," says general manager Peter Kämpfer. "The lake winds around the mountains and there's a cable car to take you up."

Set in 22,000 sq m of parkland, including its own bathing beach and private lake access, the Art Nouveau exterior houses 52 stylish modern rooms and suites, decked out with Philippe Starck lighting, Versace tableware and Murano glass. The Lalique Caviar Bar, meanwhile, is a crystal treasure trove.

The hotel boasts one of the biggest collections of wine in Switzerland, with a list of over 2,600 items on offer. Its rarer vintages attract connoisseurs from around the world. The wine cellar hosts special events, such as tastings in the dark. "You cannot even see the glass," says Peter. "You have just your nose and taste so there's nothing to distract you."

La Brasserie serves freshly caught fish and southern French specialities in a casual atmosphere. For those who prefer meat, the Park Grill dishes out prime cuts, cooked New York-style. The spa, in contrast, is a small slice of Asia in Switzerland. With three Tibetan therapists on its staff, treatments include Ku Nye massage using traditional herbs and oils. The wellness centre is set in a tranquil Japanese garden where six private Spa cottages offer complete seclusion.

Mark Twain said, "Architects cannot teach nature anything." With its mix of stunning scenery and perfectly attuned luxury rooms and facilities, perhaps Park Weggis could have changed his mind.
— www.parkweggis.ch

A TROPICAL RETREAT

The Legian Bali

ONE OF 13,000 islands in the Indonesian archipelago, Bali has for decades been a magnetic destination for tourists from across the world. They visit seeking the island's palm-fringed beaches, its kaleidoscopic coral reefs and the richly diverse, predominantly Hindu culture that suffuses life on this paradise isle.

For the past 20 years, the Legian Bali hotel has offered peerless luxury to visitors to the south of the island. Built by the award-winning designer Jaya Ibrahim, it is a haven of tranquillity set amid the bustle and thrum of the seaside town of Seminyak.

"From the immersiveness of Balinese ceremonies to the flavours of the local food, we are always curious and searching for the best expression of 'east meets west' in our service," says Director of Marketing Sarah Yana. She has been the driving force behind a raft of promotions to celebrate the hotel's 20th anniversary – recognition of the sustained excellence of luxury service since the Legian Bali first opened its doors on 15 August 1996.

Born in the Netherlands to Indonesian parents, Sarah worked in Jakarta, Shanghai, Guangzhou and Singapore before settling in Bali. Appropriately, given her globetrotting history, she says it's the cosmopolitan mixture of influences that makes the Legian Bali unique in its field, and why it provides an exclusive, experiential journey for each guest.

"Every colleague brings their own individual skills and expertise," she says, "be they Balinese, other local Indonesians or international staff, who come from anywhere from Australia to Europe." Sarah calls the appliance of Balinese Hinduism to customer care "a sacred chemistry". "Our staff all embrace and truly value the local Balinese culture," she says.

The Legian was named one of TripAdvisor's 25 best hotels in Asia, and its interior design is the embodiment of oriental elegance. The hotel's 67 suites, all seafront-facing, abound with natural wood, subtly harmonised furnishings and indigenous art throughout. The Beach House, a self-contained, three-bedroom villa with its very own pool and private-service kitchen, is the ultimate luxury venue for gatherings of friends and family.

Amid the palms and manicured lawns that lead down to the sea, there's an infinity pool, spa and yoga studio, as well as terrace bars and the hotel's main restaurant, where vibrant Asian ingredients are given the benefit of the classical French training of chef Luke Macleod, formerly of the Michelin-starred Senderens in Paris.

Beyond the five-star luxury of the Legian, Bali is famed for its coral reefs, boasting nearly 1,000 different types of fish – ideal for those who enjoy snorkelling or scuba-diving. "Snorkelling at Padang Bai up the eastern coast is a breathtaking experience," says Sarah. "The waters are crystal clear and the sea is rich with tropical fish. A top spot for the more experienced diver would be further north in Tulamben to see a US Navy shipwreck from the Second World War. Meanwhile, an hour's drive from Ubud, you'll find artisan silversmiths boasting some of the highest levels of craftsmanship in the world."

For anyone seeking adventure, mesmerising craft and culture, or simple tranquillity – or perhaps all three – the Legian Bali is the perfect base for an exquisite Balinese experience.
— lhm-hotels.com/legian-bali/en

BOMBAY DREAM

The Taj Mahal Palace, Mumbai

MANY GRAND BUILDINGS claim to be landmarks, but The Taj Mahal Palace really is. It was not only Mumbai's first luxury hotel when it opened its doors in 1903, but its 240-ft dome is still used by the Indian Navy as a triangulation point to navigate into harbour. For visitors arriving on the cruise liners of the day, the hotel's elaborate façade was the first hint of the lavish suites and ballrooms within. "The hotel is and has always been an iconic institution," says Taljinder Singh, Area Director of Mumbai Hotels and General Manager of the Taj Mahal Palace, Mumbai.

The Taj's striking 550 rooms and suites make the most of the views over the Arabian Sea and the neighbouring Gateway to India monument, with sea-facing balconies and bay windows reminiscent of Rajput window casements. The architects SK Vaidya and DN Mirza created an exuberant riot of Victorian Gothic, Florentine and Moorish details, which animate every embellished inch of the building.

The wings of the hotel conceal a tranquil courtyard and pool, with arcaded terraces for afternoon tea. It resonates with the glamour and romance of the golden age of travel in which it was built. "Clearly, we've upgraded over the years," says Taljinder, "with everything a modern traveller needs, but more than 200 of our associates have been with us for 30 years or more and they keep the golden age alive. There is real pride in working here. Many of our guests are also second- or third-generation visitors."

Jamsetji Tata, who commissioned the hotel, intended to revolutionise luxury hotels in India. To this end he embarked on a European shopping expedition to source the finest materials. "The pillars in the ballroom, for example, are made from the same steel used for the Eiffel Tower," says Taljinder. The hotel was the first in India to have American fans, German elevators, Turkish baths and English-style butlers.

The Taj also secured the first licence to serve alcohol in India for its Harbour Bar and opened the city's first 24-hour restaurant, the newly refurbished Shamiana. The hotel is a hub for fashionable Mumbai residents and visitors drawn by its history, charm and acclaimed cuisine. Sea Lounge is famed for its harbour views and afternoon tea; Wasabi by Morimoto for its Japanese food and Golden Dragon for Cantonese and Sichuan cuisine. "Our Ballroom and grand banquet spaces are some of the world's most beautiful dining areas," says Taljinder. "The Prince's Room was witness to the first ever conclave of Indian maharajahs called by the British under the Raj."

The 42 suites, which come with personalised butlers, benefited from Tata's exacting eye for quality and detail, and continue to be decorated with fine art, artefacts and silk furnishings. "Each suite is dramatically different," says Taljinder, "ranging from modern to traditional Indian sensibilities depending on our guests' preferences." The Tata Suite is decorated with authentic colonial furniture, while the Ravi Shankar Suite recalls the incognito visit of George Harrison, who came to the hotel in 1966 to study the sitar with Ravi Shankar. For as long as The Taj Mahal Palace has been a beacon for ships arriving in Mumbai, it has also been the leading light among India's luxury hotels, a taste of gracious hospitality and a remarkable destination in itself.
— www.tajhotels.com

LIVE LIKE A LORD

The Stafford London

JUST A STONE'S throw from many of London's most iconic landmarks, you could be forgiven for thinking that The Stafford London is one of the city's busiest hotels. However, set away from the nearby bustle, it is the hotel's quiet location and discreet five-star luxury that has been attracting visitors for more than 100 years.

Offering three different kinds of room, all stylish and private, and memorable dining experiences, The Stafford is one of London's best luxury hotels. The 17th-century building was once home to Lord and Lady Lyttelton and was first opened as a hotel in 1912.

"The hotel's Carriage House accommodation was converted from stables that date back some 390 years," says the hotel's manager Stuart Procter. "They once housed Lord Godolphin's horses, so they have an interesting history." They now house 12 private suites, presented in an elegant country style. Underneath these is the historic, 380-year-old cellar – a beautiful dining space for private functions, wine tastings and home to the hotel's impressive wine selection, overseen by Master Sommelier Gino Nardella.

The hotel's American Bar was opened some 60 years ago, as one of only a handful of such cocktail bars in London. "The walls are adorned with a plethora of memorabilia, autographs and photos, a nod to the US and Canadian forces that used the cellar as an air-raid shelter during the Second World War," says Stuart. "Our clients continue to leave hats, ties and photos from their time here, making it a club that requires no membership."

While the hotel's Main House offers more classic urban luxury, its 26 Mews Suites and Penthouse offer contemporary townhouse-style accommodation, with private entrances that are ideal for a lengthier stay. "Many of our clients return to The Stafford," says Stuart, "because it offers a home-away-from-home experience."

With The Stafford's discreet service, it's no wonder that Executive Concierge Frank Laino is oft-cited as the best in the world. "When it comes to informal formalities," says Stuart, "there's nothing we can't get." Quiet elegance and flawless service await those seeking a London retreat to call home, if only for a few days.
— www.thestaffordlondon.com

SMALL IS BEAUTIFUL

Small Luxury Hotels of the World

FOR MORE THAN 25 years, Small Luxury Hotels of the World has been proving that good things come in small packages. Connecting discerning travellers with the best independently minded hotels, the award-winning company has become the definitive destination for anyone seeking a truly unforgettable travel experience.

"All our hotels go the extra mile in terms of both luxury and personality," says Tim Davis, Vice President of Brand and Marketing. "Each one is a handpicked gem, offering the sort of one-of-a-kind stay that you'll remember for a lifetime, whether you're diving in the Caribbean or making your own perfume in Paris."

The independently minded company's ethos is "small is beautiful", and that doesn't just apply to hotel size. It has just 520 properties across 80 countries, each one carefully selected and regularly vetted. "We get more than 1,000 applications each year and only take on around 4 per cent," says Tim. "Hotels have to be the right fit and of an incredibly high standard. We don't do mediocre."

Unique, chic retreats include La Sultana Marrakech, a stunning collection of vaulted suites that overlook a Moroccan palace, and Kandolhu in the Maldives,

a palm-fringed private island accessible only by seaplane. "Big chains tend to offer the same experience whether you're in Shanghai or Berlin," says Tim. "With a Small Luxury Hotel, you get to truly experience a place."

In Rome, travellers can stay at the Villa Spalletti Trivelli, the elegant stately home of an Italian aristocratic family, a stone's throw from the Trevi Fountain. In Thailand, the Keemala resort offers seven tree houses suspended in the canopy of a rainforest. In Mallorca, the bijou boltholes include Cap Rocat, a 19th-century military fortress complete with a drawbridge and infinity pool behind the ramparts.

The portfolio of properties is spectacular, which is why the SLH stamp has become as reliable an indicator of excellence as a Michelin star. "Staying at a small, independent hotel can, and should, be a fantastic experience," says Tim. "Those who try it find it incredibly freeing. It's an adventure. Our customers always tell us they will never look back."
— www.slh.com

A CLASS OF ITS OWN

The Lalit Suri Hospitality Group

"WE DON'T ANSWER the phone by saying 'hello'," says Arun Kumar, the General Manager of The Lalit London. "Instead, we always greet people with 'namaskar'. From that first word, the experience of a Lalit hotel is different." The Lalit Suri Hospitality Group, which opened The Lalit London near Tower Bridge at the end of 2016, owns 12 luxury hotels across India. "All our properties have a character and a story behind them," says Arun. "The Lalit London offers the best of Indian hospitality and culture within a Grade-II listed Victorian building."

Each of The Lalit group's five-star hotels takes its character from the local area, people and heritage. The Lalit London, the group's first overseas hotel, is housed in a former grammar school designed by Edward Mountford, architect of the Old Bailey. "The rooms are called Classrooms," says Arun. "The Headmaster's Room is a luxury suite and the Governors' Room is now the cocktail bar."

Memories of school dinners are consigned to the distant past with the opening of Baluchi, The Lalit group's signature restaurant, which serves a selection of dishes from each of Lalit's Indian hotels. "Indian cuisine is among the most diverse in the world," says Arun. "There are 30 gastronomic subdivisions across the country, so there is much to discover."

The Lalit group's choice of EPR Architects, responsible for the Fortnum & Mason redesign, and interior designers Archer Humphryes Architects, the team behind The Chiltern Firehouse, is indicative of its commitment to working with elite professionals and tastemakers to create luxurious and original destinations. Outside the hotel, the tone is set by dramatic topiary and Indian sculptures designed by long-time Lalit collaborator and Paris-based landscape artist Olivier Vecchierini. "This is a boutique hotel," says Arun. "It isn't your run-of-the-mill city hotel."

Under the direction of Chairperson and Managing Director Dr Jyotsna Suri, The Lalit group has focused both on classic hotels, such as The Lalit Great Eastern in Kolkata (India's first luxury hotel, dating back to the 1840s, now restored to its full glory), as well as establishing five-star resorts in culturally important or lesser-known regions of India. The Lalit Temple View Khajuraho, for example, has been built to afford views of the Unesco World Heritage Site of Khajuraho, a city of temples dating back to 950 .

"We develop destinations, not just hotels," says Arun. "Before we opened The Lalit Resort & Spa Bekal, few tourists knew about that northern part of Kerala." The 100-acre Bekal property, fringed by tropical forest and bordered by the Arabian Sea, offers ayurvedic treatments in the group's Rejuve – The Spa and a *kettuvallom*, a floating guest cottage. "With The Lalit London, we are showing a new area to tourists who would otherwise shop and stay in the centre. There is so much to do around Tower Bridge and the building itself is a beauty."

Furnished with handcrafted chandeliers from Hyderabad, carved wooden screens and mother-of-pearl inlaid mirrors, The Lalit London mixes period elegance with Indian artistry. From the first welcoming *namaskar*, the impeccable style and hospitality are the things that unite The Lalit group's distinctive properties, whether in London, Kolkata or Bekal.
— www.thelalit.com

GALLIC CHARM

La Maison du Paradou, France

ALTHOUGH IT WAS the weather that drove Nick and Andrea Morris from Britain to Provence, the climate was not the only reason they chose this gorgeous region of the South of France as the location for La Maison du Paradou, their luxury boutique hotel. "I love this part of France," says Nick. "It is Van Gogh country and it has everything. My parents drove to the Riviera every summer and we would stop off on the way. I grew to love it."

At La Maison du Paradou, a 17th-century coaching inn a 30-minute drive from Nîmes, Avignon and Marseille at the foot of the Alpilles hills, Nick and Andrea share this love of the area with their guests. The hotel has just five impeccable bedrooms: a number that allows Nick to provide visitors with an exemplary level of service, in addition to the luxury facilities. "I help guests with their itineraries," he says, "make sure they can see things they want to see, recommend and book restaurants. We put in the time to make sure their holiday is everything we want it to be." Nick also arranges informal

drinks in the evenings so that guests can mingle with one another and swap tips about the area. "It's a friendly, clubby atmosphere," he says.

La Maison du Paradou also has a three-bedroom villa with its own pool in the grounds, available for hire on a self-catering basis. The hotel does not have a restaurant, but several excellent eating establishments nearby include a neighbourhood bistro that Terence Conran has described as his favourite restaurant in the world.

Being so far south, the climate is ideal all year round. "Although high season is June to September," says Nick, "the spring and autumn months are also lovely periods with far fewer people around. It's very pleasant indeed at those times."

So guests at La Maison du Paradou can relax in splendid comfort whatever the season. As Nick puts it, "For our guests, it's a luxurious home from home without any of the responsibility."
— www.maisonduparadou.com

SPA QUALITY

Lapinha Spa, Brazil

LAPINHA SPA IN southern Brazil is worth visiting for its beautiful location alone. Set in 1,100 acres of organic farmland surrounded by the Atlantic Araucária subtropical rainforest, the luxury spa has about as lush and green a setting as a health tourist could ask for.

However, it has much more to offer than simply stunning surroundings. Brazil's first-ever medical spa seeks to help clients to control the chronic health problems that beset modern lifestyles, such as diabetes, high cholesterol and stress. Experts and top-notch facilities here can help guests to kick-start a healthier lifestyle. A comprehensive wellness programme increases a deep revitalisation experience. "Healthy habits can be adopted more easily when a client escapes the tribulations of everyday life," says Dieter Brepohl, the spa's owner and CEO. "Our results can be seen within a week, whether they're to do with weight loss, blood cholesterol levels and blood pressure, or better indicators in the glycaemic index."

Under the auspices of trained medical professionals, every guest receives a tailored programme based on one-to-one consultations with a doctor, nutritionist, physiotherapist and personal trainer, before enjoying aqua therapy and massage treatments. The mind and soul are fortified by walking and biking tours in the grounds by day, and by meditation and musical recitals in the evenings. The subtropical climate, meanwhile, is the perfect escape from a European winter.

With experts outnumbering guests to the tune of around two to one, the spa boasts a highly personalised programme. And Lapinha's guests aren't the only ones to be impressed. In 2013 alone, it won the World Spa Wellness Award, as well as a Condé Nast Johansens recommendation. "The experience we offer is a holistic one that delivers on both health and wellness in the broadest sense," says Dieter. "Our great customer feedback gives us the assurance that we are getting things right."
— www.lapinha.com.br

REFINED STYLE

Fashion and beauty

SOME LIKE IT HAUTE

La Perla

WHEN ADA MASOTTI founded La Perla more than 60 years ago, she can scarcely have imagined that her lingerie atelier would become one of the world's leading luxury companies. However, her foundations of artisan heritage, a corsetiere's intimate knowledge of the female body and a timeless mix of innovation and tradition, all combined with a healthy dose of Italian style, have ensured that today La Perla is as desirable for women the world over as it was back in 1954 in Bologna.

"The company's core values are elegance, sensuality and preciousness. Oh, and a touch of surprise," says Nick Tacchi, La Perla's Global Marketing Director. Even its name was inspired by precious gems, with Ada Masotti's first creations presented in boxes lined with red velvet as if they were works of jewellery.

Six decades on, trends have come and gone, and La Perla has added bags, shoes, nightwear, beachwear, menswear and fragrances to its main collections. Intricate embroidery and Leavers lace combine with silk, satin, chiffon, organza and georgette, and new-generation fabrics such as neoprene.

However, craftsmanship and heritage remain at the heart of the company's creations, even if the way they're worn has changed dramatically. "Collections are created as lifestyle propositions with looks and accessories that come together to create a comprehensive style," says Nick. "Lingerie and sleepwear are the starting points for new evening looks. A bikini or swimsuit might serve as the central piece for a variety of outfits that can be worn in all different stages of a vacation." Some of the brand's most exclusive bras even feature a small sheath to cover the hooks and allow the back to be displayed.

In recent years, La Perla collections have drawn on the company's tradition of craftsmanship and luxury. The first atelier collection was presented in January 2015 during the Haute Couture Week in Paris. It also now provides a made-to-measure service in its flagship stores, which enables clients to customise a number of the brand's most exclusive creations.

Sewn entirely by hand, using gold thread and Swarovski crystals, each of these items is a one-off. "The service is aimed at couture customers who appreciate the height of luxury and exclusivity, the privilege of being unique," says Nick.

Less overtly eye-catching, but just as luxurious in its own way is the "impossible lace" that is used in many of La Perla's creations. When a scrap of fabric dating back to the early 1900s was discovered at a vintage market in Paris, a *maître dentellier* (master lacemaker) in Calais tackled the seemingly impossible task of reproducing its elaborate design. A traditional loom had to be specially modified to create the complex patterns of this antique lace without compromising its softness and lightness, resulting in a spectacular, ethereal fabric that now features in the brand's ready-to-wear garments.

Combining timeless elegance and innovation, the sensuality and luxury of this modern classic material is perhaps the best illustration of La Perla's signature mix of heritage and contemporary. "Italian heritage, the spirit of the atelier, the mix of innovation and tradition: these are the chromosomes of La Perla's DNA, reflecting the experiences of the founder," says Nick. "This heritage enables us to express the true sense of the word 'luxury' in our modern age."
— www.laperla.com

A FITTED TRIBUTE

Gagliardi

THE NAME GAGLIARDI pays homage to a man with a gregarious sense of style. The company's owner, Salvatore Borg, was usually the best-dressed man on shore leave throughout his time as a young man serving in the British merchant navy. However, it was his service as a marine during the Second World War which earned him a reputation for being more than just a dandy. On returning home to his native Malta, his fellow officers and friends conferred upon him the nickname "il Gagliardi", meaning brave and robust.

Inspired by his love of tailoring, Salvatore created both the Gagliardi tailoring brand and the Bortex (Borg Textile) Group in the 1960s. Little did he know then that he was building a legacy of stylish clothes, expert craftsmanship and fine textiles that a third generation of his family would maintain to the present day.

Peter Borg, Bortex CEO and Salvatore's son, describes the company's hallmarks. "We are inspired by Savile Row," he says, "but our approach is fresher, not as structured as traditional tailoring and imbued with a distinctive Mediterranean flair and a penchant for rich colour." It's about sharp silhouettes, luxurious fabrics and hidden details which all contribute to a relaxed aesthetic. "The Gagliardi man is a jovial, cultured gentleman who enjoys cars, fine dining and cigars," says Sam, Salvatore's grandson. "He travels extensively, loves literature, history and the arts."

This enjoyment of life permeates Gagliardi's collections. "The styling evokes the brand's origins in the 1960s jet set era," says Sam, "which is also when Malta gained its independence." Aqua blue seersucker jackets sit alongside linen shirts for a weekend feel; while the deep ochre tweed suits and business wear with a modern fit are definite nods to the original Gagliardi subversion of more formal British styles. "The half-lined jackets are definitely the brand's iconic product group," says Sam.

Gagliardi's range focuses on using Italian fabric of exquisite quality. Merino wool, cotton, cashmere, silk, linen and blends of the world's finest natural fibres contribute to a tactile wardrobe that takes the wearer from morning to evening. "It's been said that our blazers are the Maserati of sports jackets," says Sam, "and we use traditional tailoring methods to ensure a luxury finish." Through the family's garment manufacture business, the brand has cultivated strong relationships with the best fabric mills and designers. Lanificio Fili, Cerruti, Ing Ermenegildo Zegna and Ing Lanficio Loro Piana fabrics are used throughout the range. "We use the finest fibres and fabrics," he says, "so our clothes feel and look great."

Gagliardi's accessories collection also adheres to the company's classic-yet-contemporary style with perfectly proportioned silk ties, soft scarves and luxurious leather briefcases and bags. But it is its evening wear that really demonstrates the brand's understanding of fabric and fit; mohair and blends of silk allow dinner jackets to drape perfectly for understated elegance.

With Malta's capital Valletta named as 2018's European City of Culture, the island is in a great position to show off its extraordinary blend of British and Italian influences. These in turn mirror those of the founder of Gagliardi and his colourful back story. Salvatore Borg's life seems to have come full circle.
— www.gagliardi.eu

REBORN BEAUTIFUL

Environ Skin Care

"VITAMIN A IS an amazing molecule," says Dr Des Fernandes, founder of Environ®. And, after more than 25 years of working with it, he still uses that molecule as the cornerstone of his pioneering skincare brand.

Today, his company has fans far beyond its Cape Town base, selling 140 products in over 70 countries to everyone from celebrities to top dermatologists. But the discovery of just how big an impact vitamin A can have on our skin was an unexpected result of Dr Fernandes's own scientific research.

As one of the top cosmetic surgeons in the world, Dr Fernandes was already studying vitamin A in the 1980s as part of his work on skin cancer. "The skin cancer results were the real driver to find ways we could get patients to use vitamin A regularly without defaulting, because their skin started to feel irritated," he says. "Once I achieved that, I realised I was making beautiful skin."

The next breakthrough was in how the vitamin was delivered. "Because our skin can be damaged by light, the vitamin A receptors are very sensitive to it," says Dr Fernandes. "And if the receptors are damaged, we cannot absorb the vitamin properly. The paradox is that the only way we can stimulate the receptors to be rebuilt is to supply vitamin A."

So Dr Fernandes devised the "step-up system" and harnessed powerful antioxidants and peptides to build the Environ range around it. The system is designed to encourage the skin to tolerate vitamin A and build up the necessary receptors. The concentration is then increased step by step until the maximum dose is arrived at.

Because all skin is affected by light damage, everyone can benefit from the treatment based on the step-up system. "It works on men, women, dark skins, light skins," says Dr Fernandes. "We all suffer from varying degrees of the same problem – that of vitamin A deficiency caused by exposure to UV rays."

As a mark of its high quality, the Environ range has received accreditation from the respected Swiss Vitamin Institute. The company bears this seal of approval with pride. Environ also takes pride in the fact that it is one of very few skincare ranges with its own sterile manufacturing facilities and team of dedicated chemists.

This laboratory atmosphere is vital to guaranteeing the active vitamin levels in each product. The manufacturing process takes place in a vacuum and under yellow light to prevent any damage taking place to ingredients through exposure to air or light. "Natural vitamin decay means some products have short shelf lives," says Dr Fernandes. "Another company might claim a product lasts three years but we'll say you have to use it within six months."

And as the latest scientific advances are incorporated into new products, Dr Fernandes expects new discoveries to create more powerful potions to keep skin healthy, youthful and radiant as life expectancy increases. "We are constantly on the lookout for a molecule that gives better results," he says. "Perhaps double vitamin A molecules, or A mixed with vitamin E. We are one of the pioneers."
— www.environskincare.com

CITY SLICKERS

Manuela Lusso

MANUELA WILLIAMS IS a woman in a man's world. And that's how she likes it. "There aren't many of us in men's tailoring," she laughs. "It helps with the selling."

A native of Vienna, Manuela founded Manuela Lusso after 16 years of working in men's bespoke tailoring at various powerhouses throughout Europe such as Sartoriani, Fendi and Dolce & Gabbana. Her passion is to bring elegant, European style to London's Savile Row, the traditional home of the bespoke men's suit. "Professional men in London have a long and storied history of wearing unique apparel," she says. "That's the primary reason I chose London."

"*Lusso*" is the Italian word for luxury, and it is Manuela's commitment to high-end quality that ensures her company's success. Her rapidly expanding client-base is drawn mostly from the City and the financial sector, as well as from professional sportsmen, lawyers and politicians.

"These are people who want suits that will set them apart from their competitors and colleagues," says Manuela. "What makes us special is our personalised service. All sales are by private appointment, and we can meet you at your office, home, or one of our satellite offices around London. Our bespoke consultation involves detailed discussions about what a client wants in a suit, be it purpose (for instance, wedding or work), style and fit." There are also unique considerations like monograms, lining, stitching, pockets, special features and – most importantly – fabric.

"We use only the finest materials," says Manuela. "Worsted vicuña wools from the Andes, cashmere from Mongolia, merino from Australia. All are woven by Holland & Sherry or Dugdale Bros from Britain or by Loro Piana in Italy. We have around 3,000 materials in a range of colours and designs, and we're very meticulous with our portfolio – any fabrics that aren't performing are discarded, leaving only the best that have stood the test of time."

For Manuela, personal service is her priority. "Meticulous attention to detail is paramount," she says. "We guarantee quality on all bespoke suits and shirts, and always go the extra mile to ensure that our clients are treated like royalty."
— www.mlusso.co.uk

WALKING ON WATER

Sebago

SHOES AND WATER make for curious companions, yet the story of Sebago footwear is born of a generations-long affinity for the wet stuff. The name comes from Sebago Lake – literally "big stretch of water" in Abenaki Indian – one of the largest bodies of water in the US state of Maine. Rooted in its New England heritage, the firm is best known for its classic boat shoe, the Docksides.

This handcrafted, non-slip deck shoe was an instant international hit in the 1970s and is synonymous with yachting style. High-street retailer Russell and Bromley brought it to prominence in the UK in the 1980s, since when the brand has greatly extended its range of both casual and technical marine collections.

Sebago began life seven decades ago when shoe-shop owner Daniel J Wellehan Sr teamed up with two local businessmen to meet the postwar demand for quality leisure footwear. Their first invention – the penny loafer – proved so successful that, within eight years, Sebago had sold its millionth shoe.

Adam Green, Sebago's London-based brand director, says it is authenticity that sets its products apart. "Our heritage and production methods have stood the test of time," he says. "In difficult financial and political times, people turn to brands they trust." These methods are key, he explains: "Look at how we make our shoes. Our Docksides have hand-sewn uppers, true moccasin construction. Our penny loafers are fully welted – one of the most labour-intensive techniques. Other brands might develop the same look but they don't use the authentic construction."

However, you don't need to be an expert yachtsman to appreciate Sebago's products. "Our association with sailing is critical to our success," says Adam. "But whether you own a yacht or have never been on the water in your life, there's an aspect to the brand that is aspirational. Our customers might not live that lifestyle but we conjure the romance of it."

A range of limited-edition Docksides – launched to celebrate the company's 70th anniversary – has "exceeded expectations" and the company continues to look forward. "We believe in longevity and evolution," says Adam. "After all, we want to be here in another 70 years' time!"

— www.sebago.com

A CUT ABOVE

Camessi

WHEN SHANKER LAL Shroff founded Camessi, his ambition was to produce the best shirts in the world. He had been manufacturing textiles for 50 years and had come to know and admire the high-quality shirts produced in the UK, Italy and France. He saw no reason why such couture could not be produced in India.

As Shanker's son and company director Sanjiv explains: "For many years, my father had produced high-quality fabrics and yarns which were used as raw materials for various products, including garments, but he always bought his clothes from the best European designers. He was a very discerning customer and finicky with detail! But he also wanted to bring the tailoring techniques of Savile Row to India."

The young company started operating in 2006 and then spent two years researching techniques and training its team before it began manufacturing shirts for retail. "We didn't want workers with prior experience in the clothing trade, as prior experience means bad habits," explains Sanjiv. "We wanted to create our own skills in the women we employed so they would know no other way than the methods we taught them. It was the best way to ensure that there would be no corner cutting."

Camessi's philosophy is that clothes are an extension of the wearer's personality. It's why the company strives to accentuate the finer aspects of that personality through supreme attention to detail, fine handiwork and a flawless fit. Camessi's shirts are luxury bespoke products, but with a twist that reflects Shanker Lal Shroff's background in manufacturing textiles.

"My father wanted to provide a Savile Row bespoke service but in a fully industrialised manner," says Sanjiv. "Traditionally, the Savile Row businesses have a shop upstairs and the tailors below – we wanted to industrialise the back end and give the true bespoke experience but improve scalability without damaging quality."

Sanjiv's sons Rahul and Ameya both studied at the Massachusetts Institute of Technology in the US and brought an analytical, forward-thinking approach to the company when they joined as directors.

"Our company uses a similar quality system to that used in the high-end automobile industry," says Sanjiv. "For instance, most garment manufacturers will overproduce products at each stage, knowing that the substandard items will be discarded. Unlike them, we run a lean operation – there is little wastage, as we insist on excellence at every single stage of production. It's a similar system to that you'll find on luxury automobile production lines."

The company also introduced strict quality control. "Every single shirt is checked in 88 places," says Sanjiv. "In a traditional factory, one shirt out of every 100 might be checked, and not as thoroughly."

Since 2009, Camessi has slowly grown and now the company produces 2,500 shirts a month, which are available in select boutiques across the world. It has also started to make trousers, applying the same diligence that it applies to shirts, and in 2017 it will start to sell suits.

"The trousers are 100 per cent handmade but for the seams along the legs," says Sanjiv. "It's a handmade product but the process is so tight it's almost like an industrialised handmade operation. Our approach is traditional but we want to make the system as lean, efficient and foolproof as possible."
— www.camessi.com

PARISIAN CHIC

Moreau-Paris

"FRENCH CRAFTSMANSHIP IS my inspiration," says Fedor Georges Savchenko, Artistic Director of luxury leather goods brand Moreau-Paris. "My mission is to preserve and continue these traditions, such as sewing by hand. The creation of every bag is like a birth for me. It is like art."

Based in Paris, this French company has an impressive past, and Fedor is passionate about reinventing it for the present. It dates back to the middle of the 19th century when the manufacturer first established a reputation for quality, especially for its hand-stitched travel cases. All bore the distinctive insignia created from the Moreau family name.

Although the original company ceased trading in the early 20th century, this distinctive logo lives on, following the brand's relaunch in 2011 by Fedor's sister Veronika Rovnoff. Her passion for Maison Moreau's long heritage was first kindled when she chanced upon a Moreau trunk in an attic.

The Ukrainian-born siblings live by the mantra "one person, one project". That means each one of the 30 or so craftsmen working at their ateliers has responsibility for one individual bag at a time instead of mass producing them. This bespoke approach, and the use of quality dyes and leathers, as well as ancient techniques, together guarantee that a Moreau clutch, wallet or belt will last a lifetime.

The leather, for example, is sourced from several French tanneurs, who use dye and tanning methods dating back to the 16th century. Big stitching, executed by hand, is another speciality, echoing the fact that original Moreau trunks were finished this way, not with metal details. The bags also feature a print inspired by a basket-weave design historically invented by Maison Moreau.

"We are working with the best French ateliers where a particular production process was established for manufacturing Moreau articles," says Fedor who personally selects the leather and manages the production process. "The techniques we use go back centuries and our bags feature full grain leather, which is robust and ages well. It gives each piece a unique patina of charm and authenticity."

The label strives for an aesthetic that combines functionality with beauty. It is these qualities that make the brand sought after by everyone from teenagers to senior citizens. Take the Miromesnil evening clutch, for example, named after the street where the Moreau-Paris boutique is based. This has a special chain crafted to resemble a jewel, and a specially designed lockable clasp.

"Our customers appreciate quality and want to own a piece made by a very famous brand," says Fedor. "Our products are classic, timeless and made to be handed down from generation to generation."

Since the opening of the Moreau-Paris shop in 2012, the brand has established more than 30 outlets worldwide, including those in prestigious department stores such as Barney New York in Manhattan and in Tokyo, Shinsegae in Seoul and many others. The next step is to open more stores and offer customers a personalised service whereby they can choose the colour of a bag's lining, its handles and even its size.

Moreau-Paris is not only an authentically French brand, but also a heritage line in the truest sense of the word. One that has built on the tradition of centuries-old craftsmanship and introduced it to a modern audience. An inspiration indeed.
— www.moreau-paris.com

CRAFTED BY HAND

Atelier Wael

OPERATING FROM THE modern metropolis of Dubai, Atelier Wael is modelled along classic Savile Row principles but with minimalist thinking, taking quintessential London tailoring into the 21st century to produce something contemporary yet timeless.

"Our approach is modern," says Creative Director Wael Hussain. "But the techniques have been drawn out of Savile Row artistry. The focal point of our business is creating individually handcrafted suits, but we also provide the complete gentleman's wardrobe, including handcrafted casualwear. We are bound by our commitment to handicraft. This doesn't just apply to suits – it's for everything we do."

The company stems from a family heritage of tailoring. In 2008, Wael's father Asif Hussain founded his company, Threads & Tailors. With more than 40 years of experience in tailoring in the United Arab Emirates, he is often called by the UAE's royal family to tailor suits for forthcoming trips to Royal Ascot. Clientele also include European expats seeking Savile Row-style tailoring from its new base in the Middle East. Customers nearly always go back again to satiate their sartorial desires.

"We often have clients who want 25 shirts and 10 versions of the same suit, in different materials," says Wael, who has a qualifying law degree from the UK but decided to follow his father into the family business, injecting fresh blood while staying true to the founding principles. "We also do corporate clothing and uniforms for the hospitality, food and beverage sectors. We do women's clothing as well as costumes for photoshoots, TV ads and opening ceremonies. With all our clients, our goal is to excel beyond their expectations, and have friends and not just lifelong customers. We take 25 measurements, chalk out and cut a pattern that is unique to the individual. We then have the first fitting and any required adjustments, followed by a second and, if necessary, a third fitting. The Wael brand is a niche service. Our clients can actually walk through the whole process and see how their suit is made."

The company employs around 35 tailors, and takes pride in ensuring staff are treated well and rewarded suitably for their talents. The company's master cutters are able to turn their hand to anything. "We do womenswear, which is so vast with so many different designs, thus requiring our most skilled tailors," says Wael. "Our best cutters can do anything, from upholstery to soft toys. They are extremely good at pattern making and it's all based on that."

They have even been known to make a suit at short notice, providing a tailored service for those who are in Dubai and need a finely cut suit the following day. "It's not bespoke, but we can do tailor-made clothing in a very short time span," says Wael. "We can take measurements in the morning and adjust our capacity to have a piece ready the following morning."

This illustrates the way that the company has adapted to the needs of modern life while still representing the best of classic and contemporary tailoring. It also explains why the company continues to grow. "We require a minimum of 30 working hours on each suit, even if it is not bespoke," says Wael. "We believe in quality and working by hand even if it takes longer. It is worth the effort."
— www.atelierwael.ae

THE GOLDEN RATIO

Orogold Cosmetics

ACCORDING TO LEGEND, Cleopatra maintained her youthful looks by sleeping every night in a mask of gold. The tale may be myth but what is known is that this precious metal has been credited with anti-inflammatory properties and the ability to slow down ageing. It is also a signature ingredient that the US-based Orogold Cosmetics uses in all its products.

"One of the best ways to understand which skin care products to use and which to avoid is to know your ingredients," explains Brands Manager Tal Bar. "Gold has been recognised across cultures for its beautifying properties and we use tiny pieces in all of our collections. The body never rejects gold and it's one of our key ingredients, which promises our customers a luxurious and heavenly experience."

Educating a new generation of skincare "savvies" to maintain their healthy skin is Orogold's mission. Founded in 2008, this international beauty and skincare company puts the client – just as likely to be male as female, and aged anywhere from 35 to 65 – at the centre of the brand. From wrinkle-tightening serums to multivitamin moisturisers, all its ranges are tested to both Food and Drug Administration (FDA) and European standards by teams of scientists in Orogold's labs based worldwide. Free from parabens and preservatives, these beauty aids are developed to suit all skin types. "Our wide-ranging collection offers solutions for every skin concern," says Tal, "from acne to sunspots and wrinkles, while being environmentally and ethically sound."

The use of innovative technologies is evident across the brand's product range. With no fewer than eight anti-ageing treatments, 24K Cleopatra Nano regimen is one of the brand's most advanced

products. A favourite of Orogold brand ambassador and actress Alice Eve is the 24K Termica Mask, which is designed to heat up the skin, much as one would experience from being in a sauna. Once the heat penetrates the skin, it allows absorption of the mask's activating serum and all the nutrients much faster. "It leaves my skin tight, hydrated and very fresh looking," says Alice.

It is not just the products that are designed for a client's specific skin concerns. The Orogold shopping experience is about accommodating the customer's individual beauty needs at each of its 110 stores located worldwide from London to Singapore. With private suites and VIP facial rooms, the stores provide one-to-one service through skincare specialists who devote themselves to finding the right product for each customer.

The experience does not end there, however. Clients receive a follow-up call and email to ensure they are benefitting from their personalised skin "prescription". "We pride ourselves on providing an elegant and comfortable setting quite unlike that found in a department store," says Tal. "Discretion is key – the relationship with the customer is private, like that they would enjoy with their hairdresser. Our skin specialists know exactly what's in our products and spend as much time as needed with each client."

With such a successful concept, this brand has no plans to change. The future focus is set firmly on bringing the latest word in skincare to customers in order to make a difference. And, unlike Cleopatra, they do not have to wear a mask of gold every night to achieve divine-looking skin.
— www.orogoldcosmetics.co.uk

SUIT TO THRILL

Pinky Tailor

PINKY TAILOR IS a premium tailoring business with a character all of its own. Housed on three floors of a busy shop in the centre of Bangkok, the quality of its suits, shirts and other items of men's and women's clothing is beyond question. But it is the reception that customers receive at Pinky Tailor that encourages them to return time and again with such enthusiasm.

"We give a special kind of personal service," says Win Palitdejtakul, joint director of the company. "Customers make special trips to us from all parts of the world, and many have become good friends."

Win and his father, Thatsuda – the company's founder, also known as Pinky – are both master tailors, and still take part in all aspects of the process, including taking measurements and making patterns.

There are distinct differences between a ready-made suit and a bespoke one, Win explains. "If you look carefully at someone in a ready-made, for example, the sleeves will often be of different lengths," he says. "This is because many people carry things with their right arm, and their right shoulder may be a bit lower than their left. With our suits, they will be even. Having a perfect fit flatters the figure, and is noticeably more comfortable." A customer can choose every detail of a bespoke suit, including the weight of the fabric, the lining and the buttons. "Being involved in the design makes people feel special and proud," says Win.

For customers visiting the shop in person, the process is straightforward and, with a tailoring team of 35, Pinky Tailor is quick to turn orders around. A first jacket fitting can be arranged within one or two hours of measuring, and a bespoke suit can be made in two to four days. "For a first-time customer who is not able to visit, we can work from a suit that they already have," says Win. "If they send pictures of themselves wearing it, then mail the suit to us, we can use that to perfect the fit." New customers without a suit to work from can use the measuring forms on the Pinky Tailor website and describe their choices.

Win has been infatuated with the tailoring business from an early age. "When I was a boy, the shop was my playground," he says. "I even tailored my own school uniform. Seeing my father on familiar terms with the many eminent people who came to the store filled me with pride, and fuelled my desire to join the company."

The fashion world has also shown its esteem for Pinky Tailor. In *Elle Men* magazine's recent roundup of the 50 most influential people in the Thai fashion industry, the company was ranked number one in the tailoring section. In Win's mind, the message is simple. "It's the quality of our cloth and of our workmanship that customers pay for, and they love the whole experience," he says. "Once you've been blessed with a bespoke suit, it's not easy to go back to ready-made."
— www.pinkytailor.com

RADIANT RESULTS

Suqqu

"BEAUTY MUST BE polished, toned and nurtured," according to Japanese skincare and cosmetics brand, Suqqu. Taken from the Japanese word *sukku-to*, which roughly translates as "posture with attitude", this luxury beauty experience is more than just skin-deep. Developed from an innovative facial massage technique, Gankin "facial muscles" massage, Suqqu provides the luxurious gift of time, which pays dividend with its effects on the skin.

"When we launched in 2003, we'd been working with make-up artists in Japan from the film and TV industry," says UK General Manager Yuka Kaneko. "These incredibly experienced and well-respected make-up artists recognised the importance of enhancing beauty naturally, with effects that last all day." Having examined the actors' busy lifestyles and punishing filming schedules, a massage regime was developed to be applied just before make-up. The idea was that it would help release stress and build-up in the lymph nodes, and it provided instant results.

"Actors often work in harsh environments for long hours and need to be seen from 360 degrees," says Yuka. "What works for them should work for us, as real women. Together with our reputable laboratory in Japan, we created a short massage regime that should work on the facial muscles and skin. The massage to me felt painful at times, but it immediately improved the look of eyes, cheekbones and jawbones, relying on pressure points to relieve sagging muscles for 12 hours."

The Suqqu team of experts and make-up artists soon found that this three-minute regime had a huge effect on the actresses' radiance. "In Japan we're used to a lengthy bathing regime and skincare rituals," says Yuka. "For the Suqqu

woman, it is important to invest those few minutes twice a day to look after yourself."

To complement the massage, Suqqu developed a luxurious balm-like cream that also doubles as a mask. "Packed full of natural, rejuvenating ingredients from Japan, the texture is ideal for this massage," says Yuka, "ensuring time is spent working the cream."

To be treated by a Suqqu facialist or to learn the Gankin technique outside Japan, a serene treatment room at Fenwick on London's Bond Street provides an ideal environment. The service is also available at a casual facial booth at Selfridges.

Devised for women in their forties and beyond, the range of Suqqu skincare and cosmetics was launched as a whole concept. It's particularly popular with make-up artists wishing to create lasting looks for film and television from a basic foundation of good skincare. "The range was developed with make-up artists, so it had to start with rejuvenated, well-moisturised skin that could withstand a day of filming," says Yuka. "The colour collections also contain skincare properties, silicone-coated pigments and amino-acid treated powders to ensure longevity and comfort."

The Suqqu Extra Rich Cream Foundation is a perfect example, with three different stages absorbing oil and providing a rich glow throughout the day. Containing 12 natural plant extracts from Japan, the moisturising properties mean it's also good for skin, as well as improving natural confidence and radiance. "The Suqqu woman is pro-ageing," concludes Yuka. "She has a serenity about dealing with age, and with our help she can enhance the natural radiance and richness of age."

— www.suqqu.com/global

TIMELESS TAILORING

————

Apsley Bespoke Tailors, London

IT IS HARD to explain the joy, feel and comfort of a bespoke suit to those who have never worn one, but London's Apsley Bespoke Tailors has been helping its customers experience this for over 125 years. The company's heritage proves its timeless appeal, but Apsley master tailor Arshad Mahmood uses a modern analogy to explain what makes Apsley so special. "We do a lot of work with Formula One drivers," he says. "When they wear our clothes they feel the fit, the detail, the comfort – it's the same way they feel when they get in a car that's built around them, for them. Every part of their Apsley suit is cut, sewn and fitted for them. Once you've worn a tailored suit, you'll never go back to something from the high street."

The secret to Apsley's longevity is combining classic virtues of service and craftsmanship with a forward-facing focus on style. The company's roots may lie in creating suits since 1889, but its commitment to the present is equally important. "We've gone through everything from flares and double-breasted suits to all manner of hipster styles in the 1960s, not missing a beat," says Arshad. "We make clothes to the day but the ethos is about service and quality, no matter what the decade."

Apsley's clients sum up this duality perfectly. "We dress Premier League football teams," says Arshad. "It's great. You've got managers who just want to be classic in style and cut, but the players are going, 'Can't we funk this up a bit?' We had one player who said, 'Can we Pharrell this?' So nothing is standard issue – we can do classic or custom but all our suits are bespoke, with quality and service underpinning everything."

It may seem like a paradox, but in an era characterised by disposable fashion, the more enduring virtues have always remained. "Good tailoring changes how you feel," says Arshad. "A classic bespoke suit will always give you that fantastic feel and look that a high-street suit could never deliver. I call it 'coutured confidence'. Spending the time to get to know a tailor is a brilliant investment in you, your style and your comfort for the rest of your life. Your suits will never feel the same. That's the bespoke Apsley experience."
— www.apsleytailors.com

TRUSTED QUALITY

Rashmi Tailors

FROM THEIR WORKSHOP in Hong Kong, the skilled team at Rashmi Tailors have spent the past 30 years building a global reputation for the exceptional quality of their hand-made suits. It's a standing built on the firm's expertise and a dedicated, one-to-one service. "Making a suit is more of an art than a science," says company director Vijay Nandwani. "It is a skill that takes a lot of time to learn. Our youngest cutter is 55, while the oldest is 75."

Vijay believes that a trusted tailor is one of the most important professional connections a man can develop, placing it alongside those of banker, broker and barber. As he explains, clients who get a suit made by Rashmi receive the services of a tailor who spends time getting to know their style, colour and pattern preferences. The company selects the cutter best-suited for a client's build and taste, and uses only the finest fabrics, such as Italian brands Ermenegildo Zegna and Loro Piana. "We do very high-end tailoring," says Vijay. "Our work is on a par with Savile Row and the best of Milan, but our costs are lower because of where we are based."

Although it is located in Hong Kong, Rashmi Tailors boasts an international clientele and a global reach, with cutters regularly attending fittings in North America, Europe, Asia and the Middle East. Clients have often heard about the quality of Rashmi's work and wish to experience it for themselves, or may have bought a Rashmi suit during a business trip to Hong Kong and wish to repeat the experience.

"Originally, we targeted foreign customers who were working in Hong Kong and wanted the same service that they'd received at home," says Vijay. "But now, while we have our showroom in Hong Kong, we travel around the world to meet our clients, whether in their home, hotel room or office. It's a very close relationship. Most of our work comes to us through word of mouth. We are not based on street level in Hong Kong, so personal recommendations and quality of service are what drive people to us."
— www.rashmi.com

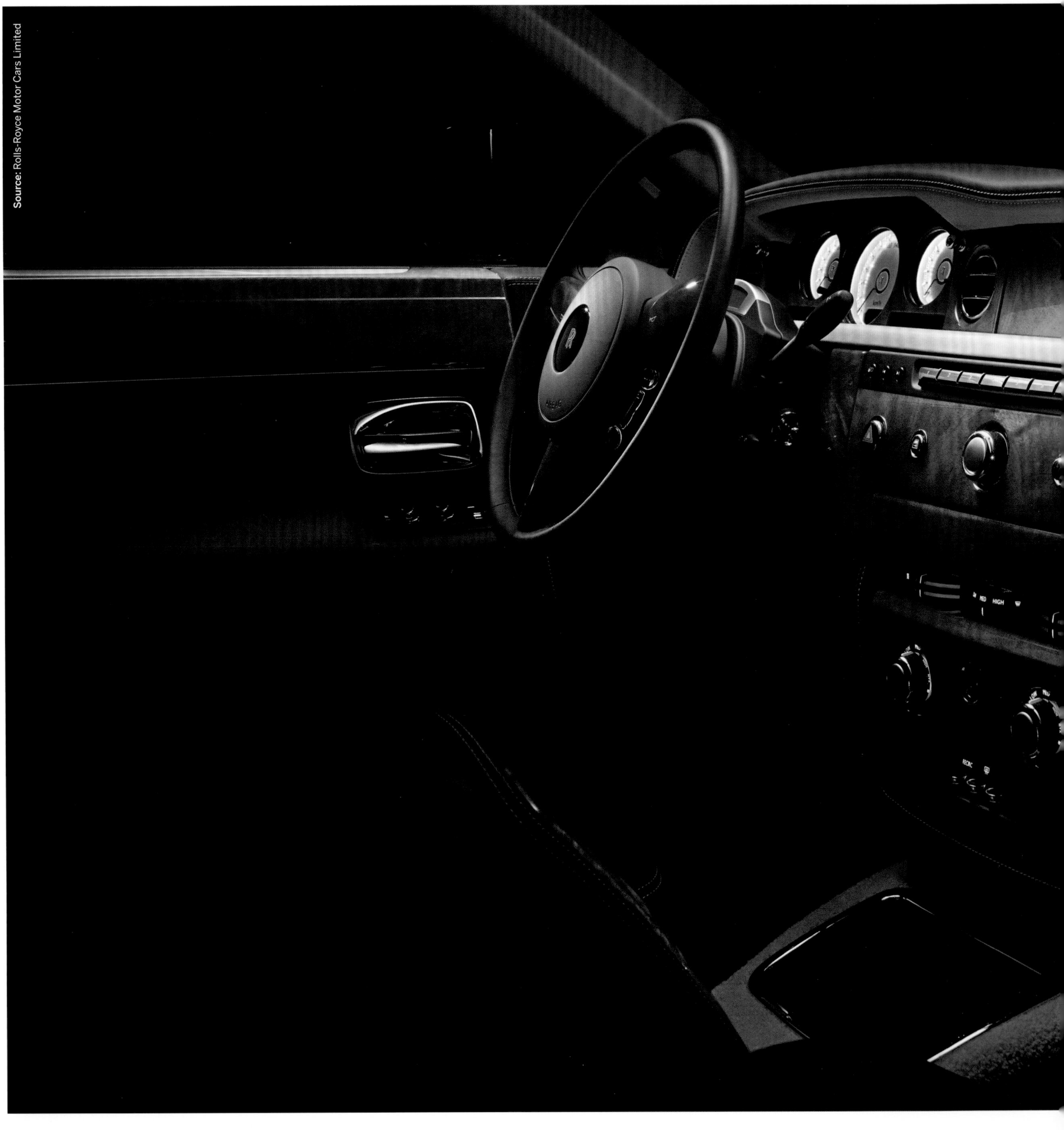

Source: Rolls-Royce Motor Cars Limited

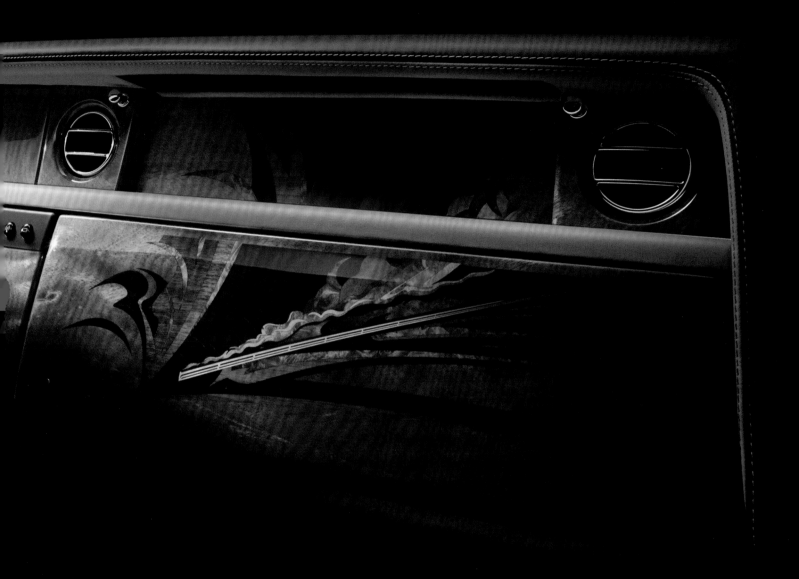

THE ART OF MAKING

From handcrafted to hi-tech

SILVER SERVICE

Topázio

FOR MORE THAN 140 years, the Portuguese company Topázio has achieved a prestigious position as one of Europe's leading makers of silverware and silver plate. "We are a fifth-generation family business, of which we are very proud," says the company Chairman Maria do Rosario Pinto Correia. "But we are always keen to look beyond tradition into the future."

To this day, Topázio employs a number of long-established handcraft techniques, and continues to produce models and lines that were developed at the beginning of the last century. The King John V baroque style, regarded as the company's signature, continues to be as popular as ever.

But Topázio also has a long record of embracing innovation, and a willingness to explore new design styles and fashions. "We were the first to put crystal and silver together," says Maria. "And in the 1970s, we introduced high-end silver-plated items, that were not regarded as an alternative until we reached an almost identical quality level. By using a good metal for the base and a thick silver plating, we were able to produce cutlery and other items that have the same feel as sterling, but are about a quarter of the price."

While continuing to apply original production methods where possible, Topázio is determined to maintain its high standards while embracing new technologies. "For example, we have always soldered with hot silver," says Maria. "But now we also use laser soldering to achieve even higher precision lines with the same quality."

No two Topázio pieces are exactly alike, although only an expert eye would spot the differences. This is because, although industrial machines are used for some parts of the process, such as stamping, engraving and soldering, their handling and that of the metals is done manually. "In this way, we are able to take special care with each piece," says Maria.

Although Topázio has a number of instantly recognisable designs, there is no record of who created some of the oldest originals. It's likely, however, that this work was carried out by various artisans in the factory. "Nowadays, we have an internal design department with a creative director," says Maria, "but we still encourage workers in all areas of the company to come up with ideas."

Topázio has been commissioned to produce a number of special collections to commemorate memorable events – such as a limited edition of pieces by African artists in honour of 40 years of the Republic of Angola. To celebrate its own 140th anniversary, Topázio gave 14 artists *carte blanche* to make anything they chose, using as inspiration a silver vase of the traditional Topázio baroque style.

"They came up with a lot of imaginative creations," says Maria. "The range of ideas was as varied as a vase, a plate or a skull." There is good reason to expect that the company's bespoke commissions will increase in value relatively quickly, and could prove an appealing prospect for collectors.

Impeccable craftsmanship has always been a pillar of Topázio's success, along with an enthusiasm for exploration in creative design. "To reflect that, we have recently introduced a new baseline for our brand," says Maria. "We call it 'Tradition is Tomorrow', bridging our *savoir faire* and experience, and our never-ending quest for the new designs that will match them. I think that perfectly describes our identity now."

— www.topazio.pt

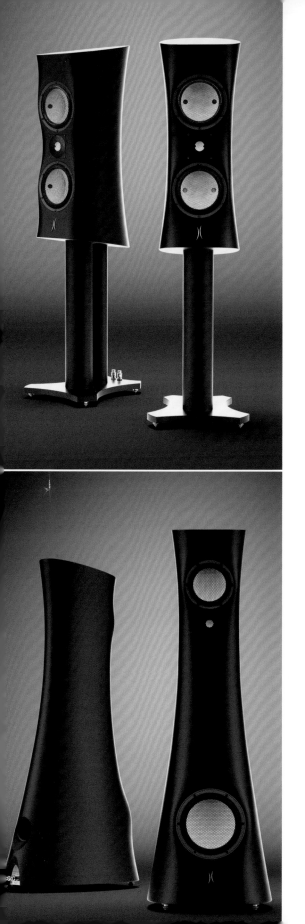

PITCH PERFECT

Estelon

THERE CAN BE few world-class firms that have been founded at the breakfast table, but Estelon – from Tallinn, Estonia – is certainly one of them. The high-end audio brand traces its origins back to a morning in April 2010 when engineer Alfred Vassilkov was having a casual discussion with his family.

"It was a lovely Sunday morning with the entire family all having breakfast together," Alfred recalls. "I had long held the ambition of creating the world's best loudspeaker. I knew what the concept would be and, rather than sell the idea to another company, I decided to try it on my own. Luckily, I already had the best key executives in the family: my daughters Alissa and Kristiina. That same evening, we decided to set up the business using our family savings. By Tuesday, the company was legally established."

Alfred had been designing speakers for other companies for over 25 years and spent five years researching opportunities to achieve his ambition of creating the world's best speaker. He always sought perfection and overcame challenges: growing up in the Soviet era, when resources were limited, he dismantled radios to rebuild and improve them. He took this interest to university, studying electro-acoustics in St Petersburg.

These experiences enabled Alfred to develop technologies and find materials with which to construct unique and innovative products. These were combined with inspiration from nature – particularly from the lush and expansive forest landscapes of Estonia – to create the perfect balance between engineering and design.

The result was Estelon, one of the world's most luxurious speaker brands. It derives aesthetic and acoustic excellence through the merger of ingenious creativity and cutting-edge science. Each decision – from engineering techniques to the materials and components used in the manufacturing process – is made with the perfect harmony of the speakers as a whole in mind.

For Alfred, this flawless synergy is what an engineer strives for in his creations. Every single detail is carefully considered, selected and tested during all stages of the production process. The result is a handcrafted masterpiece of beauty on the outside and the pinnacle of technology on the inside.

Estelon is today regarded as a leading innovator in the audio industry, having received multiple awards for its designs and technological innovations. In 2015, the company's flagship loudspeaker, the Estelon Extreme, scooped the Best of Innovation Award in the High Performance Audio and Video category at the Consumer Electronics Show in Las Vegas. In addition, the Estelon X Diamond has been named Product of the Year by *Absolute Sound Magazine*, while other Estelon products have won numerous editor's choice and best performance awards around the world.

The company's loudspeakers are today proudly owned by some of the world's most eminent innovators and global leaders. Ultimately, Alfred feels that they are intended for sophisticated individuals who appreciate the finer things in life to enjoy in their homes.

"A lifetime of designing and engineering unique audio products enabled me to blend mature character into a young audio brand," says Alfred. "This has been key in ensuring that Estelon speakers are among the best in the world."
— www.estelon.com

MUSIC MAESTRO

Audio Note

ASK AUDIO NOTE UK Ltd's founder Peter Qvortrup (yes, that's a Danish surname) why it is that he's dedicated nearly 40 years of his life to perfecting audio equipment and his answer is unequivocal. "This is my life's project," he says. "I want to do justice to the best music ever created and recorded. I'm 66 now, and the legacy I intend to leave behind is that I've created the finest audio products and playback systems with no possible practical improvements."

This ambition was ignited way back in 1978 when Peter opened his very first hi-fi shop, Audio Consult in Copenhagen, which is still trading to this day. In the UK, his company, which is based in West Sussex, employs 36 craftspeople and an additional six individuals worldwide. It specialises in producing – and revolutionising – almost every component within an audio system.

Take the humble output transformer, for instance. Audio Note goes to extreme lengths designing and making what is arguably the most critical component of any valve amplifier. The list of exotic parts for these high-quality transformers includes silver wire, high-nickel-content cores, non-magnetic stainless steel fixings and copper frames. Terminated with Audio Note silver cables, the transformers are themselves small works of art, as indeed are the additional components used in the finished products. Bespoke handmade Audio Note capacitors, Tantalum silver non-magnetic resistors and silver solder all contribute to the finest possible sound.

So what of the sound? What is hard to put into words is the sheer emotion and sense of "being" that an Audio Note system conveys. Recordings, whether played back via LP or CD, take on a lifelike persona. The recreation of the musical message enables one to delight in the composer's composition and the conductor's reading, creating a deeply enriching listening experience: cymbals shimmer, voices trill and guitar strings squeak, growl and hum.

While Peter's bespoke systems can sell for millions, he's really in the audio business for the love of music. His collection of 100,000 albums would have been even bigger had a fire at his parents' house not sadly destroyed most of his teenage collection; and he still gets a kick out of meeting new and potential customers and audio fans, and developing new products.

This is a painstaking process that can take years, with each product built and scrutinised using the finest materials and custom-made components in a new lab measuring 1,500 sq m. Yet the final checks take place at Peter's home in Brighton, where he personally tests each development in his listening room.

"You can't measure sound quality with an instrument," he says. "Try measuring the taste of a Chateau Petrus. It's not possible. We straddle the border between science and art. You don't know where one finishes and the other begins."

As for the future of the company, Peter's daughter Emily, now the CEO, is set to continue her father's legacy. Though maybe not quite yet. "I promised my wife I would retire at 75," he says. "I'm not so sure that's going to happen."
— www.audionote.co.uk

RIDING HIGHS

Prestige Cycles

WHETHER IT'S THE Tour de France victories of Chris Froome and Bradley Wiggins or the records of the likes of Mark Cavendish, Chris Hoy and Laura Trott, British cycling has been making headlines around the world in recent years. And, as more people break out the Lycra and take to the road, it's a British company that is meeting the needs of clients worldwide in their search for a high-quality, bespoke bike.

That company is Prestige Cycles – a firm that is to bikes what a Savile Row tailor is to suits. Indeed, the actual process of choosing, fitting and manufacturing is similar in many ways.

"A fitting is all to do with assessing the biomechanics of someone's body," says Stephen Roche, Managing Director of Prestige Cycles. "The body is all about hinges and all those hinges have a certain capacity for flexibility. No two cyclists are the same."

Prestige's USP is its custom-fitting service. In addition to sophisticated video and computerised measurement tools in the primary level fit, Prestige is proud to have use of a wind tunnel for advanced aerodynamic fitting geared towards triathletes or time trialists, enabling clients to try out various frames and configurations, while Stephen measures drag, analyses airflow and helps to perfect body positions.

"There are other high-end cycle suppliers," says Stephen, "but no one offers this degree of bespoke service. No one goes through the process with the precision that we do. It's similar to how a luxury car

manufacturer works. With a luxury car, you'd pick your interior; the type of stitching you want, the kind of leather. It's the same with us. It's a tailored service. You are fitted in a fitting room. You decide what bike you want and we make it up for you. We have a saddle company who make custom saddles for us. We'll bring clothing, a collection of shoes, a selection of helmets. It's comprehensive, and no one else does this."

Prestige's high standards and constant pursuit of cycling perfection have led it into some unconventional realms. The company's Hove headquarters is an Aladdin's cave of two-wheeled masterpieces, each one a testament to Prestige's search for biking perfection. For example, there are bamboo frames made by the American manufacturer Boo, each one fusing dried, hollowed-out Vietnamese bamboo with carbon joints to create a strong, ultra-lightweight and highly comfortable ride.

"We only look to work with around 30 customers a year so that gives you an idea of our exclusivity," says Stephen. "I'm proud of every job we do. We find it's popular with high-flying solicitors and bank traders, who often don't have time to take leave of their offices but do have time for an office-based fitting. I was in New York recently on the 52nd floor of a high rise overlooking a moonlit Manhattan in the small hours for a bike fitting. When clients fly you to the likes of Dubai or New York, you appreciate the people you're dealing with could go anywhere. And they choose to come to us."
— www.prestige-cycles.co.uk

THE GRATE OUTDOORS

Camp Champ

WHEN AUSTRIAN ENGINEER Franz Moser wanted to cook a meal with his family next to a nearby lake, he couldn't find portable cooking equipment that was good enough, so decided to make his own. The result is Camp Champ, a luxury travelling kitchen that contains the sort of serious equipment you'd find in a professional kitchen, that cooks for six people and can fold down to the size of a flight case.

Camp Champ is a beautiful and original item, modelled on the "campaign furniture" from the Victorian age of exploration. "Franz was inspired by watching Tarzan films as a child," says the firm's UK Brand Ambassador Oliver Roberts. "He loved the concept of 'campaign travel' – that 'Around The World In 80 Days' idea of travelling furniture that had incredibly high standards of design and manufacture and could be packed away and taken anywhere."

The Camp Champ is constructed from lightweight, robust marine plywood with galvanised steel handles, industrial steel hinges and a laminated work surface. Inside is everything needed to cook a three-course meal for six, including four powerful gas burners, integrated knife block, spice rack, kitchen utensils and even a space for your recycling. The knives and utensils are of the highest quality, having been selected by professional chefs, who also advised on the size of the work surface. "This is a fully equipped professional kitchen," says Oliver. "It's been designed to be used and to be moved."

As Oliver carefully explains how the Camp Champ folds and unfolds, he notes that it can be used in numerous situations, from garden parties and open-air concerts to hunting, shooting and fishing expeditions. "It's a kitchen that travels, so you can use it in any context you like, and even

make memories through adventure and food," he says. "It could be afternoon tea at Glyndebourne or you could set it up on the tailgate of a Land Rover during a day of country pursuits. You could take it to your ski chalet or have it in the garden for those special al fresco dinner parties with friends who want something more than a barbecue. It's a must-have for your social calendar."

The contents have been specifically chosen for Camp Champ's purposes, with Franz making careful considerations to ensure that each component is of high quality and can withstand the elements. This applies especially to the gas burners, which have to be powerful and controllable, so your food can be cooked in windy conditions. Considerable time and effort went into finding the correct balance between robustness and weight, something he finally solved with the use of marine plywood throughout the construction of Camp Champ.

The "campaign furniture" model refers to the luggage transported across continents by colonial adventurers, who travelled through mountains, rivers, jungles and deserts but always insisted on taking the best furniture with them wherever they went. Such portable furniture, which included everything from four-poster beds to candlesticks, had to be sturdy and efficient, but was also renowned for being exceptionally well crafted and was often very attractive, featuring the best wood and finishings.

Camp Champ reflects this golden age of luxurious travel, updating the concept to today but maintaining a Victorian and Edwardian sense of style and adventure. "It's about experiencing Michelin-starred dining," says Oliver, "in extraordinary places."
— www.campchamp.at

ELECTRIC DREAMS

Haibike

WITH A COMPANY motto that insists "Where future is built on tradition", Germany's Winora Group has spent more than a century developing bikes that change how people cycle. Chief among these is the Haibike range of electric bicycles which have pioneered groundbreaking innovations and revolutionised the market by creating an entirely new sport: ePerformance cycling.

Susanne Puello has run the company since 1996, when she became the fourth generation to head the family business. She is evangelical about e-bikes. "For the first time the physical strength of an athlete is combined with the dynamic of a drive unit," she says. "But the best thing is everyone can discover this special feeling, from sporty athletes to part-time sportsmen and sportswomen."

The latest bike in the range is the Haibike XDURO FullSeven Carbon Ultimate, a top-of-the-line bike made from unidirectional carbon fibres with the sophisticated monocoque method, which increases the frame's stiffness while reducing its weight. This bike weighs in at just 17.2 kg, and that includes the drive unit. Other features include a seamlessly integrated battery and a Bosch

Performance CX central motor, which is directly mounted to the frame. All this is achieved while retaining a modern, sophisticated appearance of clean lines and reduced graphics. Beautiful to look at and easy to use, it epitomises the reasons why e-bikes are becoming so popular across the world.

With everything they do, Susanne's team aim for universality. "We want to create thoughtful bike concepts for a broad variety of target groups," she explains. In the relatively new field of e-bikes, this requires a blend of innovative ideas and confident design, coupled with a robust sales channel network.

"As an innovation leader, we have consistently worked from the outset to focus on this area and expand it," says Susanne of a strategy called "on any ground" – developing an ePerformance bike suitable for every terrain. Only six years after the first Haibike XDURO was presented to the public, the brand now boasts an entire range of e-bikes from eRoadbikes to eDownhillbikes, setting new standards in the bicycle industry and beyond.
— www.raleigh.co.uk/haibike

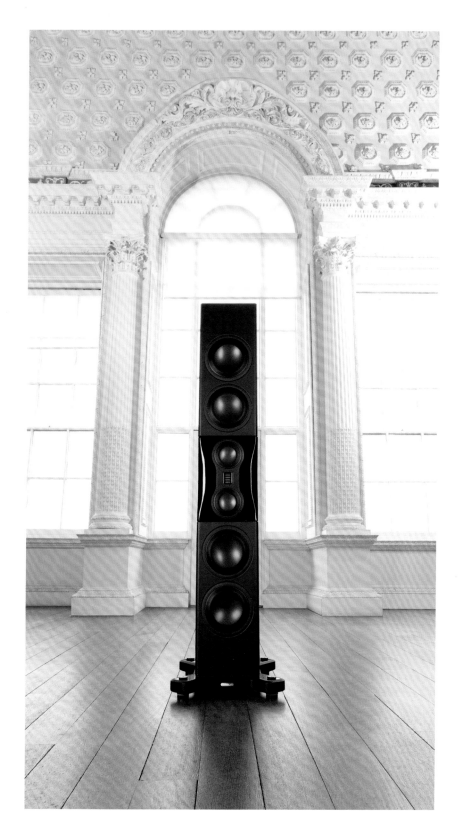

MOTIVATIONAL SPEAKER

Monitor Audio

MONITOR AUDIO'S MONOLITHIC Platinum II speaker drivers were built using the lightest and most advanced metal components available, but its production process began with something altogether more low-tech: a recce.

"We have a product development team, based in Rayleigh, Essex, who we give complete ownership of each project to," says Alex Emson, Monitor Audio's director of global sales and marketing. "They start by going out and sourcing materials."

For the leather that covers the front of each speaker, the product development team chose a 180-year-old Scottish business called Andrew Muirhead & Sons. "We had samples sent down, which we analysed, and only then did we decide whether their products worked within *our* products." It's just one example of Monitor Audio's obsession with attention to detail. Another is the wooden speaker cabinet, crafted from Santos rosewood and natural ebony, coated 11 times in clear gloss piano lacquer, which not only looks beautiful, but allows it to withstand bumps.

Then there's what goes on inside. The products in the range, from the PL100 II bookshelf speakers to the two-metre-tall floor-standing PL500 II, feature ceramic-coated aluminium-magnesium metal alloy driver cones, which, unlike the plastic ones used by its competitors, are lighter, more rigid and stronger. This doesn't just make the sound better but, crucially, the silences, too.

"Imagine you're listening to a recording of a clarinet solo backed by an orchestra," says Alex. "With our speakers, you're going to be able to shut your eyes and pinpoint where that clarinet actually is, as if it's a performance in your living room."

The range took three years to develop, but it builds on the first Platinum series, which itself took six years to create. In fact, the British-based company has been revolutionising speakers since 1972. Today, its 60-strong team distribute to 75 countries, including as far afield as Brazil, Japan and China. But why put so much effort into premium audio, when they could surely generate larger profits through simpler kit? "You can't invite The Beatles, Queen or ELO into your living room," says Alex. "Our job is to give people the best experience we can."

— www.monitoraudio.co.uk

SOUND INVESTMENT

Marantz

ONE OF THE best ways that a company can honour its proud and illustrious past is to make sure that it is always looking to the future. And that's essentially the story of Marantz. Ever since Saul Bernard Marantz started assembling his first audio product – the Consolette pre-amp – in 1948, the company has continued to push ahead, maintaining high standards of audio reproduction while sizing up the next quantum leap.

The audio world into which Marantz released his earliest products was one of analogue recordings. Even then, when the very first long-playing vinyl records were launched, there was a problem: the reproduction equipment hadn't kept pace with the delivery format. In today's digital world, this can still be the case, which is why it's essential for Marantz to continue innovating.

For Marantz's Global Brand Ambassador Ken Ishiwata, it's important that technical developments always serve the firm's founding purpose. "Of course we have electronic measuring instruments," he says. "But these can only measure instantaneously: it's like taking still photographs of a dancer. It is accurate but shows nothing of the dancer's dynamism, speed and rhythm. Some people say it's about definition, timbre, imaging, transient response and subsonics. I say it's about emotion."

In other words, the music is king. Technical development only really counts for anything if it serves Marantz's original mission: to break down the barrier between musician and listener and transmit music in its purest, most unmediated

form possible. A look at Marantz's history shows that the brand has kept apace with – and often pre-empted – developments in audio technology. Yet it has always maintained a savvy relationship with these changes, never losing sight of its core aim to deliver quality.

In early 2017, Marantz launched its Reference 10 Series: products designed with the aim of covering all music formats with a level of design, engineering and attention to detail typical of the brand. Features include a new disc-transport mechanism, which has been developed exclusively for this model; and innovative digital audio-processing technology, which maintains the company's commitment to existing formats while making the equipment future-proof.

So, even if a client prefers to stick with CDs or participate in the vinyl revival, the top-of-the-range 10 Series will deliver optimum performance. It is also designed to make the most of the next generation of digital innovations. "The series is not networked," says Ken, "but it can be connected to a PC, which will deliver digital files to the high-quality digital audio converter amplifier. This will convert and make the utmost out of any file, regardless of quality."

At a time of relentless technological change, it's comforting to know that the best way of keeping pace with developments is simply to maintain your own integrity of purpose. That's why this trusted and enduring brand continues to feel like the future.
— www.marantz.co.uk

ONLY THE BEST

Boss & Co

WALK INTO BOSS & Co's London workshop and you might be surprised at how low-tech everything is. In today's all-digital world, few expect to find craftspeople building fine guns and rifles with the same tools that have been used for centuries. But, unlike other gunmakers, Boss has not embraced modern machinery and electronic fads. It believes the only way to build the finest firearms in the world is by hand with skilled artisans.

Founded in London in 1812, Boss & Co has spent two centuries building what is known in the industry as "best guns". "Historically, a best gun was the finest shotgun or rifle a London gunmaker could make," says Arthur S DeMoulas, Chairman and owner. "We still hold ourselves to this standard."

To achieve this quality, Boss uses its unique designs, the finest materials and, most importantly, the top craftspeople in the world. Such skilled individuals are hard to find and their scarcity has always limited the number of guns that Boss can build. This is especially true today. Boss's guns are handmade, so the build process can't be rushed or held to strict timelines.

Of the shotguns and rifles built by Boss, its world-renowned "over-under" (OU) may be the most impressive. Envied by other makers, Boss patented its revolutionary OU in 1909. Elegant, lightweight and superbly balanced, it continues to be one of the most desirable shotguns made today. Most of Boss's OUs are ordered with the firm's celebrated single trigger. Patented in 1893, it was the first reliable single trigger ever created and has been refined over the years.

The majority of Boss's clients order pairs of guns for shooting driven game. Making pairs is an especially demanding task. Everything about the two guns has to be matching, from their dimensions, their engravings and their overall weight to their balance and the grain in the wooden stocks. Getting all of this absolutely right requires many more hours of work and calls for skills of the highest level.

Every Boss is custom-made and, to this end, clients are encouraged to consult with the company's craftsmen on all commissions. Boss can build whatever the client desires, be it a double rifle for deer stalking in the Scottish Highlands, a 28-gauge OU with 29-inch barrels or a father-and-son set of high-bird guns.

Regardless of features, every Boss is built to fit a shooter's measurements. A proper fit is a hallmark of a best-quality firearm. For Arthur, it's what makes a best gun feel like an extension of your body.

"Anyone who shoots a Boss will understand why top shooters and collectors have such high opinions of these guns," says Arthur. "Not only is a Boss beautiful, but it also feels alive when you handle it. Clients enjoy and admire them for decades and then pass them on to the next generation to do the same."

The company's clients include aristocrats, celebrities and business tycoons, as well as those who have saved for decades, dreaming of owning a Boss one day. Regardless of their status or bank balance, they all share a passion for fine firearms and an eye for quality.

Since 1812, Boss & Co has built the best-quality shotguns and rifles for shooters and collectors around the world. "For more than two centuries," says Arthur, "the owner of a Boss has had the satisfaction of knowing he has the best gun money can buy."
— www.bossguns.com

BOXING CLEVER

Reposo by metrica

THE PURPOSE OF a humidor – the airtight container for keeping cigars moist – is to recreate the climatic conditions of a cigar's country of origin. If this is done well, the contents will not only last for many years, but will mature with time.

"It is vital that the best cigars are kept in the right ambience," says Kai Dittmar, CEO of metrica® INTERIOR, the 300-year-old prestige design business that recently acquired the humidor maker Reposo. "If cigars are allowed to dry, the outer layers can split and become flaky," says Kai. "Too much moisture and they develop mildew."

The Reposo's humidity is kept constant by a fine, sterile vapour, which infuses the cigars with the aroma of the cabinet's cedar wood lining. It took Reposo's designer, Carsten Schroeter, several years to perfect. He sourced the finest cedar wood and metals; worked with specialist craftsmen; consulted with climate experts; and adopted an antibacterial technology used in operating theatres.

Then he had the good fortune to meet Kai Dittmar. "I met Carsten in a bar," says Kai, "and we started talking about cigars. We soon got on to his invention – which I thought was a cool idea – and he suggested we work together."

From the start, the concept was to keep Reposo completely exclusive, so only between seven and 11 units are made each year. "We have no wish ever to go into mass production," says Kai. And for those fortunate enough to own a super yacht, Reposo's "Nautic" model is guaranteed perfectly seaworthy.

"A cigar is the ultimate statement of luxury, and a Reposo is a work of art which can be customised," says Kai. "For our clients it can be an expression of themselves and of their taste. Even those who don't smoke are pleased to be able to offer cigars to their friends – in perfect condition."

The Reposo 12 bears a stainless steel plate, signed by the master craftsmen who worked on it. "These people have created a masterpiece," says Kai. "The signed plate expresses that it's just for you – as masters honouring a special client."
— www.reposo.de

BOUTIQUE BIKES

Rabasa Cycles

BIKES ARE ALL Albert Adami Rabasa has ever known. In 1922, his grandfather, Simeó, started a small repair and hire shop in Barcelona and, in the years that followed, the company spread across the Catalan capital. Before long it was not only building its own cycles but also superbikes, too, winning eight world championships under the name Derbi. "It may be true that dreams are inherited," says Albert.

Yet in 1990, Rabasa, then run by Albert's mother, ceased production. Cheap imports from Asia, combined with a brutal recession, meant it simply couldn't compete on price. "The art of manufacturing bikes in Spain disappeared," he says. "The people who made them were made redundant and the factories closed."

But Albert never gave up and, in 2011, he restarted the business with a twist – rather than mass manufacturing cycles, he now creates beautiful, handmade pushbikes tailored for each individual customer. Rabasa's team of designers, engineers and painters spend 12 days personally assembling each model from a workshop just outside Barcelona in Mollet del Vallès, using specialist materials. The frames, for instance, are made from chromoly, more rigid and durable than aluminium. Reynolds 631 tubes are imported from Birmingham because they are exceptionally strong yet light, while every model features a unique Rabasa-designed dropout – the slot in the frame where the wheel axle is attached – optimised for years of use.

These are bikes designed for city use – easy to ride, comfortable, fast and light. "We have three people in production who solder the frames, two who do the painting and two assembling," says Albert. "When something isn't perfect, it's easy to identify and correct details quickly, something you can't do in an expensive manufacturing process. It also means everything is customisable, too."

The strategy has been a commercial and critical success: Rabasa now produces 40 bikes per month, while its flagship model, Nova, won the eminent Laus Award in 2013, presented by the Spanish Association of Graphic Designers and Art Directors. By returning to the company's small roots, then, Albert has guaranteed his grandfather's legacy. "We will continue to be loyal to what we've had since we were born," he concludes. "Resistant bicycles that combine usefulness and entertainment – an urban necessity."
— www.rabasacycle.com

HIGH-SEAS TECH

Videoworks

ONLY A FEW years ago, while cruise passengers were relaxing on deck, on-board staff would ensure that their wishes were taken care of by checking on them at regular intervals. But a choice sometimes had to be made between these well-meaning interruptions and peace and privacy.

Then came Videoworks, an Italian-based entertainment solutions provider, with a range of automation systems aimed at enhancing luxury at sea in a host of ways. MyConcierge is just one of these. "When you are relaxing by the pool or in your cabin, you can order anything you like – snacks or cocktails, perhaps – just by touching a button on your tablet device," says Marketing Director Sara Stimilli. "The staff will know at once where you are and what you need."

To ensure a good night's sleep, Videoworks has worked with the Marche Polytechnic University in Ancona on the development of its Active Noise Cancelling (ANC) technology. Inside each cabin, a virtual no-noise bubble is created within a two-metre range of the bed's pillow area, to significantly decrease engine and generator sounds.

In the gym, on the other hand, a workout can be enhanced in a number of extraordinary and futuristic ways. An interactive floor can be modified to display, for example, a glass-bottom effect, showing a high-definition reproduction of coral reefs and fish. "To create a peaceful space for a yoga or Pilates session, you can turn the room into a Japanese temple – or any one of a range of environments," says Sara.

Using a variety of ingenious speakers – including some hidden away inside walls – Videoworks supplies bespoke, high-performance audio in all parts of a yacht. "We also deal with refitting projects," says Sara, "and we can carry out installations on existing craft without having to dismantle fittings and furnishings."

Videoworks uses an augmented-reality system that makes it possible to sail into a city, capture the view on a tablet, and touch a landmark to receive information or commentary about it. Guides to restaurants and places of interest can also be accessed at the touch of a screen.

All over the world at any time, hundreds of boats are at sea with Videoworks systems on board. In order to be able carry out maintenance and repairs without delay, the company has a worldwide network of experts at the ready. Sara describes the company's engineers arriving by speedboat and coming aboard to troubleshoot problems.

"It sounds like a James Bond movie, but this is the real world now," she says. "We also have remote access to our installations, and can monitor and repair problems from anywhere in the world. People need to know that their equipment will always work, so we are on the alert 24 hours a day.

"Our founder and owner, Mauro Pellegrini, believes in doing things step by step, and not taking unnecessary risks," says Sara. To this end, in July 2016, Videoworks announced the entry of a hugely experienced new COO Matteo Campana, a manager who has held important positions in several global companies. This step represents for Videoworks a crucial evolutionary step from a family-run business to a managerial company whose final goal is to make clients happy.
— www.videoworks.it

THE GREAT OUTDOORS

Skiing and adventure experiences

ALPINE ALL-STAR

Suvretta House, Switzerland

HOLIDAYS ARE WHAT memories are made of. They're about spending time with family and friends in beautiful locations, enjoying fantastic food and drink, and taking in new experiences. Peter Egli, the General Manager of Suvretta House – a luxurious escape located in the Swiss Alps above St Moritz – keeps this in mind at all times. "We aim to create special moments," he says.

Throughout the winter, snow sports take centre stage. "Our private ski lift gives guests direct access to 350 km of slopes," says Peter. "And Suvretta House is the only ski-in and ski-out hotel in St Moritz." It runs a sports school and activities include snow shoe excursions, off-piste skiing, lake skating and curling on the hotel's private rink. For children, there are nursery slopes, supervised activities and a huge ice sculpture with caves and slides in the hotel garden. If you don't have equipment, the ski shop is fully stocked for rental and sales.

In the warmer months, this winter wonderland turns gracefully from white to green. Guests can hike and mountain bike through the Engadine Valley and swim in the nearby turquoise glacial lakes that the glacier left behind. "Moss warms the lakes up to about 25°C and has properties that soften the skin," says Peter. Suvretta House also organises a weekly outing, setting up picnic tables and a barbecue in the woodland next to local waterfalls.

Food is a feature all year round. The hotel restaurants include the Grand Etage, a formal setting that contrasts with the casual atmosphere of the rest of Suvretta House. "We have a restaurant that's just for children," says Peter, "but when families come together for a meal in the Grand Restaurant, the little boys come in their suits

and ties feeling very grown up." There are also three mountain lodge restaurants, all with breathtaking views, including Chasellas, named one of *Monocle* magazine's 50 Best Global Restaurants in 2015.

For all its Alpine beauty, however, there's a distinct Britishness to Suvretta House. One of St Moritz's original grand hotels, it was opened in 1912 by hotelier Anton Bon and South African diamond merchant-turned-British Member of Parliament Charles Sydney Goldman. British touches include afternoon tea at 5 pm and the Gin'ius Club, which offers 35 carefully selected gins. "We're currently working with a botanist to create our own gentlemen's and ladies' gins using wild junipers from the local area," says Peter.

Fitting for a hotel of this calibre, Suvretta House has a 25-metre pool, gym, sauna, beauty salon and spa. But it's the lobby, with its large, south-facing windows, that initially grabs visitors' attention. "New guests go straight there," says Peter, "and people who've been coming for more than 40 years point and say 'That's why we keep coming back!' To sit on the terrace for breakfast or enjoy a drink with that stunning view is worth the travel in itself."

Combining all these elements, it's easy to see how memories are made here. "It's mainly the location that makes us so special," says Peter. "The building looks like a fairytale castle from the outside – but inside, the mood changes." Special touches such as art exhibitions, live music, culinary events and fashion shows combine with impeccable service.

"My wife and I personally welcome all the guests and say goodbye when they leave," says Peter. "The hotel is called a 'house' with good reason: we want people to feel at home."
— www.suvrettahouse.ch/en

VIRGIN TERRITORIES

Canadian Mountain Holidays

THERE IS SOMETHING very special about the Canadian Mountain Holidays heli-skiing experience. "Compared to a European resort, it's incredible," says Kenny Prevost, director of the Swiss-based sales agent Knecht Reisen. "You fly straight into the middle of nowhere. The closest civilisation is between 200 km and 300 km away. On the first day, you get to the top of the peak at 9 am, at around 3,000 metres, and the view is breathtaking. You feel like you can see into infinity."

Canadian Mountain Holidays operates 12 luxury lodges in the remote Columbia range west of the Rockies. Each lodge operates in supreme isolation from its neighbours, which means the skiing that is available cannot be surpassed.

"There are 12 different skiing areas," says Kenny, "and what stands out is that you have everything. You can have a bluebird day, where you go as high as you can into the glaciers. Or, if it is colder and snowing, you can do tree-skiing. As long as the helicopter can see the trees for reference, you can go out. In each area you have 200 possible helicopter drop-off points and, from each drop-off point, there are three or more ways to get down the mountain. The choice is limitless. It's the world's best powder, and it's the most diversified heli-skiing terrain on the planet – everything from high alpine glaciers to tree-skiing. There is no other area that has the variety which makes helicopter skiing so unique."

Founded in 1965, Canadian Mountain Holidays is a pioneer of heli-skiing. Kenny describes the experience offered by the company as "backcountry luxury". This means that the lodges are luxurious and fully staffed – with chefs, maids, mountain guides, lodge managers, bartenders – but there is no TV or phone reception. "The only thing we have is Wi-Fi," he says. "All the food is freshly made, even the morning croissants, and there is always a member of staff around if you need them – it's pretty much a 24-hour call service from the moment you are picked up at the airport – but it's not like staying at a five-star hotel. The premium aspect is the experience – the chance to ski on virgin, untouched powder, day after day, run after run."

The company looks after guests from the moment they arrive at the airport, transporting them to the lodges, serving the best food, arranging the day's skiing and providing any ski or snowboard equipment that is required. Certified mountain guides accompany skiers down the mountain in groups, with the runs decided depending on weather conditions and the desires of the customers. Holiday-goers can book in groups as large or small as they desire, depending on lodge availability – as there's no fixed format that works for everybody.

Skiers never have to travel in the tracks of a previous group, as the guides simply select an alternative route to the bottom. While heli-skiing is only recommended for those with considerable experience of the slopes, there are also guides who can help introduce intermediate and advanced backcountry skiers on special weeks to the marvels of powder skiing.

The experience is so popular that around 70 per cent of skiers are repeat customers. "It's on the bucket list as something for the special occasion," says Kenny. "But when people have done it once, they want to do it again and again. When they do it once, they are hooked."
— www.cmhski.com

WINTER WONDERLAND

Hotel Grandes Alpes Private Hotel & Spa, France

A RICH HERITAGE, state-of-the-art facilities and sumptuous attention to detail combine at the Courchevel's five-star Hotel Grandes Alpes. Part of France's iconic Trois Vallées ski region, this stand-out location provides the starting-point for a truly exceptional experience, as Galina Protsenko, Hotel Grandes Alpes' General Manager, explains.

"Courchevel is a unique place," she says. "It is the biggest skiing destination and has the highest concentration of five-star resorts. It features amazing shopping and Michelin-starred dining. We were thinking about what was missing, and we decided to create the most convenient luxury hotel in the heart of Courchevel."

This vision was realised five years ago when a historic, 45-room hotel was transformed into nine spacious and luxuriously appointed apartment suites. Originally built in 1948, the property has previously served as a post office and a church, but for its latest incarnation the interior was completely redeveloped in collaboration with French husband-and-wife design team Jean-Marc and Anne-Sophie Mouchet. They focused on "warm and soft" locally sourced materials, including wood from the region.

"It was clearly important to keep the French touch," says Galina. "But we also wanted to surprise our clients, and give them home comfort and quality. Most of our guests are families. We wanted to create a special place where they can spend quality time together in the evening, and have breakfast together. The common areas include a living room with a fireplace, and our guests have the services of a 24-hour butler. We also have some groups of friends that come to stay with us, as well as business associates who combine work with skiing."

More than 70 per cent of the guests at Hotel Grandes Alpes are return visitors from around the world. "It's a pleasure to see the children growing up, year after year," says Galina.

Courchevel's skiing season – which runs between December and early April – is relatively short yet much celebrated, and Hotel Grandes Alpes is ideally placed at the heart of the action. "You can ski directly from the door of the hotel, and that's a real privilege for our guests," says Galina. "When you sit at the bar, you can really feel the atmosphere of the place. There is something special in the air here."

From the moment of arrival in Courchevel, immaculate care is taken to cater for the needs and preferences of each guest. Hotel Grandes Alpes offers transfer services and bookings for skiing instructors and gourmet restaurants. The hotel also boasts its own acclaimed Japanese restaurant, Le Bizan, with a 25-place setting presided over by sushi master Masahiro Adachi. Alternatively, those who wish to dine in the comfort of their own apartment can book a private chef, who can even create cooking courses for the hotel's guests.

For the ultimate wind-down away from the slopes, Hotel Grandes Alpes offers guests exclusive use of its Valmont spa, including hammam, sauna and swimming pool. The hotel's therapists are specialised in a wide range of well-being treatments.

"We take time to get to know the fine details with all our guests, even their favourite flowers or ice cream," says Galina. "It's about their level of satisfaction." There is magic in Hotel Grandes Alpes' location, and an unmistakably personal touch in its brand of luxury.
— www.grandesalpes.com

A WINNING ALTITUDE

Geilo, Norway

THE SEVEN-HOUR train journey from Oslo to Bergen is one of the most beautiful – and highest – rail journeys in the world. It offers unparalleled views of the wild, unspoiled Norwegian landscape, with its rivers and valleys, forests, mountains and snowy plateaus.

At its halfway point, at the edge of the Hardangervidda National Park, lies the village and exclusive ski resort of Geilo. It's a place that has long been the home of skiing (the word "ski" actually derives from the Norwegian for "piece of wood"), and has been the destination of choice for the discerning traveller – among them the British aristocracy and Norwegian royalty – for more than a hundred years.

"Unlike many other European ski resorts, Geilo is a real, living mountain village with an old soul to it," says Trevor De Villiers, the CEO of Norway Home of Skiing. "There is nothing artificial about it. It has a community of 2,500 people, which swells to 12,000 in winter, and a fine heritage. At an altitude of 800 m, snow is guaranteed for the whole winter season, and the skiing areas and slopes are close to the town centre, with its fine hotels, spas, restaurants and boutiques."

Geilo has many fine hotels, including the renowned Dr Holms, which has been frequented by English gentry since the early 1900s. Steeped in history, the hotel started life as a health retreat – the eponymous Dr Holms was a respiratory doctor – and fell under German control during the Second World War, until the Norwegian resistance retook it in 1945.

The hotel is home to a historical art collection (guests can borrow a catalogue from reception) and features Norway's highest-altitude bowling

alley. With 125 rooms, ranging from the traditional, romantic English style, to more modern and minimalist designs, the hotel also contains a luxury spa, several restaurants, a library, a ski bar, a pub and a wine cellar.

In the heart of Geilo stands the charming and award-wining Hallingstuene restaurant, named one of the Best Restaurants in the Nordics by White Guide. Owned by renowned Norwegian chef Frode Aga, Hallingstuene is furnished like a traditional Halling cottage, with rose-paintings and two open fireplaces, and specialises in classic Norwegian fare from local producers, such as game in cream sauces, smoked sausage, rack of lamb, reindeer and trout. Guests who wish to dine in privacy can book a separate room for their party, and there is also a cognac wagon and cellar wine-bar.

"Geilo offers a world-class standard of facilities and service," says Trevor. "Everyone speaks perfect English too. The Norwegian term 'Janteloven', which places society ahead of the individual and means that nobody should be jealous of anyone else, makes Geilo the ideal holiday destination for those who enjoy privacy and discretion. I once had a very pleasant chat with a woman in a local bar, only to discover later that she was the Princess of Norway."

With daily flights out of Gatwick to both Oslo and Bergen, and packages arranged by British Airways Holidays, the resort of Geilo achieves the rare combination of being both accessible and exclusive. "Every time I take the train from Oslo to Geilo, I am blown away by the Norwegian landscape," says Trevor. It's like New Zealand on steroids. The sheer beauty of it is breathtaking."
— www.norwayhomeofskiing.com
— www.geilo.no

GET THE DRIFT

Lapland Ice Driving

FOR 14 WEEKS each year, Lake Udjaur in northern Sweden is transformed into the largest driving centre in the world. With 13 circuits carved into the ice, including exact full-scale replicas of Silverstone and Nürburgring, this is the ultimate driving experience. Customers can choose from 30 high-performance cars by Ferrari, Porsche, Maserati and others, all specially prepared for the extreme winter conditions.

"At the start of the season, I drive each car to make sure that it handles to my specifications," says Eric Gallardo, founder of Lapland Ice Driving. "We use special studded tyres and replace the cars' fluids with alternatives that won't freeze. Tough bumpers can withstand impact in temperatures of -20 °C. The pleasure is driving and drifting at speeds of up to 125 mph on ice. It's truly exhilarating."

Professional, personalised, one-on-one in-car tuition is provided, enabling clients to learn the limits of car control in a completely safe environment. There are no barriers to plough into, only soft snow. "With our intensive programme, you will drive up to 160 miles each day," says Eric. "We guarantee that you will master the art of drifting – controlling the car in a sideways skid – in two days, whether you are a complete beginner or already have some experience. Our expert instructors see to that. Afterwards, if you want to, you can then go it alone."

Since it opened in 2006, the remote village of Arjeplog's main attraction has made it a glamorous winter destination in its own right. At just a few miles south of the Arctic Circle, this is a very special destination. "A lot of our customers arrive by private jet," says Eric. "We can personalise every aspect of their stay, whether they want to drive a snowmobile or try their hand at dog-sledding."

With the Northern Lights as a spectacular backdrop, it's unsurprising that this once-in-a-lifetime experience is often anything but. "Around 75 per cent of our bookings are returning customers," says Eric. "Some people have come every winter for 10 years. The only risk is addiction."
— www.lapland-ice-driving.com

SPIRIT OF ADVENTURE

HL Adventure, Iceland

"WE'VE CERTAINLY HAD some unusual requests," says Marketing Manager Thorvardur Godi Valdimarsson of his Iceland tour company HL Adventure. "My favourite was the billionaire who wanted to throw a party so big it would register as an earthquake. We organised it on top of the Eyjafjallajökull volcano, flew in a DJ from Hong Kong and brought the biggest sound system in Iceland. And it did register as an earthquake."

HL Adventure is no ordinary tour company. Whether it's enabling clients to get up close to a polar bear, kayak in the wilds or even name their own mountain, there's virtually nothing HL can't lay on. Founded in 2003 by Jón Ólafur Magnússon, a former fishing captain and adventurer, it set out to offer high-end corporate and private clients "soft adventures", making uninhabited areas of Iceland accessible and safe.

"We cater for people who have travelled the world and seen it all," says Thorvardur. "They want a once-in-a-lifetime experience, such as our Arctic Luxury Camp – a custom-made, temporary, five-star hotel experience, with the best chefs, the finest linen, even luxury saunas, that we can build and dismantle anywhere without harming the environment. Depending who we are working with, the weather and the location, we provide guides, experts, entertainment, vehicles and vessels, sea or air, anything needed to design the experience."

Confidentiality is paramount, but Thorvardur admits that customers have included the rich and famous. One tour cost €1 million and saw 100 members of staff working on a five-day birthday party. But the company makes sure it gives something back, working with a charity to plant trees in barren areas of Iceland.

HL Adventure's innovative plans for this year include trips to the North Pole where "clients will be able to call their friends by satellite phone and toast them with Champagne from the top of the world". Next year, customers on a once-in-a-lifetime voyage to Antarctica will be able to celebrate New Year's Eve for 24 hours straight by walking directly into the next time zone. "It's all about fun," says Thorvardur, "and offering just that little bit more."
— www.hl.is

HEIGHT OF LUXURY

Obergurgl-Hochgurgl, Austria

HIGH IN THE Austrian Alps, close to the Italian border, sits Obergurgl-Hochgurgl: the region's first non-glacial ski resort to open each winter, and one of the last to shut down. This makes for a happy population, as there's great hiking, biking and mountaineering to be had here in summer, too. But most visitors come between November and April, and they are here to ski. What they find is fine snow, queue-free gondolas and great slopes – 110 km of them. Some of this is luck – nature's generosity.

But the area's residents aren't content just to rely on that. Ever since the scientist Auguste Piccard put the pretty village on the map by making an emergency landing here in 1931, locals have been steadily augmenting their natural advantages to benefit tourists. The result is 4,000 available beds in Obergurgl and another 1,000 in Hochgurgl, many of them in four- and five-star establishments with top-class spas and excellent restaurants. The views every bit as spectacular as you'd expect from a premium Alpine ski resort.

To cap it all, the place boasts the highest motorcycle museum in Europe at 2,175 m: Top Mountain Crosspoint. This ultramodern wave of a building is also the base station for the Kirchenkar mountain gondola; and home to a restaurant with a pizza oven recently imported from Italy. "It means that the pizza is seriously good," says the resort's Marketing Director, Dr Werner Hanselitsch.

Motorcycles are a theme here: the new Doppelmayr mountain gondola has one painted on every car. Maybe the pictures of these noisy machines are intended as a contrast to the silence inside the cars as skiers are transported to the peaks. "All the cars seat 10 people comfortably," says Werner. "They are very calm and spacious, and the seats are heated." And of course, the view as you climb is awesome.

There are two villages in the resort, with Obergurgl at the southern end of the Ötztal Gurgler Tal valley, but everything is smoothly integrated. A chauffeur drives new arrivals from Innsbruck airport to their destination 60 km down the valley. The restaurants and bars are open to all – even non-skiers.

The Top Mountain Star bar is a particular highlight: literally, since this glass-lined room sits at 3,030 m, with snow-bright views of glaciers on all sides. "It serves small dishes – noodles, soups – but really, you're here for the view," says Werner.

For those prepared to sacrifice a little height for a more traditional local meal, the Hohe Mut Alm, situated at 2,670 m, offers the full Tyrolean experience – local Ötztal beef and specialities like the sweet dumplings known as *germknödel* – in a wooden building complete with crackling log fire. It's also a place where you can see around 20 peaks higher than 3,000 m and about 25 glaciers.

You can ski to the restaurant and back to earn these Tyrolean treats; or relax and take the gondola. Either way, there's no danger in season of having to walk home from dinner. "We are the most snow-safe resort in the Alps," says Werner. "We have snow even when nobody else does." Really, Obergurgl-Hochgurgl has it all.

— www.obergurgl.com

MOUNTAIN EXCITEMENT

One Chalets Hakuba, Japan

JAPAN MAY NOT be the first place that springs to mind for skiers from Europe or America when planning their next holiday. However, the Hakuba Valley at the base of the Japanese Alps in Nagano – home to the 1998 Winter Olympics and fast becoming a world-renowned ski destination – could just change that.

Hakuba incorporates 10 ski resorts scattered throughout the valley and offers breathtaking views, a wide range of mountain terrains and abundant annual snowfall. Overlooking the region's most spectacular mountain, Happo One, sits one of its most exclusive properties, the One Happo Chalet.

"It is probably the most luxurious chalet in any ski resort in Japan," says Lily Kitano, Marketing and Operations Manager of One Chalets and Phoenix Japan. "Combine that with Hakuba's pristine snow conditions, beautiful blue skies and variety of terrains, and you have a snow holiday that is second to none."

The 500 sq m, five-bedroom chalet has top-notch facilities. These include wall-mounted touch screens to control heating and lighting, a fully equipped kitchen and dining area with its own cocktail bar and wine room, a large living area and heated deck, a state-of-the-art gym and a private sauna. Guests also have exclusive use of a 4x4 vehicle to explore the valley.

"We own and operate a large number of luxury chalets and hotels throughout Hakuba, but the One Happo Chalet is something special," says Lily. "Its location, size and exclusivity make it a true one-off for visitors, whether in the winter or the green season."

Lily and her team are on hand to ensure guests have a memorable holiday, whatever the season. "We operate year-round and our dedicated team love nothing more than to share our knowledge of all that Hakuba has to offer," she says. "We can arrange private catering, back-country tours, heli-skiing, an in-house massage, cultural day trips and private ski lessons with information on the best local eateries to help our guests create their ultimate holiday."

While Hakuba is predominantly known for its snow-capped mountains, in the summer, the valley is nothing short of spectacular with its scenic mountains, crystal-clear lakes and rivers, and is home to a host of outdoor activities such as hiking, cycling, river-rafting, golf and paragliding. "The whole of the Nagano 'Shinshu' region is rich in culture, tradition and beautiful landscapes with so many exciting activities to be enjoyed," says Lily, "but one of my personal highlights would have to be its abundance of delicious fresh local produce and home-brewed sake."

For those seeking traditional après-ski delights, there's Mimi's Restaurant in the Phoenix Hotel, which offers perfectly chargrilled local game and a global wine list, or the Marillen Hotel and Restaurant with its cheese-laden pleasures, homemade gluhwein and live entertainment. And for those looking to embrace Japanese culture, there is also much to enjoy.

"I'd recommend a night at our newly opened Japanese tapas and sushi restaurant, Sharaku, in Hakuba Springs Hotel," says Lily. "Reserve a seat at the Sushi Bar, where the executive chef prepares dainty delicacies and fresh sushi right in front of you, paired with the most delicious local sake. It's a lot of fun and a perfect way to enjoy your evening after a thrilling day on the mountain." A new skiing sensation indeed.
— www.onechalets.com

REFLECTED GLORY

Grand Hotel Kempinski High Tatras, Slovakia

THE BEAUTIFUL MOUNTAINS known as the High Tatras that mark the border between Poland and Slovakia have been a draw for tourists since at least the 19th century, with their relative inaccessibility ensuring that the region remains unspoilt to this day. Today, the resort of Strbske Pleso on the Slovak side is still as charming as it was 150 years ago, but it's a lot easier to get to, with direct flights from London. The result is superb, convenient skiing in a scenic location that looks as good as it did when a visit meant a hike across the mountains.

"Slovakia is still undiscovered," says Kathrin Noll, General Manager of Grand Hotel Kempinski High Tatras in Strbske Pleso. "It's a hidden secret, despite numerous Unesco heritage sites and national parks and the fantastic skiing. That will change – the country is very vibrant and is moving forward fast. For the moment, though, it is perfect for travellers who want to visit a safe but unknown destination."

The three buildings of the Grand Hotel Kempinski High Tatras, one of them dating back to 1893, are situated on the shore of a picturesque mountain lake, which reflects stunning views of the mountain peaks. Indeed, there can't be many places where a skier can look down to see the top of the run. The village, which, like the lake, is called Strbske Pleso, has all kinds of sporting activities: hiking and biking in the warmer months and, of course, skiing in winter, with snow from December till April and lots of sunshine.

"The slopes are only a few minutes from the hotel and we offer a complimentary shuttle bus for maximum convenience," says Kathrin. "The slopes are blue and red, and there's also cross-country skiing on the frozen lake. The ski pass is also valid for the neighbouring resort of Tatranska Lomnica." The après-ski scene in Strbske Pleso is very family-friendly, although guests at Grand Hotel Kempinski High Tatras have little need to venture outside the hotel once the day's sporting activities are done.

The Grand Restaurant features fine dining, using fresh ingredients from local farmers; the cosy Lobby Lounge offers Slovak and international wines in front of a roaring fireplace and stunning views of the lake; there's even a smokers' lounge. And the beautiful Zion Spa Luxury was awarded Slovakia's best spa in 2015 by the World Spa Awards.

"There are no views like those from our pool, which mirrors the mountain peaks just as the lake does," says Kathrin. "The effect of the climate is incredible and the treatments are designed to maximise that."

After more than a century of delighting tourists to the area, the Grand Hotel became a Kempinski property and reopened in 2009, after four years of thoughtful renovation and refurbishment. "That history gives the hotel its unique feel – we didn't want to change that," says Kathrin. "We restored and maintained more than 70 original features of this beautiful national heritage building during the reconstruction, and we are very proud of that."

As a result, this is still a place where the scent of a crackling wood fire greets guests as they come in from the cold, and where the luxurious surroundings have the feel of the long-vanished Austro-Hungarian Empire. Old-style luxury with modern convenience: the Grand Hotel Kempinski High Tatras seems unlikely to remain a hidden secret for much longer.
— www.kempinski.com/hightatras

PEAK PERFORMER

Hotel Le Taos, Tignes-le-Lac, France

AMID THE MILLENNIA-OLD splendour of alpine France's Haute Tarentaise, the ski resort of Tignes is a comparative youngster. Today's town was born in the 1960s following the construction of the hydroelectric Barrage de Chevril, which sank old Tignes village beneath a valleyful of meltwater from the Isère river.

This dam – the tallest in Europe when it opened in 1952 – is a dominating feature of the region, and may be familiar to the UK's Channel 4 viewers as the setting for the supernatural thriller *Les Revenants* (The Returned), which recounts eerie goings-on in a lakeside village. There's no such spookiness in modern-day Tignes, though – the resort buzzes with winter sports activity during the day and positively thrums with après-ski nightlife after dark.

In keeping with the vibrant atmosphere, the four-star Hotel Le Taos in Tignes-le-Lac combines luxury with a spirit of adventure, offering the ideal base from which to explore this glorious setting on the roof of Europe. "Tignes has a good standard of hotels but they are more traditional," says Natacha Blanc-Gonnet, Marketing Director of the Montagnettes Group, which owns Le Taos. "We wanted to offer something totally new."

Le Taos is the group's second alpine hotel. "We find inspiration from mountains all over the world," says Natacha. "Our last alpine hotel, Hameau de Kashmir in Val Thorens, focused on the Himalayas; this time we concentrated on New Mexico and the Rocky Mountains. Our CEO Agnès Girard spent two years studying in the Rockies and we loved the Taos area, which shares the same kind of free spirit as Tignes. We didn't want a pastiche: people were free-skiing in Tignes 30 years ago and

we felt that there was a shared sense of nature preserved, a real authenticity."

Le Taos opened its doors in December 2015 and has already been nominated for this year's World Ski Awards in the Best New Ski Hotel category. "It shows we've reached a standard in the first year that you wouldn't expect until the second or third," says Natacha, "when you've had a chance to assess performance and enhance the product."

Tignes has plenty of activities on offer beyond the pistes, and Le Taos also opens in July and August as well as the December-to-April skiing season. The Lac de Tignes – a short stroll from Le Taos – offers sailing, canoeing and waterskiing (even ice diving in winter), plus a lakeside golf course, mountain-bike trails and more. "There's something for kids, adults and grandparents," says Natacha. "Even if you don't ski, there's something different every day."

From the hotel restaurant guests can enjoy the panoramic majesty of the valley – a 180-degree vista from Les L'Aiguille Percee round to Grand Sassière. It's a stunning scene, but also a reminder of the unforgiving ruggedness of the region and Tignes' growing pains from half a century ago.

"It was a kind of rebirth," says Natacha, of the five villages on the shores of the lake that replaced old Tignes. "The barrage destroyed a village, and it affected people deeply. But it's a tribute to those people that, when something like that happened, they rose to the challenge and begun again. The high-altitude environment can be harsh, but enjoying that challenge informs the mountain attitude. It's a competitive, sporting spirit." Hotel Le Taos shows that this spirit is alive and thriving.
— www.hotel-le-taos.com/en

SWISS BLISS

The Chedi Andermatt, Switzerland

IN A SWISS Alpine village once used as a filming location for James Bond's *Goldfinger*, a new breed of luxury hotel has come to Europe, boasting a style that Bond himself would admire. The Chedi Andermatt opened in 2013 and, in the words of Sven Flory, the Director of Sales and Marketing: "It marks the European debut of the grand hotel for the 21st century. People come to The Chedi Andermatt for the experience and you need to come now because in a few years everybody will be coming here."

The Chedi is hot stuff – quite literally. "We have more than 200 fireplaces," says Sven. "That's more fireplaces than we have rooms. We have them in every bedroom and every public space, and lots of outside fire pits. It makes the experience very romantic."

Within this stunning mountainside fusion of Asian and Swiss themes situated just one hour from Zurich and two from Milan, The Chedi Andermatt features an award-winning spa, outstanding restaurants, luxurious rooms, incredible skiing and more. It is also open all year round: summer guests can enjoy golf, hiking and cycling, in addition to the winter delights of skiing, snowboarding, cross-country skiing, snow-shoeing and tobogganing.

While many luxury Swiss hotels are located in resorts such as Verbier, The Chedi Andermatt prides itself as being off the beaten track and therefore able to offer more than just 24-hour exposure to big-brand shopping. Instead, the experiences are more authentic, firmly entwined with the local landscape. "We can arrange packages so you can experience the local community," says Sven. "You can go hiking with the goat herds before you have a five-star barbecue in a meadow, or you can meet a dairy farmer, learn how he produces his cheese and have breakfast with him."

Luxurious touches are on offer at the award-winning spa, which has saunas, steam baths, a state-of-the-art gym, a 35 metre indoor pool beneath a glass ceiling and an outdoor pool, heated all year round, allowing guests to enjoy the breathtaking alpine scenery. For dining, there's a choice of four restaurants, including a Japanese restaurant that employs Switzerland's only sake sommelier, while the main restaurant boasts an excellent five-metre-high cheese cellar, filled with local hard and soft cheese with matching wine.

A ski butler will help guests work off their dinners on the slopes – they become sports butlers in summer, providing similar guidance for everything from golf to angling. There's a private ice rink in the courtyard, and bedrooms are spacious and equipped for luxury. "We have cashmere blankets in every room," says Sven. "You can sit in front of the fireplace with a blanket, a glass of wine and some Swiss cheese."

If all of this sounds particularly appealing, The Chedi Andermatt offers the opportunity to purchase an apartment within the luxury hotel for permanent use. The one- and two-bedroom Chedi Residences, ranging from 95 to 240 sq m living space, are fully furnished, and can be kept for yourself or rented out through the hotel while you are not there. There are also no restrictions on foreign ownership, which makes The Chedi Andermatt a truly cosmopolitan place. Either way, it provides guests with the chance to gain a permanent foothold in this gorgeous environment. "We are a year-round destination," says Sven. "It's the perfect luxury pit stop for when you want to explore one of the most beautiful areas in Europe."
— www.thechediandermatt.com

PRECIOUS PIECES

——

Jewellery and watches

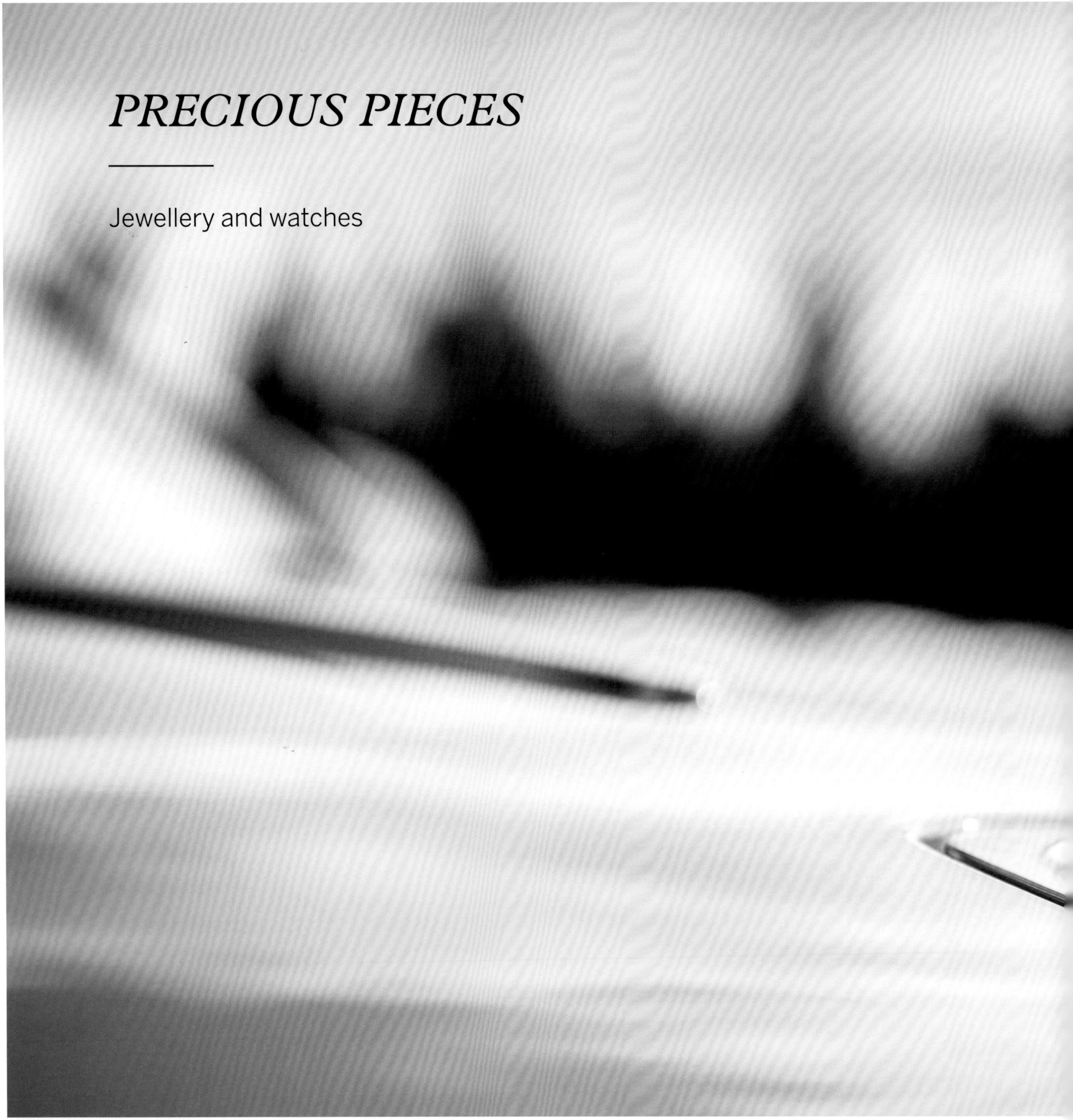

Chara Wen

TO MARK THE occasion of her daughter Krystal's 18th birthday, jeweller Rachel Wen presented her with a remarkable watch as a birthday gift. Although the watch was extraordinarily beautiful, what made it even more special was that Rachel had created the timepiece herself. It marked the beginning of the highly sophisticated jewellery brand, Chara Wen ("Chara" meaning "God's blessing and joy"), launched in Taiwan in 2009.

The inspiration for the watch came from the Parisian landmark the Eiffel Tower, but the drive behind it was pure love. Indeed, the very first collection that Rachel produced under the name Chara Wen was entitled *Gift of Love*.

"I think love is a wonderful and necessary link in our daily life between people, and it's also one of the most important lessons in our life," says Rachel. "I like to think that every piece of my jewellery is a beautiful mark of love between people, just like the gift of love. For that reason, *Gift of Love* is the most important of my collections."

But love is not the only motif that is central to Chara Wen jewellery. Both mother and daughter are passionate about art, and the second timepiece that Rachel created was in homage to a beautiful painting created by Krystal. Chara Wen's latest jewellery collection, *Classic*, takes inspiration from art deco and modern art.

"Jewellery transcends the status of accessory to become a piece of art," says Rachel. "That is because my jewellery doesn't just convey the traditional meaning of the expensive and the luxurious – I also create and present my jewellery in an artistic way. Every piece includes many thoughts and ideas that only artwork shares. My inspirations also come from many diverse and everyday surroundings, and I like to create all of them in a sculptural manner."

While the collections are relatively new, Rachel's love of jewellery isn't. As a child, she adored accompanying her mother on jewellery-buying trips, and spending hours poring over her mother's jewellery box. "Whatever my mother had, I was allowed to play with," says Rachel. "And my mother always took me with her when she went shopping for jewellery. She would ask my opinion – I had a lot of opinions even then! – and I think that was how I developed my unique aesthetic. My mother's style was subtle, conservative and classic, and it has had a profound influence on me."

When it comes to choosing the materials for her work, Rachel prefers to select each one herself, carefully choosing the right diamond and gemstone companies, with whom she has built long-lasting relationship. "I will choose the gemstones myself and they are mainly precious stones," she explains. "I like gemstones that are unique in the way of shapes and colours: sometimes I will have to cut and carve on the rough stones to fit my design.

"Black in particular is a favourite: I think of black as a deep and quiet background, with a touch of the mysterious and noble. I really like to use black gemstones in my designs, black onyx, black obsidians, black jades and black tourmalines, because they are more uncommon. I usually carve them into the shape I want or even leave them as a rough stone to fit into my design. When I combine the black stones with the glorious precious gemstones, the differences between the two textures and colours really bring out the best in them. I also like to use other semi-precious gemstones with elegant colours, such as blue-ish green tourmalines, and cut them into the shape I want. The use of colour diamonds and gemstones gives more depth to my jewellery."

Rachel's abiding aim is for her work to reach those who adore jewellery, something which she is well on the way to doing. "In 2013, we were invited to the Hong Kong Sotheby's auction," she says, "and our jewellery watch 'Gift of Love – Surprise' was successfully sold for over twice the asking price. In 2014, we joined the Baselworld watch and jewellery show. In the same year we were invited to the haute couture fashion show in Paris, and we also had our own exhibition in Le Meurice in Paris. Wherever we go, we want to connect with jewellery lovers."

Indeed, much of Rachel's work is bespoke. "To design jewellery just for the client is what I have always loved to do," she says. "I love finding out about other people's personal style and creating jewellery only for them; it just gives me great pleasure."

While Rachel's inspiration comes from many sources, the execution of it can be a more challenging journey. "My inspiration comes from basically everything in life and all surroundings," she explains. "My source of ideas could be a painting, a costume, a lamp or even a tree. That is why my jewellery has to step out of the box of traditional craftsmanship."

Every piece produced by Chara Wen features a hidden heart-shaped ruby. It's a nod to where it all began – Rachel's love for her daughter and the *Gift of Love* collection – and is a symbol that love, epitomised by the jewellery, will stand the test of time.

"There's no way to avoid difficulties and challenges during the making of the jewellery," says Rachel. "To come up with the best solution for my design, I often have to discuss my thoughts with the craftsperson. We will communicate and try out our ideas until we are all happy with the result. Therefore, we have to have a longer period of making. But I'm sure it's worth it."
— www.charawen.com

BREAKING THE RULES

AS by Atsuko Sano

BOLD, GEOMETRIC SHAPES, blocks of colour and blurred edges are not often associated with fine jewellery. But Atsuko Sano is no ordinary jewellery designer. Her contemporary brand, AS by Atsuko Sano, is fresh, free and full of juxtapositions. Encompassing both masculine and feminine design elements, the pieces are made for both men and women to wear and enjoy.

Contemporary shapes such as circles and arrow-like triangles feature strongly in the AS collections, alongside an unusual blend of coloured gold and brightly hued precious stones, making for pieces that are delightfully androgynous. While the designs may appear somewhat at odds with traditional jewellery design, Atsuko has typically ethereal reasons behind her style. "I feel that geometric shapes are the basics of design," she says, "the framework of human beings."

Atsuko takes inspiration from classical architecture, music and art, and while a Japanese background influences her design philosophy, it doesn't dictate her design style. "I feel I have my own DNA with my own ethnicity," she says. "Plus, in the world of jewellery, the influence of an artisan tends to outweigh that of a designer. The earnest nature of Japanese artisans is strongly echoed in how the pieces are polished and formed."

Highly reflective, chunky surfaces and delicately cut gems often appear on the same piece, and her *Rin* and *Architecture* series are particularly striking, with each range inhabiting an immersive narrative. "The ground design of *Rin* is composed of five elements," says Atsuko. "*Rin* is formed with five Chinese characters, and is the founding collection of the brand." The first *Rin*, which is the key to understanding Atsuko Sano's style, represents the heroic quest of the samurai; the second represents the micron unit or precision; the third represents passion and burning flames; the fourth represents reincarnation; and the final *Rin* represents ethics.

With this founding spirit, Atsuko explores elements of larger design in her small-scale works of art. "Though there are various methods, I try to pare down the characteristics of form and beauty to something very simple," says Atsuko. "As with architecture, meticulous calculation is essential for jewellery to bear light, shadow and time. It is also vital that it provides comfort and passion to people."

The impact of these influences results in stunning pieces; black gold characters, bevelled diamond shapes set with tiny stones are reminiscent of art deco style with a daring, modern edge, and the brightly coloured stones in the men's *Architecture* series soften the oversized shapes using different shades of metal. "In the world of jewellery design, it is classic theory to place gems depending on the quality of the jewellery itself," says Atsuko. "At AS, aside from when we use top-quality gems, we focus on the free, bold and fun placement of gems. We decide the balance depending on how comfortable it looks, even though the balance itself may be unstable at times. This is something very sensuous – hard to explain theoretically."

With elements to satisfy all the senses in one design, Atsuko Sano's jewellery presents an intriguing prospect for contemporary jewellery collectors; at once masculine and feminine, smooth and sharp, bold and classic, they're miniature artworks full of pleasing contrasts. "The concept behind simple beauty is one of omitting the unnecessary and keeping what's necessary," she concludes. "I prefer communicating definitely and impressively, over gently and gradually."
— www.as-by-atsuko-sano.com

NORDIC CHIC

Addalit

FROM ADDALIT'S WORKSHOP in Central London, Jonna Jarvenpaa and Laura Vilppula create stunning and unique jewellery for discerning clients from around the world. International customers fly in especially to meet with them, drawn by the quality of Addalit's work and a service that allows clients to customise any piece.

Jonna and Laura both moved to London from Finland at the same time and have been friends ever since. Jonna worked as a model before studying design while Laura studied at the Gemological Institute of America, developing an expertise in diamonds and other precious stones. In 2012, they brought together their shared love of luxury jewellery and design to establish Addalit, creating limited-edition pieces and offering a bespoke and "demi-bespoke" service. "We wanted to make something that stands out," says Jonna. "That's how it all started."

While many jewellery companies outsource production to Asia, all of Addalit's jewellery is made in London. "It's more expensive, which is why a lot of companies don't do it," says Laura. "But we think it's worth it." It also means that Laura and Jonna are personally involved in creating every piece. "We wanted to be part of the whole process," says Laura. "It's very important that it happens here so we can oversee every stage."

The pieces are designed by Jonna, who draws inspiration from her Nordic heritage and also her travels around the world hand-picking gems. "I am constantly travelling," she says, "and it can be anything about the place that inspires me – the architecture, the nature, the heritage, even the lifestyle." Clients can customise any piece they

choose, altering it to suit their own tastes. "You can make small tweaks or changes to any designs or pieces that we already have," she says. "For instance, you can change the colour of the gold, or if you have a favourite stone we can source that."

The women who wear Addalit's jewellery are confident, sophisticated and know what they want. And the bespoke and demi-bespoke service is ideal for men looking for a special gift. "For a lot of men it's not easy choosing jewellery for their partners," says Laura, describing how one customer wanted to buy a special piece of jewellery as an anniversary present but was not sure what his wife would like. Addalit sourced a unique yellow diamond, which he then gave to her as a gift. Laura and Jonna then worked with her through the entire design process to create the perfect design which reflected the client's taste.

Addalit's reputation is such that it has won most of its customers simply by word of mouth. But, in September 2016, Laura and Jonna exhibited their jewellery for the first time, featuring among a select few emerging designers chosen to show at the prestigious International Jewellery London trade event. They used the opportunity to unveil four new rings representing the four seasons in Nordic countries.

Although excited about expanding the brand, Laura and Jonna are clear that Addalit will always remain exclusive. They are committed to working personally with every customer to create something special and unique. And in doing so, they have earned a global reputation for their distinctive, luxury jewellery.

— www.addalit.com

TAKING CENTRE STAGE

George Pragnell

"THE WORD 'LUXURY' has been overused and commoditised by large fashion brands," says Charlie Pragnell. "When jewellers began being associated with this word, they wouldn't have dreamt of making two of anything, just as no artist would wish to duplicate an oil painting. It's how 'luxury' has been redefined. We deal in the original understanding of luxury. For us, true jewellery is art, not fashion."

Since 2010, Charlie has been Managing Director of the master jeweller George Pragnell. He is the grandson of the company's titular founder, a jeweller to Queen Mary who, with his wife Margaret, moved from Maidenhead in 1954 to found a new company in Wood Street, Stratford-upon-Avon.

"We're the third generation of the family to be based in Stratford," says Charlie. "But we're actually drawing from many generations of experience. My mother was the sixth generation of the Bond Street jeweller, Waters and Blott, while my wife, Emily, is a relative of the Garrard family. We've also acquired two very well-established jewellers – George Tarratt of Leicester and Philip Antrobus of Bond Street."

Charlie trained in jewellery design and gemology at the Gemological Institute of America in California, and worked in New York's diamond district before returning to England. Now he and his team of around 70 bring a panoply of different expertise to the firm.

"We have specialists in most areas," he says. "We can repair an antique Georgian barograph with a broken nib. We can have your pearls restrung, find you a matching unheated Burmese ruby if you've lost one of your earrings, take dents out of your Edwardian candlestick, fix your clock, or find a new gold chain for your pendant. We can look after it all under one roof. We have a dozen gemologists on site, and three registered valuers; we have watchmakers

and watch complication specialists who are trained to the highest level; and we have several bench jewellers who now look after customers. When my grandfather founded this company in Stratford, 62 years ago, his watchword was 'Our knowledge is your safeguard'. This is still the case."

As well as curating the firm's collection of new and antique Swiss wristwatches (made by the likes of Patek Philippe, Rolex, Jaeger Le Coultre, Omega and A Lange & Söhne), Charlie sources some of the world's finest gemstones. "It could be it a duck-egg electric-green tourmaline for an important necklace," he says, "or a 2.5 carat baby pink oval diamond for a ring." He also works on the firm's original jewellery with the talented designer Tom Crookenden, another of George's grandsons.

"Our work is heavily influenced by the art deco period," he says, "but we don't want it to look as if it's from the 1920s or 1930s. Because we have an understanding of how jewellery has evolved over the years, we are able to weave fresh and contemporary elements into the design of each piece."

The firm is still based in a wood-framed Tudor building that was designed and built in the 1590s by the carpenter Abraham Stirling, a drinking buddy of William Shakespeare's. Indeed, each April, the family hosts and sponsors the Pragnell Shakespeare Birthday Awards – previous winners have included Trevor Nunn, Kenneth Branagh, Dame Judi Dench, Sir Ian McKellen and Sir Patrick Stewart.

"It's no coincidence that we're based in the home of Shakespeare," says Charlie. "Shakespeare draws in people who are interested in creativity, and creative people from around the world are drawn to the individuality of our pieces. For us, real jewellery is art."
— www.pragnell.co.uk

PRIME TIME

DeWitt

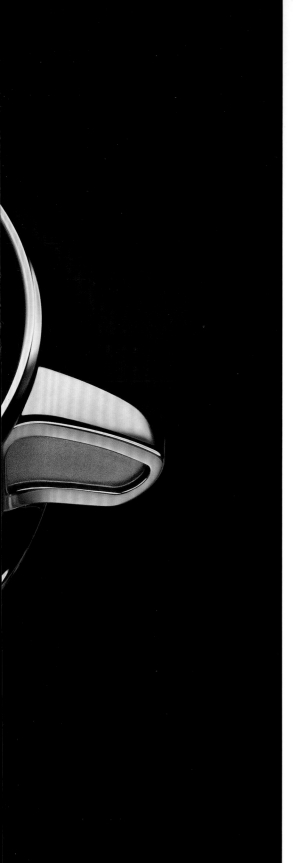

COUNT JÉRÔME DE WITT has always been determined to inject a personal feel into the watches he designs, drawing from his knowledge of disciplines such as music, architecture and mechanics. Although not a watchmaker by training – he is a former investment fund manager – his vision for DeWitt was to create non-conformist and innovative handcrafted watches.

So when his wife Viviane de Witt, who is also the company's CEO, bought two lots containing strands of Napoléon I's hair at an auction of the French emperor's memorabilia, he saw an opportunity to enable admirers of the emperor to wear some of his DNA on their wrists. The personal connection is even stronger as Count de Witt is a direct descendant of King Jérôme-Napoléon Bonaparte, the youngest brother of the early 19th-century French emperor.

Count de Witt carefully placed 0.5 mm slices of Napoléon's locks, certified by a bailiff at the DeWitt factory, inside a limited series of around 300 watches, each of which featured a likeness of Napoleon on the dial. He recalls that people contacted him from around the world wanting to own a watch that contained a relic of Napoléon. "I was astonished to see the reaction," says Count de Witt. "But I could see the pleasure on people's faces when they bought them."

While the Napoléon DNA watch made the headlines, Count de Witt has designed more than 600 different models over the past 13 years. These are made at the company's state-of-the-art factory near Geneva, Switzerland. The base of operations for some 60 highly skilled craftspeople, the factory covers all traditional watchmaking activities, from research, development and design through to production and quality control. DeWitt is also committed to perpetuating watchmaking traditions: it is one of the few remaining brands that still practises the refined 18th- and 19th-century art of guilloché engraving.

Already an avid watch enthusiast with his own private collection, Count de Witt founded the company in 2003 after meeting a watchmaker who inspired him to set up his own watch-manufacturing business. The company now sells its exquisite timepieces across all five continents. "It was a simple idea," he explains. "My inspiration is music, mechanics, architecture and beauty, and when I combine these, I can confidently say that I have produced something different from other brands. This is important for me because when you create something and someone shares your taste and buys one of your designs, they are showing confidence in you and your creation."

With a combination of respect for history, attention to detail and inspirational design, Count de Witt feels that his watches have much in common with luxury cars. "We have the same type of customers," he says. "We are dreamers who strive to make the best quality product and to create an elite club. Part of the dream is that when you make a unique product, people will be proud to wear it or to own it. The same is true of luxury cars and high-quality watches. We have the same goal."

— www.dewitt.ch

INDEPENDENT SPIRIT

Ebba Brahe Jewellery

EBBA BRAHE WAS a 17th-century Swedish countess who famously broke the heart of the king, Gustav II Adolf. Today, her legacy lives on in the work of one of her descendants, Charlotte Ramel, a Stockholm-based jewellery designer whose exquisite pieces aim to capture the power of the great Renaissance beauty.

Since she launched Ebba Brahe Jewellery in 2013, Charlotte has built up a glittering clientele including the Crown Princess Victoria and Princess Sofia of Sweden, and Mary, Crown Princess of Denmark. She creates bold, brilliant pieces that combine history with a sharp, contemporary edge. "I design for modern women who love beautiful things," says Charlotte. "Independent women. Powerful women."

Signature pieces include her dramatic, sapphire-studded "wing" earrings, inspired by Brahe's family crest, and diamond-studded feather earrings. Eclipsed moons shimmer in 18-carat yellow gold and stars are made from clusters of diamonds. Her bear-claw-shaped "Pioneer" pendant is a talismanic piece cast in silver and encrusted with black diamonds. "Bear claws are traditionally a symbol of courage and strength," she explains. "I used these symbols so that it feels very powerful."

Charlotte's fascination with jewellery began as a child, with a pearl necklace that was given to Ebba Brahe by King Gustav II Adolf in 1600. "The necklace was a token of his love and has been in my family for more than 400 years," she says. "I was fascinated by it when I was growing up. It's made from Swedish river pearls that still have an extraordinary lustre and the clasp is five big, old-cut diamonds. It is spectacular."

Inspired to work with jewellery herself, Charlotte applied to be an apprentice with the Swedish designer CF Carlman when she was just 12 years old. In her twenties she studied jewellery at Sotheby's in London before becoming an antique jewellery specialist for Stockholm auction houses. She also studied at the Gemological Institute of America in London, where she learned to grade diamonds.

Charlotte sources her stones from across the globe. "I travel a lot and choose everything myself," she says. "I often use precious stones like emeralds, black diamonds, rubies and sapphires. But I also love rare, semi-precious stones such as nummite, a black gem with flecks of colour, and green onyx. It's known as the Sorceror's Stone and it's said to carry good karma. I found that in Lebanon."

Ebba Brahe remains an inspiration, not just creatively, but professionally. "As well as being the great love of the king, she was a highly intelligent businesswoman and entrepreneur," says Charlotte. "She ran several estates, castles and a mining company, gave birth to 14 children, and died aged 78, when the average lifespan was 60. She was tough and that inspires me. It's tough to build a jewellery brand. You have to not only create and sell, but deal with PR, marketing and find new customers and new markets. With passion you become good at it."

The New York designer Donna Karan is another influence. "I had the great pleasure of meeting her twice," says Charlotte, "and I asked if she had any advice she could offer me. She told me that the secret of a successful brand is storytelling. If you have a good story, you can do anything."

Charlotte's story so far has been remarkable. Who knows what the next chapter will bring?
— www.ebbabrahe.com

STORIED STONES

Kohinoor Jewellers

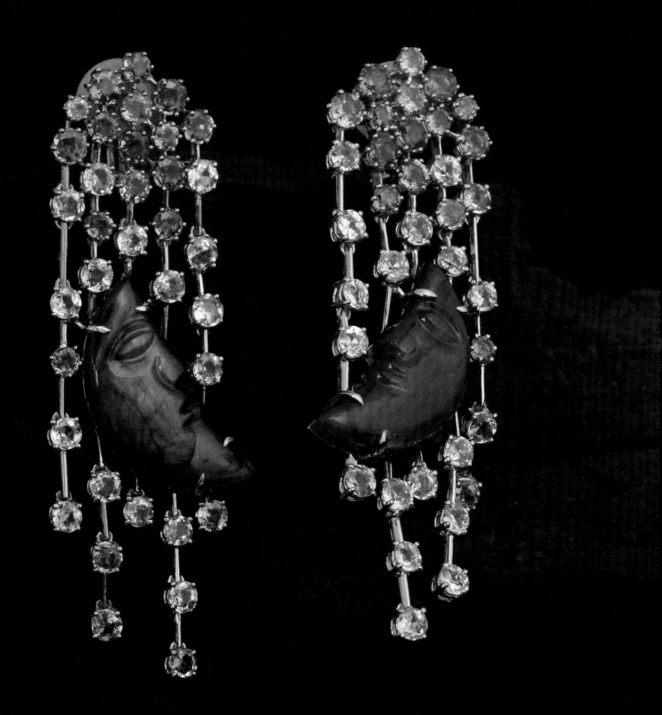

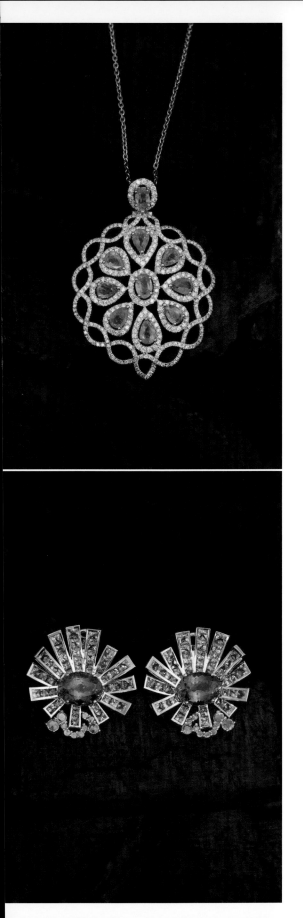

AGRA IS A city steeped in history, famous for the iconic white marble Taj Mahal, built by Mughal emperor Shah Jahan. The former Mughal capital has for centuries also been home to jewellers, artisans and artists inspired by the rich heritage around them.

Family-owned and now in its fifth generation, the exclusive, appointment-only Kohinoor Jewellers creates distinctive pieces for a discerning global clientele. "Our business developed out of our heritage," says owner Ghanshyam Mathur. "Now we work with a contemporary fusion of art and jewellery based on Indian art, architecture and paintings."

The Mathur family's ancestors came to the old walled city of Agra in 1857 with the court of the last Mughal emperor Bahadur Shah Zafar. Since then, the family has collected fine gemstones, jewellery and art, becoming experts in the intricacies of Indian art over the generations. Ghanshyam, like his father before him, is a connoisseur of Indian art collected from diverse regions, periods and religions.

"We never run out of inspiration," he says. "There is so much variety in our past. And of course we have the Taj Mahal itself, which was the inspiration for the Taj Signature Collection." Not that all inspiration comes from distant history. "My son Milind and I play golf, so we created a very successful golf-themed collection," he says. "We also created a collection based on Bharatanatyam, a classical Indian dance, using the shapes and elegance of the dancers."

The artistry and love of colour and pattern in Kohinoor's jewellery is expressed through gemstones of the highest quality. "Our jewellery is all about the stones, sapphires from Sri Lanka, for example, and rubies from Burma," says Ghanshyam. "We tend to buy stones in rough form and cut them to our specification." Often Kohinoor's jewellery begins not with a design but with the gemstones themselves, the design serving to enhance and display their particular qualities.

Fifth-generation Ruchira Mathur is Kohinoor's designer and works alongside her brother Milind Mathur, who is a graduate gemologist, certified by the Gemological Institute of America, and the company's Artistic Director. "They both have a flair for working with gemstones," says Ghanshyam, "It's in their blood." Ruchira and Milind bring a western sensibility to the jewellery collections, attuned to the tastes of the international visitors who come to Agra.

"Our jewellery is exposed to worldwide trends," says Ghanshyam. "Our customers demand the best quality and they know their jewellery. They immediately see that we offer very fine pieces." Each collection from Kohinoor Jewellers is one of a kind.

The company also offers a bespoke jewellery service, which is particularly suited to overseas visitors staying in Agra. The combination of stones and choice of settings are discussed and detailed design options created. The finished pieces are then shipped on completion.

Kohinoor Jewellers exactly defines what Ghanshyam calls "contemporary fusion": the perfect setting of expertly cut gemstones, reflecting the cultural and artistic traditions of India, and a stylish ability to bring these strands together in refined contemporary jewellery. "This fusion of modern, bespoke and heritage comes through in all our work," says Ghanshyam. As in-the-know visitors to Kohinoor Jewellers have discovered, the Taj Mahal isn't the only thing of beauty worth seeing in Agra.
— www.kohinoorjewellers.com

GLOSS LEADER

Ilgiz

RENOWNED RUSSIAN JEWELLER Ilgiz Fazulzyanov entered his profession quite by chance. Born in the Russian Republic of Tatarstan in 1968, he graduated from the Kazan Art School as a painter but a stint of training in traditional jewellery craft set him on a different career path. Friends and acquaintances began to bring the young designer their jewellery with requests to do something special with it.

"My sense of pride prevented me from admitting ignorance and so I had to learn quickly," says Ilgiz. After mastering the jewellery-making techniques and traditions of the Volga Tatars, Ilgiz opened his first workshop in Kazan and began designing his own pieces. At first he produced fine filigree work in the Tatar style and in 1994 he was even awarded a prize from the First International Islamic Artisans-at-Work Festival in Islamabad for his binding of the Quran.

At the same time, Ilgiz began experimenting with different materials and soon discovered enamelling, which quickly became his trademark. "Enamels were a great fit for me because I always thought that metals lack the necessary colours and aren't nuanced enough," he says.

In 2003, the designer established his workshop in Moscow and moved to the Russian capital where access to the Kremlin's museums allowed him to study the rich heritage of European jewellery design. Discovering the works of eminent French art nouveau designer René Lalique was a pivotal moment for Ilgiz. "His pieces conveyed the beauty of nature," he says. "He is the master who inspired me to scale new heights."

With an eye for intricate detail, Ilgiz's delicate designs are redolent of the art nouveau and art deco artistic movements: rings, brooches and pendants set with enamelwork and precious stones feature birds, irises and dragonflies. "I'm inspired by nature and its transient states," he says. "I approach the pieces as objects of art." He carefully sketches out new ideas and makes prototypes from jewellery wax; all pieces are made by hand in his workshop and enamel continues to play a central role. "I work with different enamels – Russian and French – mixing them up to achieve the perfect colour tone."

The majority of his pieces are sold in Moscow to clients who admire his aesthetic and exemplary work ethic. "I always spend a lot of time talking with my clients, learning about their lives and about what they like." Ilgiz's pieces have been bought by museums and private collections in Russia, America, Italy, Britain and Japan, while the Moscow Kremlin Museums have 18 pieces in their permanent collections, including the Butterflies pendant and earrings, which won the International Jewellery Design Award in Hong Kong in 2013. What's more, he is the first living designer to have been honoured with a solo exhibition in the Kremlin.

Ilgiz's soaring success can be attributed to his sensitive combination of tradition and modernity, his exceptional workmanship and his respect for his roots. "I no longer use any traditional techniques of Kazan jewellery," he says, "but I always strive to preserve the airiness of the piece, its lacy weightlessness, which was a signature look of our old masters."
— www.ilgiz.com/en

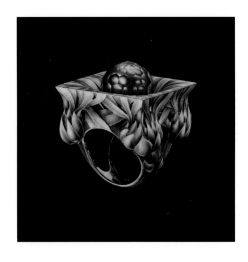

POSITIVELY PRECIOUS

Fsaadallah

EGYPTIAN JEWELLER AND crystal healer Faten Saadallah harnesses the healing powers of precious stones to create unique and personal items of bespoke jewellery in silver and gold. She runs an award-winning atelier – but not in the conventional sense.

"Last month, one of the best actresses in the Middle East was nominated for an Academy Award," she says. "But she had lost self-confidence; she told me she had no hope of winning." Nurturing personal relationships and sharing insights, Faten believes that her role is to help her clients navigate their way through such negativity. "When you open the gates of awareness, clients will embrace it," she says. So Faten told the actress to wear rubies and a red dress to the ceremony. Duly following these instructions, the actress won her award.

Faten studied the impact of stones and how to use them for many years before launching her business in Giza, in the shadow of the pyramids, in 2007. She speaks of the chakras – seven points in the body that are meridians from which energy flows – and how they affect mental and physical health. "I point with my hand and the movement of the pendulum shows me whether the chakras are in balance and where there are weaknesses," she says.

Imbalances are redressed with carefully selected stones, and Faten's clients tell her of their transformative impact. For the actress, the benefit was personal as well as professional. "Her husband didn't want to accompany her to the ceremony, but when you wear rubies, you open your heart to unconditional love," says Faten. "She told him she needed him to go and he did – but more than that,

when they read her name out as the winner, her husband wrapped her in his arms and hugged her so tightly. He didn't want to let her go to the stage to accept her award. It was all the media was talking about for a week!"

From helping a businessman close a pivotal deal with a chain of amber in his left hand to soothing a widow with a bracelet of azurite around her right wrist, "A lot of people say I have a gift – and if so, I thank God that he gave it to me," Faten says. "But I also think that through my experiences I've gained a lot of knowledge. I've travelled the world to learn about crystals, acquire skills and introduce myself to different cultures – and I've been very lucky to learn from the greatest gurus."

Collecting stones from around the world, Faten says she brings them back to her workshop "to cleanse them, alter them with sunlight or water or moonlight, and work with them." Working closely with her team of artisans, her designs range from bold modern pieces to intricate openwork, influenced by European and Arabic traditions, and Egyptian folk art. Faten's pieces are always designed to address specific needs and deficiencies. For example, "If someone lacks vision and needs to calm their fear, I'd combine carnelian and lapis lazuli," she says. It's about harnessing positive energy and protecting her clients from the negativity around them.

"I create jewellery to help people find peace and balance," Faten says. She delivers above and beyond the norm for a jeweller, helping her clients not only look good but also thrive, succeed – and even win the occasional award.

— www.fsaadallah.com

VIENNESE WHIRL

Anna Inspiring Jewellery

"I CALL MYSELF an 'inventor', rather than a jewellery designer," says Anna Ausserladscheider, the driving creative force behind her eponymous jewellery brand. After many years of working in the luxury-retail sector – designing handbags and working in interiors – Anna decided to focus on jewellery and opened her first shop in the heart of Vienna in 2009.

"I'm a positive person, I thrive on happiness and lightness, and people can feel this in my designs," she says. "I like to create pieces that are almost naive in their simplicity, that bring out the little girl in any woman; the idea is that people can feel young again."

Most of the jewellery by Anna Inspiring Jewellery is handmade in the company's workshop in Vienna by master craftspeople, while Anna looks after the designs. The majority of these are made from 18-carat rose and white gold and feature diamonds, pearls and other gemstones. Bracelets and rings come engraved with positive missives – or are left blank for customers to dream up their own good-luck charms. The brand's pendants and rings carry symbolic shapes such as butterflies, stars and hearts.

"The main idea is to deliver positive thoughts when someone wears or looks at my designs," says Anna. Her line is elegant and full of charm, with rings and necklaces fine enough to layer up for a striking look or to wear on their own. She also offers engagement rings and wedding bands, which are known for their timeless elegance.

Anna Haute is the brand's more heavyweight jewellery line, offering pieces that can be made to order. Bespoke gemstones are used and a lot of attention is paid to the interplay of matte and smooth surfaces. The jewellery often has an antique Viennese feel, while the rings from the Haute collection are more edgy.

Male customers are not overlooked by Anna, and she has created a line of minimalist bangles and simple wristbands that suit all ages and tastes. "When it comes to inspiration, I am always looking around at visual details," she says, "be it architecture or what people are wearing." Her stores also carry sterling-silver framed jewellery boxes and a selection of zesty and light eau de parfums, also created by the designer.

Aside from the jewellery, the Anna brand is known and loved for its sumptuous stores and glamorous window displays. With shops in Vienna, New York, Munich and a brand new store in London's Marylebone, Anna has created her own universe full of feminine charm and glamour. Unique pieces of furniture can be found in store, where the Anna Girls, with their trademark braids and red lips, serve customers old and new. The welcoming windows always have fresh flowers and beautifully handmade tutu dresses.

"I was experimenting with making and creating from a young age," says Anna. "I have always wanted to invent something, so I've come up with a whole universe where the jewellery and the way it's presented is really special. Everything is thought out – furniture, uniforms – I've created an entire world."
— www.annaij.com

CHOREOGRAPHED JEWELLERY

Biiju

JOANNA BOYEN, THE designer behind Biiju, has a nomadic past which influences her jewellery. "The walls of Machu Picchu look simple," she says, "but they are the essence of bespoke. Each stone is unique, yet has an intimate relationship with the others. Bespoke starts with understanding each individual element of form and function, and that includes the person for whom the piece is destined."

Joanna's clients come from all over the globe for her pieces, which are handmade in London's jewellery district of Hatton Garden. "Having something commissioned for you is a very personal experience," she says. "It's a journey that is exciting and incredibly rewarding for all involved." On delivery each client is given a keepsake – a special scrapbook tracing the evolution of the piece from concept to completion.

"Machines can make jewellery that looks good," says Joanna. "But, in the end, perfection comes from feeling. Fine jewellery needs to be handmade." Now Biiju's bespoke services are complemented by ready-to-wear collections in 18-carat gold, silver and precious stones. The "Careless Rhythm" collection evokes the sand dunes of Africa where Joanna grew up; the rose gold in the "Satin Ribbon" collection recalls her time in Russia and her professional dance training; while the exquisitely hand-woven silver pieces reflect her life in Peru.

"I think fine jewellery has to work for you," says Joanna, "otherwise you can only wear it occasionally." She is passionate about versatility and has made it a signature feature of Biiju designs, something that is captured perfectly by the "Kaleidoscope" collection. The "huggy" (a clasp) is the key element, serving as the ultimate partner which "dances" with all the other pieces. It can be used to hug a diamond pendant to an 18-carat gold chain to make a necklace, or attached to a graceful hook to be worn as an earring.

"Interchange and accessorise to your heart's content," says Joanna. "The possibilities are endless." So take a huggy and find a partner.
— www.biiju.com

SECOND TO NONE

Vacheron Constantin

ON 17 SEPTEMBER 1755 in Geneva, a 24-year-old master watchmaker called Jean-Marc Vacheron hired an apprentice and the firm known today as Vacheron Constantin was born. Ever since, his successors have produced high-quality artisanal timepieces, making it the world's oldest watch manufacturer in continuous production.

"We've been going for more than 260 years without a single gap in our archives," says CEO Juan-Carlos Torres. "It means that all our models are archived, so we can even repair one of our 18th-century timepieces if needs be. Sometimes we remake ancient tools to treat the components faithfully. We're the only company that does this."

Vacheron Constantin balances three elements of craftsmanship: technical accuracy, aesthetics and hand-finishing. All movements are hand-finished and decorated to the highest level possible, whether visible or not, exceeding even the rigorous stipulations of the Hallmark of Geneva. The firm's designers take inspiration from anything, be it fine art, travel or even nature – for example, Victorian botanical illustrations from Kew Gardens – and also update classic Vacheron Constantin models from the archives. The Métiers d'Art processes of enamelling, engraving, *guillochage* (decorative lathe turning) can be inspired by historical art and craftsmanship works dating from the middle ages, up to new artists of today.

Vacheron Constantin also provides a bespoke design service, with "cabinotiers" who work on anything from personalised engraving to watches made from scratch. One commission, known as Reference 57260 (pictured), took three watchmakers eight years to complete. "It was commissioned by a collector and is today known as the most complex watch ever made, with 57 different complications," says Juan-Carlos. "We were proud to be part of watchmaking history."

This contribution is important to Vacheron Constantin. With its continued use of apprenticeships and its educational partnerships, the firm is dedicated to the promotion of craftsmanship. "We sponsor London Craft Week," says Juan-Carlos, "which aims to put fine craftsmanship on centre stage in the UK."

The company's age-old motto sums up this ethos: "Do better if possible, and that is always possible." After more than 260 years, it's a commitment that still informs Vacheron Constantin's creations.
— www.vacheron-constantin.com

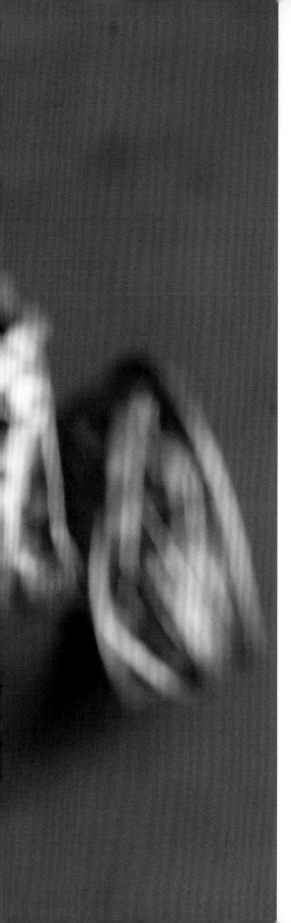

NATURE'S BOUNTY

Ann Pamintuan

ANN TIUKINHOY PAMINTUAN is a designer whose imaginative scope and love of raw materials have evolved as organically as the flora and fauna that inspire her furniture, furnishings and accessories. Romantic, distinctive and contemporary, her creative output is something of a sensation in the Philippines, where she works and lives. As one of a prestigious group of Filipino artists, Ann is exploring and pushing the boundaries of modern Asian art and design. "I wanted to be an architect," says Ann, "but my father suggested I do something more ladylike!"

Whether she is designing life-sized horses and giraffes for an outdoor park exhibit in Manila, a bespoke trunk show of her latest jewellery line, or a limited-run exhibit in a Tokyo airport, Ann Pamintuan welds her metal medium as though she were spinning satin ribbons – deliberately and gracefully in order to conjure the visions in her mind to life. These are highly sculptural pieces that are fluid and flowing, yet always disciplined and delicate.

Such impressive output makes it hard to believe Ann has received no formal design training. What she has always had, however, is a love of Ikebana – the Japanese art of flower arranging – which nurtured a fascination with natural forms. Some of her hand-made jewellery caught a local shopkeeper's eye.

"I started making jewellery and bags," she says, "eventually exploring home décor and sculpture before moving on to furniture." Ann's style is often a direct homage to nature. She works with nature's designs – be they leaves, blooms, twigs, roots, bark, chillies or even dragonflies – and renders them into finely detailed pieces, large and small.

"Everything I produce is entirely designed and completed by me," she says, "whether it is making a gold, leaf-shaped cuff, or sculpting a large piece in copper wire or cast iron." Ann will often take the source materials directly from nature – be they flowers, chillies or shells – and electroplates the organic matter in gold, silver or copper. It lends the jewellery an authenticity and ensures that nature's bounty is given permanence.

Her sculptural forms and furniture design are often more abstractly organic, taking influence from her first love, architecture. "I particularly love the Catalan architect Antoni Gaudí," she says, "especially that fluidity and movement of natural form in a building." That Ann should also work with entirely organic materials is no coincidence. Using the fifth Chinese "element" – metal – Ann shapes and bends her creations by hand at her Davao City studio, and all the art is made in the Philippines.

Ann is inspired to think beyond jewellery design and creates her *objets d'art* on a variety of scales. Recent exhibitions of her work have included the curvaceous "Cocoon" outdoors furniture collection, and an installation of life-sized horses in Greenbelt ArtPark, each of which features her signature sense of movement and spark of imagination.

Her book *Romancing Nature in Metal* is a detailed portrait of her fascination with natural forms and materials; whether reflecting the roots of a tree in a collection of stacked rings or creating a hillside sculpture inspired by bird flight.

Ann Pamintuan specialises in making the delicate and fleeting both immutable and beautiful. Using nature's materials and forms, this Filipino artist combines a wealth of imagination with a world of inspiration.
— www.annpamintuan.com

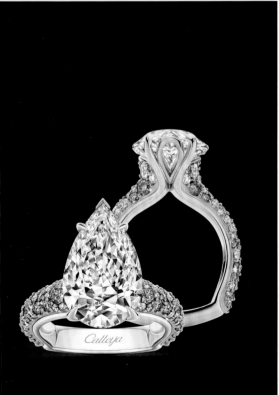

PRETTY IN PINK

Calleija Jewellers

A PINK DIAMOND is more than just a girl's best friend. This gemstone is among the world's rarest jewels and features in many designs of John Calleija, the master craftsman behind Calleija Jewellers. Based in Queensland, Australia, Calleija is a company that goes to exceptional lengths to select coveted and incomparable gems for its clients.

"While embracing new technologies, we design and create individual jewels that start with the sourcing of each gemstone," says John. "Each diamond or gemstone selected exhibits characteristics worthy of an heirloom masterpiece to be cherished for generations."

As well as quality, Calleija also insists that its jewels meet high ethical standards. Most pink diamonds are from the Argyle mine in Australia's East Kimberley region. For more than 30 years, Calleija has been an Argyle Pink Diamond Select Atelier, part of an exclusive network exercising the highest standards of care and custody in the supply chain. Calleija's Argyle pink diamonds were even worn by the celebrity campaigner Livia Firth not once but twice at the Oscars Green Carpet Challenge, the sustainable and ethical fashion initiative she founded. Calleija's strict moral credentials in sourcing its gems made the bespoke brand an ideal choice for Livia.

Another high-profile partnership that Calleija enjoys is with Zara Phillips MBE. In 2015, John and the Olympic medal-winning horsewoman and granddaughter to Her Majesty The Queen created an eponymous equestrian-themed collection. Exclusive pieces include a "Saddle" platinum ring edged with white diamonds. "What we created reflects the spirit of unbridled elegance," says John. "It intertwines my passion for precision with Zara Phillips's passion for all things equestrian."

No request is too much of a challenge – or too unusual – for John and his team to execute. They have created diamond-covered buttons for one woman to wear on her designer jeans, as well as the world's most expensive champagne glasses (made from platinum and featuring 1,600 pink diamonds). For The Queen's Diamond Jubilee, the mining corporation Rio Tinto commissioned Calleija to make something special. John obliged with a diamond, pink diamond and platinum sculpture complete with its own security showcase displayed at Kensington Palace.

"It's a joy to sit with a client to create a one-off piece that resembles their personality and style," says John. "The essence of what we do is treating our clients to a magical combination of beauty, artistic flair and integrity."

Of course, a business is only as good as the people who work for it, and Calleija is no exception. Its three boutiques – in London, Sydney and the Gold Coast – are run by a talented team who are "driven by passion and who strive for perfection", according to John. It is the strengths and abilities of the team that give Calleija its competitive edge in the marketplace. "The company is creative and progressive," he says, "and we nurture these qualities by employing people who share our obsession with the best jewellery design, with innovation and proficiency."

Although Calleija is expanding on its boutiques to showcase its global brand partnerships, the aim is to maintain a service that always offers clients handcrafted jewellery designs, rather than generic and mass-produced items. With its combined appeal of being an ethical brand and one that crafts bespoke pieces, Calleija looks set to be the jeweller of choice for many generations to come.
— www.calleija.com

RENAISSANCE WOMAN

Elizabeth Gage

FOR CELEBRATED BRITISH jewellery designer Elizabeth Gage, inspiration always starts with the stones. "When I see a jewel I like, I immediately know what to do with it," she says. "It could be a South Sea pearl that I'll string onto a necklace or a fire opal that I'll set with black jade. It's very instinctive."

This approach has served her well for over five decades. Ever since she began crafting bold, original jewellery in the late 1960s, Elizabeth's achievements have been as dazzling as her creations. She won her first commission from Cartier in 1968 and was awarded the De Beers Diamonds International Award in 1972. In 1989, she received the prestigious Queen's Award for Export Achievement, and her diamond encrusted Agincourt ring, which has been hailed as a masterpiece, now sits in the permanent collection of the V&A Museum in London.

Elizabeth's creativity and craftsmanship has influenced generations of designers, yet she remains unaffected by modernity. Instead, her inspiration comes from the Renaissance courts, the romance of the Knights Templar and the vivid colours of the natural world. Catherine the Great is also an enduring muse. "I first became aware of the intense beauty of jewellery from admiring pictures of her in a book," says Elizabeth. "She had great taste. She loved to wear beautiful things. What woman doesn't?"

Elizabeth was inspired to create her first ring after a visit to the British Museum in her twenties. "I was looking for a ring that I could wear from day into night, but I couldn't find one I liked," she says. "Then I chanced upon a collection of Roman rings.

They were exactly the kind of thing I wanted. They had soul. I could hardly believe my luck."

After training at the Sir John Cass College in London, she made her first ring – a wide gold band studded with amethysts and peridots. "I wanted diamonds and rubies but I didn't have the money," she says. "When it was finished, to my surprise the very small stones made it look like an ancient carpet. It didn't look modern at all – I loved that."

Nowadays, her virtuoso vision transforms white opals into unicorns, yellow tourmalines into owls and spotted agate into leopards. Her Belgravia showroom glitters with mandarin garnets, luminous moonstones and enormous diamonds, each set in a one-of-a-kind ring, necklace or pin. No two pieces are alike.

Clients have included Lauren Bacall, who commissioned Elizabeth in the 1980s and 1990s. "She was a very beautiful, strong-looking lady of quality," Elizabeth remembers, "and her style was unusual." An Indian-inspired pin she created for Bacall made the news in 2015 when it was auctioned at Bonhams for £16,597, more than four times its pre-sale estimate.

"Making history wearable" is how one client has described the way Elizabeth weaves the past into her own exquisite museum pieces. "Like every artist, I learned to walk in the steps of others until I could walk on my own," she wrote in her 2003 book, *The Unconventional Gage*. And, after half a century at the forefront of British jewellery design, Elizabeth isn't just inspired by history. She has earned a place in it, too.
— www.elizabeth-gage.com

QUEEN OF THE STONE AGE

Doris Hangartner

"WHEN YOU FIND the right gem, magic happens," says Doris Hangartner, founder of the Swiss jewellery company that bears her name. And, if quality, cut, colour and clarity are at the heart of every piece, it is individuality and understated flair that set her bespoke creations and carefully sourced stones apart.

Based in Zurich, Doris works with select lapidary companies to track down the perfect stones, many of which have an unusual provenance. Master goldsmiths in Switzerland then bring all her clever designs to life; these might include, for instance, earrings with stones that can be interchanged to ensure they suit any occasion. Her goldsmiths also specialise in finding contemporary materials in which to set Doris's favourite coloured gems, such as the bright blue and green Paraiba tourmalines, mined first in Brazil in 1989 and more recently in Mozambique. Lavender blue ceramic makes the colours in a tanzanite sing, for example, while matt-black carbon offsets a dazzling mandarin garnet.

Always sleekly elegant with a modern touch, Doris's creations appeal to a more discerning buyer or collector. "You need to be a bit of a connoisseur to really know and appreciate what you're wearing," she says. "These gems are so fascinating, so intricate, they have these different colours and you need to know more about them and where they are from."

Much of Doris's inspiration comes from the stone itself, which dictates how it should be used. As a result, she's both particular and determined when it comes to finding the right gem. One red spinel was sourced from Mahenge in Tanzania after two years searching for a gem with the perfect warm orange-red flashes. Others come from closed or nearly worked-out mines, such as an aquamarine from the original Santa Maria mine in Brazil, adding interest and rarity to its value.

"It's all in the ingredients," she says. "It's like enjoying simple but very good food – imagine eating the freshest pasta with delicious tomato sauce. How does one gem resonate with another? What enhances them? Which combinations are best?"

This deep appreciation has inspired other product lines that appeal to all five senses: first came a range of perfumes and scented candles, which was followed by a collection of handmade chocolates. Calming peridot, uplifting Paraiba tourmaline, fiery red diamond or red spinel, and warm imperial topaz are the starting point, with each creation attempting to capture the sensation that the gems provoke, such as a pop of vodka in the chocolate, inspired by the invigorating colour of a Paraiba tourmaline.

After sight, touch, scent and taste, Doris moved into the worlds of music and dance. She collaborated with dancers, choreographers and musicians to create the Gem Dance Collection's first ballet with tango music, all inspired by the red spinel. Doris has also collaborated with contemporary artist Lisa Sharpe, whose paintings are matched to a particular gem. Together they have created "gem art fusion", appealing to those investors who also enjoy collecting loose stones.

At the heart of her approach is the individual and his or her affinity with a particular stone. "There's the perfect harmony, a piece that's completely in tune with your personality, with your presence," she says. And that is when the magic happens.
— www.dorishangartner.com

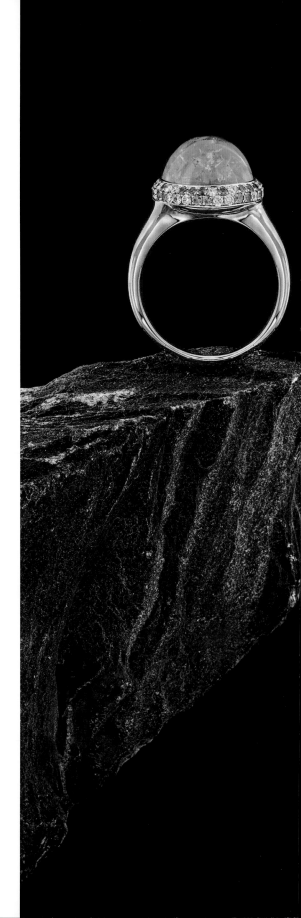

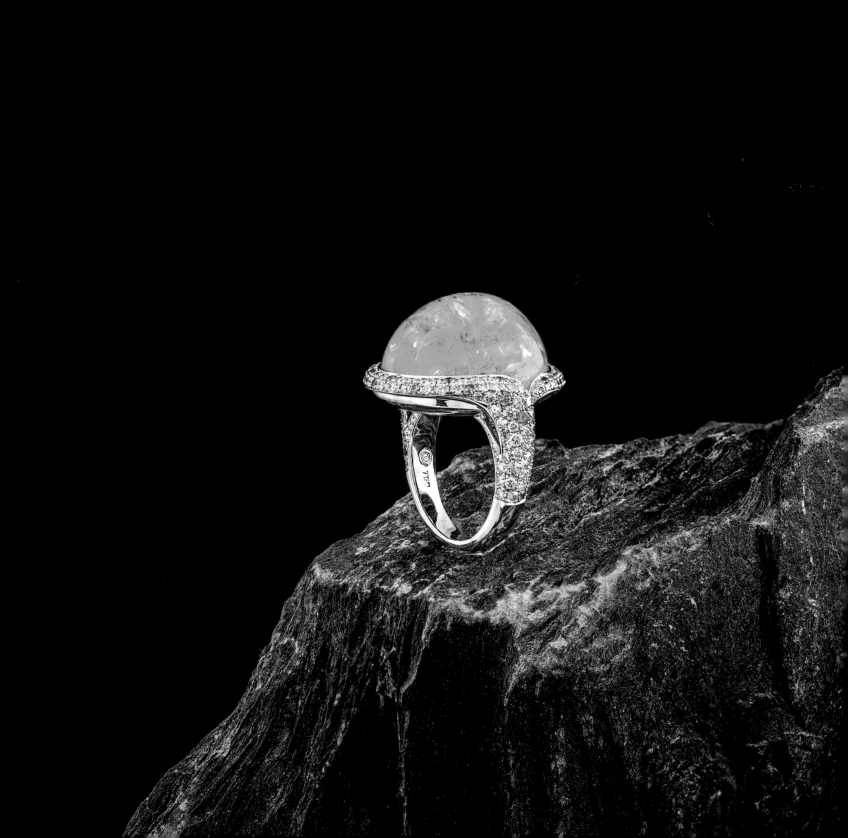

A SPARKLING CELEBRATION

Gems Pavillion

"JEWELLERY IS THE universal language of celebrations," says Piya Ahchariyasripong. "By creating exquisite pieces of fine jewellery for our customers we give them something that makes every day feel like a celebration."

Piya is Sales and Marketing Director of the exclusive Bangkok-based jewellery house Gems Pavilion. He talks animatedly about what he sees as the life-enhancing properties of perfectly crafted, limited-edition and one-of-a-kind jewellery.

"When Gems Pavilion was founded in 1996," says Piya, "the aim was quite simply to be the best jeweller in Thailand. Perfectionism is in my DNA, and this quality has been passed down to everyone in our company." In 2017, Gems Pavilion celebrates its 20th anniversary as one of Thailand's preeminent jewellers, and it also has plans to expand locally and internationally in the near future.

A standout bespoke commission from 2015 was a dazzling 236-carat tiara. It took more than six months to source the round- and pear-shaped diamonds set within it and a further eight months to create it.

"We have 20 years of expertise in making beautiful designs," says International Relations Director Pranisa Achariyasripong, "and every year we offer something new and special to our customers."

From an initial team of three, Gems Pavilion has expanded to employ more than 200 highly skilled designers, gem experts, stone setters and precision jewellery manufacturers. "Creating fine jewellery means that both the design and the materials need to be of the finest quality," says Piya. "If you have a magnificent design but use poor quality materials, you can't create marvellous jewellery, even with the finest craftsmanship."

The company's team of expert Thai and Italian designers produces some 12,000 designs each year. "But we only consider one in 50 for possible production," says Pranisa. "Our customers demand that level of perfection."

When working on bespoke creations, a preliminary interview with the client about personal taste and lifestyle will guide the designers towards an initial concept, using sketches and computer-assisted-design imaging. "Actually, we know most of our customers and they trust our style, designs, taste and craftsmanship," says Pranisa.

The balance and elegance of each piece combine, as Piya puts it, "to make women beautiful, to enhance their own beauty without overpowering it." Gems Pavilion creates contemporary classics that celebrate a woman's distinctive style. While each piece is unique, it is made with such intuitive skill and understanding of the client's taste that it perfectly suits her and complements her look and lifestyle.

"When we make jewellery pieces, we believe that love and happiness are the most important components," says Piya. "We also believe that this positive sentiment is passed on, through the artisan production process, towards the customer."
— www.gemspavilion.com

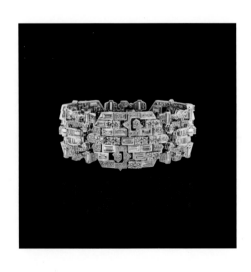

PIECE DE RESISTANCE

Lito Jewellery

WHEN A CUSTOMER entered Lito's Athens boutique asking why the opal in the centre of the custom-made, coloured diamond pavé ring she'd bought kept turning transparent, the designer wasn't perturbed.

"While travelling in India, I'd learned that real opals change colour when they are placed in water, losing their milky whiteness," says Lito Karakostanoglou. "After a bit of detective work, it turned out that my customer was keeping the ring on when she washed her hands, getting it wet. I was able to reassure her that it is the nature of opals to absorb water, so her ring was a pure original!"

Lito travels all over the world – from Africa to Mexico to Japan – to source gems and materials for her handmade, unique jewellery designs. She designs and sells both her own themed collections and bespoke pieces for clients. "For me, jewellery is the most powerful, personal expression of individual style," she says.

Her collections offer a rare combination of luxurious, time-gone-by craftsmanship alongside a refreshingly modern take on jewellery, producing pieces that are not only decorative, but also become everyday objects of desire. "I blend contemporary techniques and influences with older ones, creating diverse and original styles that are timeless."

She began her career almost by accident, while studying for a master's degree in advertising in Boston. "A friend and I went to a bead shop and started experimenting and making bracelets for friends," she recalls. "I loved being creative and I realised that this was, in fact, what I was meant to do with my life."

In 1999, she returned to Athens and opened her first shop. Five years later, deciding that she needed to acquire more skills, she moved to Paris to study sculpture, drawing and wax technique. Apprenticeships with Kenzo and Jean Paul Gaultier followed, before she returned to Athens and, in 2006, reopened her boutique, Lito's Cabinet de Curiosites, together with her own atelier and distribution company.

Her jewellery can now be bought in stores across the world and also online via websites including Net-a-Porter, Luisaviaroma and Twistonline, with a wide range of prices. Her most popular collection, "Tu es Partout", is made up of pieces, such as pendants and earrings, with a bejewelled eye at the centre. Each eye is hand painted by a Russian iconographer and then enamelled and crafted with diamonds, sapphires or rubies.

"The eye is traditionally a culturally diverse symbol of protection," says Lito, "but for me it symbolises something more modern too. It's about being present in the moment, mirroring your soul, and observing the beauty and truth both inside of you and in the world. It's a surrealistic 'talisman' with a different story for each person, that winks playfully at the world and reminds you to keep your eyes open, to look, observe and create."

Lito's personal favourite collection is titled "Scarabées de Beauté" and was designed for Galerie BSL in Paris in 2009. Inspired by the mythical properties of the sacred scarab and its innate beauty, it uses both real insects – preserved specimens from the Philippines, Peru, Costa Rica, Thailand and Madagascar – set in gold and diamonds, and jewelled ones, which are then inlaid into boxes and frames, with mirrors, silks and velours. Pieces can either be worn on the body or displayed in cases or frames, like works of art.

"It's all about how you can imitate nature at its best, and bringing this small animal back to life," she says. "Nature has always been my biggest inspiration – particularly light, which is nature's greatest wonder."

The "Hive" collection is based on the beauty of honeycombs, using rose cut diamonds to play with light and form. The influence of nature can also be seen in the "Peacock" collection, which is inspired by the colours and patterns of the creature's magnificent feathers. "From Hinduism to Christianity, the peacock feather is a symbol of good fortune and immortality," says Lito. "This collection is full of art deco and art nouveau influences, using enamel through a traditional *vitraux* stained-glass technique."

Lito often works on more than one collection simultaneously, and she doesn't always start the design process by sketching: "Often it begins from sourcing an interesting material, or a stone, which leads my creativity and dictates how the piece will evolve," she explains. "It is a spontaneous, organic process. I work directly on the model

and, depending on the seasons, or my mood, this can develop in the most unexpected ways. My early, self-taught years in jewellery-making have worked to my advantage, giving me the freedom and spontaneity to create with no preconceptions or set rules, so I can come up with unorthodox designs and unconventional combinations."

Her newest collection, "Infinite", is all about going back to basics, to the "essential". Influenced by vintage watch quadrants, it employs sleek lines, simple shapes and gentle curves in geometric shapes, fashioned in pure gold.

Featured in *The New Jewellers* (Thames & Hudson), an anthology of rising talent, Lito's designs attract the avant-garde and the unconventional. Celebrity clients have included music producer and rapper Jay Z, actors Dakota Johnson, Tilda Swinton, and Kate Beckinsale, and fashion designer Tory Burch.

Lito believes that the jewellery you choose shows your personality: it embodies the sort of person you are, or the person you'd like to be. "The type of woman who wears Lito jewellery embraces life," says Lito. "She is modern, unpretentious and fresh. She's the kind of woman who mixes vintage fashion with the latest trends, a classic blazer with sneakers. She has a style of her own. I'd call her Bobo – a combination of bohemian and bourgeois. She is chic, open-minded, at times a bit eccentric, but always free and confident to be herself. Lito is about celebrating your individuality."
— www.lito-jewelry.com

GLAM ROCKS

Karp Jewellery

FOR SMIT VIRANI, the jewellery we wear needs to fit not just the body but also the personality. "It doesn't matter if it's a pendant or a bracelet," says the high-profile Director of Karp Jewellery. "Our designers create each piece individually in the same way a tailor makes a bespoke suit. At Karp we try to exceed our customers' expectations – to craft pieces that even the customer could not have imagined."

Karp is able to achieve and maintain such standards through its dedicated design centre, Studio 361. "Our designers work with our management team to identify and respond to the latest trends and customer designs to create captivating designs," says Smit. Studio 361's work is supported by manufacturing units in China and in Surat, India. These state-of-the-art facilities are able to execute the most demanding designs with consistent perfection.

Karp is also one of the select few companies to have Sightholder status, something granted by De Beers Global Sightholder Sales in 1993. "This privilege allows us to source the best diamonds in the world," says Smit. "We also endeavour to ensure that our diamonds are conflict-free and conform to the most stringent ethical standards in the industry."

Karp designs pieces in all varieties, from simple to luxurious. They can also grace any occasion, from intimate moments to grand events. "We know how much a piece of jewellery can mean to someone," says Smit. "A person can form an emotional connection with a piece, and we always seek to give that the ultimate respect it deserves, through our attention to detail in every aspect of the piece. Each small detail integrates precisely into the larger design."

At the same time, Karp strives to create pieces that a client will feel is worth the price.

"We accommodate each design within those specifications and requirements," says Smit. "We aspire to make each moment special with our jewellery."

The centrepiece of Karp's range is the FengHuang collection, named after the legendary Chinese firebird. "It epitomises all the best in Karp," says Smit. "The smallest of details is an exposition in fine artistic detail on its own, and the design as a whole is grand and luxurious, fitted with diamonds of exquisite colours and varying sizes, In Chinese mythology, the FengHuang is known for its vibrant plumage and reigns over all others." At the mass-market end, the jeweller has enjoyed considerable success with Karp Cluster – a range which gives the illusion of a large diamond by "clustering" stones tightly together.

Diamonds are a core speciality for the company, including rare, D-grade diamonds, sought after for their pure, colourless quality. Only a handful of 20-carat D-grade gems exist in the world – but exclusivity is everything for those among Karp's customer base, which includes celebrities and the super-rich.

"Our customers are looking for pieces which are unique," says Smit. "They are seeking investment-based luxury. Everything we create has unparalleled detailing, quality and finish. This means I know what rough diamonds I need to buy, and at what time to ensure that our clients' demands are always met."

Through a combination of keeping ahead of fashion and being obsessed with sourcing the finest-grade gems, Karp lives up to its reputation for exclusive gems of the finest quality. This is a firm that deserves its motto: "a synonym of perfection".

— www.karpjewellery.com

A STAND-OUT SUCCESS

Carolyn Lo

ANY SHOPPER WHO has wasted hours trudging round stores and searching the internet in vain knows what it's like to be Carolyn Lo. "I wanted to wear beautiful jewellery but I couldn't find designs I liked," she recalls. "They just weren't for sale!" Carolyn's solution was possibly more extreme than most people's, however: "I started to design for myself."

As it turns out, this was the perfect plan. Today, the Taiwan-based jeweller's one-of-a-kind brooches, earrings, rings, necklaces and bracelets sell for between $5,000 and $45,000.

Carolyn's work has a unique freedom, fluidity and creativity that possibly stems from the very thing she feared might hold her back – her lack of formal training. "There are no rules," she says of her methods and style. But this has brought challenges.

"I hand-sketch designs," she says, "and, when I started out, my concepts weren't what the goldsmiths were used to. The gold they used tended to be heavy and bulky. I like fine and delicate things with a lot of detail. That's a lot of work to produce! So I really had to search for people who would make my pieces." Luckily, the grace and popularity of the results enabled Carolyn to build a strong team of craftspeople. "They're all based in Taiwan," she adds. "I'm very proud to be able to say that."

Initially designing for friends, her reputation and client base grew quickly. Pretty soon, Carolyn had blossomed from a passionate consumer into a skilled designer and successful businesswoman.

In 2013, she opened her boutique in the fashionable Tien Mu neighbourhood of Taipei – which is particularly popular with well-heeled expats from the UK, the US and Japan. There, she sells both her own pieces and custom work. "People bring me their ideas, stones or jewellery to redesign," she explains.

Defining Carolyn's style is as easy as it is broad. "It's about celebrating the stones," she says. "Until I find a setting and a design that honours each gem, I won't touch it." Her pieces are therefore complex and considered – elegant, intricate and joyful, sensitively embracing colour. "It's all about finding harmony."

As for the future, while Carolyn hopes to open a second shop in London or New York, she is determined to keep her business bespoke.

Trade shows in Hong Kong and Singapore in 2014 brought international customers, as well as offers to work with new companies and manufacturers. "I'm happy the way I am," says Carolyn. "Everything is hand-made. I'm not interested in mass production. Everything becomes ordinary then; nothing stands out."

That's crucial to this designer, whose very raison d'etre was to buck the trend and fill a gap in the market. "It's why I don't repeat my designs," says Carolyn, "and that sometimes gets me into trouble with the customer! They see something they like and want one the same, but I say no. I'll make them something in the same style, but the colour or size of the stone will be different, or some element of the design will change."

It all stems from that original, frustrating shopping dilemma. "People come to me because they want something different – so I'll give them that. And when I show them the finished piece," she concludes, "they understand that it's perfect for them, and that it's the only one like that in the world." — www.carolynlo.com

JEWEL IDENTITY

Joanna Dahdah

JOANNA DAHDAH IS busy tidying her desk. Torn-out magazine clippings and sketches on the backs of shopping lists flutter out from between scattered papers as she sweeps everything aside to clear her work surface. Next, she lights a scented candle and puts out a vase of fresh flowers, then lines up a set of new drawing pens ready for the creative process to begin.

"This is the little ritual I go through before creating a new collection," says the 29-year-old jewellery designer, who works out of her base in Beirut's exclusive Achrafieh district. Today, Joanna is focusing on her latest line, a collection of delicate, diamond-orientated designs entitled Constellation, in which stones of different sizes are arranged to mimic stars in the night sky. "I draw inspiration from the things I see, such as nature and art," she says.

Edgy, but eminently wearable, Joanna's early designs were quick to attract attention, appearing on the pages of Italian *Vogue* before winning her Best Newcomer 2010 at London Jewellery Week and launching her onto the design scene.

Joanna's debut collection, Muse, was inspired by the works of Gustav Klimt – an approach influenced by her education at London's prestigious Central St Martins School of Art and Design. "We were taught to always think outside the box," she says. It was there that she developed an unconventional sense of beauty paired with an instinctive understanding of materials and unique craftsmanship. After graduating, she gained gemologist credentials at California's Gemological Institute of America before returning to her native Beirut to launch the flagship Joanna Dahdah boutique.

At present, the firm is busy expanding in the Middle East, with two new boutiques in Beirut and a growing presence in Dubai, establishing its place among leading jewellery designers in the region's most dynamic and fashionable cities. However, Joanna was born in Paris, and plans to launch a store there in the future. "Having been brought up in Europe," she says, "I appeal to both European and Arabic markets. I manage to mix both worlds in my work."
— www.joannadahdah.com

DRAWING ON TRADITION

Augustine Jewels

WHEN ALEXANDRA MORRIS Robson founded luxury jewellery brand Augustine Jewels in 2013, she brought her contemporary vision to a historic London site. The art nouveau setting of Augustine Studios was originally part of the famous design group Silver Studios, which produced fabric, wallpaper and metalwork for British institutions such as Liberty between 1860 and the 1960s.

"We have tried to incorporate the heritage into the brand," says Alexandra. "With Augustine Jewels, the focus is very much on reviving the tradition for design and exquisite craftsmanship in England; everything is made here. Our showroom is in West London, our workshop is in East London, and we source diamonds and stones from all over the world."

Alexandra is highly qualified in this field, having earned international qualifications and awards in fashion and bespoke jewellery design, as well as training with the GIA (Gemological Institute of America) in diamond and coloured-stone grading. These days, Augustine Jewels commissions may lead her to source an exceptional yellow diamond or a Burmese pigeon's-blood ruby to create a unique luxury piece, and a key point is that all of the natural gemstones and fine metals used are also ethically sourced, with reference to the Kimberley Process Certification Scheme.

Augustine Jewels produces two fine collections each year, and was recently shortlisted by the National Association of Jewellers for Jewellery Designer of the Year 2015. The company's jewellery has also drawn attention on the red carpet, as worn by screen and music stars such as Amy Willerton. Alexandra collaborates with her Creative Director Jazz on both the collections and the bespoke commissions, and everything is based on Alexandra's own hand-drawn designs, rather than conventional computer-aided designs. It's a technique that reflects the intricate attention to detail and personal touch at the heart of Augustine Jewels.

"When you draw by hand, you're extremely focused; you're thinking about nothing else but this person's engagement ring," says Alexandra. "The piece is always better when there is a reason or emotion behind it. By working with people, we're creating things that you wouldn't find anywhere else."
— www.augustinejewels.com

HANDCRAFTED
GLAMOUR

Aurum of Jersey

IN A CHIC showroom in the heart of St Helier, Jersey, you'll find a perfect replica of Nelson's warship, HMS *Victory*. Two-feet long and handcrafted out of sterling silver, it was made by the renowned jewellers Aurum of Jersey. "It took a year to create," recalls goldsmith and owner Richard Blampied. "Made for The Coombe Trust, a UK-based charity, it was originally displayed at Lloyds of London before we bought it back. It's a very special piece and we'll never sell it."

Aurum, which specialises in original, one-off pieces, was also chosen to make a silver replica of Jersey's 17th-century Royal Mace, originally given to the island by Charles II in 1663. It was presented by the States of Jersey to Her Majesty The Queen, commemorating her visit to the island in 1989.

Set up by Richard Blampied in 1968, Aurum is very much a family business. Richard's wife Alexa is the designer; one of his daughters, Sandie, is the firm's accountant; while Sandie's twin sister Julie is a trained gemologist and goldsmith who works alongside her father in the day-to-day running of the business.

Unlike much of today's mass-produced jewellery, Aurum uses old-fashioned techniques, creating handmade pieces designed without the use of computer-aided design. Its gemstones are ethically sourced and the larger diamonds are certificated, with each stone serving as the inspiration for the design of a unique piece. "We take huge pride in covering every aspect of the process," says Richard, "from sourcing to designing, to goldsmithing and setting."

Prices start at £2,000 for a ring or pendant, rising accordingly to fit the size and quality of the gemstones used or the complexity of the piece. The latest collection is called *Choisir*. "Each piece has a dual purpose," explains Alexa. "There are, for example, some rings in which the centrepiece, set with precious stones, can be turned over, in effect creating two different rings, and earrings that come apart creating one look for daytime and another for evening."

Alexa's designs have won Aurum international acclaim, including the Lonmin platinum Diamond Design Award in 2011/12. "Inspiration might be sparked by architecture, art or film could spark my imagination. The sight of the Chrysler Building on a recent trip to New York inspired me to create a tanzanite ring in an art deco style. Sometimes a customer may have personal requirements, like incorporating words or symbols that are significant to them into the design."

Aurum's customers – who include celebrities and visitors to the island, as well as locals – can be a little absent-minded. "We made his-and-hers wedding rings for a bride and groom, and he forgot to pick them up," recalls Richard. "On the morning of the wedding, the groom sent in his wife-to-be on her push bike to collect them. I think they're still married!"

After over 40 years leading the market in Jersey, Aurum is expanding. It recently exhibited at London's International Jewellery Show for the first time, following shows at Somerset House and the Saatchi Gallery in the capital. Staff numbers continue to grow and Aurum now has a UK-based marketing manager.

"It's great to be in this line of work because you're dealing with people's emotions," says Alexa. "You get to share in their happiness, in something lasting and significant to them that they will pass down. You can't get much better than that."
— www.aurumjewellers.co.uk

A GLITTERING LEGACY

Michael Young Jewels

IT IS IMPOSSIBLE to pass Michael Youssoufian's Hong Kong jewellery boutique, Michael Young Jewels, without pausing to gaze at the pieces in the window. Exquisitely wrought necklaces of diamonds, rubies and emeralds glitter enticingly. Magnificent cluster rings spill over with sparkling stones. Delicate earrings in the art-deco style are finished with tiny, lustrous pearls. Each is a work of art in its own right.

Part of the magnetic allure of these pieces is down to the stones themselves. Like many of the finest jewellers down the generations, Michael has an innate sense of the qualities possessed by each gem stone he picks up and an ability to draw designs to suit wide-ranging tastes and requirements from this simple but powerful starting point.

It might be a delicate pendant in which a particular sapphire or ruby will occupy pride of place. Or it might be a thick cuff bracelet composed of many different stones. Regardless, Michael will work closely with each client to produce a piece that fulfils their ideals of beauty and design.

"Every request is taken personally," he says. "Building lasting friendships with clients is one of the most rewarding aspects of the business."

While many contemporary jewellery brands subscribe to modern trends tending towards the stark and minimal, Michael speaks to a particular kind of shopper who seeks artistic quality in a piece of jewellery. "Art is a form of expression unlike any other," says Michael, who studied at the High School of Fine Arts in Geneva before following his family's footsteps into the field of jewellery. "All forms of art help to shape my ideas."

He gestures towards a cabinet housing an eclectic array of designs marrying multiple influences from across the ages. His appreciation of the classics is always evident, not only in the rare collection of antiques that form part of his collection but also in the touches and techniques that characterise his custom creations.

As the fifth generation in a long line of jewellers, Michael has always understood the importance of the past, learning from the mastery of his forebears, one of whom was appointed jeweller to the Royal Court of Egypt from the 1920s to 1950s. With both British and Armenian ancestry, he has honed his skills in some of the world's greatest centres of jewellery, spending time in Alexandria, London and Geneva before establishing his own brand in Hong Kong in 1997.

He now combines his passion for the past with an astute understanding of current markets, translated into a ready-to-wear collection that speaks to a current generation of buyers. These pieces harness the time-transcending quality that have come to characterise Michael's works, capturing the essence of contemporary style in a way that will be beautiful forever.

For Michael, it has never been about following trends. Instead, he stays true to his initial source of inspiration – the world of art, keeping his gaze focused on great works, past and present, as he ponders each new creation. "We don't adapt our lines to the markets," he says, firmly. "We stamp our own style on the jewellery world with each unique piece."
— www.michaelyoungjewels.com

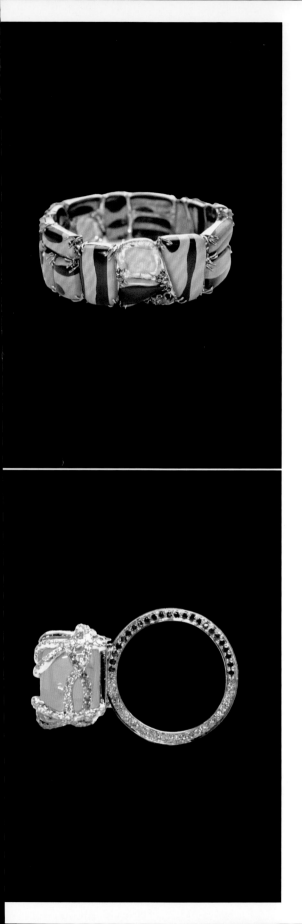

ART OF THE MATTER

Sharon Khazzam

"JEWELLERY IS WEARABLE art," says Sharon Khazzam. "That's the common denominator in my work – the meeting of art and fine jewellery." The New York-based jewellery designer's pieces – with their bright colours, whimsical designs and handcrafted quality – are certainly as unique as any work of art. Mixing traditional techniques with unusual stones and contemporary cuts, this is jewellery that appeals to those who appreciate individual style.

The first to use diamond slices, an approach that has now become widespread across the industry, Sharon is constantly searching for the latest unusual element to include in her jewellery. "I look for other gem stones," she says. "I've used emerald slices, which are gorgeous but not traditional. Some have inclusions that people don't like, but I think they are more interesting than the perfect stone at times."

Often featuring a perfect or precious stone next to something that some might consider imperfect or term semi-precious, Sharon's work is all about the overall effect. Her favourites include the increasingly rare Paraiba tourmaline from Brazil, where mines are almost depleted, equally rare tanzanite from Tanzania and the pinky peach padparadscha sapphire.

"Precious stones are not something we see too many of," she says, with such stones appreciating and becoming more prized as their rarity rises. "But they're mixed with the more commonplace – it has to be wearable and enhance the person who's wearing it."

Sharon's clientele recognise the intrinsic value of her jewellery. "It takes a more sophisticated customer," she says. "Someone who doesn't need the assurance of letting everybody know what they have spent."

While a particularly spectacular stone may occasionally inspire a design, which Sharon draws free hand, it's the idea that normally comes first. She describes her style as "elegant but with whimsy", with an element of surprise in each piece.

The Reeni necklace, for example, features three subtle insects, which have flown onto the stones. And the apparently understated Nidar bracelet, with its peridot and black diamonds, hides a complete underwater world on its back with octopus, coral and sea anemones carved in 18 carat gold. "No one sees but you know it's there," she says. "Like the lining of a jacket, it's as important to me as the front." Other designs, such as the multi-strand Vessny necklace, come apart to suit different situations.

This attention to detail extends to buyers receiving a book that provides an overview of the piece, with a description of each stone, guidance for those pieces that come apart, and a number to certify authenticity and ensure lifelong assistance. As much care is taken in the presentation and preservation of these collectable heirlooms as for any work of art. Indeed, this is a theme that runs through every aspect of Sharon's jewellery: even her studio has a gallery in the downstairs space, run by her daughter Alexandra Ainatchi, who has a degree in art history.

As with her jewellery, the gallery's exhibitions are curated to showcase the unique and the unexpected, to encourage people to consider something in a different way. For instance, one focused on photos by the top food photographers on Instagram, reminding the viewer of the beauty of something that they might otherwise take for granted. "It's unusual, not immediately recognisable," says Sharon. "You may not have ever thought of this as art." But as with her own jewellery, there's more to it than meets the eye.
— www.sharonkhazzam.com

FACE VALUE

Urban Jürgensen

THE MOST ENDURING icons are built on solid foundations. This is certainly true of the luxury wristwatch brand Urban Jürgensen, which still carries the name and ethos of its original family dynasty of Danish master watchmakers and innovators. The past is always present in Urban Jürgensen's ultra-fine handcrafted contemporary collections, and the brand remains true to three core pillars.

Firstly, there is its unique legacy. "We have had an uninterrupted existence since 1773," says CEO Søren Petersen, "And our company's founder is counted as one of the original masters of the art of precision horology."

Copenhagen-born Urban Jürgensen continued the groundbreaking watchmaking of his father Jürgen Jürgensen, and his own award-winning work was succeeded by his sons Louis Urban and Jules, who started production, also in Switzerland, in 1834. The 21st-century incarnation of the brand retains its Danish ownership, with expert production based in Biel – upholding the second pillar, of exceptional craftsmanship.

"Our tag line is 'honouring timeless traditions'," says Søren. "We want to re-establish the art of taking time to create very detailed work: Our watches are all handmade, and directed at collectors and connoisseurs. It is niche production; we'll never work with high volumes – but we also believe that a beautiful, handcrafted mechanical watch is something that anyone can appreciate."

Key to this are the exclusive movements developed by Urban Jürgensen's watchmakers, including a patented "detent escapement", based on the exceptional precision of classic naval chronometers. The resulting watches have won numerous awards over the centuries – and they continue to be recognised for the very highest achievements in watchmaking. These include selection for the 2016 edition of the prestigious Grand Prix D'Horlogerie De Geneve, Men's Category, an award the company won previously in 2014.

Another inimitably fine detail is the "grenage dial" technique. It creates a beautiful, pearled protective surface finish by hand-brushing a secret compound of silver, salts and other elements onto individual dials. This exemplifies Urban Jürgensen's blend of aesthetic style and old, traditional craft skills.

The third pillar is elegance. Urban Jürgensen timepieces stand out because of their exceptionally subdued elegant quality. "Our watches are not designed to be flashy or outrageous," says Søren. "They are stylishly subtle and classic. You can wear them with your jeans or with your tuxedo." It is a quality that unites watch connoisseurs of all ages. "Younger generations are looking for something with true value – and something they can tell an authentic story with," he adds.

There are personal stories and revolutionary visions at the heart of this brand – as well as an international scope that echoes the original Urban Jürgensen's experience. The young Urban honed his skills in world cities including Paris and London, and his successors took the company's reputation much further afield. "Back in the day, if you were a craftsman, you were required to become a journeyman," says Søren. "You'd travel around the world to learn from masters and improve your craft."

In the 21st century, Urban Jürgensen watches represent rich traditions and hallmark classic designs – a creative collaboration between Denmark and Switzerland – that are coveted all over the world.
— www.urbanjurgensen.com

TIMELESS TREASURES

Shen London

WHEN SHEENA GILL was 11, she watched in awe as Prince Charles got engaged to Lady Diana Spencer. Captivated by Diana's beautiful engagement ring – a 12-carat Ceylon sapphire surrounded by 14 diamonds, created by Garrard of London – she decided that, one day, she too would design her own fine jewellery. What she could never have dreamed was that, 30 years later, she would be holding the hand of the new owner of that ring, Catherine Middleton, following another royal engagement.

"I've been designing jewellery for 25 years," says Sheena. "But, until I set up Shen London, my main career was in magazine publishing and, latterly, as co-owner of GGMR, a digital technology business. The Duke and Duchess of Cambridge were one of our clients and we ran the Royal Wedding Gift Fund Website. After the wedding we were invited to Buckingham Palace for tea. It was then that I held Catherine's hand with the ring on. I nearly cried!"

Shen London (the name derives from a mis-spelling of Sheena) was created to produce exquisite, bespoke, high-end pieces, featuring only the finest gemstones, and using the same cutting process as the Swiss watch industry. Creative Director Sheena works with renowned diamond expert Marie Chalmers – named this year as one of the top 100 most influential people in jewellery by *Professional Jeweler Magazine* – who hand-selects every ethically sourced diamond.

"Unlike most jewellers," says Sheena, "we don't buy our diamonds in packets. We buy them direct from site-holders and choose only perfect rounds and squares, the best colours and precision cuts."

Sheena's designs aren't fashion-driven. "They are timeless, but contemporary," she says, "wearable investment pieces that will be the classics of tomorrow. They let the diamonds do their job –

to sparkle. All the designs are cohesive, so you can wear one piece, several together or a whole suite. My customers are women who know what they want – independent, discerning individuals who understand quality and are comfortable outside of brands."

As all Shen London pieces are either bespoke or semi-bespoke, they're not available in retail outlets and can only be purchased via appointment. Prices start at £4,000 for a pendant, rising to around £40,000. The debut collection – the Goddess Collection – features nine designs, each comprising earrings, bracelets and pendants, crafted in white 18-carat gold with diamonds and sapphires. Simple and elegant, each design is named after a Greek Goddess. "My inspiration comes from everywhere," says Sheena, "from buildings, from nature, sometimes from the diamonds themselves."

Sheena is currently working on a new collection for 2017 and is soon to announce an exciting celebrity collaboration. Shen London has also had work displayed at Walpole luxury exhibitions and is moving into the "experience package" area, teaming up with luxury concierge services.

Client satisfaction is of the utmost importance. In fact, Sheena says she'd rather a client didn't buy a piece unless they were 100 per cent in love with it. "Choosing jewellery should be a wonderful experience," she says. "That's why we always hand-deliver pieces. We're soon going to start letting clients choose their own diamonds. We want people to feel part of the making of their jewellery, and to wear it with pride. Last week we did a delivery and the lady was so excited she was shaking and couldn't undo the clasp. That to me is what it's all about. I know she will treasure it forever."
— www.shen.london

ONE TO WATCH

David Duggan Watches

When you enter the David Duggan Watches showroom in Mayfair's elegant 19th-century Burlington Arcade, the welcome is warm and the attention to detail is meticulous. Founder David Duggan's seven-strong specialist team has 180 years of collective horological experience, their knowledge matched only by their passion for the pre-owned luxury timepieces that the company specialises in. The showroom focuses on Patek Philippe and Rolex models, along with other world-class brands including Cartier, Vacheron and Jaeger-LeCoultre.

"A watch has a life; it has a heartbeat and its own eccentricities," says Managing Director David Hagon. Hagon was first drawn to working with watches in his youth, just like David Duggan himself. Duggan began working with his brother John in 1975, dealing in rare coins and pocket watches, before establishing his own business in 1983, focusing on luxury timepieces.

"We buy, sell, repair, and restore modern and vintage watches," says Hagon. "Nobody else carries the depth of stock that we do. We're a Rolex-approved service centre, and a member of the British Horological Institute. If you walk into the Patek Philippe showroom and explain that you're considering buying a pre-owned watch, we are often the place they recommend. Myself and others in the team are ex-Patek, and we endeavour to maintain the same level of service that they offer selling their new watches."

The company has always focused on craftsmanship that transcends fleeting trends. Clients are introduced to the intricate details of the watches that make them akin to fine art – from the tiny hand-finished tourbillon components to exquisite dials displaying the moon and constellations. The staff are attuned to the exact tastes and needs of their international clients and collectors, many of whom have become friends over time.

"Sometimes, the popularity of pre-owned watches stems from the waiting lists; Patek Philippe produces just 38,000 watches a year," says Hagon. "For a lot of people, it's also a safe way to invest. A wristwatch purchased in mint condition from a reputable dealer, such as ourselves, could be half the price it might cost new. Instead of owning one piece, you could own two and start to grow your collection. Plus, if you're planning to leave something to your children, there's no inheritance tax to consider."

In the Rolex-approved service centre, as well as the showroom, there is a continual focus on maintaining the most exacting standards. "Our Chief Technician, Ian Forster, trained in Switzerland," says Hagon. "He was an expert watchmaker for both Patek Philippe and Cartier and also has Rolex training."

The oldest timepiece that has ever been repaired at David Duggan Watches was a Patek Philippe pocket watch dating from 1850. "It had been badly treated over the years and was in need of meticulous care," says Hagon. "But at the Geneva factory, they were happy enough to share information with us, so that Ian could create a new part to restore the watch to its former glory."

It's this level of service, attention to detail and close affiliation with luxury Swiss makers that has kept clients coming back for over 30 years – because, with David Duggan Watches, they know they can rely on quality that stands the test of time.
— www.daviddugganwatches.co.uk

DIAMOND LIFE

Salima Thakker Jewellery

"THERE IS NO 'typical' customer who buys my work," says jewellery designer Salima Thakker. "It often attracts striking and distinctive individuals. I'll never forget the man with a weight fascination who commissioned a particularly heavy bracelet. The price was prohibitive, so in the end I made a bracelet in gold that weighed almost half a kilo. He came to see me later to show me his collection of bracelets. He rolled up his sleeve and his arm must have carried four kilos of precious metal."

The 41-year-old artist, whose work combines traditional materials and techniques with contemporary design, is based in Antwerp, the city of diamonds. After training at the Royal Academy, Salima moved to Italy to learn handcrafting techniques, then studied at London's Royal College of Art. She worked with Italian companies Damiani and Salvini where she also learned computer-aided design. She returned to Antwerp in 2001 to open a workshop, which became the first of her two shops.

"I get my inspiration from many places," she says. "From daily life – architecture, nature, my imagination and from other people, those I collaborate with and who commission me, asking for things I might never have dreamed of. One woman requested a unique piece of jewellery to embrace her arm. I ended up making her a silver-and-gold sleeve, like chain-mail armour. I have six core collections, and I regularly create individual pieces. Everything is still handmade; I like to give it the personal touch."

Salima admits that her often avant-garde designs are not always universally popular. "People tend to either love or hate them. Some of my pieces are in the shop for a week, others for two years, but sooner or later every piece finds its wearer, its match."

She travels around the world to source stones – her personal favourite is tourmaline – and to display her work at shows and trade fairs. Salima hopes to come across many more exclusive challenges but, for her, the key thing is maintaining balance between her quality and her artistic control, and by focussing on that personal touch with her clients.
— www.salimathakker.com

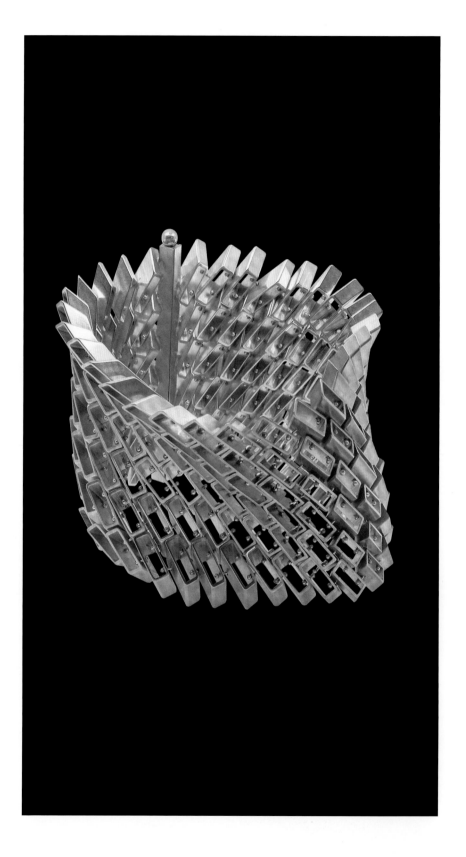

SPARKLING PRIZE

————————

Jade Jewellery

SUKAINA MACKIE COMES from a family of Lebanese diamond dealers. "I grew up in a small town in Sierra Leone by the diamond mines," she says. "I spent long hours dallying with diamonds and I was always mesmerised by their beauty."

Hardly surprising, then, that Sukaina became a jeweller herself, founding Jade Jewellery and opening her first shop in Jeddah, Saudi Arabia in 2002. After a globetrotting childhood, living between Sierra Leone, England, Lebanon, Belgium and Saudi Arabia, she journeyed to Antwerp to pursue her dream of studying diamonds, and worked with her brother, who is also in the trade.

"Returning to Jeddah, I put on a successful exhibition in November 2001," she says, "so I opened our flagship store a year later. Since then, we have been growing slowly but steadily."

In 2007, Sukaina partnered with Rola Krimmley, who, like her, enjoyed a nomadic childhood, living in Saudi Arabia, Lebanon, France and London. The two have since brought the company to global attention, establishing a strong UK presence.

Jade Jewellery works with top designers from Italy, France, Greece, the UK and the US, including the likes of Stephen Webster, Staurino Fratelli, Paulo Piovan and Crivelli, to create collections that transform classic cuts into vibrant contemporary creations. Standout pieces include a beautiful art deco necklace by Nikos Koulis and a pair of white gold, emerald and diamond Crivelli earrings. The results have proved to be extremely popular.

"Our jewellery has been worn by members of the Saudi royal family and other Middle Eastern luminaries," says Sukaina, "as well as many celebrities." Jade Jewellery caters to all jewellery lovers – women, men and children alike. "We give every piece and every customer the same attention and care," she adds.

The company's pieces are almost all one-offs, and any that are designed in multiple feature different precious stones. "It means that each one is unique," says Sukaina. This makes for happy customers but can be hard on the designers, as each item of jewellery has its own look and personality. "Sometimes," says Sukaina, wistfully, "it is really hard to detach oneself from these pieces and sell them!"
— www.jade-jewellery.net

BEAUTIFUL INSPIRATION

Viviane Debbas

SOMETIMES, TRAVEL REALLY does broaden the mind. Viviane Debbas didn't choose to bring up her young family in Paris – she was there because of the civil war in her homeland, Lebanon. But, while there, she began designing her own jewellery. When friends admired her pieces and asked her to make more, she was inspired to take a gemology course.

"I just loved precious stones," she says. She proved it by launching her first collection in 1990. By 1993, she had a shop in the smart 8th arrondissement. However, her loyalty was always to Lebanon and, when the fighting abated, she took her family, and her thriving business, back home.

Lebanon's long war scattered its citizens far and wide across the globe, but Viviane has spent her career swimming against that current. She opened her first Beirut shop in the Sofil Centre and then another in the prestigious Phoenicia Intercontinental Hotel. In 2009, she moved to a sumptuous shop in the heart of the city, on Park Boulevard, and that is now her sole outlet.

Just as Viviane has created a "home" for her jewellery, she also has a "family" – her staff have been with her for years. And this warmth and wish to nurture are apparent in her relationship with her clients. "I want to reflect a woman's beauty," she says, "which may be why I love pearls so much – they reflect the loveliness of their wearer at any age, from 10 to 90."

She also loves diamonds, but a fondness for traditional adornments doesn't make Viviane a designer of conventional jewellery. "I like to blend materials," she says. "I use wood, old coins, precious stones, semi-precious stones." She also likes to

blend Oriental and Occidental cultures, having experience both at first-hand.

But the most important thing is that the customer is happy with her piece. "If a woman wants a particular stone," says Viviane, "something very special, I will do something original that suits her needs." She will offer tactful advice on what suits the woman's shape while always being careful to stay true to that person's desires. The results are both beautiful and, often, surprisingly informal. "I like to create pieces that a woman can wear at all times," she adds. "The same piece should work equally well with an evening dress or with jeans."

As befits such a well-travelled woman, Viviane is inspired by the objects around her, whether natural or man-made. "I do a lot of Hand of Fatima and Evil Eye designs," she says. The former are exquisitely jewelled hands that reference Fatima, the daughter of Mohammed; the latter are good-luck charms in turquoise or semi-precious stones that are popular in the Arab word. They are traditional, but she makes them new. "I like to play," she says, "mixing and mingling stones and settings."

As for the men, they aren't left unadorned. As well as cufflinks in diamonds or gold, Viviane plays with pieces for men, too. "I like the chance to do something funky or funny," she says, and her Middle Eastern heritage is apparent here in the worry beads in amber, haematite, ruby or pearls. Some pray with them, some play with them, others just collect them, but rubbing them is considered good luck. And, as anyone who has lived through troubled times knows, none of us can have enough of that.

— www.vivianedebbas.com

TRANSFORMING DESIGN

MyriamSOS

AWARD-WINNING JEWELLERY designer Myriam Soseilos of MyriamSOS Fine Jewellery has had some interesting commissions, but none have been more unusual than the request to turn a woman's spine into a body chain.

"The client said she'd had an accident five years before and wanted a piece of jewellery that looked identical to her permanently injured spine, but in miniature," explains Myriam. "She sent me her MRI scans and I created a white and rose gold pendant with diamonds. She was very happy with the result."

Myriam's design career began while she was working at a top communications agency, making jewellery in her spare time. By 2008, people had begun asking if they could buy her pieces and requesting bespoke designs. "I started to ask fundamental questions about jewellery. Why should rings be round? Why should a ring with red gems look red? Why should a piece of jewellery have only a single function?"

Myriam employed a design tutor and set up a workshop below her house, studying jewellery techniques every night after work. In 2010, she quit her job, moved to London to study at Central Saint Martins, and set up her eponymous company.

Since then, she hasn't looked back. Myriam now works with a team of 15 craftspeople. Her designs – which have been worn by celebrities including actress Jodie Whittaker and singer Alexandra Burke – are sold online and in high-end stores in the UK (where she is based), the UAE, the US, Italy, Hong Kong and her homeland, Cyprus. She has delivered a TED talk on her work, and creates ready-to-wear collections which can be bought as seen or customised to suit a client's desires and budget. She also undertakes original

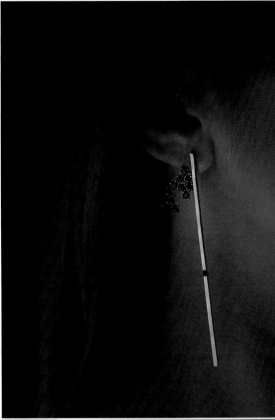

commissions: prices range from £500 for a simple piece to several thousands, depending on the materials and gems used.

She is known for her innovative approach to design. "I've never been conventional," she says. "I always look for something different. My USP is my multi-functional jewellery, encapsulated in the 'Transformers' collection. It's jewellery that is flexible, moveable and playful, which can be worn in many different ways. It is designed for today's woman, who has so many different roles in life. A pendant can become a ring, for example, or turn inside out. A pair of long earrings and a ring can be transformed into a pair of short earrings and a bracelet. One of my pieces can be worn in 18 different ways!"

She also designed bespoke rings in rose gold and silver for Candy Crush, replicating the phone app's distinctive designs using rubies, citrine, amethyst and emeralds. Her latest work in progress is a piece of jewellery containing a microchip. "I don't yet know if it will be a ring or a bracelet," she says, "but it will execute a number of commands, such as the gems moving or lights coming on with the press of a button. I'm getting technical support from watchmakers."

Her awards include Designer of the Year 2013 at London Jewellery Week and at the 2015 International Madame Figaro Women of the Year achievement awards. She was also a finalist in New Designer of the Year 2014 at the UK Watch & Jewellery Awards.

With plans to expand into new territories, such as Asia, MyriamSOS will continue to be at the forefront of innovative jewellery design. "Inspiration can come from anywhere," says Myriam. "But I always try to go one step further and challenge myself."
— www.myriamsos.co.uk

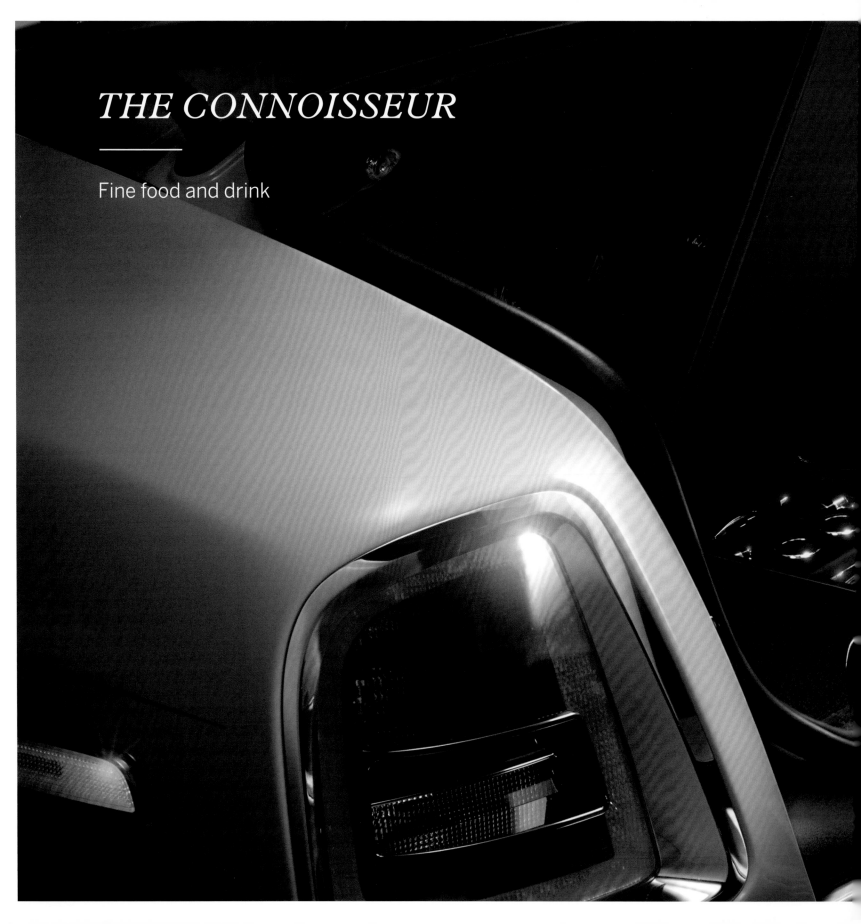

THE CONNOISSEUR

Fine food and drink

PURE AT HEART

———————

FoodsCross Natural Products

IT ALL BEGAN, several years ago, with a conversation about honey. Panos Kirnidis was talking to his wife Aliki Vasilopoulou and his friend Thomas Tsilalis – the three co-founders of FoodsCross Natural Products – about food and nutrition. "My wife said we had to eat honey for our health," says Panos. "When I offered to buy some from the supermarket, she said: 'No, not the mass-produced stuff – the real, healthy, unprocessed honey'. And, to this day, we've been searching for real, raw, natural, unprocessed food."

Panos soon realised that his wife – who is passionate about the value of nutrition and well aware of what is lost during the process of mass production – was referring instead to the real, raw, natural food. It was in this moment that FoodsCross was born.

From its base in Greece, FoodsCross seeks out and sells the highest-quality unprocessed food it can find. The range originated with thyme honey from the Aegean island of Astypalaia and now includes a variety of delicious products that use black and white Greek truffles in different forms: olive oil, butter, salt and paste.

"FoodsCross people are travellers, explorers, connectors, little treasure hunters," says Panos. All three founders believe that it is important to understand the environment from which each ingredient comes, to appreciate its history, time and place – its breeding. "Pure, crude, unprocessed – such food is a gift from nature," says Panos. "FoodsCross is determined to protect and share it as a luxury available to all."

FoodsCross honey is a case in point. By law, any honey that contains 18 per cent thyme pollen can be labelled thyme honey, but FoodsCross's thyme honey boasts an astonishing 80 per cent. This illustrates the company's unique level of commitment to quality, along with its refusal to be swayed by the vagaries of the general market.

It also goes above and beyond the demands of legislation. Even if it is entirely legal for bees to be fed with artificial food and antibiotics, FoodsCross resists such measures. Bees, in their natural wild existence, live on honey and even if this is a demanding and costly process to replicate, FoodsCross does it with care and persistence. The company's founders believe that it is worth it – a revival of the forgotten knowledge and respect that people once had for the land and the creatures that live on it.

"Laws are written by humans," says Panos. "We are seeking out the food that is much better than the law. We absolutely believe that bees should consume honey, it's their natural food. Bees are very sensitive and the honey also acts as a natural antibiotic. So our bees live on honey and they do not need artificial food and antibiotics, even if those things are allowed by law. This is far more demanding, but it's what we believe."

Panos insists that the difference can be discerned in the taste and also in the stimulating, restorative effect that this pure, unprocessed nectar has on the body. "Thyme honey is extremely good in terms of nutrition and many other areas," he says. "It's a bit spicy on the throat and you don't need to consume very much – a small tablespoon is enough to give all of the flavour as well as the daily required nutrients. Because with this food, it's not just about the taste, it's about the benefits. This food is like medicine."

The firm's truffle products are sourced just as carefully from the Greek mountains. "We spend a year, maybe two, investigating each product," says Panos. "It's not just about the aroma and taste, it's also about the fundamental nutrition. We have chemical labs to analyse the products and see how pure they are. We hunt the wild truffle with our dogs, send them to Italy, where they package the product to our standards, then it comes back to Greece for the commercial part. The process is very expensive and very difficult, but this is not any ordinary product. Often truffles have synthetic perfumes, which is allowed by law but not by us. We use only pure truffle in our products."

Panos likens his team to "explorers or food hunters", travelling the world to find the finest raw products that provide a taste experience unlike anything else available. They share the restless spirit of true pioneers and appreciate food as a need and a pleasure for body and soul. Panos places the FoodsCross founders and clients within a context of historical wanderers, who recorded their experiences, discovered valuable and overlooked data, made drawings of objects, buildings and works, and created precious cultural archives. In their minds, food is important, but so is provenance and cultivation, and they hope that this sort of understanding becomes integral to our enjoyment of food.

The company's packaging is emblematic of its attention to detail. The food may speak for itself but FoodsCross extends the same care to how its product is presented to the world. "Design is part of the food ritual, and we respect it as much the food itself," says Panos. "A number of international design and taste quality awards have come as recognition of our choices, and FoodsCross is committed to preserving its ethics of curiosity, care and attention in all its food-related endeavours. If taste is a vehicle of memory and a trigger of imagination, then FoodsCross is gradually creating a cabinet of taste wonders."
— www.foodscross.com/en

THE WORD

IN NOVEMBER 1790, **GEORGE SANDEMAN** EXPLAINED, IN A LETTER TO HIS FATHER (ON WHOM HE DEPENDED TO LEND HIM £300 TO START HIS BUSINESS), THAT HE URGENTLY NEEDED THE MONEY BY CHRISTMAS IN ORDER TO MEET THE COSTS OF A WINE VAULT HE HAD TAKEN. IN HIS OWN WORDS, GEORGE WROTE, 'THE WINES MUST BE LAID IN THEN, IF CAN'T BE DONE SOONER, ON ACCOUNT OF THE WINTER, AND I NEED NOT OBSERVE THAT THE CREDIT OF A MAN DEPENDS ON HIS PUNCTUALITY TO A DAY'. CLEARLY, YOUNG GEORGE HAD LEARNED THE WAYS OF BUSINESS BY TRADING IN THE CITY OF LONDON, WHERE DEALS WERE SETTLED ON A GENTLEMAN'S WORD, AS REFLECTED IN LONDON'S STOCK EXCHANGE MOTTO:

MY WORD IS MY BOND.

2000 VINTAGE PORTO
BOTTLED IN 2002

SANDEMAN

225TH ANNIVERSARY COLLECTION

The Word · N°1 from a collection of 6 · Limited Edition

VINTAGE PORTO 2000
BOTTLED IN 2002

THE SPIRIT

SANDEMAN

225TH ANNIVERSARY COLLECTION

The Spirit · N°2 from a collection of 6 · Limited Edition

VINTAGE PORTO
2000
BOTTLED IN 2002

THE JOURNEY

(Porto to London, to Vila Nova de Gaia to Jerez)

SANDEMAN

225TH ANNIVERSARY COLLECTION

The Journey · N°3 from a collection of 6 · Limited Edition

CRAFT

VINTAGE PORTO 2000
Bottled in 2002

SANDEMAN

225TH ANNIVERSARY COLLECTION

The Craft · N°4 from a collection of 6 · Limited Edition

VIN

PI

The Pioneer

225TH AN

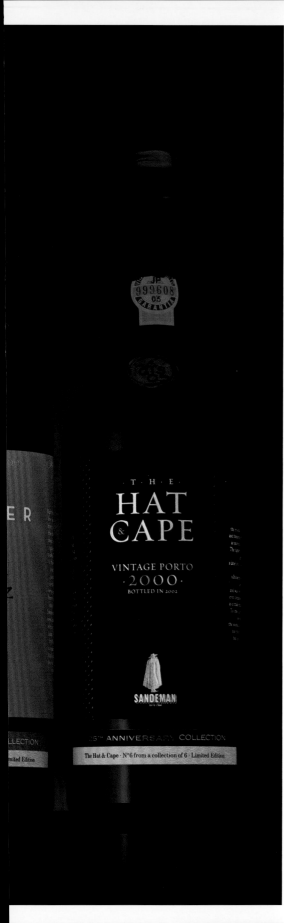

PORT OF KINGS

Sandeman

"PEOPLE OFTEN THINK of Port as something you only drink with Stilton at Christmas, sitting by an open fire," says George Sandeman, the seventh-generation descendant of his namesake, who founded the company in 1790. "We are trying to change that image of Vinho do Porto from what your grandfather would drink to a drink all ages and genders can enjoy."

The first George Sandeman, a young Scot, started the company with a £300 loan from his cabinet-maker father, which he used to buy a cellar of wine. He made his fortune in just seven years. "He was a very colourful person," says George. "He used to wear a wig – which was totally out of fashion by then – to the Stock Exchange. It earned him the nickname Old Cauliflower. He also had a reputation for being extremely honest. If he went travelling, Rothschild would advance him money to buy wine just on the strength of his word."

Over the centuries, the company evolved from being a wine merchant to a wine producer, buying up vineyards in Spain and Portugal. By the early 1950s it was specialising in Ports and Sherries; and, although it is now owned by the Portuguese Sogrape Vinhos group, it has remained true to its roots with a focus on quality and innovation. "We own and manage all of the production, bottling and ageing of our wines, which means we get a better consistency and a guarantee of quality," says George. "It always tastes the same."

The brand has many celebrity fans, including musician Steve Winwood and George's teenage crush, Michelle Phillips from The Mamas and The Papas. Sandeman is concentrating on its portfolio of 12 Ports, ranging in vintage from a single year to 40 years, and featuring white, tawny and ruby varieties. Sold in more than 50 markets worldwide, they are available in Britain at Waitrose and Majestic.

"They have a great finesse and balance," says George. "They give a vibrant explosion of flavour in your mouth, leaving your palate clean and refreshed. Drinking a ruby Port is like eating a plum, while a tawny is like a dried apricot with an almond in it. The aroma is very important."

Sandeman was one of the very first wine companies to use branding, advertising and a trademark: its famous Don, a silhouetted figure wearing a black Portuguese student's cape and a flat brimmed hat, is instantly recognisable. His illustrated figure has graced the labels since 1933, when he appeared on the biggest outdoor billboard ever seen in London.

That spirit of innovation continues to this day, as the brand targets a younger, less male-dominated demographic. "We're working with mixologists to create new Port-based cocktails, using things like cinnamon and hot peppers, and we have created a cocktail app. There is a trend towards drinking sweeter drinks and Port is a much more of a naturally sweet drink than, say, Irish cream or limoncello. All the sweetness comes from the part of the grape that hasn't turned into alcohol. Port can also be a refreshing summertime drink: try it on ice with a slice of orange."

It sounds as if George is well on his way to accomplishing his mission to change the image of Port from being a fusty old Christmas staple.
— www.sandeman.com

A TASTE OF ITALY

Prosciutto di Parma

WHEN THE FRENCH magazine *Madame Figaro* interviewed Hollywood actress Scarlett Johansson some years ago, they asked the secret of her beauty. Her answer? Not a skin cream, or cosmetic treatment, but eating Parma Ham.

Although it's not typically used as a beauty product, Parma Ham has long been regarded as one of the purest foods available. Prosciutto di Parma – *prosciutto* is from the Latin *perexsuctum*, meaning dried – was first produced in Roman times. It received official recognition in 1963, when the Parma Ham Consortium was founded to promote and protect its production and designation.

"When the Parma Ham producers, who are all located in a small area to the south of Parma, began to distribute the product worldwide, they realised they needed protection against imitators and counterfeiters," explains Elke Fernandez of the Parma Ham Consortium. "They gave themselves some strict production rules and defined our organisation's role. Later, these rules became part of EU legislation."

Parma Ham comes from specific races of pigs born and reared in Italy, and it must be cured for a mandatory 12 months, using only sea salt and no additives. This is how Parma Ham gets its mild, sweet taste – known in Italian as *dolce*.

A genuine whole Parma Ham must be trademarked with the Ducal Crown on both sides, visible even when the meat is cut in half. Packets of sliced ham bear the same Ducal Crown printed in gold on a black triangle.

Parma Ham is a very healthy food, used as a protein replacer by athletes and a pre-match snack by Italian footballers. "It has a high protein content and is easily digestible because the curing process breaks down the proteins into amino acids," says Elke. "People have a tendency to discard the fat but it's very important to the taste and not unhealthy because during the curing the fat components change from saturated to unsaturated."

Parma Ham is renowned for its versatility. "In Italy it's traditionally eaten with bread, cheese or cantaloupe melon," says Elke. "It goes well with all kinds of fruit, especially figs, and can be used in salads or pasta dishes too. More recently, chefs have used it to wrap around fish. I've seen Parma Ham Belgian chocolates and even an ice cream. It's all a question of personal taste."

The Parma Ham Consortium represents 150 producers and exports Parma Ham to around 90 countries worldwide, selling 79 million pre-sliced packs a year. After Italy, the US is the biggest market, closely followed by Germany, France and Britain.

Even a product as successful as Parma Ham can't afford to rest on its laurels. "We're involved in a lot of new initiatives," says Elke. "We're running programmes financed by the EU, such as Legends of Europe, which is a way of getting European products better known in the USA, educating the American trade and consumer on what Protected Designation of Origin means. We also run a Parma Ham Specialist programme, recognising and rewarding restaurants or points of sale which have a big commitment to Parma Ham. That way we can speak directly to consumers and make them feel important."

— www.prosciuttodiparma.com

LAND OF INFUSION

No. 3 Clive Road

FOR ITS FOUNDER Radhika Chopra, luxury tea brand No. 3 Clive Road is all about home. It's about both returning to her homeland, India, after growing up and working in the US, and the simple, everyday act of relaxing after a day at work. "To me, tea represents and encompasses the idea of coming home," says Radhika. "When I arrive back in my apartment, the very first thing I do is to have a lovely cup of tea."

Set up in 2015, the company specialises in exquisite hand-blended teas, premium letter-pressed stationery and bespoke locally produced accessories. Using the best-quality materials, together with state-of-the-art design and innovation, it perfectly combines the traditional and the modern, bringing the values of a bygone era into the homes and lifestyles of today.

Despite its youth as a brand, No. 3 Clive Road is steeped in history, taking its name from the New Delhi home where Radhika's father was born in 1931. The address features prominently in Radhika's grandfather's diary, which he kept for more than 50 years from 1914, chronicling both his family history and that of India through its most turbulent and fascinating years.

"For me, the brand is a way of preserving our family history," says Radhika. "And while the idea of high tea is the legacy of the British, and we export tea to the rest of the world, until No. 3 Clive Road, there wasn't a luxury packaged tea brand in India."

No. 3 Clive Road currently offers 10 unique, natural tea blends, each named after a region of India and packaged in a beautifully designed box. Radhika's current personal favourite is Madurai Masala blend. "It contains chai spices with a twist," she says, "and it keeps me warm in the winter!"

Partnering the teas are accessories, such as traditional Indian clay khullars and luxury stationery featuring illustrated vignettes of Indian cities, made from the finest papers with lined envelopes. Later this year, to coincide with Diwali, Radhika will also be launching scented candles that celebrate India's temple towns.

"For me, the three areas perfectly complement each other," she says. "They are all things you do to relax at home: you have a lovely cup of tea, write a note to a close friend and light a candle. And all the products make perfect gifts."

The brand is growing fast, even beyond Radhika's expectations. No. 3 Clive Road now retails in several outlets across India and is sold online via its website. It has recently signed a contract to provide in-room tea service for a luxury hotel chain, and has just received an order from a US gourmet delivery company for 24,000 tea boxes.

Radhika says her customers tend to be well-travelled individuals with discerning tastes. Recently, she created a special blend for the Maharaja of Maheshwar, whose son was getting married. The box was designed to reflect the renowned Maheshwari sari weave.

Future plans include expanding its hotel and international presence and bringing out single estate teas packaged in tins, which will be marketed like fine wines. Radhika also hopes to open a tea shop in New Delhi. "Ultimately," she says, "I want No. 3 Clive Road to be known as an international brand that celebrates India and represents the elegance of a bygone era."

— www.threecliveroad.com

NO.3
CLIVE
ROAD

KASHMIRI KAHWA
A CLASSIC BLEND FROM THE VALLEY

IN THE SERVICE OF GOOD TASTE

Café Royal

THE ONGOING QUEST to make good coffee and the work of a secret agent have much in common, according to Raphael Gugerli, CEO of Delica. And he should know. Delica produces the Café Royal brand, a premium coffee from Switzerland that was launched in 2012 and has already won fans and customers across the world. "We are both on the same mission," says Raphael. "A mission in the service of good taste."

To emphasise the point, Café Royal has brought in pop star Robbie Williams to play the part of a secret agent in a series of videos, representing the mission of this coffee house to supply only the very best in good taste. How did Raphael find the former Take That wild boy? "Smart and charming," says Raphael. "And he is a coffee lover – it was a natural fit." So was Robbie's legendary sense of humour. "Our secret agent doesn't take himself too seriously," he adds. "He reflects the company and how we would like our customers to enjoy high quality."

It helps that the team in charge of the brand is a young group. "We have this open spirit with which we work towards bringing a new lifestyle and a new drink to the customer," says Raphael. By "new drink" he means the expanding range of Café Royal coffees, around 40 in all, targeted at every consumer taste, from Blonde City Roast to Italian Dark Roast, from classic espresso blends to flavoured coffees. Café Royal makes fairtrade, organic, single origin and limited-edition ranges – available as beans, instant, iced and capsules for the Nespresso system – as well as a range of teas.

From sourcing the beans to product research and development, marketing and advertising, everything is done in-house. "It means that we can really control the quality of our coffee," says Raphael. "It starts with the culture of collaboration inside our company and it goes right through to the distinctive packaging, which we designed ourselves."

Café Royal sources its coffee from 25 countries worldwide, including Costa Rica, Vietnam and Ethiopia. "We work with a very few local producers rather than with thousands of different suppliers," says Raphael. "As much as we can, we work with them directly. This means that the contact is very transparent." The social, environmental and economic impact of coffee growing also matters a great deal to this company. All its products are certified under UTZ, a programme for sustainable coffee, cocoa and tea farming.

Based in Birsfelden, near Basel and the German border, Delica was founded in 1954 and is one of the largest coffee-roasting companies in Switzerland, processing around 12,200 tonnes of green coffee beans annually. Having found success in the home market, the Café Royal brand has expanded rapidly across Europe and now the rest of the world, including Japan, Russia and Australia. Its sights are firmly set on finding new markets and continuing its mission to bring good taste to the masses.
— cafe-royal.com

CACAO POWER

Felchlin Switzerland

IN A BUSINESS world that requires growth, it can be hard for any firm to emphasise tradition and stability. But tradition is crucial when the manufacturing of your product requires patience, discernment and age-old techniques that cannot be compromised. This requires a different business approach, and any brand that can achieve returns while practising perfection is doing something remarkable.

Swiss chocolatier Felchlin is such a company. Founded in 1908 and initially trading in honey, it began in-house production of couverture in 1936. "Couverture" relates to the higher percentage of cocoa butter in the chocolate, and the couvertures manufactured by Felchlin are uniquely refined and delicious. Inevitably, they do have their price.

CEO Christian Aschwanden locates the company's product within particularly rarefied culinary and sensory parameters. "It's comparable to wine," he says. "We buy beans for their specific terroir, which carry their very particular flavours. Felchlin is well known for its wide range of different flavours, which hardly anyone can compete with."

This tradition of knowledge and craftsmanship offers unique opportunities. Felchlin works directly with carefully selected farmers and cooperatives – from Ecuador and Bolivia to Madagascar and Costa Rica. This careful selection not only results in long-standing relationships, but also in consistent quality.

"We have a chocolate hunter called Felix Inderbitzin, who travels around the world in order to find the best beans for us," says Christian, describing the evolution of a particularly enjoyable-sounding job within the company. "Felix used to really have to go looking for the beans, whereas today we get approached by cooperatives and partners wanting to work with us. One of the reasons is surely because we foster sustainable relationships and planting, while paying well above Fair Trade prices. This ensures that the farmers and their families are doing well."

Still, there's a basic simplicity at the heart of what Felchlin does. "We want to accentuate the quality of the bean rather than add additional flavours," says Christian. "We use only Swiss milk and sugar and source all our raw materials carefully."

Such perfectionism requires diligence. "Once the cocoa bags arrive at our premises after their long journey, we check that the beans are in an impeccable state," says Christian. "We ensure that the beans are immaculate and also that the taste profile matches our reference sample. For the latter, we have our sensory panel: they ensure that all our goods, whether received or produced, are of the highest standard. If they are not, we decline them, as we must maintain excellence in everything that we do at all times."

For all of its expertise, Felchlin remains a tastefully understated enterprise. There's clearly a real reluctance to sacrifice exclusivity for visibility. Christian is pleased with the company's sky-high reputation among people who know their chocolate.

"Our business is well known among chocolate connoisseurs," he says. "Felchlin is not like any other brand because we put so much passion into our chocolates. It's not only the ingredients; it's how you treat them, from the beginning through to the end of the process. It's our employees and their expertise that make us what we are. Every detail works together in harmony to create this wonderful product." Certainly, it's inspiring to know that, for some companies, quality will always beat quantity.
— www.felchlin.com/en

THE BEST CELLAR

Octavian

AROUND 100 FEET below the Wiltshire countryside is a mine, from which miners once extracted the Bath stone used to construct some of the finest homes in England. Now, these vast underground spaces have been turned into Octavian Vaults, a subterranean cellar, one million square feet in size, containing tens of thousands of cases of fine wine in the ideal conditions.

"The size can be a bit disconcerting for new staff," says Vincent O'Brien, the Managing Director. "We have to escort them for a month before they get their bearings. But for our clients, people who are passionate about wine, from the moment it arrives on our doorstep to the moment it leaves, we ensure that their wine has the best possible care."

It's widely known that wine needs to be kept in certain strict conditions if it is to retain its taste, colour and value. Octavian Vaults promises that wine in this vast natural cellar will be stored at 13 degrees (plus or minus one degree), with a humidity of 80 per cent (plus or minus 5 per cent), with no natural light or UV and minimal vibrations. For people who care about wine, this is essential.

"Whether you have bought wine with the intention of selling it for a profit or sitting down to drink it with fine food and good company, we make sure it's kept in the condition people expect," says Vincent. "Our customers often have no physical interaction with their wine for years – the average case spends nine years in our care – so we inspect the wine and take the responsibility of being their senses very seriously. We want our clients to be confident that this is what they paid for."

Octavian provides a Certificate of Pristine Storage, so clients can show that their wine has been laid down in the best conditions, and they also have excellent insurance and security. The company has contracts with wine merchants and private individuals all over the country, with 30 per cent of its clientele based outside the UK.

"We want to ensure that when a wine leaves us it is finer, safer and more valuable because it has been in our care," says Vincent. "We work with a fine-wine clientele who are often buying and selling among themselves, so transactions take place without the wine having to move from our four walls. That makes it easier and is much better for the wine."

That wine includes a bottle of sherry from 1775, as well as individual cases worth well over £100,000. But there are also cases that have more of an emotional value, bought on birthdays or graduations and intended to be opened at a later anniversary. This demonstrates the range of people interested in wine and every case is treated with the same care.

"We have a combination of clients; some are collectors and some have wines as an investment," says Vincent. "The common goal is that they care about the enjoyment of wine and they want to get a return on their investment, whether that's financial or from drinking it. The value of wine is increasing all the time and people need to think who they trust to look after that investment. With us, people know it has been looked after and is worth buying for that ultimate moment when you pull out the cork and pour the first glass."

— www.octavian.co.uk

WHOLLY SMOKED

Ritchie's of Rothesay

IN A LOCKED safe in a lawyer's office in Glasgow sits the secret of Ritchie's of Rothesay's success. The safe contains the secret marinade recipe for the firm's famous smoked salmon, a product that is still produced in a 19th-century smokehouse on the Isle of Bute where the walls are thick with aged tar. "As soon as you walk into this oak-beamed room you absorb this amazing smoky atmosphere," says Head of Marketing Vittoria Recchi. "The process is essentially the same as it was in 1888 when the smokehouse opened."

Ritchie's began life as Barr's, providing smoked kippers for the Balmoral breakfasts of Queen Victoria, who was just one of thousands of customers. In the 1960s, the firm switched the focus of its production to smoked salmon – although it still smokes kippers and trout – as it was taken over by the Ritchie family. It is now owned by the Marquess of Bute as part of a group of companies that collectively celebrate the island's traditions and heritage.

"The Marquess was brought up on Ritchie's smoked salmon and recognised what an asset it was for the island," says Vittoria. "It is run alongside two other Bute brands – the historical house and gardens of Mount Stuart, and Bute Fabrics, a mill that produces contemporary fabric that is exported all over the world, to everyone from American banks to Japanese airports. These three inter-related family brands reinforce the heritage and values of the island and its people. We're a major employee and a central part of the island's economy and life." And the royal connection is still sustained – a recent visitor to Bute Fabrics was the Duke of Rothesay, also known as HRH The Prince of Wales.

With smoked fish, meat and cheese becoming increasingly fashionable, the staff at Ritchie's pride themselves on their ability to move with the times, producing contemporary products such as smoked haddock scotch eggs while always using traditional, artisanal methods.

"We buy the fish in Glasgow and then cure it in Ritchie's secret recipe for two days and two nights," says Vittoria. "Then the side of salmon is hung on tenterhooks and smoked over smouldering oak shavings from Scotch whisky barrels on racks inside the 100-year-old kiln. The entire process, including the slicing of the salmon, is done by hand in the traditional method."

It's this mix of old and new thinking that helps make Ritchie's so distinctive, with the firm coaching apprentices in traditional styles of food production but also encouraging them to apply these techniques to exciting new concoctions of their own creation. The company's range of products is sold from its shop in Rothesay and via its website, and it supplies an international range of wholesalers, distributors, speciality retailers, hotels and restaurants.

All of this helps to spread the Bute message. "The family has always been very innovative and forward-thinking," says Vittoria, "and that is a philosophy we maintain across all our brands. We focus on the heritage but we try to be modern, sharing the message that the Isle of Bute is a special, wholesome place that creates brands in a very sustainable yet timely fashion."
— www.ritchiesofrothesay.co.uk

HIGH SPIRITS

Ben Nevis Distillery (Fort William) Ltd

NESTLED AT THE foot of Britain's highest mountain, the Ben Nevis Distillery is set against an impressive backdrop – one that also plays a vital role in the production process. Ever since it was founded in 1825, the distillery has drawn its water from a river high up on Ben Nevis. "We were the first distillery to be set up in the area and we still get our water from Ben Nevis, which is what makes us unique." says General Manager Colin Ross. "We draw the water supply from a burn that runs on the northern face of the mountain."

The distillery, a few miles north of Fort William, is owned by Japan's Nikka Whisky Distilling Co Ltd, and produces a range of blended whiskies, a blended malt and various ages of single malt, aimed at a growing international market. "Scotch whisky has always been seen as the best," says Colin. "The Irish have always been there, as have US bourbons, and we now have the rise of Japanese and Indian whisky. There is a wider choice and more people are building distilleries."

Around two million litres of whisky will be produced this year by the Ben Nevis Distillery. "Ours is a fairly full-flavoured whisky," says Colin, "with its own distinctive taste. It's intense without the smokiness." It is usually finished in sherry, claret and bourbon barrels, although the distillery also occasionally uses Californian red and white casks, Burgundy barrels and Port pipes and butts. The decision as to whether a batch is ready to be bottled is taken collectively. "We take samples from the casts and select," says Colin, who has worked in the trade since 1965. "We take samples and a few of us will nose them and taste them to get a consensus of opinion."

The distillery also has a visitors' centre, so tourists to this beautiful corner of the Highlands can see the production process and sample the wares. "We have a small audio-visual presentation and then we give a tour of the distillery followed by a tasting," says Colin. With its enviable location, much like savouring Ben Nevis Distillery's exceptional whisky, it's a singular experience.
— www.bennevisdistillery.com

MILLIONAIRES' ROE

Caviar de France

OPERATING AT THE top end of a niche market, Caviar de France is a powerful fish in a small pond. "In France, we're a symbol of luxury: haute couture caviar," says Marketing Director Heather Ducretot.

Founded in 1993 and based in Biganos on the Arcachon Bay in south-west France, Caviar de France has just 12 hectares. "We're small and beautiful," says Heather, referring to its farming methods as much as its size. Fish tanks are fed by river water. "Water comes in at one end, goes through the tanks, and goes back into the river. There's no intensive farming here, so our fish can take time to grow. We're the best-tasting caviar because we're not in a rush; we harvest at the average age of 10 years, whereas some companies harvest at seven." Sustainable and ethical methods are prioritised. "Our farm gives maximum space to the fish," she adds. "We have no chemicals and no antibiotics. We run a very clean farm."

A destination in itself, Caviar de France is located in an old flour mill that dates back to 1834. An exhibition space now occupies the original grinding room. "We do high-profile private tours, and group visits by appointment for the public. People can come and discover how we work," says Heather, adding that each trip ends with a tasting.

"The caviar is harvested by experts and transformed in our on-site laboratories with our special salting techniques," she says. One brand, Diva, only uses natural salts. "It's buttery in flavour and the taste of salt is much lighter," says Heather. Another, Ebène, is matured for several months. "It's slightly softer and much longer lasting. A lot of people think that caviar is very salty – and a lot of caviars are! – but that will kill the flavour. That's why we produce in small quantities using very little salt."

The company sells internationally to upmarket shops and Michelin-starred restaurants, as well as to private buyers seeking a unique, high-quality product. "People really do appreciate the difference," Heather says. In this overcrowded luxury market, Caviar de France stands out as something special.
— www.caviardefrance.com

WINE IN THE BLOOD

Domaine Ponsot

AS THE FOURTH generation of his family to run one of France's most prestigious wineries, Laurent Ponsot could be forgiven for focusing on the proud history of Domaine Ponsot. But instead, he wants to talk about innovation. "This morning I met with a company that will produce connected bottles for us," he says. "We have already the intelligent case and the intelligent bottle, but next they will be connected as well. I can't tell you what 'connected' means though – this will be revealed in the future!"

Domaine Ponsot's success, since it was founded in 1872, lies partly in its constant desire for innovation – with advances in bottling, corks, farming equipment and increasingly sophisticated heat indicators to ensure wine is handled correctly after leaving the winery. "We are not very big but we must be the only winery in Burgundy that produces 12 Grands Crus," says Laurent. "We use every technique we have at our disposal today, after 2,000 years of history of winemaking in Burgundy, and if we don't find anything that corresponds to what we need, we invent it. We produce 20 different appellations and the Grands Crus represent 80 per cent of our output. They are the crème de la crème, the top 1 per cent of all wine in Burgundy, and only 33 Grands Crus exist. So this makes us a little special."

Laurent has worked at the winery for more than 30 years, having succeeded his father as owner in the early 1980s. "You could say I have a little blood in my wine, or is it vice versa?" he laughs. Laurent spent the first few years expanding the winery's international reach, building on work pioneered by his grandfather, who introduced Burgundy to the US in the 1930s. "I was visiting Japan, Hong Kong, China, Singapore and Thailand, as well as the US," he says. "As we began to produce the most authentic wines, I travelled everywhere to share them with people and the result is that Domaine Ponsot is one of the most famous wineries outside France."

The winery produces around 2,500 cases a year from its various vineyards, refusing to bow to contemporary trends, fads and fashions but operating along a set of defined principles that include not using any chemicals or pesticides. "I want to produce the most natural and authentic wines without being in accordance with the current fashions," says Laurent. "We have been producing wine on this planet for more than 8,000 years and in the last 40 years we have reinvented everything.

"We love nature in my family – she's the only one that can give a great vintage, a great wine," he continues. "We are one element in the chain that starts at the roots of the vine and ends with a glass of wine. We want to give whoever opens one of our bottles an emotion that relates to one tiny piece of this planet, represented through the appellation. These are mysteries, fairy tales, not standard wines."
— www.domaine-ponsot.com

GRAND HAM

Joselito

FOR NEARLY 150 years, five generations of the Gómez family have, through their company, Joselito, been producing what many believe to be the world's finest ham. Its products are made with such care and attention to quality that certain years are labelled as "vintage". "There is no doubt," says José Gómez, the company's fifth-generation manager. "A Joselito vintage ham that has been cured naturally over more than eight years has unique sensory qualities."

Variations in the aroma of the ham from one year to another are influenced by the weather, which dictates the type of food that is naturally available in the countryside for the pigs. Joselito can claim unreservedly that its animals are free-range: with three to four hectares each of oak forest in which to roam freely, they live in a semi-wild state. "Because the pigs live only on what the countryside gives them," says José, "the quality of the acorns and the fresh grass and flowers that they eat will significantly affect the ham."

Although Joselito's animal husbandry methods and curing techniques have changed little since it was founded in 1868, the company is not averse to harnessing modern technology in pursuit of quality. "Every Joselito ham has a microchip attached with an ID number," says José. "This carries a library of information, such as details of the animal's parentage, what it has been eating and so on. It enables us to exercise supreme quality-control."

Every Joselito ham takes an average of six years to produce. Each pig lives for two years, and the curing process takes place over three to five years. Being able to monitor the produce over the whole period enables the firm to make modifications and improvements along the way. "Uniquely, we control the whole cycle of production," says José, "from breeding and management of our own countryside and our own animals, right up to the processing of the ham."

Every year, Joselito plants between 70,000 and 80,000 trees, and is the only food company in the world to have been awarded FSC Forest Management certification for sustainability. "We'll not see the direct benefits in our lifetime," says José. "But it's a way to help preserve the ecosystem of the pigs for decades to come. It's a way to give something back."

Joselito has the distinction of being the only producer not to add any additives or preservatives to its ham, adding nothing but sea salt from the south of Spain. In the past four years, the company has established a culinary research project, JoselitoLab, to explore the gastronomic possibilities of its products. "We collaborate with three-star Michelin chefs around the world," says José, "creating different recipes combining their know-how with the most precious product from Spain." Past editions include Ferran Adria (a partnership with El Bulli in Spain), Massimiliano Alajmo (with Le Calandre in Italy), Jonnie Boer (with De Lebrije in the Netherlands) and Seiji Yamamoto (with RyuGin in Japan).

Joselito's culinary excellence owes much to the equal respect that it pays to tradition and continuity. It's an excellence that the proud custodians of its name look certain to hold far into the future.
— www.joselito.com

A RECIPE FOR RELAXATION

Bodega Garzón, Uruguay

"IT ALL STARTED with the idea to make extra virgin olive oil in Uruguay," says Christian Wylie, Managing Director of Bodega Garzón. The company is owned by Alejandro P Bulgheroni, the Argentinian oil man who is fast becoming one of the most renowned wine and olive oil producers in the Americas. "Mr Bulgheroni is extremely passionate about the area," says Christian. "Since 1999, he and his wife Bettina have been building a 4,300-hectare estate near the village of Garzón, an hour's drive from the Punta del Este resort area – known as the St-Tropez of South America – with its stunning beaches and beautiful people."

Today, Bulgheroni makes award-winning extra virgin olive oils – under the Colinas de Garzón name – in his boutique production plant, using the fruits of its own olive groves. In 2015, his were the New World's only extra virgin olive oils to be mentioned in the World's Best Olive Oils shortlist. He also handcrafts prize-winning wines in Bodega Garzón's state-of-the-art winery. The wines and olive oils are available in key markets and distributed in London by the prestigious fine wine merchant, Bibendum.

"Mr Bulgheroni planted his 220 hectares of vineyards high up in the hills, where they benefit from granite soils and cool Atlantic breezes," says Christian. "Garzón is on the same latitude as the emblematic wine-growing regions of Argentina, Chile and Australia. Here, led by oenologist Alberto Antonini, more than 1,000 individual blocks were planted, including Tannat and Albariño, Uruguay's signature varietals."

Quality is paramount in everything the company does, as is sustainability. Bodega Garzón uses only renewable energy – eight wind generators are on the estate – and recycles all its fertiliser. Bodega Garzón will be the first sustainable winery with LEED (Leadership in Energy & Environmental Design) certification outside North America: that includes the winery, vineyards and hospitality facilities in accordance with the stringent requirements of the United States Green Building Council (USGBC).

Yet there is more to Garzón than its olive groves, vineyards and wineries. Despite a population of fewer than 200 people, the village is home to the hotel of Argentinian celebrity chef Francis Mallmann, known for his open-fire approach to cooking. As a global ambassador for Garzón, Mallmann oversees Bodega Garzón restaurant, serving delightful seasonal dishes.

The estate is a 2015 TripAdvisor Certificate of Excellence award winner, and visitors can choose to enjoy a variety of activities. These include a scenic ride in a horse-drawn carriage between the olive plantations; a visit to the extra virgin olive oil mill to learn about and take part in the production process; wine and olive oil tasting sessions; a hot-air balloon trip over the spectacular local countryside; bicycle rides in the estate; and a barbecue among the olive trees with spectacular vistas of the vineyards.

The Bulgheroni family vineyard estate in Garzón also houses the most exclusive golf course in Latin America, designed by the champion golfer Angel Cabrera. A private members' luxury club has recently opened at the winery, and a Posada spa is being built among the vineyards. Next year, an exclusive beach resort will be constructed in the chic and charming José Ignacio village on the Uruguayan coast.

"This area is so unspoiled and laid-back, with a slow pace and excellent gastronomy," says Christian. "Everything here is about quality and quality of life. It's the perfect place to escape from it all."
— www.bodegagarzon.com

A GROWING HERITAGE

Domaine Faiveley

ALTHOUGH EVE FAIVELEY, along with her brother Erwan, is part of the seventh generation of her family to run Domaine Faiveley, she tries not to think too hard about family responsibility. Instead she focuses on producing exceptional wine from one of Burgundy's great domains.

"Erwan and I realise we have something very important that we need to preserve but it's not something we think about every day – it's too heavy," she says. "Each generation makes different wines but we are all trained in the same way of working the vineyard. We have a viniculture training that sees us working the vineyard in the best way for nature and our wine."

Despite her protestations, Eve Faiveley is steeped in a rich tradition of great winemaking. She had her first glass when she was four or five, she admits, and has grown up surrounded by vineyards. Domaine Faiveley was founded in 1825 by Pierre Faiveley and now has around 127 hectares split between Côte de Nuits, Côte de Beaune and Côte Chalonnaise. There are two wineries – one in Côte Chalonnaise and the other in Nuits-Saints-Georges – and these vineyards produce 12 Grands Crus and 25 Premier Crus, with a further six vineyards (climats) classed as monopoles.

"We are the biggest producer of Grands Crus and Premier Crus," says Eve. "That is because each of the seven generations of my family has purchased something new and there's never been an issue with succession." This deep association with the region brings with it an innate appreciation for nature and preservation, a respect for the people, land and buildings of this historic area, especially since 2015, when the climats of Burgundy were made a Unesco World Heritage Site.

Although Eve and Erwan Faiveley differ from their father in their favoured style of wine, they still consult him regularly, maintaining the generational links. "My father handed over to Erwan ten years ago, but if we have a big decision to make, we always make sure we speak with him," says Eve. "We know that we have to preserve what we have and want to make sure that we leave the domaine to our kids as our father left it to us."
— www.domaine-faiveley.com

FISH AND WOOD CHIPS

———

Frank Hederman

FRANK HEDERMAN WAS born and raised in the attractive port town of Cobh, on the south side of Cork harbour in Ireland. His excursions with local fishermen as a boy spawned his love for fish, and led him to set up the most renowned and respected smokehouse in Ireland, now in its 35th year.

Ireland is fast gaining a reputation for fine food. Frank has played his part in this, but remains refreshingly unpretentious about it. "I started out hoping to make a living for my wife and myself," he says. "I was always close to fish and fishing, so I didn't see what I'm doing as some ghastly 'artisan' lifestyle choice. We started smoking wild salmon, and stayed at it until we got good at it."

From the age of 13, Frank fished in a dory boat for mackerel with local fishermen in the summer. In those days he'd sell his catches in the nearby market town of Midleton – nowadays his products are stocked by Fortnum & Mason and Selfridges. He also supplies his friend Rick Stein in Padstow.

Frank had to teach himself the smoking technique. "There was no point in talking to any of the other smokers," he says. "It was all a big secret. So we built

a small smoke room – rather like an old-fashioned wardrobe – to contain the smoke. We'd burn the chips in a brick kiln, and pipe it through to the smoker, where we'd hang the fish. It was a rather slow and painstaking process – I used to sit in an armchair for hours, feeding the chips in by hand! Now, thankfully, we have a larger smokehouse and a smoke generator, which is slightly more automated."

After curing the fish in salt, preservation continues in the smokehouse as oil molecules in the raw material absorb the smoke, adding flavour and character. "It's important to have well-produced organic fish," says Frank, "and Marine Harvest provide us with a product that is consistently good, week in, week out."

There are now six full-time Hederman employees, constantly innovating and refining, but the smoking itself is still done in the traditional – and rather rare – hanging style. "We now also smoke cheese, salt, butter and oats," says Frank. "And we're always looking for new things to do with fish. This is a fun, fun business, and I have no intentions of retiring. It's the joy of it that keeps us doing it."
— www.frankhederman.com

WELL OILED

Olio Verde

EVERY DAY, THE Olio Verde family inspects its estate's 3,000 olive trees. Thanks to decades of care and an eco-friendly approach, any issues with the fruit are identified early. This dedication is shared by all of the founding family and is one of the reasons why its olive oil has an international reputation for quality.

Valeria Becchina and her two sisters now own Olio Verde, a company founded in 1985 by their parents and based in the west of Sicily. There is only one type of olive they grow – the Nocellara del Belice. Fleshy and green, the Nocellara was traditionally eaten as a delicacy until Valeria and her family turned the fruit into oil.

"We were the first company to do this," says Valeria. "It is one of the most precious varieties in the world for curing and table consumption, and doesn't yield much oil. But the oil it does produce is like an elixir – rich and fruity with undertones of banana and ripe fruit. And the special process we use to make the oil means it is of exceptional quality and sought after by chefs and those who appreciate the best."

The process Valeria refers to includes harvesting the crop very early, at the beginning of October or even the end of September instead of late October or November. "The longer the wait then the more oil," says Valeria. "But this means losing our exclusive flavours of freshness and fruitiness, which people fall in love with. It also means less polyphenols, which are a health-protecting anti-oxidant."

The polyphenol content is also preserved because the olives are immediately milled and crushed, which prevents fermentation and acidity.

These factors both undermine the anti-oxidant content, which is also preserved through cold pressing, a technique where the temperature never rises – in this case – above 21ºC. Special purified water is even used at every stage of production and fruits are grown from trees fed with organic fertiliser.

"The legal limit for olive oil acidity is 0.8 per cent," explains Valeria. "Most oils are around 0.4, but ours is 0.1 per cent – years after production it still tastes perfect. Our approach is incredibly meticulous – we only select the best olives – and we control the whole process from producing to selling."

With an output of 100,000 bottles a year, Olio Verde's oils are in demand globally, selling well in the US and even in Japan where people enjoy drizzling it over raw seafood. Many leading chefs are great fans and appreciate the way Olio Verde offers the perfect extra virgin olive oil for each recipe from two brand lines. It is also a key ingredient in Valeria's animal-fat-free chocolate cake for the family parties.

The company discloses the harvest week of each extra virgin olive oil to ensure maximum transparency and versatility. Through these precise production methods, it is able to obtain varying flavours, tones and colours.

Olio Verde is very much a family affair that is set to continue. Valeria's teenage son Daniel is already learning the art of olive-oil making from his surroundings. "Looking after olive trees is like bringing up children – you have to nurture them," says Valeria. "And no one does this better than this great family."
— www.olioverde.it

AN ARABIAN AFFAIR

————

Soucolat

A SUBTLE HINT of cardamom comes through as the hard chocolate shell gives way to a pale, creamy centre. Next, an unexpected wave of rosewater washes over the tongue, balancing other spices, including saffron and cinnamon, which are delicately discernible in the soft praline centre. These are flavours more commonly found in a Middle Eastern market than in a Belgian-style chocolate, which, for Kuwait-born chocolatier Nada Al-Jouan, is precisely the point.

"I have always loved cooking," says Nada, "and I became fascinated by creating beautiful food products that looked as good as they tasted." In 2007, she established Kuwait's premium artisan chocolate company, Kakao, which focused on producing quality chocolates infused with Middle Eastern flavours. It proved an instant hit in Kuwait, quickly expanding to attract a client base from across the Gulf.

Nada attributes this rapid growth to the "east meets west" quality of her chocolates. "Using the finest French and Swiss chocolate, we create and develop original recipes containing traditional Arabic and Kuwaiti flavours," she says, explaining that the company satisfies a demand for products that reflect local heritage. Earlier this year, she changed the brand's name to more closely reflect its roots, settling on Soucolat, which combines the Arabic word for marketplace – *souk* – with the French word for chocolate.

Some of her most popular creations are based on traditional Kuwaiti desserts. The Muhalbiya, topped with Middle Eastern candy floss, was inspired by a rosewater and mastic powder-infused milk pudding that's popular in Kuwait. Another best-seller is the salted pistachio chocolate slab, which, like many treats on offer in Soucolat's flagship boutique, tastes best with a shot of strong Arabic coffee.

An important feature of the creative process for Nada is an emphasis on using the best and most natural ingredients possible. "We source top-quality ingredients from all around the world then prepare everything by hand," she says. "We only use natural flavours." Every step of the creative process is carried out in-house, right down to caramelising and roasting the nuts and making the pralines and ganache.

This attention to detail extends to the packaging, which is a labour of love for Nada, who places particular emphasis on the appearance of each chocolate. "I am obsessed with the way things look and have a flair for beautiful packaging," she says. "I am self-taught and constantly learning as I go, so I rely on my palate and imagination, and the inspiration of beautiful things."

Nada also drew from the work of the renowned pastry chef, Pierre Hermé, creator of the best-selling Ispahan Macaron flavoured with lychee, rose and raspberry. "I have humbly taken the elements of his creation and transformed it into a chocolate piece, blending rosewater and raspberries with almond," she says. This is the latest in a line of new creations sold at Soucolat, which supplements its permanent collection with seasonal and special-edition lines built around national and religious holidays.

But it's luxury weddings, baby receptions, private parties and corporate gatherings where Soucolat excels, often creating customised chocolates and new flavours according to a theme. Soucolat customers are always eager to celebrate special occasions with Nada's exquisite Arabian chocolates.
— www.soucolat.com

CURED BY NATURE

Salumi Subissati

THE TUSCAN HILLSIDE town of Roccastrada has an idyllic location, and the beauty of the surrounding countryside is reflected in the food produced by Riccardo Subissati. Founded in 1963, Salumi Subissati produces Italian cured meats, salamis and sausages using traditional methods. This requires time and effort but it results in exceptional, award-winning products – the company won three gold stars in the International Superior Taste Award.

A new production site is underway, but this will not change how the company produces its range of prosciutto, soppressata, salami, capocollo, rigatino, ham and sausages of all kinds. "Our aim is to increase the production of high-quality, free-range pigs reared in the wild woodlands," says Riccardo, "and bring traditional and modern-day technologies together, where the quality of the meat is one of excellence."

Ricardo continues the family tradition of personally selecting the finest Italian pork and supervising every stage of the process. His father Giancarlo was just as forward-looking when he started the firm, selling products via a mobile shop, so they were available in towns further afield. Now, Salumi Subissati's products can be found in Sweden, Denmark and Luxembourg, as well as throughout Italy, where the company is a byword for outstanding quality. This comes from ingredients, recipes and the method of production.

"We use traditional curing methods, and only include pork, salt and herbs," says Anne-Marie O'Brien, the company's Export Manager. "We don't bulk out the sausage with anything. It is pure meat. We want the taste to be high quality; we don't want an everyday experience. The process we use means we can have a lower salt content. Lots of our salamis are popular because of the things we add, such as pine nuts or truffle. Tuscan herbs is our big seller. Tastes change, but we always use traditional methods."

With a view to maintaining the authenticity of these extraordinary, organic cured meats, Subbisati is currently collaborating with a local farmer who breeds pigs that roam free in extensive woodlands dominated by the dense Mediterranean bush. The pigs feed off whatever they can find – acorns, berries, wild mushrooms, organic cereals and grains. It is a long-term, slow project but the outcome promises to be exceptional. The quality is also helped by the perfect climatic conditions found in Roccastrada, high in the hills and caressed by the scent of the sea breeze. "The position of the village, 460 metres above sea level, means the product can be cured more naturally," says Anne-Marie.

Riccardo and his family are determined to maintain this quality rather than take short cuts, and this helps the company stand out from its competitors. "When my father started the business in 1963," says Riccardo, "it was part of everyday life to butcher and cure meats. In those days, with only four or five products on offer, the competition waned or increased within the boundaries of a very limited market. Things slowly began to change and, in just two decades, the number of high-quality producers increased and the art of pork butchery exported worldwide. Today, with an ever-evolving food industry, some brands have chosen to focus on quality. We are one of these."
— www.subissaticoldmeats.com

TEA'S COMPANY

The Tea and Herb Company

SENAKA KOTAGAMA GREW up on his family plantation in the highlands of Ceylon – now Sri Lanka – where, since boyhood, his senses have been inspired by the aromas and rich colours of the plants. "I have been experimenting with ingredients since I was a child," he says. "After leaving school, I trained as a tea taster, and have dedicated 32 years of my life to producing subtle flavours and fragrances."

Senaka is now Chairman and founder of Silkenty Designer & Gift Tea – a proprietary brand of The Tea and Herb Company. Founded in 1998, the company sources, purifies, processes and exports the finest natural and organic Ceylon teas, its forte being garden-fresh, unblended 100 per cent pure Ceylon tea in its unadulterated condition. All teas are harvested, processed and packed for export in a matter of a few days, using cutting-edge technology and the best packaging, thus locking in each tea's full flavour and freshness.

To the many connoisseurs around the world who appreciate Silkenty's generous selection of tea and allied blends, good taste is not limited to flavour. The company's flair for visual design is also evident in every detail – from its packaging, adorned with a selection of romantic poems, to its elegant website. As well as leaf teas, Silkenty's products include other unique teas, herbs, spices, berries and other fruits, sourced from around the world. The company's team of expert blenders and tasters regularly get together to pool their creativity and imagination.

"We are really bold in our experimentation, continually questing to create exotic and exciting new flavours," says Senaka. From the robust richness of black Bombay Chai to the delicate bergamot orange bouquet of the aristocratic Earl Grey, there are blends to suit every taste. Sensual rewards are delivered by a range of fruit and flower infusions –

from honeydew melon and apricot to hibiscus flowers blended with rose hips. Traditionalists can savour the delicate fragrance of the white tea beloved for centuries of Chinese emperors and their courtiers.

Silkenty's signature silk-like tea bags are made in a pyramid shape, large enough to include rough-cut leaves, herbs, buds, petals and whole berries. Each bag is loosely filled to augment the taste by enhancing water circulation, and is created from a variety of corn starch – strong enough to withstand boiling infusion, but also entirely biodegradable.

These days, high-quality tea is appreciated by connoisseurs in the manner of a fine wine, and Silkenty is attracting the attention of high-end luxury hotel customers with a gourmet palate. The company's elegant gift boxes are also proving popular around the world, and it is possible to choose ready-made or bespoke selections from the company's easily navigable website.

Of all of his company's numerous blends and creations, Senaka's favourite is Real Berry Iced Tea. "When I created it, I submitted it for the World Tea Championship in Las Vegas," he says, "and the judges awarded it Best Iced Tea. I was delighted."

At Silkenty, experimentation is a continual and never-ending process, born out of the joy that the team derives from finding new flavour combinations. "Our teas are always evolving," says Senaka, "and we never stop surprising ourselves. They truly are a feast for the senses. As the great Victorian prime minister William Gladstone famously put it: 'If you are cold, tea will warm you; if you are too heated, it will cool you; If you are depressed, it will cheer you; If you are excited, it will calm you.'"
— www.silkenty.com

WELL WORTH THE WAIT

Domaine Pichard

PATIENCE, IT IS said, is a virtue. Oenophiles who wait a decade or so before opening a bottle of Cuvée Renée from Domaine Pichard will be rewarded with a ruby-gold wine with hints of spice typical of the Madiran appellation. "Madiran was considered on a par with Pomerol and Pauillac," says Domaine Pichard Director Rod Cork. "Queen Victoria drank it at royal banquets. In reviving Domaine Pichard, we are investing in a wine that we believe is the jewel in the crown."

Domaine Pichard lies on a south-facing slope looking towards the Pyrenees in south-west France. "The location is fantastic, very unspoilt, a bit like living in a time warp," says Rod. When he and his brother-in-law Jean Sentilles bought the 12-hectare domaine in 2005, they planted new vines, renovated the cellars and installed new *foudres* (door-height kegs) for vinification. After four years of a clean soil programme, Domaine Pichard received its organic certification. "We have 100 per cent traceability of each row of grapes," says Rod, "from harvest through vinification to bottling."

Today, the domaine extends to 22 hectares, planted with Tannat, Cabernet Franc and Petit Manseng. "In order to have the Madiran appellation, you must use a minimum of 50 per cent Tannat," says Rod. "Our prestige wines, Cuvée Renée and Cuvée Aimée, contain 80 to 95 per cent Tannat and up to 20 per cent Cabernet Franc. Many of the Cabernet Franc vines are more than 50 years old and give a unique and recognisable taste of coffee, tobacco, blackberry and black fruit."

With the vinification process taking between 24 and 36 months, it isn't just the wine drinker who has to show patience when investing in Domaine Pichard's Madiran. "The most recent wine we have been selling is the 2011," says Rod. "This is because so much work goes into assembling and maturing the wine."

Rod and Jean also grow a tiny acreage of the rare Pacherenc grape, which produces a sweet, light white wine with a low sugar content. "Depending on the climatic conditions, it tastes of grapefruit, pineapple, honey or vanilla," says Rod. "I think it's the future." Domaine Pichard produces 10,000 bottles of Pacherenc a year and between 50,000 and 70,000 bottles of Madiran. "We are not looking to sell wine on a large scale, but to connoisseurs," he adds.

The cachet of Madiran wines lies not just in their quality, but in the scarcity of the Tannat grape. The phylloxera epidemic at the turn of the 20th century devastated swathes of vines and, by the 1950s, only a smattering of Tannat vines had survived. "Wine production in the Madiran area is still minute," says Rod, "probably 5 per cent of wine produced in Bordeaux."

Tannat has long been prized for its health benefits. It contains no sulphur and four times the amount of polyphenol of other grapes. Polyphenol, which protects against heart disease, is the root of the "French paradox", where Madiran wines offset the richness of the duck and goose dishes eaten in the region.

"For those with the cellar space and the patience, Domaine Pichard is creating wines that are the equal of any grand Bordeaux," says Rod. "We are demonstrating to the world that Madiran is a first-class wine and Pacherenc is a wine of enormous potential."

— www.domainepichard.com

VIRGIN TERRITORY

Ritual Bloom

THERE ARE MORE than 132 million olive trees growing on the sun-soaked hillsides of Greece, where the tradition of harvesting the fruit for oil dates back thousands of years. Today's farmers draw on expertise passed down through countless generations, and as the world's leading producer of black olives, the country plays a leading role in the international olive oil market, exporting around half of its crop each year.

While Europe's other olive oil giants, Spain and Italy, have carved out a space for premium varieties, Greece's output is predominantly bulk exports, with only around 5 per cent reflecting the origin of the bottled produce. That's why the founders of Ritual Bloom decided to establish a boutique brand, building on the time-honoured traditions to create a luxury, organic olive oil with a full-bodied flavour that captures the essence of Greece.

"Our aim is to promote Greek olive oil," says Constantin Athitakis of Ritual Bloom, "both in the domestic market as a fully certified organic product but also abroad in order to strengthen the image of this high-quality, traditional and typically Greek product." Constantin founded the brand with his business partner Filippou George in 2015. Today, Ritual Bloom can be found in gourmet food shops across Greece and in high-end food stores and restaurants worldwide, in addition to its growing sales base online.

The brand's success, says Constantin, is encapsulated by its motto: "Earth, trees and sun are our ingredients." Come harvest time, hand-picked fruits are chosen for their colour, ripeness and condition, with two varieties of olive used – Athinolia, known for the intensity of its flavour, and Koroneiki, which has a high ratio of skin to flesh, giving the oil its coveted aromatic quality.

A blend of time-tested cultivation methods and new technologies is used to manufacture the product. "It is a ritual, steeped in custom and tradition," says Constantin. "Olive oil is a live product. It requires care at every stage of the production process, from the olive grove to the bottling, from the storage to the final placement of the product on the shelf."
— www.ritualbloom.com

GOURMET GOES GLOBAL

Bazzar, Brazil

ANY CONVERSATION ABOUT which country produces the best food is unlikely to include Brazil – largely because the average consumer lacks knowledge about the quality of Brazilian ingredients. It's something that husband-and-wife team Cristiana Beltrão and André Paraizo wanted to address when they opened their first restaurant in 1998. Bazzar was established in the heart of Ipanema and offered a new concept in Rio de Janeiro's food outlets: farm-to-table fresh food.

It was an unusual approach but critics were soon praising the restaurant for its innovative and health-conscious approach. Before long, customers – who came to the restaurant in their droves – wanted to know how to recreate the delicious meals they encountered there – and so the Bazzar Factory was born.

"All Bazzar products come from recipes made in our restaurant," says Cristiana, co-owner of Bazzar. "The cooking sauces, the desserts – each item comes from the inspiration and expertise of our chefs." Its range includes the Açaí Dessert, a Brazilian sweet typically eaten at the start of the day and made with guaraná berry and banana, and Brigadeiro, a traditional rich chocolate dessert.

In time, palates from further afield have also been able to enjoy the Brazilian treats. Bazzar is now stocked in some of the major department stores across the world, including Harrods in the UK, La Grande Épicerie at Le Bon Marché in Paris and Sogo & Seibu in Japan. "We are also very proud to be currently distributed by premium supermarkets like Marks & Spencer in the UK and Fairway Market in the US," says Cristiana, "in addition to more than 900 points of sale throughout Brazil."

Among Bazzar's many awards is the World Packaging Organisation Innovation Award. "That was especially important to us," says Cristiana. "We were recognised for innovation and quality while in contention with the biggest global brands."

Two factors have dominated the firm's rise to success. "We are driven by a passion for food and a passion for bringing the essence of Brazil to consumers everywhere," says Cristiana. "Our range is made with natural ingredients from our country that were, until now, a Brazilian secret. Bazzar's ambition from here is a simple one: to bring a slice of Rio de Janeiro to every plate in the world."
— www.bazzar.com.br/en

ELEGANT SPACES

Interiors and architecture

SUPERIOR INTERIORS

Louise Jones Interiors

LONDON-BASED INTERIOR designer Louise Jones has a single aim with every project she takes on – to deliver an end result that surpasses all expectations. Over the years she has built a reputation for working on residences where the owners are "starting again", be it a new build or a complete redesign.

"Our clients have very specific tastes and desires," says Louise. "We're often dealing with people on the *Forbes* Billionaire List or the *Sunday Times* Rich List. They know what works and what doesn't work. They've been to all the best hotels, they've been to the nicest houses; they are very particular. Some will want me to run with the look, others will want to get involved with the look and adapt it as the project goes on."

Louise lives and breathes every project that she and her seven-strong team take on. "These clients want something completely bespoke, and they have very high expectations," she says. "It's why I deliver far more than they expect, in terms of the quality and beauty, and practicality of the end result."

She gets to know the client well enough to establish a firm grasp of what they do and don't like – often meeting up every week – before producing hand-drawn sketches. After this comes a close consultation, and then the design, look and feel evolve, until the very last detail is complete. Projects start at around £500,000 and can cost as much as £35 million, taking anything between one and six years.

"We deal with some new builds, and some older properties that have been completely gutted and rebuilt," she says. "One West London property, for instance, had been reduced to what builders describe as 'shell and core' – complete bare bones. The emphasis then shifts to the architect, although we still have to discuss with each client the room layouts, the position of kitchens and bathrooms, the lighting and the electrics. Then come the hard finishes – the timber floors, the fireplaces, the bathroom marble. Finally, we'll work on the soft furnishings and furniture."

These final details might include every last cushion, mirror, artwork or *objet d'art*. "These always vary massively, from one project to the next," says Louise. "For instance, we recently worked on a property in Belgravia, where the lady of the house was from Syria, and she was keen to have something that reminded her of home. Before the terrible civil war started, I managed to commission some beautiful art pieces from Damascus and had them sent over.

"Other times I might be dealing with traditional country homes and working with patterns and colours that are very English and traditional," she continues, "but in a not-too-stuffy way. We recently worked on the extension of a country estate in Scotland where we wanted it to look like it had been used for hundreds of years. We got in specialist

Architecture
in the 20th Century

100 INTERIORS AROUND THE WORLD

LELEU

cabinet makers to create something with distressed wood and we used deliberately aged fabrics."

Sometimes, clients will require something more hi-tech. "I've designed houses with golf simulator rooms, shooting simulator rooms and discotheques," says Louise. "There are some clients who demand swimming pools with underwater sound and projector screens. I've worked with some of the top specialist companies around the world, and I've become adept at integrating all of these requirements into my designs."

Louise Jones Interiors has designed restaurants and a high-end bespoke boutique hotel, but tends to concentrate on a varied selection of residential properties. The firm is as expert at transforming an Australian villa as it is a Swiss chalet, a Georgian chateau or a Moscow mansion. Indeed, some clients have more than one property being revamped at any one time. It means that Louise's contact book reads like a who's who of international interior design. She can bring items to the design mix that simply aren't available anywhere else, whether in terms of specialist finishes, bespoke furniture or unusual textiles.

"That's what makes the job so exciting," says Louise. "Going that extra mile to source something, or sourcing something that you haven't sought previously for anyone else, these things are par for the course. I'll always end up somewhere I haven't been before, or working with someone I haven't worked with before."

Louise initially embarked on a successful career as an accountant for Price Waterhouse Cooper in Manchester before switching jobs. "I desperately missed doing something creative," she says. She moved to London, retrained at the Inchbald School of Design and served her apprenticeship at top interior designers Todhunter Earle before setting up her own firm – based in Lots Road, Chelsea – in 2001. Her work has since been feted by the press, with Louise recently appearing on *House & Garden*'s list of the top 100 interior designers and featuring in *The Sunday Times* and *Essential Kitchen Bedroom Bathroom* magazine.

Yet, after 20 years in the business, every project is still unique. "I would never want to repeat myself," she says. "If I did, I wouldn't be a designer, I'd be a shopper! I try to give clients exactly what they want – beyond their expectations, actually. In terms of the beauty of the end result, and the practicality of the end result, I use all my experience and all my contacts to give the client something really special. It's where my sense of style comes to the fore. I not only have a knowledge of materials and finishes, but also I've developed the ability to visualise the end result."

It is this level of attention to detail that has earned Louise an international reputation, with most of her work coming from recommendations and via word of mouth. "That's because it is in the nature of me and my clients to insist that nothing less will do."
— www.louisejonesinteriors.com

DOWN TIME

Ringsted Dun

SLEEP ISN'T SOMETHING to be taken lightly at Ringsted Dun. From the quality of the down which fills its duvets and pillows to the equally high ethical standards the Danish company sets itself, a lot of effort goes into ensuring a good night's sleep.

"We want to deliver our customers' dreams," says CEO Peter B Petersen. And their recipe for utter relaxation mixes the best handcrafted luxury with the latest technology to help create the perfect duvet for each individual person.

Founded in 1947, the company is still privately owned, with a staff of 80 based at its headquarters a few hours west of Copenhagen. "It's important that we're able to produce in Denmark," says Peter. "We have been using duvets in Denmark for a thousand years and the process of filling has been done this way for decades. Even the Danish royalty use our duvets."

Fittingly, the bedding is inspired by Hans Christian Andersen's Fairy Tales, with duvets called The Snow Queen, The Nightingale and The Princess and the Pea (whose handmade silk cover and rare Icelandic eiderdown filling is one of the most exclusive and luxurious creations in the collection).

While Ringsted Dun will never sacrifice its individual, detailed approach to fully automated production, it has embraced technology in some respects. Special machines speed up the more repetitive parts of the factory process, reducing to five minutes the time it takes to make one duvet.

What's never compromised is the quality of the down and feathers, sourced from across Europe as a by-product of the food industry. Everything from washing and sorting to testing, filling and shipping is then carried out on the Danish site. "Everything is sorted by hand," says Peter. "We also have our own laboratory to check for different parameters such as the down quality. It's very important to us that we actually meet the highest criteria for the world, not just for a given country."

Ringsted Dun is a member of the European Down & Feather Association, which ensures that suppliers are regularly audited to prevent animal cruelty. Its membership has an impact on the quality of its merchandise, too: birds in Europe enjoy a longer life, resulting in more mature feathers and a longer-lasting, more luxurious product.

This ethical approach to production, combined with the use of natural materials in the manufacture of duvets, has helped to extend Ringsted Dun's customer base to around 60 countries. While its biggest markets are Scandinavia and Asia, there are plans to expand further into both Asia and Britain.

"Ringsted Dun produces superior duvets and pillows of outstanding quality and craftsmanship," says Freddy Svane, Denmark's ambassador in Japan. "It has set high standards within the sector and has impressively lived up to the strictest expectations which must be set."

Ringsted Dun's latest forward-looking project is to build a sleep laboratory in collaboration with the Technical University of Denmark. Because with ever-changing technology helping to create the ultimate night's sleep, the company isn't about to be caught napping. Unlike its happy customers.
— www.ringsteddun.com

DREAM WEAVERS

Leitner Leinen

NESTLED IN THE green, undulating hills of Austria's Mühlviertel is a tradition that goes back five generations. Once scattered with the blue flowers of the flax fields, the hills are alive with the sound of weaving, and the rich linen tradition of the Leitner family continues in the village of Ulrichsberg, near the Bavarian and Bohemian borders.

Leitner Leinen was founded in 1853 and is now a leader in Austria's textile industry. The company produces table, bath and bedlinens elegant enough to completely transform a room, whether contemporary or classic. Jakob Leitner, from the family's sixth generation, outlines the company's commitment to quality and design. "The product is totally crafted in Ulrichsberg. We use flax from France and Belgium now, and threads spun exclusively for Leitner in Italy and Hungary add to the quality." The weave itself is unusual: 40 warp threads per cm contribute to the exclusive luxury finish of the product.

With Leitner products available across Europe and the rest of the world, Jakob credits his father, director Friedrich Leitner, with creating a brand that boasts both modern appeal and timeless designs. "Leitner today is a byword for fine, natural yarn," says Friedrich. "We have learned over the years how to process the finest and most difficult fibres, to consider the significance of colour, and by using subtle shades in richly varied nuances, the items in our collections may be harmoniously combined." Designs include pure, plain bed linens that are at once fresh and subtle, discreet botanic relief designs and traditional Austrian textile motifs.

The introduction of terry linen and soft, tactile loungewear adds to the versatility of Leitner Leinen's products; and, as all the products are available by the metre, creating custom products is simple. "We introduced our first capsule collections in 1995," says Jakob, "and more than 20 years on, most of these designs are just as popular."

Design inspiration comes from woodcuts, paintings and the natural environment from different regions of Austria. These are given a modern touch with a natural colour palette. "Our in-house designer has been producing our exclusive collections for 15 years, and her designs are exciting yet classic," Jakob adds. Interior designers and lifestyle stores alike love the ease of ordering fabric by the metre, allowing them to create their own Leitner curtains, upholstery and home textiles, as well as taking advantage of Leitner's own bespoke made-to-measure services.

Fusing tradition with contemporary design, Leitner Leinen is a brand synonymous with luxurious, tactile fabrics. Not only do Leitner Leinen textiles feature in the private spaces of Europe's design-conscious, they can also be found in some of the top restaurants and hotels around the globe, including the Armani Hotel in Dubai and Le Bailli de Suffren in Saint-Tropez. And because Leitner textiles combine modern neutrals with pared-back classics, they have the kind of timeless appeal that makes them popular in stylish homes from Germany to Japan: a far cry from the hills of the Mühlviertel.

— www.leitnerleinen.com

PRIDE OF LACE

———

Geraldine Larkin

IRELAND HAS A rich history of producing some of the world's finest textiles, from its crisp linen to its intricate lace designs. However, Irish designer Geraldine Larkin has taken traditional textile techniques and used her architectural background to turn them into covetable and contemporary works of art. While hand embroidery might conjure images of gentle domesticity, Geraldine Larkin's home textiles are couture pieces – small-scale art installations that elevate hand embroidery to true heirlooms.

Geraldine began her design career at University College, Dublin, where she studied architecture, but her love of surface detail and textiles took her to Central Saint Martin's in London where she worked with some of the UK's leading fashion designers. "I undertook an internship with Jasper Conran, among others, and loved his work as a colourist," says Geraldine. "He really encouraged me and gave me the freedom to explore my surface textile work."

Geraldine's pursuit of learning museum-quality embroidery techniques led her to some of the world's best craftspeople, many of whom she still works with today. "These artisans helped me use traditional ways to realise more contemporary designs," she says. "Part of the beauty of these textiles is their esoteric quality – somehow part of these craftsmen's spirit and passion goes into each finished piece. Somebody has put their time and skills into it and that's very important."

After working for more than 20 years in fashion in London, New York, Paris and Milan, Geraldine turned her skills to home textiles. Her background in fashion has given her a new perspective on home decoration. "Originally, I was designing embroidery for evening wear or accessories, but moving into interiors showed how differently embroidery can be presented," she says.

Everything from cushions and curtains, to table linen, wall panels and lampshades can be adorned with Geraldine's designs, but it goes beyond the usual home textiles. "We can add designs to anything – fire screens, wardrobe door panels, upholstery, you name it – and the beauty of hand embroidery means that we can use almost any fabric, even fur and leather."

Each piece is custom-designed and, due to the nature of hand embroidery, each is truly unique. Like a snowflake, each stitch is different to the next, although a central thread of design runs through all of Geraldine's pieces. "Every single piece is drawn by me," she says. "I originate all the artwork, and it's like my signature or handwriting throughout all the work."

Her team of specialist embroiderers is global, and Geraldine has been working with her main atelier in India for more than 20 years. Bespoke designs can be refined or produced from conception to completion at the Geraldine Larkin studio in London's Notting Hill, which is also where her archive of some 10,000 samples is housed for those who wish to visit, by appointment only.

"I love the process of designing and no project is too challenging," says Geraldine. A recent project took her back to her origins in fashion design when she embroidered pieces for British fashion designer Giles Deacon's Paris couture show. "We're passionate about modern interpretations of this artisanal skill," she says, "and really the only limit is one's imagination."
— www.geraldinelarkin.com

SPINNING GOLD

———

Cecchi e Cecchi

ALTHOUGH PRATO IN Tuscany has been the home of Italy's textile industry for centuries, it was true serendipity when two men named Mario Cecchi met there in 1958. It transpired that both weavers were expert in producing luxury home textiles, so they decided to pool their experience and keen eye for texture and pattern to form a company. And thus Cecchi e Cecchi was born.

For more than 60 years, the company has continued to produce artisan textiles, and to this day Cecchi e Cecchi's plaid blankets, wool throws and scarves are made entirely in Italy. "Everything we make is designed in-house, using fibres that are spun here in Tuscany," says the company's President Roberta Pecci, whose family took ownership of Cecchi e Cecchi in 2007. "My family has been weaving various fabrics for renowned apparel brands around the world since 1884, even throughout the wars. We are proud to continue this tradition in Prato.

"Some of our designs go back 50 years," she continues, "and we have huge jacquard looms, which means we're able to incorporate traditional techniques into even our contemporary designs." The company's collections of throws and blankets feature a range of styles including soft and drapey damasks – often based on Venetian designs – richly tactile cable-knit throws and cosy mohair bedspreads. "We use a high percentage of natural fibres, such as cashmere, lambswool and silk," says Roberta. "Ultimately, this creates a luxurious product that lasts for a long time. Our artisan textiles are unique and can maintain their beauty for 20 years in some cases."

Cecchi e Cecchi's consistent high quality has resulted in its textiles being featured in some of the world's best-dressed hotel rooms, thanks to the company's bespoke design service. "We work closely with interior designers to produce custom ranges," says Roberta. "Because of my family's rich textile heritage, we're able to produce the fibres and colours that work well with the Cecchi e Cecchi aesthetic." With a typically Italian dedication to quality, texture and design, Cecchi e Cecchi is proud to maintain Prato's traditions, weaving a beautiful legacy in decorative living for generations to come.

— www.cecchicecchi.it

THE ART OF GLASS

Aristide Najean

Aristide Najean's home and furnace are so full of his own colourful, elaborate glass works that they could easily be mistaken for private galleries. Delicate cherry blossom chandeliers inspired by Japanese poetry – each 5 ft wide – flourish in the living room, while a series reminiscent of monastic candelabra, with opaque glass dripping like wax, adorn the kitchen. In the furnace, the constantly boiling oven fuses minerals together, ready for the next stunning glass creation.

Born and bred in Paris, Aristide arrived on Murano in 1986 to study the Venetian island's renowned, centuries-old glassmaking techniques. Originally a painter, he saw glassmaking as an extension of this, and it became his preferred material. His chandeliers are thus inspired by both painting and glassmaking, which mutually interact and are each pushed to their limits. "Aristide observes everything consistently, methodically, analytically," says Sylvie Plassnig, his partner of 19 years. "He is always open to inspiration and his oeuvre is completely different to anything else."

Aristide's glass art is inspired by its Muranese heritage, but his creativity, his appreciation of colour, and his fresh, poetic and innovative light creations represent a new approach, raising its status to that of contemporary art. In a quest for excellence, Aristide drives forward his team of highly skilled masters. He works with Baccarat Crystal, and their *Zénith sur la lagune* collaboration brought the rival French and Italian glass traditions together for the very first time. The result is spectacular, with Aristide's brightly coloured stags bursting from Baccarat's intricate, sparkling, cut-glass chandelier.

Aristide's work has caught the attention of world-renowned designers including Starck, Jouin, Wilmotte, Moinard and Manku, and can be seen in such high-end hotels as The Dorchester in London, Le Royal Monceau in Paris and the Palazzina G in Venice. He also receives many private commissions.

"Meeting a customer is always exciting," he says. "It involves balancing their requirements with what I feel for them. I want to create works of art that fit them exactly, and bring happiness into their home. Using my intuition and sensitivity, I quickly conceptualise the artwork they're looking for." Aristide's commitment to the craft is palpable – and it is forever crystallised in each of his masterpieces.
— www.aristidenajean.ch

HISTORY IN THE MAKING

Baldi

THE BALDI FAMILY boasts an impressive creative heritage that dates back to its ancestor Vincenzo Consani. A prominent 19th-century Italian sculptor, Vincenzo created the marble statue *La Vittoria* (Victory), a masterpiece that is currently housed in Florence's Pitti Palace.

This artistic talent is still evident today in the luxury furniture and home accessories produced by Vincenzo's descendants at the Baldi design company. Founded as an atelier in 1867, Baldi is now run by Vincenzo Consani's great-great-grandson Luca Baldi, Luca's sister Francesca Baldi, and head of R&D and Production Leonardo Boni. "We are a historic Florentine company that specialises in creating one-of-a-kind, custom-made statement pieces that are nothing less than jewels for the home," says Luca.

Baldi's artisans are masters of traditional Tuscan decorative art techniques, from mouth-blown and hand-engraved lead crystal to precision casting, stone cutting and bronze chiselling. With an emphasis on splendour and attention to detail, Baldi's furniture, lighting and accessories collection *Home Jewels* often mixes two or three elements – bronze, crystals or gemstones, and marble or mosaics.

The decorative techniques enhance and reveal the natural beauty of the finest materials gathered from around the world – light shining through rock crystal, the vivid colours of purple amethyst, green malachite and blue lapis lazuli, and the iridescent patterns of tiger's eye. Among Baldi's most striking pieces are rock crystal bathtubs, carved from a single block sourced from the Amazon rainforest in Brazil and retailing at nearly €1 million. One especially dedicated client commissioned a bathroom in malachite mosaic and gold-plated bronze, a seven-metre-high, stone-and-bronze clock decorated with gilt carving and lion heads, and a Steinway grand piano clad in gilt-edged malachite veneer.

"The use of colourful stones in the production of decorative objects has been popular in Italy since the Renaissance," says Leonardo Boni, "when work with precious stones was flourishing in Florence under the influence of the Medici family."

The talent behind the company's artistic vision is the renowned designer Luca Bojola, the company's Creative Director, assisted by a young team from Florence's leading industrial design university. Together they combine traditional crafts with the latest 3D scanning, printing and rendering technology. "We have mastered the art of creating unique and timeless pieces that represent the quintessence of Italian style and centuries-old craftsmanship," says Luca Baldi. It is particularly apparent in the company's most challenging project to date, its Jewel Home, Casa Baldi, where clients can customise any room in a house in the Baldi style.

Baldi has a flagship boutique at Harrods in London and 13 other outlets, including ones in Dubai, Moscow and Muscat. Luca credits the company's "creative members" throughout the generations as the inspiration for its designs. "Today, as in the past, the secret of Baldi's success remains our refined taste, our great aesthetic sense and our long-standing tradition of craftsmanship," he says. Vincenzo Consani's natural talent lives on in his descendants at Baldi, who are dedicated to preserving his legacy – and to creating masterpieces of their very own.
— www.baldihomejewels.com

A PERFECT BLEND

―――――

Gentili Mosconi

SOME MARRIAGES ARE made in heaven. As long ago as 1988, the creative flair of Patrizia Mosconi and the business acumen of Francesco Gentili came together to found the luxury interiors company Gentili Mosconi. Still united in both love and business nearly 30 years on, it was a meeting of hearts as well as minds.

"We are optimists," Francesco says of the couple's long-term success. "We don't have delusions of grandeur, but we are aware that, through our shared passion, we can achieve even the most arduous of goals."

Established during a period of significant growth within the Italian textiles industry, Gentili Mosconi identified clear objectives from the outset, choosing to focus on impeccable quality and to combine traditional handicrafts with new technology. Initially headquartered in a humble apartment in Como, northern Italy, the company started out producing ties and silk scarves.

Today, it develops textiles for the world's most renowned haute couture and prêt-à-porter brands, while also producing exquisite interior textiles for private clients and companies from Europe, the US, Russia, Japan and the Middle East. Gentili Mosconi's reputation continues to grow via social media and word of mouth. And, to keep up with demand, the company now works from three locations and employs more than 60 skilled artisans and office staff.

The founding duo are still central to this success, guiding the company forward while remaining true to their original ambitions. Patrizia's expertise is primarily in design, working with fine satin, silk, linen and cotton, and embellishing fabrics with jacquard patterns, embroideries and classic Italian hemming techniques. She creates elegant household linens,

towels, bathrobes and customised quilted rugs, ensuring that each product is unique.

With much of Patrizia's inspiration drawn from the sea, it comes as no surprise that she has experience producing interiors not only for homes but also yachts. The super yacht Wider 150 called *Genesi* is her latest interior project and is pictured opposite. "My family's company worked with the Italian navy," she says. "Decorating a yacht is always a great challenge as it requires the utmost attention to detail."

Francesco, meanwhile – with his strong leadership and unwavering tenacity – is the driving force behind the business side of Gentili Mosconi. "He combines creativity and management ability, and he's the touchstone for everyone," says Gentili Mosconi's Style Director, Neera Tana. "He is always in control – nothing gets past him. But what makes him an exceptional person is his innate sensitivity towards every single member of the company. He believes he should be responsible not only for their wealth, but also for their well-being."

Employees are made to feel part of a big family, but what makes the company really stand out is that every item is produced locally. This is, unquestionably, one of the cornerstones of Gentili Mosconi, empowering highly specialised artisans – whose skills have been handed down from generation to generation – to oversee industrial production.

"Being made in Italy," says Francesco, "is emblematic of our quality, prestige and refinement. Creativity is innate to the genetic makeup of every Italian and allows us to develop original products, different from those offered by our competitors. We have at our disposal an unmatched heritage and we work tirelessly to get the best out of it."
— www.gentilimosconihome.com

CHARACTER BUILDING

BC&D International

HONG KONG'S FAMOUS skyline owes much to its cosmopolitan society. It is a city that accommodates huge numbers of people in a limited space, and its vibrant blend of cultures has contributed to the development of a distinctly modern urban setting.

Within this dynamic architectural environment, Hong Kong design firm BC&D International creates unique and engaging structures that capture the city's contemporary aesthetic in new and interesting ways. "Our design is typically clean cut and functional but with an eye for exquisite details," says Brian Chan, BC&D's Managing Director. "We always approach building and interior design as bespoke tailoring, in that our clients' needs are carefully attended to and expressed in a highly individual manner."

Where BC&D stands out is through a strong focus on the human quality of a building, not just from a structural perspective but in the look and feel that will make a project inviting for human interactions upon completion. "This is the humanistic DNA of our design," says Chan. "It's one that emphasises various elements that are essential to *joie de vivre*. I take cross-cultural lifestyles and put them together."

He points to past projects, which include a boutique hotel in Beijing, private residences in the heart of Hong Kong, and large-scale office developments and headquarters for major global companies all across Asia. This diversity is enabled by the multidisciplinary services that BC&D offers, including architectural design and planning, interior design and corporate branding.

"The design field is frequently split into distinct disciplines," says Chan. "Companies will typically focus on just architecture, interior design, landscape, urban planning, graphics or branding. Our vision is to combine all of these elements to create a holistic and harmonious whole." Perhaps this "Vitruvian vision" can be credited to Chan's education at that pillar of American architectural training, Cornell University.

Upon receiving his professional degree at Cornell, Chan worked on large-scale institutional structures and residential developments in the US before moving back to Hong Kong to begin his own architectural practice. Since 1992, his firm has consistently produced quality work and earned accolades in the field.

Today, BC&D's teams work out of studios spread across Hong Kong, Thailand and China, with an eye on new opportunities further afield, including several small-scale ventures in Paris and New York. Current projects include a private hospital and a training school for the Hong Kong Fire Services Department, which is the largest institution of its kind in Asia. The company has been commissioned by one of China's foremost technology companies to design the public spaces of its trophy headquarters building, which Chan is particularly excited about.

"It's a great opportunity to showcase our expertise and design sensibility," he says. "We strive to strike a balance between classical principles and avant garde visions, and we embrace the future without losing all the wonderful ingredients that helped to form great civilisations." The marriage of old and new is evident in many of Hong Kong's contemporary structures but Chan's "Renaissance Man" vision sets BC&D apart, giving it a distinct identity in the crowded cityscape.
— www.bcd-intl.com

SMOOTH OPERATOR

Lameirinho

"THE FINISHING STAGE of the production process is the secret of my business," explains Paulo Coelho Lima. In the world of luxury home textiles, it is the feel of a fabric that sets it apart from the competition. That is why Paulo's family-owned business Lameirinho is dedicated to ensuring that only perfection will do. "It's the soft touch and smoothness of the fabric that we achieve that makes our product a 'must have' for those who value quality," he says.

This Portuguese company specialises in bedding, bath and table linen, and owes its success to the dedication and vision of the Coelho Lima family. It is they who have been instrumental in creating and maintaining for 68 years a team who are focused on satisfying their customers.

Now in its third generation, the company was founded by Joaquim Martins Coelho Lima in 1948 in Portugal's textile capital Guimaraes. Back then, Lameirinho had just two mechanical looms. Today, this leading home-textile brand is a considerably larger operation with 163 looms, a team of nearly 700 and an international reputation for quality. The production capacity can reach 8 million pieces per year, although the nature of the weaving and textile production is still firmly based on traditional and local skills.

To maintain its reputation for making the finest textiles, Lameirinho controls the entire production in-house, from the weaving and finishing to delivering the product to its customers. A dedicated design team is in charge, creating innovative ranges on a regular basis both for its eponymous labels and for household name brands. It works with a wide range of fibres and blends including silk, cashmere and linen, as well as bamboo, tencel and modal. From satin to jacquard, its organic cotton ranges are chemical-free, demonstrating the importance Lameirinho places on protecting the environment.

This ethical stance has earned the company a GOTS (Global Organic Textile Standard) certification for organic bed linen. "Like health and safety, the environment is important for us," says Paulo, who is also a member of the board of directors. "Lameirinho is a certified company of the highest quality, whether that means health and safety or our attitude towards the environment. This applies to the conception, development, production and commercialisation of all our products, such as ensuring that our organic cotton items are allergen-free."

The Lameirinho brand and licensed fabrics can be found in retail shops, in its seven stores in Portugal and on the company website. The next goal is to have top-class hotels and cruise ships using its bed linen. "It will ensure that their customers are guaranteed a serene and restful sleep," says Paulo.

Although rooted in the ancient techniques of textile production, this brand is certainly not old-fashioned. Indeed, its team of weavers and designers are unrivalled in their interpretation of contemporary elegance and tireless in their pursuit of innovative products such as a new type of linen with a special non-iron finish. Over the decades, Lameirinho has been guided by the values of integrity and trust. "The success of our customers is our own success," says Paulo. These principles also ensure that quality can be guaranteed by the Coelho Lima family from start to finish, both now and for decades to come.
— www.lameirinho.pt

SHIP SHAPE

Carpentry and Boat-Building Services

FOR NEW ZEALANDER Brendon Jost, boatbuilding has been a lifelong passion. "It's pretty much all I've ever wanted to do since I was about 10," he says. "I geared my whole schooling towards it and I've been immersed in it ever since."

This devotion led him to Palma de Mallorca, the west Mediterranean island that has become the main hub of the superyacht industry. After years working as a shipwright, it also led him to strike out on his own and launch Carpentry and Boat-Building Services (CABBS) in 2007. This steadily expanding, skilled and versatile team of expert craftsmen has since become an exemplar of quality in the highly competitive field of yacht carpentry.

"We started out with the smaller boats," recalls Brendon, "and, from there, they just got progressively bigger and bigger. We're now working on some of the most prestigious yachts around." The key to this growth is, perhaps paradoxically, a desire to keep things exclusive. Brendon is not someone who is willing to sacrifice quality for quantity. "I'd rather grow slower and grow stronger," he says. "I hand-pick the people who work with me and make sure that the people I take on know what they're doing and are as passionate about it as I am."

This approach has resulted in some truly striking results; builds that are notable for both their functionality and their beauty. Brendon's passion is for traditional materials such as teak. But he's keen to point out his team's flexibility. "My guys are right up there in terms of the newer ways of doing things," he says, "with new laminates, Perspex and so on."

Essentially, the CABBS service is about choice, with a bespoke ethos. "Pretty much everything we provide is handmade," says Brendon. "All boats are slightly different and you have to be able to work with the different shapes and dimensions. We work to a very high standard. The whole idea is to give people what they want, and we can do just about anything. You could come to us with an unusual idea for a sculpture, for example, and we'd be able to help you out. We can take almost any idea and work with it."
— www.cabbs.es

A SPA IS BORN

Howard Spa Consulting

A MEMORABLE SPA experience is one in which the guest's progress from treatment room to relaxation area is enticing, serene and meticulously managed. With decades of expertise in the luxury sector, Howard Spa Consulting has designed award-winning spas for, among others, Armani/Spa in Dubai and Milan, the Coral Reef Club in Barbados, Dormy House in the Cotswolds and a major showcase project – opening early 2017 – at the five-star Lanesborough Hotel in Knightsbridge.

"When we design a spa, it's about creating a story and an identity that will enable it to stand out from the rest," says owner and Managing Director Neil Howard. "It is about understanding the character and philosophy of the property in which the spa will sit and developing a unique combination of facilities for it. We also advise on staff selection and training – a nice-looking spa isn't anything without exceptional, five-star service."

Neil's attention to detail begins at the architect's drawing stage and encompasses feasibility studies, competitor analysis and a full interior-design specification, down to treatment couches and products. In 2012, Armani/Spa in Milan and the Monastero Santa Rosa Hotel & Spa on the Amalfi coast were both named in *Architectural Digest*'s top 11 "Best-Designed Spas Around The World". Monastero Santa Rosa was also named Best Newcomer in the 2013 *Tatler* Spa Awards. "When we met with Giorgio Armani," says Neil, "the design themes centred around fragrance, texture and a palette that included metallics and obsidian – a hard, glass-like volcanic rock. Delving into what a client wants, layering the themes, balancing the look and treatment menu is a very important part of what we do."

Spas for villas, palaces, gated communities and mega-yachts are a growth area, and Howard Spa Consulting is adept at establishing when and how the owners want to use their spa.

"Our designers have worked with high-end brands, they know the luxury world, yet they aren't egotistical," he says. "They don't put their personal stamp on a project, it's all about what the client wants. We offer a bespoke service from design to soft opening and operation. If you look at our portfolio, none of our spas look the same, which says a lot about our adaptability and skill at interpreting a concept."
— www.howardspaconsulting.com

A FORCE OF NATURE

Simone Naturally Inspired

MANY INTERIOR DESIGNERS talk about "bringing the outside in". Few mean it quite as literally as Simone Arora, whose eponymous store in Mumbai is filled with furniture, homewares and artefacts crafted from wood, sand, crystal and stone. The earthy textures and muted tones form a design concept she calls "nature luxe".

Desks are made from burnished driftwood and mirrored tables are cut to look like pools of water. The showstopping centrepiece is an enormous, 25-ft chandelier that cascades down from the atrium. It has branches made from twisted metal and crystals that are suspended like icicles. "That is my signature piece," says Simone. "It was designed exclusively for the store and made in Europe. It is spectacular."

Simone Naturally Inspired features 140 brands under one roof and is spread over two levels of a beautiful old heritage building, once owned by the commander-in-chief of the Eastern Fleet. "We restored it from the ground up," she says. "It has stunning arched windows, high ceilings and stone walls. The interiors are tranquil and soothing, in natural colour schemes. I wanted to create a haven from the hustle and bustle of city life."

Browsing the store is an immersive experience. The ambient lighting changes three times a day and the air is scented with Simone's signature fragrance. "I want to enlighten and involve the customer from the moment they step in," she says, "it's meant to be a total sensory pleasure."

Simone, which opened in 2014, is the expression of a lifetime's interest in interiors. Its owner was born in 1971 into an artistic family: her father, Sanjay Khan, is a filmmaker and actor, and her mother, Zarine, is a successful interior designer. "Our mother kept a beautiful home full of carefully curated art and furniture," says Simone. "I remember the way she decorated the dining table with fine crystal, fresh linen and flowers for dinner parties. I still count on her eye and sense of aesthetics when choosing merchandise."

Simone married entrepreneur Ajay Arora when she was 21 and together they launched D'Decor, now the largest manufacturer of furnishing fabrics in the world. The idea of launching her own brand came four years ago. "I had always been a silent creative contributor to D'Decor," she says, "and I felt a strong desire to express myself. To create an identity of my own."

Inspiration came from her suburban Mumbai home, Juhu, which she designed with the renowned Indian architect Hafeez Contractor. "I was intensely involved in every aspect of the build," she explains. "I personally sourced all the furniture, accessories and art from Europe. It took years. Now it's an extremely relaxing and rejuvenating place. Every window looks out on lush natural greenery and trees."

This passion for detail explains her new business venture, Project Simone. "With this offering, we provide turn-key project solutions, from conceptualisation to implementation," she says. "We showcase our design concepts via mood boards that encompass a complete look and feel of a space."

Nature remains her inspiration. "The natural world brings us tranquillity and soothes and rejuvenates our minds and senses. Simone is an oasis in the heart of Mumbai and I hope that every customer who comes to my store experiences that."
— www.simone.com

BLUEPRINT FOR BEAUTY

KCA International Designers

LONDON, SHANGHAI AND Hong Kong are some of the most architecturally diverse yet exciting cities on earth, constantly surprising design obsessives with their cutting-edge buildings and luxurious interiors. KCA International Designers is present in each of these cities, quietly creating some of the world's most contemporary and covetable interiors for the penthouses, hotels and even palaces of its clients. Each is based on a philosophy of discretion, balance and a deep passion for great design.

Khuan Chew and Associates (KCA) is a global interior design agency that has its roots in the UK and employs around 100 designers and architects around the world. Founder Khuan Chew first fell in love with architectural and interior design in the 1980s, working in New York, Hong Kong and London, Khuan continued to work internationally, creating private residences for the likes of the Sultan of Brunei, as well as building an international reputation with the Four Seasons, Waldorf Astoria and Sofitel hotel groups. Her reputation gained momentum, which led her to set up her own London firm in 1988.

"The jewel in our design crown is the Burj Al Arab, which rightly warrants a special mention," says CEO Raj Sanotra. The interior of this palatial seven-star hotel serves as an impressive portfolio for KCA's work. "This prestigious project was bestowed upon us by Sheikh Mohammed bin Rashid Al Maktoum, the ruler of Dubai, to whom we owe much of our success," says Raj. "Since opening in December 1999 it has been KCA's biggest claim to fame, winning many awards and gaining us worldwide recognition: 17 years on, it is still the talk of the industry."

Dubai's expansion means that more than 40 designers are now based at KCA's United Arab Emirates' office. "Around 80 per cent of our work is five-star hotels," says Raj, "though we also work on very exclusive private residences and prestigious public spaces."

KCA International's current roster of clients represents a hugely diverse design portfolio. "We're currently working on an £800 million project in London's Canary Wharf," says Raj. "Our mission was to evolve a unique identity for an exclusive development. The end result is a cohesive scheme which very much compliments the elegant architectural towers and meets with the demographic tier of its clientele and lifestyle."

A unifying element of KCA's various projects is, in fact, the style itself. "We used to be very much led by the client and the build to create an interior, but over the years it's become clear that we have a house style," says Raj. "It's opulent, but not ostentatious; it's clean and classic but certainly not minimal. Our signature interiors are built to last, with contemporary and cutting-edge design elements to suit each building."

Consulting on new developments means that KCA International can produce interiors with no conflict of interests either financially or artistically. Whether it's working on the shared spaces of a disused building in London or a luxury hotel in the Mediterranean, KCA's team of designers means that cutting-edge interiors are crafted from experience and enthusiasm to add real value to a property.

"Our spectrum seems wide enough," concludes Raj, "but really we are creating timeless spaces with comfortable, couture design that is recognised instantly the world over. As Khuan herself says: 'There is no limit to perfection.'"
— www.kca-int.com

INSIDE STYLE

C&C Milano

WITH THE GREAT and the good of the fashion world jetting in for its twice-yearly fashion week, it's little wonder that Milan has been Italy's style capital for decades. Emanuele Castellini has been part of this fashion heritage since the 1970s, producing some of the finest silks and linens for design houses such as Gianfranco Ferre and Giorgio Armani. Since the 1980s, he and his cousin Piero have been creating a new kind of style – making beautiful textiles for the home, right in the heart of glamorous Milan.

"The 1970s fashion industry in Milan was such a special, inspiring place to work," says Emanuele. "Supplying fashion fabrics to houses such as Donna Karan and Kenzo meant I was constantly surrounded by creativity." However, when it came to creating his own concept store, Emanuele looked a little closer to home. "My cousin Piero has a strong background in architecture and interior design, and when we decided to combine our talents a lifestyle brand was born."

Piero's design experience and Emanuele's flair for fashion and business led to the cousins creating C&C Milano, a concept store in Milan's fashion district that inspired with its original, welcoming boutique and garden. "The store was really an opportunity for people to come and touch the textiles and see how they would work in their homes." The luxury curtains, upholstery fabrics and linens are now on display in London, Hong Kong, Moscow and Munich showrooms, making these typically Italian home textiles accessible to a world of style-lovers.

"The design inspiration comes from all over, but Tuscany – its colours, the sea, the gardens and the architecture – is the main narrative thread that runs through our collections," says Emanuele.

The saturated coral pinks, deep aquas, natural sand and grey tones in the linen collections, and the rustic simplicity of the firm's bed linen demonstrate this influence. However, the geometric patterns, modern damasks and soft neutrals also demonstrate a more contemporary, urban style. "Our collections are never complete," says Emanuele. "Unlike fashion, we're able to make small changes, and the products evolve." This adaptability makes C&C Milano an ideal choice for interior designers who are searching for something uniquely special. "We're very flexible with our design choices, so we're able to offer a complete interior design service with Piero's expertise," says Emanuele. The curtains, upholstery fabrics, trims and even wallpaper can be customised to create comprehensive interior schemes for homes and hospitality, or even vehicles.

"We've created interiors for yachts and private aircraft," he says. "I also have C&C leather trim and linen upholstery in my car!" The raw materials used by C&C Milano for the fabrics and carpets are some of the finest natural fibres in the world – silks from China, merino from Australia, French and Belgian linen, Egyptian cotton and cashmere from Mongolia are all spun, woven and hand-finished in Italy, ensuring high quality.

"Every single detail is important for the quality of our products," says Emanuele. Creating screen-printed bespoke table linen or a soft bedroom retreat, the rich array of textiles at C&C Milano is an ideal resource for those wanting to curate a warm interior with charm and provenance – one that's entirely Made in Italy.
— www.cec-milano.com

CURTAIN CALL

Sevinch Passementerie

EGYPT, WITH ITS links to the historic Silk Road, has always attracted some of world's finest textiles. Hand-dyed silks, woven brocades and braided ropes can all be found by the adventurous treasure-hunter in Cairo's bazaars. When Sevinch Deman unearthed an antique tassel in an Egyptian market, she was enchanted by its faded beauty and unusual charm, and started to think in earnest about how she could bring hand-made interpretations of her newly discovered treasure to the world.

"I was attracted to this tassel as it shone out like a jewel," says Sevinch, of the day she discovered her first curtain dressing. "It was just beautiful." Stepping into the vibrant Cairo workshop of her company, Sevinch Passementerie, one is struck by echoes of that, and with the thrill of rummaging through a great atelier or textile market. Craftspeople busily weave, dye, braid and carve bespoke curtain accessories and trimmings, preserving skills and techniques that date back over 200 years.

"The raw materials are wood, hanks of yarn and wire," says Sevinch, "and the metamorphosis into these beautiful, miniature pieces is exquisite." Although the decorative art of passementerie is often associated with French design, Sevinch was determined to use Egyptian skills and knowledge to create passementerie for an international clientele, and her eponymous design house was born.

"Everything starts with the dyeing process," says Sevinch's husband Michael Deman. "The hanks of yarn are hand-dyed, and Sevinch is a ferocious perfectionist – every single finished product is truly bespoke, and therefore must match the fabric specifically." Once a new design is commissioned, Sevinch's creative experience and intuition take over, whether it's creating a piece for an art-deco inspired Parisian apartment, reproduction fringing for a 19th-century London townhouse, or trimming for a drapery in New York's Metropolitan Museum of Art.

"The designs don't come from a seasonal collection or catalogue," says Michael. "Each one is unique." Once the yarn or luxury fibre is dyed by the master dyer, it is finely spun within the workshop, before the woven tapes and fringes are created on hand-built looms on site. Skilled craftspeople then twist the delicate strands, embroider the tapes or hand-stitch the details, such as beads, sequins and jewels, onto the tassels.

"Our designs are often complex," says Michael. "A commission of 20 metres of a historical reproduction fringe for the Biltmore Estate in North Carolina took six months and featured more than 20,000 handmade components."

Sevinch's love of the intricacy of such pieces has led her to design her own range of custom jewellery, which features the same ornate detailing as her passementerie. Whether adorning a client or their home, however, it is the quality and originality of the work that makes Sevinch Passementerie so in demand around the world.

"Our creations often catch the eye of museum curators, as does our work with Watts of Westminster in London" says Michael. "A faithful execution of an original, sometimes moth-eaten sample is an exhilarating challenge." This almost forensic attention to detail is what makes the beautiful *objets d'art* at Sevinch Passementerie so desirable. Texture, form and handcrafted detail all combine with a warmth and passion for something seemingly so innocuous, but which is created to be treasured for a lifetime.
— www.passementerie.org

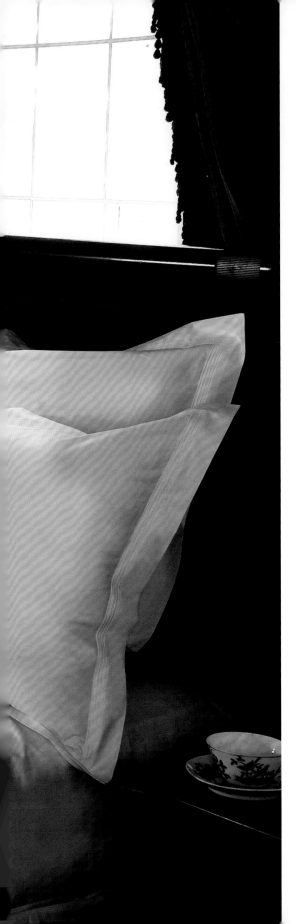

BY ROYAL APPOINTMENT

Peter Reed

LUXURY LINENS RETAILER Peter Reed has very deep roots. The company has been selling quality bed linen for 150 years since it was founded in 1861 in Lancashire, at the heart of the cotton industry. General Manager Sean Clayton attributes its success to its heritage. "We have a story to tell," he says.

"The company is probably best known for its signature cord design," says Sean. "Historically, the one-row cord bed linen was for the servants while the five-row cord was for the lord of the manor. Each cord represents a different quality of fabric." The range is still just as popular today.

Yet, while the company is proud of its past it is determined not to stay stuck there. New lines are introduced each year in recognition of its customers' changing needs. "We draw inspiration from our archive, pulling design ideas from our history and adjusting them to contemporary tastes."

One aspect that never changes, however, is the sheer Britishness of the brand. "We're proud to be made in England, using local skills," Sean says. The raw material – Egyptian cotton – comes to us from Italy where the cloth is woven. It is then delivered to the factory in Nelson, Lancashire to be cut, sewn and finished by hand by local seamstresses.

"Peter Reed is part of the local community," says Sean. "The people who work here are passionate, and they're proud to see their work in Harrods, and to know that the linens they make are being used in Buckingham Palace. That's a very big thing for us."

And well it might be. "We have the royal warrant," says Sean, "and to get that, you need to have supplied a royal household for five years. Then you go before various panels and, if your products and services are deemed to be of sufficient quality, your warrant is signed off by a member of the royal family." Peter Reed's warrant is by appointment to the Queen, meaning the company supplies bed linens direct to Buckingham Palace. "To us, that's the highest mark of quality you can get."

And while she may be Peter Reed's most high-profile customer, the Queen is in good company. "Some of the names that come to us make my jaw drop," says Sean. As well as selling through retailers in 37 countries – among them Bloomingdales, Saks Fifth Avenue and John Lewis – Peter Reed offers bespoke services to private customers. "We make whatever people need – so someone might have a circular bed and need a fitted sheet made specifically to fit, or a client with a super yacht might want monogrammed bath linens," he adds. "We will create samples and send them over." No request is too outlandish, too big, or too small. "A gentleman in Texas recently wanted just a single pillowcase with his name on. Because we make each and every item to order, that's no problem at all for us."

"There's a lot of modern thinking to move the company forward," says Sean. He's clearly looking forward to working with his colleagues and clients on the next chapter of the Peter Reed story.
— www.peterreed.com

MESSAGE IN A BOTTLE

Gilchrist & Soames

WHEN OSCAR DE la Renta was invited to create a collection of bathroom products for Peninsula Hotels in 2013, he needed to partner with a company that shared his commitment to excellence. The natural choice was Gilchrist & Soames, the bath and body brand that has been supplying luxurious English toiletries to the world's finest hotels, spas and resorts for more than 30 years.

Together they created a shampoo, conditioner, shower gel and body lotion that was to be the designer's first and last hotel collection before his death in 2014. Fragranced with an exclusive scent by de la Renta, it came in stunning bottles capped with blue roses, which paired the glamour of his fashion house with Gilchrist & Soames's commitment to responsible luxury.

The company's ethos is innovative and ethical: since 2007, its products have been free from petrochemicals and synthetic ingredients. Natural conditioning agents include honey and food-grade glycerine. Packaging and bottles are recyclable and produced using green manufacturing processes.

This combination of a forward-looking approach and exceptional products has attracted collaborative partners such as Parisian perfumer Diptyque and Beverly Hills hair cosmetics company Neil George. The firm's clients in the hotel industry include the luxury chains Mandarin Oriental, Hand Picked Hotels and Ritz Carlton. In 2013, the May Fair Hotel in London commissioned Gilchrist & Soames to create a collection based on the scent of freshly cut grass.

In recent years, with the cosmetics industry's focus on "clean beauty", the brand's retail presence has grown, particularly in the US. Its smart, sophisticated skin treatments appeal to people who care about the purity of ingredients. Lotions are made with nutrient-rich botanical extracts; and exfoliators contain wax-based emollients rather than plastic microbeads.

"Our customers are increasingly looking for clean, green products," says Natalia Brightmore, international marketing manager. "All our formulations are rich in organic ingredients and essential oils. People want the confidence that they're doing the right thing by their skin and by the planet." Gilchrist & Soames has managed to bottle that, too.

— www.gilchristsoames.com

MIDDLE EASTERN PROMISE

———

Decoration One

THE TRADITION OF Islamic art dates back centuries, spanning cultures and continents, and incorporating a huge variety of genres and influences. From glasswork, pottery and calligraphy to carpet weaving, painting and architecture, the creative output of the Islamic world is enormous in scope.

It's this huge body of tradition that sisters Sally and Susanne Baalbaki tapped into when they launched their boutique home accessories store Decoration One in Amman, Jordan in 2010. The enterprise began as a hobby, with the sisters making their ornamental arts and crafts at home, but they soon realised there was a wider demand for their designs.

"We started out making festive items for the holiday season at Ramadan," says Susanne, "but we found that people were interested in seeing these patterns repeated in other items too." The sisters decided to expand their range, branching out into tableware and home accessories that fuse the past with the present in a combination of delicate arabesque designs and bold geometric patterns.

The response was extremely positive and now Decoration One sells its handcrafted items to boutiques across the Middle East with clients in Saudi Arabia, the UAE, Kuwait, Bahrain and Qatar. Increasingly, Sally says, they are looking to broaden their appeal beyond the region, attending overseas trade shows, such as Ambiente and Christmasworld in Frankfurt and Spring Fair in Birmingham.

Recently, the Baalbaki sisters' efforts to expand their European client base paid off, with a large order from a major European department store. With this foothold in Europe and a successful online store that sells internationally, Decoration One is now setting its sights on the USA.

"When we started attending overseas trade shows in 2010 we were often the only exhibitor from the Arab world," says Sally. "Now, the market is growing and people are really interested in our collection. Our vision is to create, develop and promote contemporary Arabic style through quality products." In today's bustling international market, Decoration One looks set to achieve its global goal.
— www.decoration-one.com

CAPTIVATING YARN

Jim Thompson

THE FACT THAT beautiful, colourful, handcrafted Thai silk is known the world over is down to one producer, Jim Thompson, maintaining the legacy of the company's visionary founder of the same name. When the US entered the Second World War, Thompson – then a New York architect – joined the organisation that would later become the CIA. For five years he travelled extensively, but it was his time as military attaché in Thailand after the war that sowed the seeds of his future venture. When his military career ended, Thompson resumed his life as an architect. One of his first projects was the restoration of the Mandarin Oriental Hotel Bangkok, and it was during this time that Thompson first came across exquisite Thai silk.

Thompson would go on to transform the industry. In the 1940s, the art of silk weaving was a dying trade. Production was erratic and the traditionally used vegetable dyes left colours looking muted and faded. Thompson saw and appreciated the exceptional quality of Thai silk. By imbuing the traditional fabric with vibrant colours from high-quality dyes, and through improving the weaving techniques, Thompson is recognised for making Thai silk the beautiful, sought-after fabric it is today.

Thompson moved to Bangkok in 1948 and formed The Thai Silk Company, operating out of a small shop. Thanks to his contacts, Thai silk began to appear on famous American costume designers' tables – most notably in the Broadway musical *The King and I* and the film epic *Ben Hur*. It was not long before the coveted silk began to appear in fashionable women's wardrobes and on the walls of Windsor Castle. "Everyone became enamoured with it," says Ou Baholyodhin, Creative Director of

Home Furnishings. "There's an iridescence and a sense of handcrafted luxury about it that's difficult to match. It needed Jim's fresh pair of eyes to see its potential."

From the outset, Thompson operated on the principle that The Thai Silk Company would be majority owned by Thai people, so that the livelihoods and culture of the local weavers and silk farmers would be sustained. He conserved the traditional elements of silk weaving, but introduced innovations that raised the standard of production, from better looms and a strict cocoon inspection regime, to permanent dyes, lustrous colour schemes and new designs.

Today, The Thai Silk Company is a design powerhouse. The company has grown from its original 100 employees to more than 3,000. "Our customer service is really second to none," says Ou. "These days the company spends a great deal of time working very closely with designers on creating exclusive products, matching a particular shade, colour or texture. We offer worldwide representation and quality control. The consistency of our fabric is key; every inch is inspected.

"We continue to be an entirely vertically integrated company, growing our own silkworms, producing the yarn, dyeing it and weaving it," Ou adds. "We're where we are today because of Jim's vision and his sensitivity to south-east Asian culture. His house is now a museum, the Jim Thompson House. It has become the second most visited site in Thailand and is still used by our design studio. We continue to refer to our archives of his early designs and prints, only making small tweaks and changes to make it relevant to today."
— www.jimthompsonfabrics.com

SCENTS OF INDIVIDUALITY

IPG Fragrances

"LUXURY IS ALL about being unique," says Isabelle Maillebiau, Head Perfumer of IPG Fragrances in Switzerland. Using only the finest ingredients, and made for the world's most discerning customers, the company's Per Fumum Ex (PFX) service is the perfume equivalent of haute couture. Haute Parfumerie – creating your own bespoke scent – aims to return perfume making to its highly individual origins.

"The perfume industry has changed considerably over time," says Panayot Gueorguiev, Managing Director of IPG. "Many fragrances today lack character, as ingredients have been brought to the bare minimum and formulations have to respond to the latest trends. Nowadays people who are completely different wear the same scent, losing their individuality and personality. Our service returns to the intimate art of creating your own perfume and product line, skilfully and delicately designed to capture your very essence, emotions and character. A perfume that is unforgettable and that will leave your unique *sillage*, or projection."

The entire process is individually tailored to each client, creating a bespoke perfume and product line with a wide choice of products for personal or home use. These include hair and body perfumes, bath cosmetics, massage products, room and bedroom sprays and waters, scented candles, diffusers and much more. Everything is of the highest quality, from the rare, pure natural oils to the handmade packaging. Ingredients are chosen with as much care as grapes for a vintage wine. "It's for our clients who know what they're buying and appreciate it," says Isabelle. "From one summer to the next, a rose will never smell the same. When you crop

it this year or next, it's different, like a rare wine. Connoisseurs understand this."

The final luxury is the time taken to create a perfect a personalised fragrance and line of products, a process which usually takes more than six months. During this time, the customer works with the perfumer to review hundreds of reformulations as they narrow down the finished product.

The sensual properties of the service make it an exquisite and unique gift. Popular both for weddings and anniversaries, it is intimate and exciting, offering a voyage to an entirely new world. Over time, many clients seek out an entire wardrobe of fragrances.

"The perfume should evolve with us, with our lifestyle, habits and moods," says Isabelle. "We will modify the formula accordingly, so as to create variations that will suit every occasion." PFX also offers a collection of finest quality, pure natural oils and non-alcohol perfume compositions, particularly sought after in Asia and the Middle East. These use pure Indian and Cambodian oudh, Indonesian patchouli, Bulgarian rose oil, jasmine from the south of France, iris from Italy, vanilla from Tahiti, osmanthus from China and many other rare ingredients. PFX also occasionally launches ready-to-use, limited-edition products, based around an exceptional ingredient.

The names of the company's global clientele are as closely guarded as the finished formulations, ensuring that no two people will ever have quite the same perfume. And that is, perhaps, the ultimate luxury. "It remains a very personal service," says Panayot. "Very intimate, created from a true understanding with the client."

— www.ipg-fragrances.com

THE ART OF CRAFT

Eidsgaard Design/Pegasus Design

YOU COULD BE forgiven for thinking that Eidsgaard Design's interiors – with their huge glass panels, contemporary upholstery and luxurious flooring – belong in a chic penthouse or exclusive boutique hotel. In fact, the company creates amazing spaces of a different kind: ones that float.

Director Peder Eidsgaard founded Eidsgaard Design in 2005, and has notched up more than 20 years' experience in designing luxury yachts. "At the age of 12, I saw a magazine feature about London's superyacht designers," says Peder. "Since then I have wanted to do this job." He and his business partners Ewa Eidsgaad and Ben Harrison bring their design, architecture and project-management expertise to the interiors of superyachts (such as the 66 m *Vanish*, pictured opposite); while their London-based sister company, Pegasus Design, works on interiors for private jets (such as the ACJ319 *Belville*, pictured left).

Eidsgaard Design's bespoke projects have attracted an international clientele, but each project is unique, and approached as such. "I would say our style is contemporary, but our success lies in the way we do things," says Peder. "Building a yacht is often a lengthy process, and from the very beginning we aim to incorporate different structures and respect the architecture. Saying that, we can be very creative with our yacht interiors, and we love to open them up so we can maximise the available space."

It's no surprise, then, that Eidsgaard Design interiors feature vast glass windows to let the light pour in; but they also include cosier, more intimate spaces. Harmony is considered hugely important, as is functionality. "Building a yacht is very costly," says Peder. "So we have to resist the temptation to use expensive materials and instead exercise restraint with our design. Creating a cohesive interior that is an extension of a client's taste and personal brand is what we love doing."

Eidsgaard Design's sister company, Pegasus Design, shares this open-yet-comfortable approach. "Jet design is slightly different," says Peder, "in that we are limited by the size of the fuselage. We try to create big spaces that make an impact when you walk on to a jet, yet make you feel cocooned and safe once you sit down for a long flight."

Building relationships with clients before embarking on a project is of paramount importance to Peder and his team. "We like to visit clients at home and in their office to see what they need from a personal space," says Peder. "It's important that we meet up to discuss a project, as some clients have specific ideas that may not translate to yacht or jet design, and some may have no design experience at all. We have to make them comfortable enough to express what they really want."

The team at Pegasus Design is careful to match a jet's exteriors to its interior, even devising bespoke paint finishes. "The exterior paint lines need to wrap the fuselage perfectly so it looks dynamic from every angle," says Peder. "We want the outside to have as much impact as the interior. After all, this is a status symbol."

With each project presenting different challenges and solutions, Eidsgaard Design and Pegasus Design creations nevertheless share the same well-considered, elegantly finished quality. They reflect an individual client's personality, and are sure to impress all who sail, or fly, in them.
— www.eidsgaard.com
— www.pegasusdesign.mc

ORIENT EXPRESSION

Lala Curio

UNEARTHING ANCIENT TREASURES and creating new ways to use them in modern homes is not only an inspiration for interior designer Laura Cheung, it is her passion. Her luxury interiors brand Lala Curio is a playful take on Chinese artisanship, incorporating Laura's love of antiquity, her respect for ancient decorative skills and modern sensibilities.

Laura was born in Sydney, schooled in England, raised in Hong Kong, and has worked internationally in the worlds of fashion, art, interior design and brand strategy. She trained at Parsons School of Design in New York and obtained her master's degree at Sotheby's Institute of Art in London, where she studied 500 years of furniture and ceramics from Europe and China. Lala Curio has thus developed a thoroughly global outlook on design.

"I'm somewhat of a melting pot myself," says Laura. "And, by helping to preserve forgotten arts from around the world and bring them to a modern clientele, we hope to foster a younger generation to continue the legacy of these lost techniques."

Located on a quiet residential terrace in Hong Kong's Starstreet Precinct, Lala Curio's flagship boutique is designed to look like a home, with its own dining room and salon. "The shop appeals to tastemakers who take a thrill in the theatre of life," says Laura. "It might be the lady of the house who wants a fashionable abode, or the curious minded who appreciates craft and embraces modernity."

The boutique is filled with whimsical objects – all designed and created in-house – as well as meticulously crafted furniture, lights and decorative accessories. But pride of place goes to the imperial craft cloisonné tiles and the hand-painted and embroidered silk wallpaper – creations that reinvent traditional chinoiserie. They balance traditional craftsmanship with contemporary playfulness.

Laura comes from three generations of furniture artisans. "My family is my rock," she says, "and my parents my biggest inspiration." Her work draws upon those traditions. "After completing my master's degree, I spent three years visiting workshops throughout remote parts of China, India, the Philippines and Europe," she says. "For our hand-painted wallpaper, I visited artisans all over China who were painting, embroidering or sculpting. There is a long history of decorative arts in China that we can learn from."

This theme is followed throughout her range. "All our products follow this pattern of taking Chinese craft and making it accessible to a modern, worldly audience," says Laura. "Cloisonné tiles, for instance, are so intricate and time-consuming to create, and the skills are being forgotten." The lengthy process – which includes bronze castings, bending delicate wires into shapes, enamelling and multiple firings – carries a high risk of *craquelure*, the dense cracking that often comes from ageing. After a long process of development with the few remaining workshops of the forgotten art, Lala Curio has invented new ways of applying cloisonné to make the art more accessible.

The brand continues to evolve with its loyal clientele, many of whom take advantage of Lala Curio's bespoke interior design service. "I love that feeling that comes with finishing a space, curating a show, creating an event, a house or a restaurant," says Laura. "The best thing about Lala Curio is that like-minded people can come together to appreciate the passion and creativity that goes into each project."
— www.lalacurio.com

THE FABRIC OF LIFE

Amalia Home Collection

FOR ALMOST 100 years, the Coelho Lima family has been weaving fabric that is redolent of the Portuguese landscape. Back in the 1920s, its mills in northern Portugal created textiles that typified the colours and designs of this region, and that practice of drawing inspiration from the area continues to this day. The family owns Amalia Home Collection, a brand that combines old-world craftsmanship with innovative modern techniques to manufacture exquisite bed linen that is designed to last a lifetime.

"The Amalia Home Collection draws its inspiration from the very place where the product is produced," says owner and Chief Designer António Coelho Lima. "The collection represents the landscape and the people of Portugal. From coastline to mountainside, from stone street to rolling hills, each design is made to bring a little piece of Portugal to your home."

António takes great pride in producing textile collections that combine a strong sense of history with an eye to the future. Developed with the high-end consumer in mind, these employ a wide variety of thread counts and carefully selected raw materials. The result is a product that is ready to compete with the most recognised home-textile brands. "We create our products with passion," says António, "and we aim to adequately respond to customers' highest expectations. These products have been developed and positioned to be a top-of-the-market offer to the consumer."

The co-creator of the collection, Maria José Lima, believes that the offering has something for every household. "From crisp percales to silky sateens," she says, "to perfectly woven jacquards and finely detailed prints and embroideries, there is something for every linen closet in this product line."

The 2016 collection presents four different themes reflecting different inspirations that warrant a wide range of designs, adapted to give the consumer more choices for their bedroom décor. The four themes – Aurea, Oceano, Aroma and Salinas – each represent a small piece of Portuguese life. Oceano reflects the many shades of blue found on the Atlantic coast; Salinas evokes the salt flats of central Portugal and the clean, neutral shades found there; Aroma's wide colour palette conjures up the essence of life in Portuguese villages and cities; and Aurea (from the latin word *aurum* meaning "gold") is reminiscent of the golden light and warmth associated with the Portuguese climate.

This collection has all been created with a great sense of history and an eye to the future. "These are products that stand at the crossroads of old-world craftsmanship and modern innovation," says António.

António's greatest inspiration, however, is clearly his family. He talks effusively and affectionately about his father João, his daughters Sara and Lia, and his chief collaborator, his wife Maria José – all of whom are woven into the company's vibrant heritage.
— www.amaliahomecollection.com

RUGGED GOOD LOOKS

La Manufacture Cogolin

THE NAME COGOLIN does not only refer to the village in the Côte d'Azur. It is also synonymous with the high-end, hand-knotted or geometric-patterned woven rugs that have been handmade there for nearly a hundred years. La Manufacture Cogolin was established in 1924 in the ateliers of a silk producer. In 1928 textile manufacturer Jean Lauer purchased the workshop and moved south, bringing his Jacquard looms and skilled weavers from Lyon and the famous tapestry town of Aubusson in central France.

In the beginning, La Manufacture Cogolin produced hand-knotted rugs in one part of the workshop and fabric in another. Inspired by the three-dimensional style of traditional hand-knotted Mediterranean rugs, Lauer eventually modified his fabric looms to weave the distinctive carpets for which Cogolin is known today.

"It's not something that can be replicated," says Managing Director Sarah Henry. "All these narrow pieces are sewn together by hand, piece by piece. It's an economically crazy thing to do in a world where most rugs and carpets are woven on wide, mechanical looms."

Yet the company is managing to expand globally while keeping the brand's extraordinary heritage intact. "We don't want to modernise," says Sarah. "That is not who we are. We continue to develop new patterns to be relevant to the contemporary market, but the historical aspect of our production is very important."

La Manufacture Cogolin has also begun reissuing collections of hand-knotted rugs from its rich archives, collaborating with a workshop in Nepal. Its latest collection, "Idylle", is drawn from a series of designs by the inter-war artist Christian Bérard, who worked often with Lauer. His work reflects a strong art deco influence but looks very up-to-date.

Cogolin has been part of the House of Tai Ping since 2010. The group's investment has allowed the brand to make repairs to its workshop and looms, and expand internationally. In Hong Kong and Shanghai, Tai Ping and Cogolin textiles share their showrooms. In Paris, however, Cogolin is shown exclusively. "Our cultural history is unique," says Sarah. "Lauer worked with Cocteau, Leleu and Jean-Michel Frank among many others, and the company is a very important part of the history of French decorative arts."

All Cogolin rugs are bespoke, produced according to the request of each client. "We work with clients to choose a design from our catalogue and colours from our palette, and then weave to their requested size," says Sarah. "Our clients regard their purchase as an heirloom piece. They often start with the rug and build the room around it."

Cogolin launches new collections every year, one from Provence in January and another from Nepal, usually in September. Its main focus now is to expand its reach in the US and Asia, where its rugs are less well known than in Europe. Wherever its clientele may be, quality always comes first. "We are preserving these fantastic techniques," says Sarah, "making something completely handmade and very couture. That's a great thing to be part of: we are keeping alive this very old, very simple way of making something extraordinary and we are all very proud of that."

— www.manufacturecogolin.com

TOUCH OF CLASS

———

Christian Fischbacher

IN 1819, 16-year-old Christian Fischbacher, recognising the quality of the handcrafted fabrics produced in his home town of St Peterzell, Switzerland, made a name for himself by trading them in the neighbouring town of St Gallen. The company's linen and fabric ranges expanded throughout the 19th and 20th centuries, eventually catching the eye of such eminent fashion houses as Dior and Versace. With a sixth generation of Fischbacher now at its helm, the firm that bears its founder's name continues to produce design-led and bespoke fabrics, sumptuous bed linen and sustainable home textiles for a global clientele.

Managing Director Michael Fischbacher runs the firm, and – alongside his wife Camilla – oversees the exclusive ranges, which are still designed at the company's St Gallen headquarters. "We have five designers here in our studio, each producing original drawings and surface pattern designs," says Art Director Camilla Fischbacher. "While we use modern technology, we still value the integrity of hand-produced designs. We take luxury through to its finest details. We have inspired design and innovative production techniques, but the end result has got to be beautiful to touch."

The company's range of upholstery and drape fabrics, merino wool rugs and linen, cotton and silk home textiles is testament to this tactile obsession, and to sustainable quality. "It's about choosing materials that last," says Camilla. Sustainability also means taking the environment into consideration, and Christian Fischbacher's Benu Flow fabric, made from a pioneering use of recycled PET bottles, earned the company the prestigious Red Dot Design Award.

As well as pioneering new eco-conscious products, Christian Fischbacher continues to develop its creativity with home-interior solutions. Working with interior designers, architects and clients that include prominent hotel groups, the firm can offer bespoke soft furnishings for any room or space.

With some 200 years of expertise, Christian Fischbacher is a company that serves a global market, but manages to produce luxury on an intimate level. Indeed, the family firm's beautiful textiles look set to appeal to many generations of design-conscious customers to come.
— www.fischbacher.com

RISE TO THE TOP

Kevala Stairs

HAVING RECENTLY VISITED Kevala Stairs' design studio to discuss plans for a new house, a client was so taken by the shape of a beautifully curved staircase that it became the inspiration and focus of the design for the rest of the house. Looking at Kevala Stairs' portfolio of work, this client's actions are perfectly understandable. These really are heavenly stairways.

Co-founder and director David Saw has 45 years' experience in the construction industry; first in bespoke joinery, then as a house-builder. With a thorough understanding of building construction, proportion and balance, he insists that form, rather than function, drives each project. "We look at what complements the space in an ideal world," says David, "then ask how to achieve it."

Kevala Stairs prides itself on the bespoke nature of each project. Its design team works closely with clients to achieve the staircase they desire. "We use the latest computer software for a creative design," says David. "Once drawings are agreed, materials are carefully selected and all parts precision-cut and hand-finished in state-of-the-art production facilities. They are then delivered to site, assembled and installed by one of our expert installation teams."

For each individual project Kevala Stairs sources the best materials. "Maybe stone from Italy, timbers from America, or stainless steel parts from within just 100 metres of our office in High Wycombe – we insist on the best quality," says David. "Kevala" is an Indian word meaning "whole, complete, in search of perfection" and, in projects such as Ashridge House in the Chilterns or The Halcyon in London, that quest nears fulfilment.

The latter – a luxury home in Hampstead – is a remarkable feat of design and engineering, offering a sinuous, organic contrast to the minimalist interior. "The vine motif is an invitation to climb the stairs," says David. And, with a wrought-iron balustrade running over four floors, a 51-metre handrail in stained oak and treads of Portuguese Moleanos limestone, that invitation is compelling.

Since forming in 2006, Kevala Stairs has been expanding rapidly to keep up with demand. It is evident that this team has the enthusiasm and focus to climb to the very top.

— www.kevalastairs.com

DEEP DOWN COMFORT

Royal Eiderdown

"WE SAY THAT eiderdown is soft like a cloud," says Hreggvidur St. Magnusson, co-owner of Royal Eiderdown. "It is incredibly light, but gives superior insulation. This means you need a smaller quantity of pure eiderdown to fill a duvet." Pure eiderdown, certified as such by the Icelandic government, is a very rare and completely eco-sustainable resource. It is all that goes into Royal Eiderdown's Skarð duvets, which bring a 600-year-old Icelandic tradition up to date with a contemporary luxury collection.

An eiderdown duvet is only genuine if it is filled with the down from the eider duck and isn't bulked out with goose down. Iceland produces between 85 and 90 per cent of the world's annual supply, which amounts to around 3,500 kg. "The eider duck is a wild bird and its population has never grown," says Hreggvidur, "so the supply of down is very, very scarce."

As it takes on average 1 kg of pure down to fill a single duvet, there can never be more than around 3,000 authentic eiderdown duvets made each year. Each Royal Eiderdown duvet has a Certificate of Authenticity and Origin from the Icelandic government, proving the purity and source of the filling. "The duvet is given a specific serial number and is signed by a government assessor," adds Hreggvidur.

Hilmar Kristinsson, co-owner of Royal Eiderdown, represents the 28th generation of Skarð eiderdown farmers. "The pride he has in his heritage is inspiring," says Hreggvidur. "When he talks of his family and their history you see a spark in his eyes."

The first documented evidence of the prestige of Skarð eiderdowns appears in 1455, when Ólöf

the Rich and her husband Björn of Iceland sailed to Denmark with gifts for King Christian I. "They brought a small duvet for the king's youngest child," says Hreggvidur. "Such is our history."

The eiderdown harvest today has changed very little since the 15th century. Eider ducks nest on the grassy islands of the Breidafjordur off the south-west coast of Iceland. The harvest begins by boat, with family and friends gathering to carefully pick the down shed by the female eider ducks. "It is a game of patience," says Hreggvidur. "Once the eggs have hatched, we hand-pick the down from 50 to 60 nests to fill a single duvet."

The down is gently dried, teased out, cleaned and checked for any twig or grass fragments. Once certified, it is stitched into Egyptian cotton duvet covers woven to order in Japan. It is a painstaking and labour-intensive process. "Our duvets are made to order and each one takes six weeks to complete," says Hreggvidur. "We sell everything directly ourselves so as to control the quality at every step. As soon as a client experiences the lightness and warmth of our duvets it is the start of a long-lasting relationship with us."

Royal Eiderdown is continuing the proud tradition of eider duck farming on Iceland, with its painstaking industry and rigorous quality control. Skarð Eiderdown Duvets only came into being as a luxury brand in 2014, so the lucky few who manage to order a cloud-like duvet are only now catching up on the centuries-old secret of a delicious night's sleep.
— www.royaleiderdown.com

LOVE IS THE RUG

Tai Ping

TAI PING CELEBRATED its 60th anniversary in 2016, marking a milestone in the company's history and a chance to reflect on six decades of quality, craftsmanship and success. Since it was established in Hong Kong in 1956, Tai Ping has grown from a local carpet-maker to a global brand adorning the most luxurious of floors, from palaces to private jets.

Tai Ping was founded by a group of seven businessmen in a time of turmoil for Hong Kong, as refugees poured in from Japanese-occupied areas of mainland China. Its founders' aim was to protect Chinese artisans and provide employment for the city's growing population by producing high-quality, handcrafted carpets.

Since then, generations of families have worked for the company, building on ancient techniques and traditions. The skill and experience of its artisans remain at the heart of Tai Ping, and it prides itself on the artistry that goes into custom-making its carpet and rugs, as well as the time and effort devoted to creating the best product possible.

"Everything we do is bespoke, there isn't a thing we do that is run-of-the-mill," says Kathryn Hallam, Managing Director of Tai Ping's UK operation. "It all starts from scratch – we spin the yarn to spec and dye the yarn to achieve the desired colour."

It can take up to six years to master the skills needed to produce the most complex carpet designs, but Kathryn says it is not just the artisans who become immersed in Tai Ping's heritage and legacy. A great number of Tai Ping's employees have worked for the company for many years, developing a deep understanding of the business. "We are all very proud of what we do," says Kathryn.

The passion that runs throughout the company means that there is meticulous attention to detail at every stage of designing, making and installing the carpets, to ensure that the finished product is absolutely right. "We take it very seriously," says Kathryn. "We want to make sure that the end user is happy and that the client – who is most of the time the designer – is happy. And we want the people who make the carpet to be proud. It's a very personal, emotional journey."

This expertise and passion for creating bespoke carpets also means that Tai Ping is perfectly placed to take on the most complex or exacting of projects, and thrives on demanding commissions. "We are happy to be challenged," says Kathryn.

Tai Ping's commitment to meeting clients' requirements, down to the smallest detail, has made it the company of choice for a host of luxury locations, from top hotels and designer stores to super-yachts and the homes of the wealthy and elite. Kathryn is understandably discreet, but clients have included Hollywood A-listers and heads of state from around the world.

Over the past 60 years, Tai Ping has grown into a global company, recognised as one of the best in the business by those in the know. And while it may now count celebrities and superyacht designers among its customers, it remains devoted to its founding principles of quality and craftsmanship, and respect for the artisans at its heart.
— www.houseoftaiping.com

MATERIAL WEALTH

Vividgrey

"I WANTED TO create simple but emotionally engaging furnishing," says Sabine Fajana, who started Vividgrey as a new brand with its own online shop in 2013. Since then, she has been designing and making home furnishings and lighting from her beautifully restored studio in Vienna. Her company now sells pieces in luxury shops and children's concept stores around the world.

The collection, which includes cushions, throws, rugs and lighting, often invites nature into the home. Each piece is full of imaginative detail and there is often a sense of discovery. "The brand evolved from combining my work as an interior architect for prestigious luxury brands in London with being the mother of a small son," says Sabine. "Both experiences led me to put my heart into developing a brand full of soul, with aesthetics that resonate with grown-ups and children alike."

Vividgrey's simple yet sophisticated products are as tactile as they are charming. "The balance between raw and refined materials and techniques is at the heart of the brand," explains Sabine, who picks out contrasting textures with tremendous care. "This could be coarse linen voile embellished with tiny leather hearts, soft cotton embroidery or metallic print details on thick linen, or torn strips of fine cotton batiste filtering light ever so gently." The muted colour palette is devised to help the products mix harmoniously in the home.

Social and environmental responsibility is key to the brand's success. "All our fabrics are certified organic or locally woven and dyed by us," says Sabine. "We source from certified Fairtrade organisations. Any timber used for the collection is reclaimed or sourced sustainably in Europe. The packaging and stationery is made from recycled paper that we emboss by hand."

Each item that leaves Vividgrey's workshop is unique because of the entirely handmade process it has undergone, from fabric-dyeing to logo screen printing. All the textiles are washable and the materials are chosen to age gracefully, so that they evolve into contemporary heirlooms for each generation to use and love.
— www.vividgrey.co

TEXTILE MESSAGING

La Gallina Matta

A LITTLE MORE than 10 years ago, Claudia Petruzzi Granato decided to indulge her longstanding passion for interior design and established La Gallina Matta, a home decoration company specialising in textiles for the table and for furnishings. Before long it had expanded into a global concern, exporting to a dozen countries around the world.

Yet despite her clear acumen as an entrepreneur, Claudia derives the most pleasure from the creative side of her work. "I'm still the designer," she says, "and this is definitely the part of the business I love the most. I spend a great deal of time coming up with new ideas for lines that will enhance our customers' homes." La Gallina Matta's products, all proudly made in Italy, are defined by fine materials, multiple colours and bespoke service. Showcase items include the Parentesi collection of stylish linen placemats, which are embroidered in mercerised cotton and coated – or "oil-clothed" – to make them resistant to stains and wrinkles.

The company's house style speaks of cosy informality, with a range of vivid fabrics – although many of Claudia's designs are equally compatible with formal settings. Her look has been described by some as "French with an American influence". "But I'm also influenced by my Italian-ness," she says. "Which means taste, creativity, luxury and tailoring. I strongly believe in creating an environment where table settings and furnishings all belong to the same style."

Claudia was inspired to call the company La Gallina Matta – "mad hen" – after a trip to Sardinia, where she bought an impish sculpture of a chicken that is said to bring good luck. Since then, La Gallina Matta products have been featured in a host of international magazines, and Claudia has been honoured with the Prix Découverte award at the Maison&Objet interiors show in Paris.

She admits to feeling pleased and proud that her style has become so popular – appealing to everyone from young professionals with families to royals and heads of state. "What delights me most is to see a product that I have created being used for occasions like family lunches and dinners," she says. "It is wonderful to be part of such precious shared moments."
— www.lagallinamatta.com

INTELLIGENT DESIGN

Privilege

CASH RICH, TIME poor is the lament echoed among the world's jet-setting, empire-leading elite, none more so than in Russia. The business acumen, not to mention the hours, demanded to sustain business success rarely allows the time needed to create a dream home. To make those dreams come true, Privilege, a leading design studio based in St Petersburg, offers its discerning clients a comprehensive design, build and fit service.

"We stand out because we offer something luxurious and special, plus a service from start to finish," says founder, owner and lead designer Elena Konovalova. From intimate apartments to gracious new houses, Privilege offers its clients the reassurance of working with a sole contractor who can realise their design vision from initial plan to final fit.

Since Elena set up Privilege in 2011, she and her team, which now numbers 15, have worked across Russia on a variety of projects that have brought the company critical acclaim. In 2011, Privilege won the top interior design prize from a field of 70 at the Arch-Idea international design awards. And in 2012, Elena won the Russian interior design award at Interia for her design of a St Petersburg apartment.

"We have worked on everything from cafés to hotels, restaurants and office spaces, but most of our work is private commissions for homes and apartments," says Elena. "Our clients are wealthy and we offer them a high-end, elite service."

Living and working in St Petersburg, Elena has developed a style that embraces the baroque splendours of her city, updated in a contemporary combination of exquisite wood and stone finishes, richly textured fabrics and light-flooded interiors. Her earliest commission was from John Stuart, who founded the Russian Department at Sotheby's auctioneers. She realised his dream of renovating his St Petersburg apartment as a showcase for his collection of Russian art and furniture.

Elena is trained as an antiques restorer as well as an interior designer and she carries this appreciation of authentic finishes and craftsmanship into her projects today. "Our design studio specialises in classical design," she says, "with furniture sourced from Italy and France, and we also supply refurbished antique furniture."

As the team at Privilege has grown, its expertise have expanded to include every aspect of project management, from the initial architectural designs and overseeing construction to the design and manufacture of bespoke furniture. "We make time to come and see the space," says Elena, "then we take care of all the paperwork, order all the furniture and do all the decorating work. All that remains is to hand the keys to the client at the end." She makes the business of specialist paint finishes, polished marble flooring and sourcing imported crystal chandeliers sound easy. Privilege only works with around 50 clients a year, ensuring it can deliver a personalised service with commissions completed to schedule.

For the most discerning of its clients, Privilege offers a specialist service called Private Design, for which Elena works one-to-one with a client to create anything from a yacht, a private jet or a car interior to houses and apartments. "As a starting point, I am inspired by a certain object, a specific colour or specific space," she says. "These things inspire me and inform the whole project." Within the time frame stipulated by her client, she will source furniture, furnishings and decorative objects from across Europe, principally Italy, the UK, France and Germany. Suppliers include not only larger brands, but also small, well-established family businesses whose master craftspeople have been making collectable pieces for generations.

Elena will also purchase paintings and antiques at auction and from private collections on behalf of her personal clients. "Luxury interiors are, at the same time, hugely enjoyable and challenging to fulfil," she says. "That is exactly why my clients need my help – I know how to make their ideas a reality."

Keeping work to a strict schedule is a key part of Privilege's commitment to its clients, who, says Elena, "find us through word of mouth." Each stage of construction is carefully monitored, as is the progress of the decoration and the final finishes. Assessing a client's requirements in detail in the early stages of a commission eliminates the need for protracted meetings once work has begun.

Privilege offers its clients a 3D visualisation of their future home, which gives a clear impression of how the rooms integrate and the proposed layout of fixtures and fittings, and even household appliances. Clients are able to see the projected effect of colour schemes and lighting plans, enabling them to make

decisions early on in the design process. Once signed off, Privilege has the breadth of skills to complete every aspect of the scheme, saving its clients time and money.

Projects generally take around 18 months to complete, depending on the complexity and style of the brief. The design team at Privilege works intuitively across contemporary and traditional styles. "We try to combine both of these approaches in our work," says Elena. "But this has to be done with taste."

Recalling Elena's early training in antiques restoration, Privilege has become known for its expertise in gilding and silver-plating. In a nod to the famous facades and interiors of St Petersburg's imperial residences, elaborate plasterwork and light fittings can be gilded to add richness and refinement to private apartments and penthouses. The specialist painters and decorators who work with Privilege can also pick out pastel details in ceiling mouldings and recreate murals, paintings and antique maps to order. "We put our heart and soul into every detail of a project," says Elena.

With projects such as the design of the business lounge at St Petersburg Pulkovo Airport, Privilege is continuing to expand its portfolio. And in the domestic arena, with each new residence, Elena comes into her own, however complex, detailed and painstaking the process. Indeed, as she puts it: "I help people realise their dreams."

— www.privilege.spb.ru

THE GLOBETROTTER

Travel in style

CRUISE CONTROL

Crystal Cruises

IF ALL THE awards and accolades garnered by Crystal Cruises over the quarter-century since its founding were to be listed below, there would be no space to mention anything else. Year after year, the company wins World's Best in such industry-leading magazines as *Conde Nast Traveller* and *Travel + Leisure*, being recognised across multiple categories in the process. These awards are particularly significant because they are voted for by readers, from their crucial perspective as paying customers.

Crystal's Vice President of International Sales and Marketing, Helen Beck, is obliged to sample the firm's voyages in the interests of quality control. Many would regard this as one of the world's most enviable jobs.

"Over the past two years, a change of ownership has opened up an abundant range of new choices," she says. "Our two beautiful ocean vessels, *Crystal Symphony* and *Crystal Serenity* remain our heartbeat, and we've now also introduced Crystal River Cruises and Crystal Yacht & Expedition Cruises."

Crystal's distinguishing feature has always been the volume of space aboard each ship, combined with a lower-than-average number of guests. An additional luxury is an unusually high service-crew-to-guest ratio on all vessels.

The first of Crystal River Cruises' river yachts, *Crystal Mozart*, was recently launched in Vienna: the largest, most luxurious vessel to sail the Danube. In 2017, *Crystal Bach* and *Crystal Mahler* debut with voyages from Amsterdam, sailing the Rhine, Main and Danube rivers through Central Europe.

"On our river cruises," says Helen, "everything is highly exclusive. All suites come with butler service, and we have an open dining system that creates a relaxed atmosphere." A dinner in a Michelin-starred restaurant onshore is included for each guest, and liveried coaches are laid on for Crystal's wide selection of complimentary land excursions. Crystal applies the same standards to its yacht, with customary attention to service, space, quality and choices.

The luxury *Crystal Esprit*, which made her debut in the Seychelles in December 2015, offers suites for all 62 guests, who are outnumbered by the crew. The vessel's shallow draft enables her to come close to coasts and beaches, and make unscheduled stops. The aft of the vessel is equipped with water skis, jet skis and paddle boards – and there is even a miniature submarine for exploring reefs.

Every Crystal voyage includes meals, as well as beers, wines, spirits, soft drinks, tea and coffee, with complimentary tours offered in every port on Crystal River Cruises and Crystal Yacht & Expedition Cruises voyages. In addition to the simplicity of this policy, the price often compares favourably with many competitors that offer non-inclusive cruises.

More adventurous travellers can now embark on one of the company's newly launched Air Cruises. "Visiting some of the world's most iconic destinations and with a dining room, lounge, wine cellar and concierge on board, you could describe our Crystal Air Cruises as ocean cruises in the air," says Helen.

It is hardly surprising that many voyagers return to Crystal time and again, and many plan their annual trips to coincide with friends made on previous adventures. And now, the profusion of new offerings may well tempt them to try some novel experiences.
— www.crystalcruises.co.uk

TOUR DE FORCE

Vilasa Luxury Travel

"IN LUXURY TRAVEL, what makes the difference is people," says Gursharan Singh, Vice President of Minar Travels. The company – one of only a few family-owned Indian tour operators – offers dedicated, carefully designed experiences of India and its neighbouring countries through its high-end tours brand Vilasa Luxury Travel.

Whether visitors wish to see the Taj Mahal or something more off the beaten track, Vilasa prides itself in ensuring a seamless travel experience, from airport pick-up to luxury hotels and the sights and encounters of the Indian subcontinent. While Minar offers a formidable range of services, including chartered flights and corporate travel, Vilasa is dedicated to providing the smoothest and most luxurious experience possible – and the key to this is the people who make it happen.

"The travel business is entirely experience-driven," says Gursharan. "You have to have the right knowledge and attitude. Our staff usually have 10 or more years in the industry; they know how to talk to people, how to really understand what wealthy travellers desire and have the experience and dedication to provide it." Vilasa also places a priority on enthusiasm in its team. "They have to listen carefully to what the client wants," says Gursharan, "and then go that extra mile to make the experience something really amazing."

Vilasa has a vast network of exceptional heritage properties across India, Nepal, Bhutan, Sri Lanka and the Maldives; and a foolproof infrastructure to move clients effortlessly between them. It also combines the top people with all the right connections. This all makes for a superior luxury travel experience.

The company has had the prestigious National Tourism Award conferred upon it by the Government of India nine times, and owes most of its success to the vision of Managing Director Harvinder Singh Duggal. He left the prestigious Tata Group – which owns Jaguar and Land Rover – to found his own boutique operation, Minar Travels, 24 years ago. The company has risen from its small beginnings to become one of the foremost Delhi-based tour companies, with an aviation arm and offices around the world.

Another factor in the company's winning formula is its ability to appeal to high-end travellers across the globe, from Russia (where it has the exclusive contract to handle travel for top government organisations) to Europe, China and Latin America. The needs of these very different travellers vary greatly, but the company meets them all confidently, and offers a range of incentives to strengthen its appeal. Vilasa provides the experts, including people fluent in Russian, Korean, Chinese, French, Spanish, English and a host of other languages, as well as the languages of the Indian subcontinent. The parent company, Minar Travels, offers the contacts and expansive infrastructure without which no great travel experience is complete.

"At Minar Travels, we value personal integrity, honesty and a hands-on approach above everything else," says Harvinder Singh Duggal. He knows that in an age of luxury travel, with the cultural riches of the Indian subcontinent becoming accessible to ever greater numbers of global travellers, it is the expertise of his employees that really make the difference.
— www.vilasaluxury.com

TOP-FLIGHT SERVICES

AMAC Aerospace Switzerland

WHEN WALEED MUHIDDIN wishes to explain the business philosophy behind AMAC Aerospace, he likens it to the hotel industry. "If a client wants something, we will do everything in our power to make it happen," explains the company's Vice President of Strategic Operations & Business Development. "We are specialists in the business aviation market and were established on the simple basis that there were not enough aircraft maintenance repair and overhaul [MRO] centres around the world."

The company – AMAC is an acronym for Aircraft Maintenance and Completion – operates four flagship hangars at Basel airport in Switzerland on a 35-year lease, but also has offices in Zurich and hangar space in Istanbul and in Bodrum, Turkey, as well as hangar, workshop and office space in Auch, France. These secure, state-of-the-art facilities allow it to manage and maintain a variety of aircraft used for business purposes, which can be anything from a small private jet to an entire corporate fleet.

There are four divisions to the company: maintenance; completion and refurbishment; aircraft management and sales; and charter. Through these divisions the company is able to do everything related to business aviation, always ensuring that it uses its own team of experts to maintain complete control of the job.

AMAC is now the industry's largest privately owned facility in the world, offering narrow- and wide-body completion and maintenance for the corporate and private aviation market. Its growth is largely due to a determination to complete every job on time and on budget, and the company's structure.

"All our competitors are publicly funded or have shareholders," says Waleed. "But we have three owners so can make decisions instantly, within 24 or 48 hours, rather than a week or more. We can make rapid choices about what will work for the benefit of our company and our clients. We don't dawdle."

The largest area of work is maintenance. "We offer maintenance packages where you can choose whether to have minimum maintenance or something more intense," says Waleed. "We can perform this on Boeing, Airbus, Gulf Stream, some Bombardier and the PC-12."

AMAC can also design, refurbish and refit aircraft, working on interiors from small-sized aircraft all the way up to an A380 to whatever design the customer desires. A team of expert craftspeople ensures the fabrics and material are of the highest standard, and the company can accommodate any request for modification. The extraordinary quality of these flying palaces has delighted an international portfolio of customers. "Some people consider these interiors to be works of art," says Waleed.

AMAC also helps with the daily running of aircraft in areas such as crew, meals and cleaning. "These services are small but integral," says Waleed. "The client always wants to know that they have a full crew to fly whenever they are ready, that they have food and drink on board and that the craft is clean." The company can also ensure satisfying results for clients wishing to purchase, sell, part-exchange or charter an aircraft.

"If a person is interested in AMAC, they will not be disappointed," concludes Waleed. "We are purveyors of Swiss excellence. You can buy a penknife from a market and it's cheap but will only last a year. Come to us and it's like buying a Swiss Army knife."
— www.amacaerospace.com

PUSHING THE ENVELOPE

Bugaboo

BUGABOO MAY BE renowned for its high-end strollers but, for designer and founder Max Barenbrug, buggies have only ever been one part of his vision. "We are a mobility brand," he says. "We are first and foremost about mobility and performance. And we want to have a relationship with the consumer that lasts longer than the four years that someone's child needs a stroller."

Now, that vision has become reality with the launch of the Dutch company's latest innovation, the Bugaboo Boxer, which aims to make people think again about suitcases. Bugaboo Boxer is a revolutionary luggage system made up of interlocking bags and cases that create an ergonomic, easy-to-manoeuvre system.

Bugaboo (literal meaning: "tiny, teasing ghost") started life as Max's 1994 graduation project, to redesign the stroller. Noticing that parents were struggling with their buggies and bicycles and kit – and that existing strollers were ugly, cheap-looking and not very functional – he set out to design something that not only looked good but was also adaptable and could perform well in all manner of environments, including beach and mountain.

Received with great acclaim and press attention, the original Bugaboo hit the market in 1999. Since then, with the launch of several new models, including the Bugaboo Cameleon and the Bugaboo Bee, and collaborations with designers including Marc Jacobs, Diesel and Missoni, Bugaboo has been consistently rated as the best pushchair brand by consumers and reviewers for its versatility, beauty and user functionality.

Bugaboo strollers are also popular with celebrities, from actual royalty – both the Dutch Queen and the Duchess of Cambridge have purchased strollers – to pop royalty. "We got a phone call from our retailer in Los Angeles," Max recalls. "She was literally shouting down the phone with excitement: 'Madonna is here and she's buying a Bugaboo!' It was really funny."

For Max, inspiration comes "from the stomach, not from the brain". "I don't look at what competitors are doing," he says. "I look on the street, at what's needed, and I always do my own thing. When a design is right, my heart, brain and stomach all say it's good."

With his design for the Bugaboo Boxer, Max has reinvented the wheel – or rather four wheels – once again. "Luggage is a boring market, like the stroller market was when we started," he says. "It's just plastic pieces with wheels. The Bugaboo Boxer is about performance and manoeuvrability and modularity: it pushes like a stroller in front of you, instead of being dragged behind you, and you can control the steering. You don't need to bring a separate laptop bag or day bag – they are all integrated into the system."

Aimed at families and business travellers, the Bugaboo Boxer launched in September 2016 on the company's website, in Bugaboo brandstores in Amsterdam and Berlin, and at pop-up shops in London and New York. Customers can choose the colour and configuration they desire. A system including chassis, case and cabin case with inner bag costs around £1,140.

The future for Bugaboo looks exciting. "We now have a stroller and a luggage business, and we're going to continue to work on new designs and models and to improve our products," says Max. "There is also a third business area that we're working on, but I can't tell you anything about it. All I can say is that it's going to have wheels. It will be revealed in two years."
— www.bugaboo.com

FLIGHTS OF FANCY

Fly Me To The Moon Travel, Greece

"I AM NOT a travel agent, or even a travel designer," says Elena Papanicolaou, founder and CEO of Fly Me To The Moon Travel. "I want to show my clientele every single good thing there is in Greece – or at least, every one that will interest them."

After 15 years as CEO of a large chemical company, flying frequently for work, Elena knew just what top-end travellers wanted. She also knew that, in her native Greece, they weren't finding it. So, three years ago, she started her company. "I only do Greece," she says, "and I do the whole of Greece."

Elena was born in Athens and has spent years building up her knowledge of her homeland and a formidable network of specialist contacts. "We offer authenticity, uniqueness, imagination," she says. "I am not interested in the typical. True luxury is not necessarily about five-star hotels: it's a fabulous, unrepeatable experience. It might be a gorgeous cottage in the middle of the forest, with a fantastic hiking route and a local person to show it to you then take you to his home for a meal."

Thanks to her network of people on the ground, Elena can find everything – from the local artisan nobody knows about to the special permit that requires connections in a government ministry. She also plans the whole trip, from yachts to guides to meals to special activities, and meets every client at least once before their journey begins.

"It is a highly personalised service," she says. "My philosophy is to keep doing something I really know well, and just do it even better. It is my job to know the people who are the experts and to be able to select what is really good, authentic and a little bit edgy, and then use the right people to set it up and make it fly."

For instance, Elena might work with a university professor when putting together a cultural trip, or with a fashion consultant if the request is for an exclusive shopping trip. She gives the example of a recent birthday party for a group of 50, mainly from the US.

"They arrived by yacht on the island of Symi in the Dodecanese – a very small island that's incredibly picturesque, it looks like a jewel," she says. "They had fun relaxing, riding scooters round the island, and for the actual celebration I had rented a deserted monastery on an unoccupied island seven minutes' boat ride from Symi with a huge seafront patio. I set it up with hanging lights and linen tablecloths, brought in a DJ, a sax player and a local team of expert restaurateurs who grilled meat and fish and served it with salads."

It was, she says, all very upmarket but with a local style. The guests arrived in typical small wooden boats, to a typical Greek feast full of tiny thoughtful touches. "It was something amazing," she says. "The food, the wine, the dancing. They left at 5 am!" Elena would have left rather later, since she has to do all the serious stuff as well as enjoy the fun ("all the logistics, safety and efficiency, those things are very important"). Meanwhile, guests can relax, knowing that everything is taken care of, every whim catered for. And that is surely the greatest luxury of all.
— www.flymetothemoontravel.com

HAPPY RETURNS

Invest in Andalucía

MANY ARE AWARE of the holiday charms and exquisite golf resorts of Andalucía, a stretch of southern Spain that takes in Seville, Granada and the sun-dappled coast around Almeria and Malaga. But not everybody knows that Andalucía is also, for many foreign companies, one of Europe's most attractive areas for investment.

"Great training and education nourishes a huge talent pool of well-qualified, motivated and loyal employees," says Vanessa Bernad González of Invest in Andalucía, an initiative supported by the regional government to assist foreign investors. "It's embedded in an area with more competitive business costs than the rest of Europe, with great flight connectivity, modern transport infrastructure, many business incentives, international schools and an amazing quality of life. These are key issues for foreign executives."

The team at Invest in Andalucía is proud to list the benefits and advantages of the region: "Andalucía has the population of Austria," says Vanessa. "It offers access to a large internal market and a rapidly expanding North African market. Productivity is growing, there is dynamic R&D activity and the infrastructure is

very strong. In biotechnology there are initiatives for advanced therapies and stem-cell research. We have impressive CSP solar plants. the ICT hub Malaga Valley, and Seville is home to a final assembly line of Airbus, including the A400M aircraft. Next to Gibraltar you'll find Spain's number-one container harbour, Algeciras."

Invest in Andalucía makes life easier for investors, whether they are making their first move into the region or are looking to expand existing interests. "We are a single contact point," says Vanessa. "Our account managers hold the hand of the investor, so they will find all the information and contacts they need."

Regional specialisms include biotechnology, chemicals, ICT, agroindustry and aeronautics, with companies including Accenture, Acerinox, Pfizer, Glaxo, Renault, Oracle, KPMG, Vodafone, Atos, PwC, Everis, Bayer, DuPont, Huawei, Fujitsu, Ericsson, Siemens, Heineken and IBM. "All take advantage of the business environment and the exceptional quality of life," says Vanessa. "It's always been a great place to live, but it's now much more than that."
— www.investinandalucia.es

THE MEMORY MAKER

Cashel Travel

IT BEGINS WITH a seaplane ride, soaring over the Scottish landscape and gazing out onto the glorious wilderness of the Highlands below. Then, the plane dips and glides over the calm waters of a remote loch, pulling up alongside a secluded beach. Here, in this remarkable setting, a private tent awaits where a gourmet chef is preparing a spectacular feast for two, featuring the finest Scottish fare.

This is one of many bespoke experiences available from Cashel Travel, a boutique, family-run company that crafts unique itineraries around the UK's most extraordinary regions. Based in Edinburgh and with 30 expert staff members, it is one of Britain's leading bespoke tour operators. "As people have more time to travel and more destinations open up, they are increasingly looking for experiences rather than just amazing hotels," says James Aitken, founder and joint owner of Cashel Travel. "People now are looking to do things that aren't possible to organise on their own, whether it is to stay in a castle, dining with the owner, or playing on an exclusive golf course on a private island, or blending their own whisky."

For Cashel Travel, the first stage in planning a holiday is to establish the client's expectations. "Everyone has different levels of comfort and luxury," says James. "Some clients want to meet locals in a village pub. Others want to be pampered throughout." New venues are carefully assessed by James and fellow company director, Marta Kucharczyk, who spend much of the year scoping out restaurants, hotels and experiences. "The only way to make sure our clients enjoy their precious leisure time," says Marta, "is to check everything in advance and not trust online guides, which are frequently out of date or plain wrong!"

It's not just the luxury leisure market demanding unusual activities. The so-called MICE sector – an acronym for "meetings, incentives, conferencing, exhibitions" – is increasingly looking to create memorable itineraries for businesses. "We are experiencing a change in clients' requests," says Marta, "with a demand for more experiential and experimental activities that emphasise meeting the locals, dining in unusual settings and staying in amazing places."

That's where Cashel Travel really stands apart as they scour the UK in search of the exceptional, always on the lookout for places, people and experiences that will perfectly suit each individual client.
— www.casheltravel.com

DECK IT OUT

Oyster Yachts

WHEN OYSTER YACHTS launched its first "deck saloon", the designers were unaware that they were pioneering a class of vessel that would soon become a world favourite. Thanks to the simple concept of an indoor saloon and navigation area with panoramic views, the world of sailing was opened to people who are attracted to the idea of going to sea, but not as a rugged sport. Instead, deck saloons provide a pleasant and luxurious experience, with all the enchantment of being under sail.

In the 1970s, Oyster's founder, Richard Matthews, funded a race boat of his own by making 10 and selling all but one, and formed a company that has been building yachts ever since. These days, Oyster builds between 15 and 18 bespoke sailing yachts each year.

"All our boats are built to order," says CEO, David Tydeman. "We have our own boatyards – in Hoveton, Norfolk and Southampton – and we welcome customers to come and visit, and enjoy being involved in the planning and design."

Oyster's output is in three groups. At one end of the scale are yachts between 47½ ft and 62½ ft, which are suitable for family and friends, without needing a professional crew. At the other end are boats above 80 ft – classed as Superyachts – which are large enough to provide separate facilities for crew and owners. Many are equipped for luxury hotel-level service. In between are boats, nicknamed the coupés, that require one or two crew, but do not have that social separation.

"We make what we call blue-water cruising boats," says David. "Our signature themes are the wrap-around window in each saloon, and the siting of the owners' cabins at the back – which is the quietest and most comfortable place to sleep."

Many Oyster owners start with the dream early in life, waiting for the time and opportunity to cruise the oceans. In contrast to motor yachts, which are restricted by their need for fuel and hence confined to local cruising, sailing yachts have the freedom to cross oceans and roam the world. "A sailing yacht is the perfect hybrid machine," says David, "because you can switch the engine off and let the wind take you."

One of Oyster's proud creations is *Maegan*, an 825 Superyacht, which won Best Interior Design of a Sailing Yacht at the 2016 International Yacht and Aviation Awards. "We've just sold another 825 – similar to *Maegan* – to a couple who had only done a week's sailing before coming into some money," says David. "We've found them a skipper and a chef, and we're arranging for them to go round the world in the exclusive Oyster World rally. It will be a great adventure."

As well as running a brokerage service for pre-owned vessels, Oyster regularly hosts owners' events. There are two regattas each year in the Caribbean and the Mediterranean and, in January 2017, 34 other Oyster yachts will join the new owners of the 825 in the two-year circumnavigation.

Oyster has twice been honoured with a Queen's Award for Export. "We employ 400 people, and we build everything in England," says David. "We're a proud, privately owned British company."
— www.oysteryachts.com

SAIL OF THE CENTURY

Superyacht Seven Spices, Egypt

A QUARTER OF a century ago there was little in this part of the Egyptian Red Sea coast but sand, sea and an idea. The idea – and then the land – belonged to Samih Sawiris, the now-billionaire Egyptian-Montenegrin businessman, who was scouting out opportunities for his family's development firm. With investment and a certain topographical flair, Sawiris has created from the desert a leisure complex that some have called the Red Sea Riviera – El Gouna.

From this network of man-made canals springs every size and shape of vessel. But one leisure craft in particular has earned a name for unparalleled luxury. Run by South African couple Debbie and Captain Peter Dickens, *Seven Spices* is a superyacht for hire, and the only such craft operating out of El Gouna.

Peter and Debbie landed in Egypt three years ago, having previously plied their nautical trade in the British and US Virgin Islands. In that time they've become accustomed to the Egyptian way of life, its language and customs, and built a loyal, high-end clientele. "We've had movie and TV stars – even Saudi princes," says Debbie. The attractions of *Seven Spices* are evident enough from the impressive

raw numbers. The yacht is 40 m in length, with 550 sq m of space on four levels, six guest staterooms accommodating 13 guests, two bars, a saloon, formal dining space for 14, plus four outside deck areas and a Jacuzzi. Guests have unlimited access to the latest scuba gear, plus an onboard dive instructor and a host of other water sports, all-inclusive, alongside food and non-alcoholic drinks.

But it is the personal touches that make the experience so special. "El Gouna is a secure little bubble of calm where you are the focus of our attention," says Debbie. "We'll sort your visa, a VIP meet-and-greet, and transport you in luxury to the boat. Whether you want to spend your time diving, kite-surfing, snorkelling, being pampered by our masseuse or taking a tour to visit the Pyramids, we will create an itinerary that suits you." The more traditional treasures of Egypt are only a couple of hours away. "If you have the time, it's really exciting," says Debbie.

From the Pharoahs to fine dining, *Seven Spices* offers a mixture of activities from cultures ancient and modern that you genuinely won't find anywhere else.
— www.luxurymotoryachts.com

A WORLD OF DIFFERENCE

Captain's Choice

FOR THE PAST 20 years, top-end travel company Captain's Choice has been going the extra mile for discerning travellers. It specialises in once-in-a-lifetime voyages to the world's most remote and exotic places, from the North Pole to the Andes, from Burma to Botswana.

"We source our destinations with incredible care and always ensure that we show travellers the very heart of every country," says Katie Panagou, the UK Manager of Captain's Choice. "We create itineraries to places that are not easily accessible, and use local tour guides, who are always happy to talk about their culture."

The company, which was established by travel enthusiasts Phil and Kaye Asker in Sydney, Australia, offers fully inclusive tours on a luxury jet, with every detail of its two- to three-week-long trips coordinated by an experienced Tour Host Team that even includes a doctor. Travelling on a privately chartered 90-seater Boeing 767 is not only a luxury experience, but also it frees the holidaymakers from the hassles associated with scheduled air travel, such as long check-in or security queues. "We make sure that travel only happens during the day," says Katie, "so customers will always get a good night's sleep."

The three tours scheduled in 2016, for instance, included an exploration of the equator (with stop-offs in Cuba, Panama and the Galapagos Islands); a voyage around South America (which took in Argentina, Peru and Easter Island); and a tour of Asia and Africa (which took off from Sydney and landed in London, via Cambodia, India and the Serengeti, among other places).

Captain's Choice takes care of every detail, from point-to-point luggage transfers to tips, meals, drinks, excursions and five-star accommodation. "Once you are on our tour, you won't have to open your wallet," says Katie. "It really is a fully inclusive product."

The company launched a UK office eight years ago to accommodate its European customers, who usually make up around 30 per cent of every tour group. Captain's Choice tours also attract single travellers who are reassured by the safety of group travel but also by the promise that there is considerable flexibility on every trip, from what to do during the day to where to have dinner in the evening. From stunning sights to travelling in style, it's safe to say that Captain's Choice shows its customers the world of difference.
— www.captainschoice.co.uk

FAMILY MATTERS

Big style for little ones

YOUNG AT HEART

Cashmirino

"CHILDREN'S CLOTHES ARE my passion," says Maria Busquets, the creator and founder of Cashmirino. As a fast-growing children's clothing company, the brand prides itself on using luxury fabrics and artisan techniques to create traditional styling.

Cashmirino's cosy London store is located in Burlington Arcade – the exclusive, covered shopping gallery that connects Bond Street with Piccadilly – and is immediately recognisable for its unique window displays. The shop is warmly decorated and located over two floors, one for babies and the other for children aged up to 10 (although some boys' designs go up to age 14).

"Children are my main inspiration, with their innocence, love and enthusiasm," says Maria. "They want to feel comfortable and they like to wear colours. They shouldn't be dressed like mini adults."

Born in Venezuela and educated in Venezuela, Europe and Canada, Maria began her career at Merrill Lynch, before deciding to pursue her real ambition. "I wore cashmere myself and wondered why my first daughter, Sofia, shouldn't wear it too," she says. "So I decided to create my own line." In 2000, the year her second daughter was born, Maria started Cashmirino in Italy.

In 2008, with all her children at school, Maria opened her first flagship store in the brand's home city of Milan. "My three children have been my real teachers," she says. "They showed me what they wanted, in the colours that they picked and through their dreams and the games that they played. Love was my main motivation. I also understood how to design for boys so much better when my son Nico was born."

Maria begins her design process by disconnecting and meditating, until her mind is clear of everyday stress, and she is in her "in-love mood". Once her designs are final, Cashmirino's pieces are handmade and hand-cut by people across the globe. "Quality and care are our main concerns," says Maria. "We use natural fibres in which we carefully select fabrics and materials."

In the store, customers will find hand-embroidered smock dresses and Korean-collared detailed shirts made from the finest cotton and linen, all made in Italy. The brand's signature cashmere sweaters, cardigans and dresses are hand-knitted or hand-finished by an artisan manufacturer in Inner Mongolia. Detailing is key, with paisley handkerchiefs tucked into shirt pockets and contrasting floral underskirts hidden under dresses.

After 19 years in Milan, Maria is now based in London and is concentrating on expanding the online side of her business through a re-launch of the brand's website. "We want our customers to feel like they are part of a community through our new site," she says. "Through playful storytelling in the form of our Cashmirino bear characters, we hope that children will be entertained with surprises whilst also enjoying choosing their own clothes with their parents.

"At the end of the journey," she concludes, "we hope that the children will witness something original and fun while understanding exactly where the clothes came from and how they were made. With our new website we want to create a Cashmirino family world – a world that is inspired by and dedicated to children. The most beautiful expression of love."
— www.cashmirino.com

ON THE GOOD FOOT

PèPè Shoes

WHEN ACTOR HELENA Bonham Carter came into PèPè Shoes' Paris store to buy shoes for her children, she liked it so much that she ended up buying the shop fittings. "We had some jumping jacks as decoration," recalls Paola Pizzetti, co-founder and co-owner (with husband Dario) of PèPè. "She was so enthusiastic, she asked if she could buy them too!"

PèPè was started by Dario's father in 1970. When Paola and Dario took over, they expanded the range from infant shoes to children's walking shoes, and set out to create a unique and recognisable brand, using the best quality materials and craftsmanship, and mixing retro and contemporary details.

"We started doing things that others didn't anymore," says Paola. "Like using leather soles on some shoes, not just for style but because it's good for children to feel the ground beneath their feet. It stimulates their sense of touch."

PèPè shoes are handcrafted and made entirely in Italy using traditional techniques. Already using vegetable-dyed leathers, it plans to make its production processes even more environmentally friendly in the future.

The firm is based in Vigevano, Italy, a town which specialises in high-end shoe production (it is also the home of Manolo Blahnik, Moreschi and Gravati). The company has two standalone stores, in Paris and Milan, where customers are able to order some styles customised with their own choice of materials. The brand's shoes are also stocked in retail outlets worldwide and an online shop is currently in progress.

"PèPè shoes have an understated elegance – there are no logos and they're not shouty," says Paola. "Our customers are people who love quality, style and detail, and understand the importance of accessories. You can have the best dress in the world but if you have a poor shoe you spoil everything."

The most popular style is a T-bar shoe made for both young boys and girls, which comes in a multitude of colours and materials. "We even make them in yellow," says Paola. "It's bright and fun. After all, children have all their lives to wear blue and brown shoes."
— www.pepechildrenshoes.it

SOLE PURPOSE

————

Young Soles

CHILDREN OFTEN STRIVE to grow up too fast and the fashion world generally urges them on. In contrast, the success of luxury children's footwear brand Young Soles has been to create a small and stylish collection of shoes with the joys of childhood firmly in mind. "I like kids to look like kids," says Stuart Anderson, Director of Sales and Marketing. "Our shoes are inspired by childhood memories, so the look is retro meets modern."

Like many good ideas, Young Soles is a business born out of necessity, or at least frustration, on the part of shoe designer Louise Shill, Stuart's life and business partner. "When our first daughter Rosie was born, Louise couldn't find any shoes she liked for her so she decided to design her own," says Stuart. "She had some samples made up of the Rosie T-Bar and straight away got orders to make more."

The design principle is simple. The company uses lightweight soles and the softest leather that moulds to the foot. It also puts a twist on classic British designs, such as white patent-leather Chelsea boots, high-shine oxblood brogue boots or nude pink sandals. The Hattie monkey-boots are tied with Liberty cotton laces. "We were influenced by British shoe makers like Grenson and Hudson, who make edgy versions of their classic styles for adults," says Stuart. "But there wasn't anything similar for children."

Less than two years after Louise and Stuart began to produce a full collection for toddlers and juniors, they were awarded gold – in 2015 and 2016 – at the *Junior Design Awards* and "highly commended" in the prestigious *Drapers* footwear awards. "People love nicely crafted, well-made shoes," says Stuart. "And we've put a lot of care into the product. Our shoe box is like a small suitcase so that kids can keep things in it."

Young Soles has been snapped up by stockists across Europe and beyond, with a huge amount of interest from China and the US. Its reinvention of classic British shoe styles with a witty dash of street-cred means that kids can still be kids and look stylish at the same time. "They are beautiful products, something that customers want to be involved in," says Stuart. "Young Soles has been a joy to work on."
— www.youngsoles.co.uk

A DREAM DRIVE

Fun Furniture Collection

IF YOU'VE EVER dreamed of sleeping in a Mini Cooper, a classic camper van or even a Rolls-Royce, then Fun Furniture Collection is the company for you – or at least for your children or grandchildren. Since 2008, Mark Turner and Llinos Mair Pritchard have been constructing high-quality children's beds in the shape of iconic cars and trucks, with each item handmade to order, allowing for an extraordinary degree of detail and individualisation.

"Yes, these orders do tend to be parent driven," laughs Mark. "But the children know what they are, and it inspires them to learn about the vehicle."

It all began at a classic truck show in 2008. "I was wandering around and saw an AEC Matador and suddenly had this idea that it would make a really fantastic bed for a child," says Mark. "I designed it on my computer and then went into the workshop and cut and assembled it. The finished bed received acclaim. It grew from there as we began to take on more commissions, but things really took off when we introduced the camper vans."

Mark is a trained industrial designer and self-confessed car fanatic, which is why Fun Furniture beds are so carefully constructed and accurate in their detail. "We do make other products – storage units, desks, toy boxes – but everything is road-vehicle themed as that's my passion," he says. "I research, take photographs and then add as much detail as possible. For the camper van, I spent weeks making a sliding door from plywood because I really wanted to get it right."

It's why Fun Furniture Collection's designs are becoming so sought after, with the company taking commissions from customers that include members of Middle Eastern royal families. "The devil is in the detail," says Llinos. "A lot of people make themed furniture, but what we try and offer is tremendous detail, as well as the strength, quality and durability of the material. We see these as heirlooms, something to be passed down from generation to generation, and so make everything double strength to ensure it can really withstand the rigours of play."

Mark may be a stickler for detail, but he is more than happy to be driven by the desires of the customer, changing colour schemes and number plates to suit. For the popular London Routemaster bus model, for instance, customers can choose their own route or destination – Neverland was one customer's choice.

The most popular beds are the camper vans, with the Mini, Land Rover and Routemaster also selling well. Mark is happy to try anything – his dream commission is a Lamborghini Countach – but only if the bed is recognisable as the vehicle, something that requires some innovative design. "I can't just do the ones I want," he says. "We prefer to make the ones people will buy as it takes time and money to design, build and promote each prototype."

The final result is, however, well worth it as these beds are more than just furniture. They look so realistic that children immediately co-opt them into their creative play, allowing the imagination to run wild. "You hear them go straight into this different world as soon as they see the bed," says Mark. "It really sparks their imagination."

— www.funfurniturecollection.co.uk

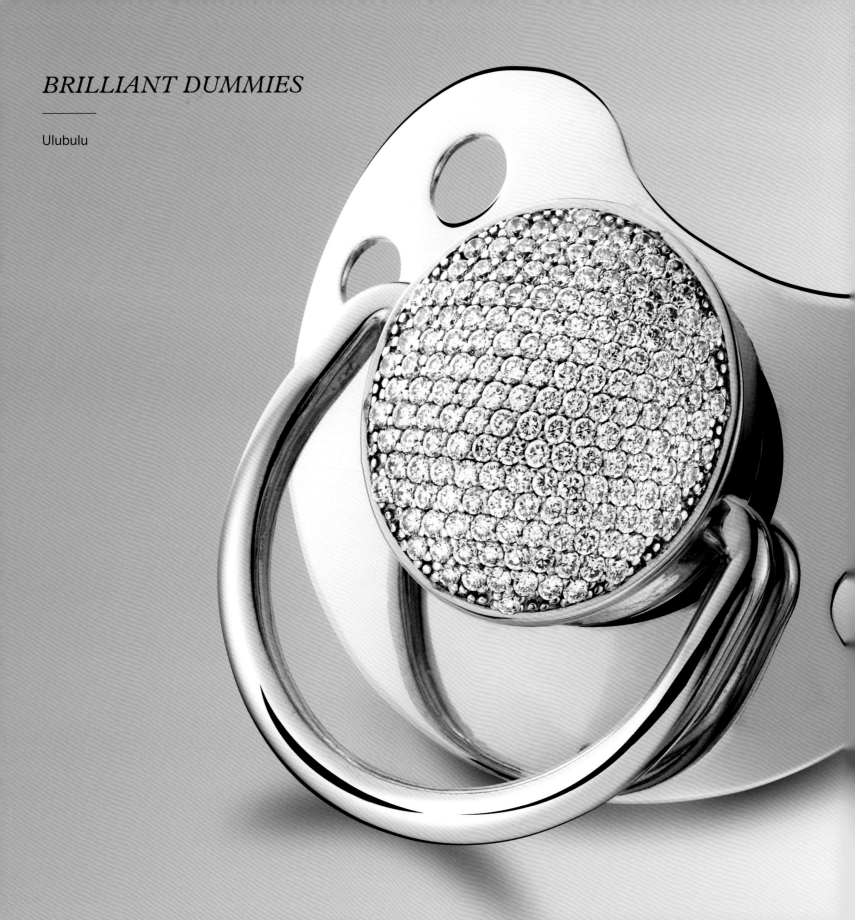

BRILLIANT DUMMIES

Ulubulu

THOUGHTS OF BABY paraphernalia normally conjure up pastel-coloured plastic, disposable nappies and slightly whiffy clothes smeared with (at best) food. But since 2005, Ulubulu's Creative Director Mathis Riiber has been on a mission to design hitherto unremarkable baby accessories along more original and stylish lines. "When my wife and I had our first son," he says, "I often found I had collected him from day care with another child's dummy! We came up with a concept of quality soothers unique to each child, so even dads could remember which dummy belonged to them."

Meaning "Hullabaloo" in Danish, the firm's name is taken from a traditional nursery rhyme. The manufacture of Ulubulu's primary products is done in Germany, using high-quality BPA-free materials and orthodontic silicon teats. They can then be personalised with a child's name; or carry moustache designs or witty slogans such as ''Mute button'' and "Pull to sound alarm," which stand out from the average powder blue or baby pink dummy.

"It's important that these are design-led products," says Mathis, whose background is in luxury jewellery. "Parents want something cool. These products are original, giftable keepsakes, and although they're everyday objects such as teethers, we really pay attention to detail." The eminently chewable teethers Mathis refers to are available in different shapes: a knuckleduster, a hashtag and a camera. He has also designed an eye-catching range of brightly coloured silicon bibs, whose similarly humorous and engaging style makes it easy to see why these products are so popular in an increasingly competitive parenting market.

At the very top of Ulubulu's range is an 18-carat gold pacifier, pavé-set with more than 150 diamonds. This extremely precious, exquisite keepsake drew international attention to the US-based company; and for good reason. "We created this pacifier as a gift for Brad Pitt and Angelina Jolie's first child, Shiloh," he says. The 18-carat white gold shell is a scale model of Ulubulu's everyday pacifiers, and even features the silicone teat; but since it weighs 100 g, it isn't suitable for a baby to suck. For the lucky few who can afford it, though, the famous Diamond Pacifier can be made to order as a completely cherished, one-off gift.

"The pacifier is hand-engraved with the baby's name, birthdate and weight, and there's no reason we can't use different stones instead of the pavé-set diamonds," says Mathis. As each deluxe dummy is made to order, it's easy to alter the details: the 18-carat white gold could become rose gold, for instance, while the diamonds could be swapped for emeralds. "I have some more designs on my drawing board that incorporate the mother and baby's fingerprints," says Mathis, "so ideas are always evolving." These bespoke items can take up to eight weeks to make but are most definitely worth the wait.

But whether it's to cause a hullabaloo in the press with an extravagant diamond-encrusted baby gift, or to treat a baby or toddler to something irresistible to drool or chew on, Ulubulu has something for every family. "They're wonderful keepsakes," says Mathis. "These designs are absolutely what we'd like for our own children."
— www.ulubulu.com

PLAY TIME

Mr Uky

IN MANY WAYS, Zeynep Akpolat encountered the same trouble dressing her son as every other new mum. "He started walking when he was eight-and-a-half months old and one week later he was running," she explains. "He still won't stand still! But it was impossible for me to find a decent pair of trousers to fit him."

It wasn't just fit, either. While girls had the pick of stylish and colourful outfits, boys made do with drab greys, navy jogging bottoms and cartoon-character tops created from the kind of overpriced yet mass-manufactured materials that didn't survive the rigour of, well, all that racing about. "The mainstream fashion industry is very sexist," says Zeynep.

So, in 2014, she set up her own blog asking other mothers for help, and inviting tips on where to hunt down good items. The site quickly gathered thousands of loyal followers. Realising she was onto something, Zeynep took things one step further: teaching herself to sew and then making clothes for her son and, soon after, for her friends' little boys. "How hard could it be?" she thought.

Today, Mr Uky – named after her son's initials, naturally – is an independent business with five staff creating the items she initially struggled to find. Inspired by the cool, unisex 1970s-style outfits that she wore as a child, Zeynep's clothes ignore current trends and aim to be timelessly smart and durable. "The looks are dapper," she says, "but there is nothing preventing a girl from wearing them, too."

Zeynep stops at nothing in her search for quality and diversity. Knitwear is handmade in rural Istanbul, jackets are sourced from bespoke tailors, while heavier materials such as tweeds sit in her collections alongside trousers with durable, elasticised waists. All her clothes use the highest-quality wool, cotton and linen normally reserved for adults. Or, as she more succinctly puts it: "Comfortable for the children and practical for mum."

There is one final inspection that makes Mr Uky truly unique. "When I work on a new design or fabric I have a test period," she says. "My son wears them every day for a couple of weeks. I wash them and put them in the dryer. Only those that pass are good to go. So they really are kidproof."
— www.mruky.com

HAPPY FEET

Bibi

BIBI'S CHILDREN'S SHOES have long been a Brazilian institution, and they look set to gain a foothold with even more youngsters around the world. The company was founded in 1949 and made its mark as the first Brazilian footwear brand to produce shoes specifically for children.

It is the only footwear of its type to have won approval from the Brazilian Association of Foot and Ankle Medicine and Surgery, and combines this crucial physiological endorsement with an imaginative, fashion-forward range of styles that has proved a firm favourite with youthful fans and their families.

"Bibi is a well-established and really successful Brazilian brand that is also sold across 65 countries outside Europe," says Gerry Walker, the Head of Sales at European distributor Ghetz Ltd. "But, until now, it has only dipped its toes into the European market. We were looking for an anatomic footwear product for children, and this was a perfect match."

For Gerry's colleague, Office Manager Tania Malaspini, Bibi is a modern phenomenon with a rich heritage. "Growing up in Brazil, I wore these shoes when I was little, like so many children," says Tania. "They are very contemporary and fashionable, and they're also designed to last."

The company's shoes are manufactured in Brazil, using the highest-grade soft leather, and each has an innovative core that is key to the brand's sustained, and growing, popularity. "We have a properly fitted product in an age when shoes are often treated as convenience goods," says Gerry. "Bibi shoes are designed to cradle a child's foot and give it solid support, while also giving it room to grow. They have a unique Fisioflex insole, so they're really convenient and comfortable. Bibi prides itself on contributing to the child's natural and happy development."

Bibi's tagline – #letkidsbekids – and its latest range of designs are pitched at busy young adventurers. "The colours are fun and eye-catching," says Gerry. "They have all the technology and lights that kids love, with lots of stars and sparkles for the girls' shoes." Indeed, Bibi enables both girls and boys to step out in 21st-century style, with support that has stood the test of time.
— www.bibi.com.br/en

COOL KIDS

Alex and Alexa

OFTEN DESCRIBED AS the Net-a-Porter for under-16s, Alex and Alexa is a one-stop online department store for parents searching for children's clothing and shoes that combine a keen eye for individual style, quality and practicality. "With everyday essentials from Mayoral to stylish streetwear from Nike and blow-the-budget-beautiful shoes from Sophia Webster Mini, we bring the greatest collection of brands to our customers," says Senior PR Manager Jenny Slungaard.

The site is part of the leading multi-channel children's retailer, The Luxury Kids Group, along with Babyshop and Oii Designs, and was founded in 2007 with a selection of high-end labels such as Burberry, Fendi, Stella McCartney and Chloé. It has since broadened its offering to encompass sportswear, premium brands, shoes, accessories and toys. "The concept was to make time-poor parents' lives easier when shopping for their kids' clothing," says Jenny. "We have everything they need in one place, delivered directly to their door anywhere in the world." This balance of content and quality has paid off, with Alex and Alexa winning the *Junior Magazine* Best Online Fashion Retailer Award four times since 2011.

Customer engagement and feedback is a driving force behind Alex and Alexa, and its website features comments and articles from customers, tastemakers and fashion bloggers from around the world. "We work with editors at the world's leading consumer titles," says Jenny, "creating magazine content that sets us apart from our competitors, meaning we are able to reach new customers worldwide."

Alex and Alexa regularly introduces new brands to its customers, but only after careful vetting. "We are very selective," says Jenny. "The fabrics and the quality need to be right, so we usually watch a new designer for a season or two before we would stock them." Provenance is also vital and the site's buyers first ensure that a product's supply chain is ethically managed before they commit to selling a party dress or a wooden train. Alex and Alexa's Made With Love Christmas campaign showcases, among other things, clothes made with organic fabrics and Fairtrade alpaca blankets, sourced from weavers in Peru.

The range of products at Alex and Alexa is expanding, with the focus on footwear through the introduction of brands such as Ferragamo and Minna Parikka, as well as traditional toys. "We are known for stocking classic, well-made toys from the likes of Le Toy Van, Vilac and Djeco," says Jenny.

Also expanding is the personal-shopping service. "We work with high-net-worth customers, sports stars, actors and royalty," says Jenny. "We show the latest season's collection at their homes and help them find what they are looking for." Such style direction is particularly valuable when it comes to teenagers, who increasingly want to dress like celebrities. "We stock a number of brands that are aimed at – and are age-appropriate for – those often hard-to-dress years," says Jenny, "from cool, Scandi boys-brand Someday Soon to tween-appropriate Bang Bang Copenhagen, a brand that epitomises dressing-up style."

For parents looking for fresh, beautifully designed children's fashion, from intricately embroidered Dolce & Gabbana party dresses to technical yet stylish sportswear, Alex and Alexa offers a stress-free and enticing shopping experience.
— www.alexandalexa.com

HIGH-END PROPERTY

Homes and happy returns

CREATIVE DEVELOPMENT

District //S, Lebanon

WITH ARCHITECTURAL INFLUENCES that range from 400 years of Ottoman rule to the French colonial era of the early 20th century, Beirut's wide boulevards and winding lanes are a reflection of its rich and multifaceted history.

Today, the Mediterranean city is enjoying a renaissance and is recapturing the glamour that once earned it the name of the Paris of the Middle East. Lebanon has never stopped rebuilding and reinventing itself. Nowhere is this more evident than in the new, award-winning District //S neighbourhood.

Due for completion in December 2017, District //S represents an entirely new style of urban living, offering a mix of housing, luxury dining and vibrant retail, as well as everyday amenities. "We have not just built new homes, we have created a whole new neighbourhood," says the project's Marketing Manager. "Residents can go out to buy bread, go to the book store and then out for dinner all in one area."

Saifi Modern SAL, the owner and developer of District //S, has taken into account the varying requirements of its residents by including everything they might need: from laundry to concierge services to space for storing a wine collection. "It is as if you're living with the convenience of a five-star hotel," says Chairman Anthony Stephan, "but in the privacy of your own luxury apartment."

The 42,000-sq m, pedestrianised development benefits from being in the historic heart of the city, nestled between the lively Gemmayzeh area, the elegant Saifi Village and new developments in the west. This means that schools, museums and nightlife are all accessible without the use of a car.

The architects have recreated an old Beirut street ambience by building the neighbourhood on three levels: shops, galleries, restaurants and gardens are at street level; residential space inhabits the second level; and, above that, airy roof gardens, penthouses and sky terraces abound. Trees and greenery keep the pedestrian paths around the residences cool; and these lead out onto a sunny, public piazza bustling with cafés and restaurants.

On the street level, columns and glass-fronted shop fronts create vistas in and out of the buildings. There's a gym, swimming pool and spa for those wanting to get fit. For those seeking retail therapy, there are four retail lanes of luxury boutiques worthy of any cosmopolitan capital.

The 17 five-storey residential buildings feature 100 apartments suitable for everyone from families to young couples, with an offering of eight penthouses, four townhouses and 30 studios. Saifi Modern SAL worked closely with London-based architects Allies and Morrison, who studied the topography of old Beirut for inspiration. To make the district blend in seamlessly with the rest of the city, buildings are clad in five different types of stone, including a local yellow one. Much like the French colonial homes nearby, the residences are fitted with tall, louvred shutters that are closed against the sun to keep the rooms cool.

The penthouses overlook a series of connecting rooftops with terraces, creating a private landscape raised above the city. "We put a lot of emphasis on outdoor spaces," says Alfredo Caraballo, a partner at Allies and Morrison. "We've created large balconies and lodges that act as rooms, which is what

Lebanese residents expect from a comfortable home." While there is some subtle variation between the buildings, all the residential blocks reference each other. "It's like looking at a family portrait," says Anthony Stephan. "No building is the same but they all have something in common."

The homes are delivered as finished products but those moving in are free to consult with Saifi Modern SAL's Beirut-based architects and bring in their own designers to alter the interiors to their own specifications, choosing from Cararra marble floors or teak wood finishes.

The design of District //S has impressed architecture professionals at home and abroad. It won the Francis Tibbalds award for Best Practice Project at the National Urban Design Awards 2013, for its "comprehensive response to the historic character of Beirut, going well beyond the superficialities of appearance to reflect the cultural and functional nature of the city".

In recognition of its green credentials, the 2014 Real Estate Awards Lebanon awarded it the prize for Most Eco-friendly and Sustainable development. District //S is, in fact, the first eco-friendly neighbourhood in Beirut. "Residents are not going to be here just for a year, but for the long run," says Anthony. "They want to invest in their future." Street lights use energy-efficient fixtures; and rainwater is collected to decrease the

neighbourhood's water consumption. In addition, the roof gardens not only answer Beirut's demand for al fresco living, but also keep the buildings (as well as their residents) cool. The wood used in construction is sustainably harvested and most building materials have recycled content.

"The environmentally sustainable nature of the district offers residents and visitors a better quality of life," adds Anthony. With District //S, Lebanon will be the fifth country in the world to set its sights on the Leadership in Energy and Environmental Design for Neighbourhood Development, an internationally recognised green building certification.

The new homes are popular with Lebanese expats, who appreciate the cosmopolitan feeling of District //S and the architecture's nod to Lebanese heritage. "We have also sold apartments to Lebanese residents who do not live in Beirut but who come here every weekend and would rather not stay in a hotel," says the Marketing Manager.

More than 70 per cent of residential space has already been sold and interest remains high. It is clear that with District //S's thoughtful design and layout, luxury amenities and eco-friendly credentials, Saifi Modern SAL has created a brand new type of neighbourhood living for a forward-looking Beirut. "District //S is a jewel of a city within the city," says the Marketing Manager.
— www.districts.com.lb

PLEASURE ISLANDS

Azores Business Development Society

WHEN DR ARNALDO Machado, President of the Board of Administrators of the Azores Business Development Society (SDEA), speaks of the region's "beautiful natural environment", he isn't kidding.

The Azores is a group of nine breathtaking Portuguese islands, where a great deal bubbles beneath the surface. The picturesque holiday vibe belies an area ripe with foreign investment, tourism and trade, and its geography is equally deceptive: the islands are in fact the peaks of some of the world's tallest mountains, reaching up from the deep bed of the Atlantic.

The volcanic archipelago, located about 850 miles west of continental Portugal, is thriving, and the SDEA was established in March 2013 to nurture local businesses, promote innovation and attract foreign investment. "We are a public society whose mission is to design and manage economic policy and reinforce the competitiveness of the region," says Arnaldo. "We act in several areas, including promoting the potential of the Azores and giving financial support to local companies."

When it comes to opportunities for foreign investment, there are three main areas of focus for the period up to 2020. These are the tourism sector, the economy of the sea and the agriculture and dairy industries. The Azores' greatest natural asset is the sea. "We have an economic marine zone of around 1 million sq km, which is about 30 per cent of the total exclusive economic marine zone of the EU," says Arnaldo. "So we have great potential there, with fisheries, with the canning industry, with nautical tourism and with biotechnology."

The Azores' success in the dairy sector is down to the mild climate all year round, with temperatures rarely rising above 28ºC or dipping below 11ºC. "We have very good conditions for dairy products," says Arnaldo. "We therefore produce about 50 per cent of the total consumption of cheese of Portugal, and about 30 per cent of its milk.

"And when it comes to tourism," he continues, "we have no shortage of areas for investment, including real estate, holiday resorts, golf, water and nautical sports, hot springs, health and well-being services."

Arnaldo believes the Azores' future is blue and green – dependent on the sea and sustainability. Given its geography, this is a necessity. "The Azores is a green oasis in the middle of the blue Atlantic," he says. "We are a region with unique and attractive characteristics, and vast opportunities yet to be explored. So we have put a strong emphasis on the green and blue economies, considering environmental and sustainable best practices and adding value to locally produced goods and services."

The SDEA has seen great successes in its short lifetime, and this is something Arnaldo puts down to teamwork. "We have a good balance of people who specialise in different areas," he says. "We work together, but sometimes the specialists in a certain field will take the lead and we will form a team around their expertise."

This way of working is natural to the Azores – maximising its skills and resources, in keeping with its goals of local development, best practice and sustainability. Foreign investors are attracted by this long-term vision, as much as by the region's potential, which, like the islands themselves, has barely scratched the surface. "We are a long-term society," concludes Arnaldo, "working into the future."
— www.investinazores.com

ONE OF A KIND

Mohammed Bin Rashid Al Maktoum City – District One, Dubai

ELITE LIVING MEANS having the utmost in luxury every way you turn, and nowhere does this quite as emphatically as Dubai. At the heart of this city lies the latest in luxurious living: the Mohammed Bin Rashid Al Maktoum City District One, an exclusive residential community and expansive development that is due to be completed by 2020. Phase one of the project, which comprises villas and mansions, commenced handover in October 2016.

Its developer Meydan Sobha celebrated a milestone in December 2015 when the 8.4 km-long cycle path and running track was inaugurated. The District One track is part of the vision of His Highness Sheikh Mohammed Bin Rashid Al Maktoum – UAE's Vice President, Prime Minister and Ruler of Dubai – and also the desire of Meydan Sobha to provide a world-class amenity, not just for its residents, but for the community as a whole.

In an aspect that has come to epitomise the work of Meydan Sobha, the running track's surface is state-of-the-art and not only lowers the risk of injury, but also enhances speed and is slip-resistant. This isn't the only sporting endeavour available to the development's residents.

The Crystal Lagoon at District One will become the first of its kind in the United Arab Emirates and, upon completion, will become the world's largest man-made lagoon. It will offer residents of District One exclusive access to swimming, paddleboarding, kayaking and other non-motorised aquatic leisure activities.

"District One is one of the lowest density developments in the heart of any international city, with 60 per cent dedicated to open spaces and green areas," says a Meydan Sobha spokesperson.

"The luxurious residential community will lie along sublime beaches and sweeping parklands with Dubai's breathtaking architecture as the backdrop."

The District One mansions range from 16,400 sq ft up to 38,000 sq ft and are available in three architectural styles: Modern Arabic, Contemporary and Mediterranean. "All mansions are crafted to a meticulous level and are the very highest quality," says a spokesperson, "nestling amid a beautiful pastoral retreat."

The Modern Arabic mansions use traditional Middle Eastern architecture as a starting point and blend practical functionality with aesthetic splendour. The Contemporary villas feature clean and minimalist lines, with calm open spaces that interlink to create open-plan living, perfect for the way many families now want to interact. Full-height glazing and strip windows create an incredibly light ambience, breaking down barriers between interior and exterior, and helping to bring the outside inside. To enhance the feeling of space, the visual palette is clean and neutral, using natural materials and several shades of grey.

The Mediterranean Villas reflect a harmonious blend of Mediterranean and northern European architecture, and feature the cutting edge of interior design, delivering homes that offer complete privacy.

District One lies close to all the major routes into the city, with quick access to Downtown Dubai, Dubai International Financial Centre, Dubai World Trade Center and the airport. "District One is for the buyer who craves exclusivity," says a spokesperson. "as this project offers the opulent life right in the heart of the city – a life for the elite."

— www.meydansobha.com

A GOLDEN OPPORTUNITY

Golden Tree Real Estate, Algarve

THOUGH THE ALGARVE has long been a popular holiday destination, the south coast of Portugal is undergoing a significant transformation. "The Algarve is re-inventing itself," says Ana Paula Marques, owner of "creative real estate company" Golden Tree. "Old houses are being replaced by modern houses, many built by prize-winning architects, and the infrastructure, resorts and facilities are all completely renewed. All over the coast we have contemporary bespoke villas with concierge service, ready to be moved into, and resorts around are booming. Construction in the Algarve boasts high-quality materials, high-end technology and energy efficiency, as well as environmental friendliness."

Located in the central Algarve "golden triangle", Golden Tree is ideally placed to help clients find or build their dream property anywhere in the region. "We offer integral services by advising our clients and their representatives on site with regard to the procedures with solicitors, architects, interior designers and construction services," says Ana. "We make sure things are done properly and we guide the buyer through the whole process until they move into their new property, making it smooth and trouble-free."

There are lots of attractions to life in the Algarve, explains Ana, with the climate being, decisively, the most important one. This doesn't mean residents spend all their time on the beach, but it does mean life is lived outside, on a restaurant terrace or playing a round of golf. "You can spend all your time outdoors, visiting national parks or playing sports," she says. "You can enjoy the sun, the wind and the water in any way you like."

Golden Tree services are custom-tailored. The real estate company not only helps clients find their ideal holiday or permanent home, but also provides support to clients looking for strategic investments. "We take pride in holding a portfolio with a wide array of real estate products, including modern properties, dwellings to build, traditional properties, apartments, hotels, golf courses and even wineries," says Ana. "There is such a great deal of potential, be it in terms of architecture, design, construction, technology or even "hidden jewels" that people don't know about. The Algarve is a true paradise and we take great pleasure in guiding our clients in the treasure hunt."
— www.goldentree.net

POWER TO THE PEOPLE

Battersea Power Station

BATTERSEA POWER STATION, one of London's most recognisable landmarks, stood empty for more than 30 years before the arrival of an ambitious scheme to totally reinvent it. "This 42-acre site will be a new and vibrant neighbourhood, with community at the heart of everything," says Georgia Siri, UK Sales Director of the Battersea Power Station Development Company (BPSDC). "It will have an identity as distinct as the Left Bank in Paris, giving people who live and work here and nearby a sense of membership and belonging."

The enthusiasm of the Malaysian shareholders of the project and their commitment to long-term involvement sets this project apart from most urban development schemes. The renowned Uruguayan architect Rafael Viñoly, as Master Planner, and David Twohig, as Chief Development Officer, share a zeal for fusing big-city life with village culture. The project has also enlisted a number of visionary architects, including Gehry Partners (best known for Bilbao's Guggenheim Museum) and Foster + Partners (the company behind the Gherkin).

To ensure permanence and consistency, Battersea Power Station will continue to manage the estate following completion. "We have been tasked with creating places that people will want to make their homes," says Georgia. "We are also building a mix of residential and commercial properties, to bring life to the area by night and by day." The Turbine Halls inside the Power Station will contain retail, restaurant, office and leisure space – including a venue for events. The Power Station will favour the best of British brands and new concept stores, while the riverside village of Circus West will favour small, local brands. There will be generous provision of park-like gardens and a spectacular 1.5 acre roof garden.

At the heart of the redevelopment of the area is a new Northern line tube station – Battersea Power Station – along with a dedicated River Bus service. "We call the people who are choosing the 253 loft-style apartments in the Power Station 'Luxury Adventurers'," says Georgia. "Many of these pioneers are creative people, who care about space and light. They also want to know their neighbours."

There has been considerable interest from local Londoners and movers from outside London, many attracted by the emphasis on community. "One of our mottos is 'Don't Do Ordinary'," says Georgia. "It's incredibly exciting and we all feel very privileged to be part of it."
— www.batterseapowerstation.co.uk

ESTATES OF GRACE

Navarino Residences, Costa Navarino, Greece

BOASTING 4,500 YEARS of history and seven different "Natura" areas of protected landscape, Messinia is one of Greece's most attractive and fascinating regions. It's also home to the award-winning Costa Navarino, an upscale but sustainable Mediterranean destination which includes hotels, golf course and residences – all intimately tied to the local culture, history and nature. "It is luxurious in an understated manner, aligned with the local flora and community," says real estate director Evgenios Dendrinos. "Authenticity and the impact on the environment and local community have always been pivotal."

With several of Costa Navarino's hotel resorts and golf courses already open for business, attention has now moved to the luxury villas. "Navarino Residences are 50 exclusive villas, all with unobstructed sea views from ground level," says Evgenios. "The villas come in three different types, in terms of size and location, but share several characteristics. Residents will enjoy sea views from their gardens and watch exquisite sunsets. Owners can customise their villas, within a framework governed by our architectural guidelines, to guarantee the end product will integrate harmoniously with the local environment and work aesthetically with the surrounding buildings."

The villas are impressively contemporary and immaculately finished; but they still feature architecture that references the area's history and landscape. This is in keeping with a determination to make sure the Costa Navarino development, which will consist of five separate areas of around 1.2 sq km each, is not only harmonious with its surroundings but is also the most environmentally responsible development of its kind worldwide.

Residents can enjoy seasonal local products, including wine and olive oil harvested from a dedicated garden (its branded products – Navarino Icons – are already being sold around the world in exclusive shops such as Harrods, Marks & Spencer and Dean & DeLuca). There are also authentic experiences on offer, such as cooking sessions with local villagers; and "philosophical walks" – a historian-guided activity which enables guests to discuss important modern-day issues through the prism of Ancient Greek philosophy. "It's the holistic experience of living in Messinia with all the perks and luxury of a five-star resort," says Evgenios.

Messinia is served by Kalamata International Airport, with direct BA flights from Heathrow and EasyJet flights from Gatwick. The ambitious development is the brainchild of Captain Vassilis Constantakopoulos, who grew up in Messinia before establishing the giant shipping company Costamare Inc, listed on the New York Stock Exchange.

The region is close to numerous significant historical locations, including Mycenaean palaces, 33 castles and three Unesco World Heritage Sites. Residents will also have access to nearby areas that will be developed with the Costa Navarino resorts, including numerous eating, drinking and coffee-shop venues and commercial outlets, as well as dedicated beachfront all-day restaurant and bar facilities. Residents will enjoy privileged access to resort amenities such as hotel swimming pools, a gym and two signature golf courses; a huge variety of activities such as cycling, scuba diving and yachting; and extensive facilities for children.

"Our future owners will have all the facilities of a high-end resort but also access to a unique natural environment and huge history," says Evgenios. "That makes for a unique living experience."
— www.costanavarino.com/residences

INVEST IN PARADISE

Soneva Private Residences, Maldives

THE MALDIVES HAS long been synonymous with secluded paradise escapes, white sands, turquoise water and gently swaying palm trees. For more than 20 years, visitors to the Soneva Fushi resort have been welcomed by sustainable barefoot luxury, and now a lucky few can own their very own piece of paradise.

Alongside its sister resort, the award-winning Soneva Kiri in Thailand, Soneva Fushi was the brainchild of Sonu and Eva Shivdasani, whose luxurious escapes encourage a philosophy called SLOW LIFE: Sustainable-Local-Organic-Wellness Learning-Inspiring-Fun-Experiences. Set on a private island covered in lush jungle and located within a Unesco Biosphere Reserve in the Baa Atoll, Soneva Fushi inspires the imagination with its back-to-nature luxury living. Opening in October 2016, Soneva Jani is one of the most anticipated openings in the Indian Ocean. It also offers a limited number of private residences for sale, with some signature plots still available.

Soneva made history in 2011 by being the first in the Maldives to offer high-quality homes for foreigners. These extraordinary villas, ranging in size from one to nine bedrooms, are built to meet the owners' individual requirements, while being constructed using time-tested techniques and materials from sustainable sources.

Benefitting from abundant natural light, lush foliage and picturesque views, the sprawling villas all feature private pools, dining, study and lounge areas, steam and sauna rooms, spa suites, private gyms, fully fitted walk-in kitchens, wine cellars and spacious bathrooms, with Soneva's signature indoor and outdoor showers and water-features.

"Life here is dominated by relaxed indecision," says Sonu Shivdasani, founder and CEO of Soneva. "It is a refined, rustic, relaxed sort of luxury – with a cold towel on a tray. Aside from unwinding at the Six Senses Spa, guests can watch classic movies at the stunning outdoor Cinema Paradiso, count Saturn's rings at the state-of-the-art Observatory, or learn to blow glass at the only Glass Studio in the region."

Other highlights include some of the best snorkelling and diving in the Maldives, eight different dining outlets, a wine cellar with more than 7,000 mostly organic and biodynamic wines, an unmatched Children's Den, and dedicated cheese, chocolate, ice-cream and charcuterie rooms.

"The idea is that you don't just buy into a week's vacation or holiday home, but into a philosophy," says Sonu. "We call it intelligent luxury. It's about understanding the daily lives of our guests and offering them experiences that are both 'new' – in that they are rare and exceptional – but at the same time 'true', in that they are highly desired and cherished. We specialise in creating sanctuaries where you can return with your friends and family, year after year, at your own island home-away-from-home."

Each fully serviced villa comes complete with a personal butler, and full access to all the island's facilities, with special "owner's rates" being offered in the restaurants, bars and outlets.

Soneva offers the ultimate in paradise property, with all the conveniences and luxuries of a holiday. With no cars, no news and no shoes as part of the philosophy of Soneva, the escapism is absolute, and – for a lucky few – can be accessed whenever they so desire.

— www.soneva.com/residences

DRIVE OF A LIFETIME

PGA Catalunya Resort, Spain

ALTHOUGH IT BOASTS access to Spain's number-one-rated golf course, the PGA Catalunya Resort is more than just an incredible golf destination or exclusive residential complex. "The project has been designed for owners to fully enjoy the Mediterranean lifestyle in an exceptional setting, with the best facilities and first-class services," says Jurriun van Naerssen, PGA Catalunya Resort's real estate sales director. "It's ideal for those seeking an exclusive, modern home, who wish to enjoy a unique, year-round lifestyle."

The resort opened in 1999, and in 2011 introduced its low-density residential project. These signature homes can be designed to fit the owners' tastes and requirements but each respects the beautiful local environment and the consistent modern style of the resort. "We offer generous plots with stunning views, contemporary design villas, comfortable semi-detached villas and modern apartments with golf views," says Jurriun. "All mix modernity, quality and considerate integration into their surroundings."

These surroundings are, quite simply, exceptional. The resort features two 18-hole golf courses and the five-star Hotel Camiral. It is close to Barcelona and Girona, as well as the beaches of the Costa Brava and the skiing facilities of the Pyrenees. "We are surrounded by some of the most beautiful and fascinating villages, beaches and mountains in Catalonia, with award-winning gastronomy, and wonderful wines, art and culture," says Jurriun. "Our Residents Club is exclusive to property owners and it's the perfect way to start the day, with a little exercise, swimming a few lengths in the pool under the morning sun, jogging while the resort awakens, or playing golf or tennis. There is also a spa, children's park and pool."

PGA Catalunya Resort also offers a residential management programme, including 24-hour security, maintenance, personalised administration and rental of the property, gardening and landscaping consultancy, babysitting and a concierge service. "This is a very attractive destination for anyone looking for a more sophisticated experience with all the comforts of the Mediterranean lifestyle," says Jurriun. "You can explore unique gastronomy, medieval history, the art of Dalí and Picasso, or other memorable experiences. And PGA Catalunya Resort is right in the centre of it all."
— www.pgacatalunya.com/real-estate

FAIRWAY TO HEAVEN

Quinta do Lago, Portugal

FOR GOLF LOVERS, there is nowhere quite like Quinta do Lago, the Algarve resort that, for more than 40 years, has been the home of five outstanding golf courses, as well as gorgeous beaches and five-star luxury facilities. When the resort first opened, it offered unprecedented access to world-class leisure. Now, with the completion of a €50 million investment programme, Quinta do Lago has secured its exceptional appeal well into the 21st century.

"The vision of 40 years ago for such a complex resort was very ahead of its time," says Director of Sales Jamie Robinson. "This forward-thinking infrastructure and overall layout has held the resort in great stead over the last four decades, combined with ongoing improvement and investment programmes."

The recent investment programme has seen the resort's North Course redesigned by world-famous golfer Paul McGinley and US golf architect Beau Welling. It also includes the creation of one of the finest driving ranges in Europe, the first ever Paul McGinley Golf Academy, a gym and a mini-golf course that replicates the most famous nine-holes in the world. The resort has also upgraded its gastronomic offering to 10 bars and restaurants, including the new Bovino Steakhouse, while there is also a new programme of events and entertainment. In addition, Quinta do Lago has a new Sports Centre, offering 25 different activities. All of this set within the beautiful Ria Formosa Natura Park. "We are renowned for our golden beaches, 300 days of sunshine per year, the friendly Portuguese people and great fresh food from around the country," says Jamie. "We offer an idyllic holiday resort within easy reach of many European capitals, year-round flights and some of Europe's best lifestyle amenities."

Quinta do Lago also has a residential portfolio, providing the chance to build a luxury home within the resort, working with the some of the world's best architects, landscape gardeners and interior designers. "We have a limited supply of real estate within the resort," says Jamie. "It's unique in that we have control of so many aspects of the resort, and people really value the fact that we are a renowned brand with a long experience in the luxury market."
— www.quintadolago.com/en

A HELPING HAND

Health and happiness

THE BETTER LIFE

Bupa Cromwell Hospital

"PRETTY MUCH THE only thing that you can't do here is have a baby," explains Ahmed El Barkouki, Commercial Director of London's Bupa Cromwell Hospital. "You can see an in-house GP, get diagnosed, referred, treated and discharged, all under one roof. Each year, we perform around 4,000 procedures and see some 120,000 patients."

Purpose-built in 1981, the hospital was bought by Bupa in 2008. Since then it has earned a reputation for complex surgery and for providing excellence in both clinical care and service. Its list of specialities runs to more than 70 areas of expertise, with, for instance, orthopaedic surgery performed by members of the Fortius Group – leading surgeons whose clients include major sports stars.

"Unusually, for a private hospital, almost all of our key specialities are backed up by a multidisciplinary team," says Ahmed. "This means decisions around complex cases are made collectively, not just by a single consultant."

Located in a quiet, residential area of South Kensington in West London, the Cromwell is accessible by public transport and is close to Heathrow Airport. It also offers a valet parking service. In addition, many of London's best hotels are nearby, which is ideal for visiting families.

"We are an international hospital," says Ahmed. "Around half of our patients come from overseas, from more than 140 countries around the world. Our dedicated international patient centre acts like a private concierge to arrange accommodation, meet and greet, and provide free interpretation."

The Cromwell is a leader in cardiac services, employing the TAVI (Transcatheter aortic valve implantation) technique to insert artificial heart valves via a balloon catheter. For patients with prostate cancer it can provide minimally invasive high-intensity focused ultrasound (HIFU). It is also one of the few centres in the UK that uses a Gamma Knife treatment for brain tumours. Infection control is of the utmost importance, and rates are extremely low at the hospital. The Cromwell even uses a microbiology app to ensure the most efficient and safe use of antibiotics.

The hospital has recently refurbished all patient rooms, which offer hotel-style comfort as well as the very highest levels of care, and the outpatient reception area is being remodelled into the equivalent of a first-class check-in lounge. This will provide patients with one-to-one privacy as soon as they walk through the doors.

For those who want the ultimate in luxury, there are four suites available, including the 200 sq m Royal Suite, which resembles a central London penthouse.

"Our patients tell us that we have a 'family feel', which is not something that you hear very often about a hospital," says Ahmed. "We are friendly and there's a calm, relaxed atmosphere. The hospital is spacious, and the huge glass dome in the middle of the lobby makes it feel light and bright. There's even a roof garden terrace, with tables and umbrellas, for patients who want to enjoy the outdoors."
— www.bupacromwellhospital.com

RETHINKING CHARITY

Mercy Corps

WHEREVER THERE IS human need, or whenever there is crisis caused by disaster, conflict or poverty, the global organisation Mercy Corps is likely to be there, working to provide relief, drive recovery and build long-term resilience. Its work is not confined to places where disaster has struck, such as earthquake-hit Nepal; it also aims to build lasting stability in fragile countries, including Afghanistan (where it has been working for 20 years), the Democratic Republic of Congo, South Sudan and Colombia.

"We span the spectrum from relief to recovery through to development," says Mercy Corps' media and communications manager Amy Fairbairn. "We are more than an aid organisation. We think collaboratively and act boldly."

This international body, with headquarters in the US and Britain, was set up in 1979 in response to the flight of Cambodian refugees from famine, war and genocide. Today, it runs the largest NGO-led aid operation inside Syria and has helped more than 7.4 million people affected by the crisis.

Its mission is to alleviate suffering, poverty and oppression by helping people build secure, productive and fair communities. But its work is far removed from the traditional model of "truck and dump", where food and supplies are collected and dropped off at a crisis zone with no follow-up support. "Our strategy is to work in partnership with local communities, government bodies and the private sector to find sustainable solutions," says Amy. "We work with the local population and leverage their knowledge and expertise to make those communities more resilient." Around 93 per cent of staff come from the areas where they work.

Recently, Mercy Corps has been working with local restaurants and hotels to provide food and shelter for refugees from the Middle East who have made their way to Greece and the Balkans. "Rather than give refugees what we think they need," says Amy, "we give them debit cards so they can buy what they need when they need it from local vendors, helping the local economy in the process."

In 2015, a year of unprecedented humanitarian crises, Mercy Corps reached 30 million people with urgent assistance and lasting solutions to save and improve their lives. This statistic is made up of individual stories of survival, such as that of Maysaa, who fled Syria with her three children and now lives in Lebanon. She received cooking training under a Mercy Corps programme geared to helping displaced Syrians and their host communities by fostering self-reliance. She developed her skills and went on to secure a part-time job.

Mercy Corps has learned to work on the basis that people facing crisis are resilient. "We want to support them to recover," says Amy. "That means arriving at smarter solutions by using local knowledge, our learned expertise and new technology." She describes how the organisation set up Wi-Fi hotspots for Syrian refugees in Greece, and created a website in six languages.

The geopolitical reality is that Mercy Corps is still working with refugees now, just as it did when it was founded. The charity continues to evolve to address new challenges as they emerge. "We know more now than ever before how to help people quickly and for the long term," says Amy. "We can do it together."
— www.mercycorps.org.uk

WELL TRAVELLED

Jet Well Soon

YOUR FINGERS, YOUR hand, sometimes your whole arm are, by turns, numb, fizzy and painful. And your GP has confirmed the news: you are suffering from carpal tunnel syndrome and you would benefit from surgery. But, sadly, there's a waiting list. It'll be neither days, nor weeks, but months till your number comes up. What are the alternatives?

Dr Arvin Rodrigues has a solution. His company, Jet Well Soon, specialises in luxury healthcare for those prepared to travel to secure the best and quickest medical attention.

"What we do," he says, "is offer high-quality, efficient, safe and quick treatments in top-class private hospitals in the United Kingdom, Portugal and Spain." If the treatment or procedure you require is non-urgent, then Jet Well Soon will take care of everything – travel, accommodation, the necessary clinical attention with the right surgeon in the right hospital – and ensure that all of this comes to pass in the lap of luxury. And quickly.

Dr Rodrigues is happy to provide a scenario. "If you have been diagnosed with the need for carpal tunnel surgery, then you could contact Jet Well Soon," he says. "You would tell me your preferred destination in the UK, Portugal or Spain. We'd try to narrow it down to one city.

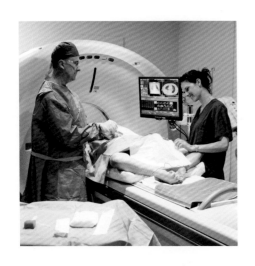

"If, say, you chose Lisbon then we would give you two different alternatives: surgeon X in hospital A or surgeon Y in hospital B," continues Dr Rodrigues. "The price difference between the two would be negligible. We would provide you with information about those two surgeons or you could have a Skype conversation with both before you decide. We want you to be comfortable with your surgeon before you leave home."

Clients can then specify a week when the procedure can be carried out in. "We try, within reason, to make that work," says Dr Rodrigues, "with the potential always that it might be possible within a very few days. Then, once a time and a place have been agreed, we can deal with the travel and accommodation arrangements with you." With direct contracts with a range of luxury hotels already in place, the company can arrange a place to stay with no additional costs involved.

A representative – who will usually speak several languages – will always meet a client at the airport to drive him or her to the hotel. "You can relax, maybe have a drink," says Dr Rodrigues. "Then, that same day or the next morning, you would be taken in a chauffeur-driven car to the hospital, still accompanied by our representative. You would be met at the hospital and introduced to the surgeon, who then makes sure that everything is in place for you to undergo the procedure."

"If it's a carpal tunnel operation you will be able to leave hospital that same day, so you'd return to your hotel and have dinner with your travelling partner. If you'd prefer to go to a restaurant, we can arrange that too. And then, after a good night's sleep, home ..."

Jet Well Soon is an enterprise wholly led by physicians such as Dr Rodrigues, and is growing partnerships all the time with reliable agencies in both the UK and across Europe. "Let us know what you need," is their mantra, "and leave everything to us." — www.jetwellsoon.co.uk

SAVING YOUNG LIVES

The Lullaby Trust

WHILE MANY CHILDHOOD diseases have been eradicated, the leading cause of death in infants between 1 and 12 months remains unexplained. It's called SIDS – or Sudden Infant Death Syndrome – and it claims the lives of five babies in the UK each week. The Lullaby Trust was set up to raise funds for research and to support parents bereaved by SIDS. "Losing a child is very traumatic, so our service is crucial," says Francine Bates, the Lullaby Trust's Chief Executive. "We reach around 70 per cent of families who are unexpectedly bereaved through SIDS. Our bereavement team offers one-on-one support, sometimes for many years."

The charity was founded in 1971 by Nancy Hunter-Gray, who lost her grandson Martin to SIDS, then known as cot death. She was appalled to discover that, at that time, around 2,000 babies were dying each year for reasons unknown, and set up the charity originally known as the Foundation for the Study of Infant Deaths to fundraise for research to discover why.

In the early 1990s, it was discovered that the biggest risk factor was babies sleeping on their tummies. Alongside TV presenter Anne Diamond, who had just lost her son Sebastian to cot death, a national campaign was launched telling parents that all babies should sleep on their backs. This became one of the most successful public health campaigns ever, cutting incidents of cot death in the UK from around 2,000 a year to 300 by 1996.

Today, the Lullaby Trust estimates that it has saved the lives of more than 20,000 babies by promoting Safe Sleep advice: a remarkable achievement, given the fact that it gets no government funding and relies entirely on donations. As well as being the leading national body in promoting safer sleep to parents, it is also the UK's largest funder of medical research into sudden infant death.

"We're still trying to understand why certain babies die," says Francine. "It's likely that a combination of factors come into play when young babies are at their most vulnerable, and there are key steps parents can take to help reduce the chance of tragedy occurring. But more research is vital."

With the right breakthrough and suitable funding, Francine believes that SIDS, like smallpox, can become a thing of the past. "With the necessary support, we hope to crack it in the next 10 years. We just need one last push."
— www.lullabytrust.org.uk

LIFE SUPPORT

Royal Trinity Hospice

"PEOPLE DON'T UNDERSTAND what we do, and they're scared," says Dallas Pounds, CEO of Royal Trinity Hospice. The irony is, of course, that Britain's oldest hospice specialises in coping with the fear and incomprehension that so often accompany terminal illness.

Royal Trinity Hospice is housed on the edge of Clapham Common, London, where a light-filled Georgian building with 28 beds overlooks beautiful gardens. It was set up in 1891 by William Hoare of the Hoare banking family. "He was concerned that people had nowhere to go to die comfortably," says Dallas. "That is a service we still provide, but we also offer all sorts of outpatient and community care: doctors, nurses, therapists and social workers."

Patients would rather stay put at this difficult time, and Trinity Hospice facilitates that. "We can send nurses or specialists to people wherever they call home," says Dallas, "whether that's a care home, a hostel or even prison." Less than a third of the £12 million annual cost comes from public funding. "The rest is split between income from our 25 shops and fundraising. We rely on the generosity of the community. Some people don't understand what hospices do: they think of them as somewhere dreary and scary, somewhere to die."

The hospice turns 125 this year. "We want to open an outpatient and community-based centre in central London," says Dallas. "A place the healthy can come to find information on helping loved ones with life-limiting illnesses. Somewhere to plan for death and dying, with a café – a place that will be a resource for the whole community. There's a real need for more community services."

Hospices don't replace hospital treatment, says Dallas – they supplement it. "We address the physical, emotional, spiritual and psychological issues that a hospital may not have the time or expertise to look at," she says. The earlier Trinity becomes involved, the more it can do, helping people to navigate their way through a sometimes bewildering health and social care system.

"We support people to live the way they want to, insofar as that is possible, and to make informed choices until they die," says Dallas. "Then we support those close to that person in whichever way suits them." That is a vital part of Trinity's main responsibility: helping people with life-limiting illnesses to live every moment.
— www.royaltrinityhospice.london

FIT FOR PURPOSE

HumbleFit

WELL-BEING AND MINDFULNESS are recognised as practices that can greatly enhance the quality of all kinds of lives. Yet it is still rare to find a professional health and fitness company that focuses on both mind and body – a scarce blend of expertise that the London-based HumbleFit specialises in.

The company's founder and CEO Alice Humble draws from her own experience of competitive sports and fitness management. "I've been interested in sports since I was a child and became a nationally ranked pole vaulter in my teens," says Alice. "Pole vaulting requires a lot of mental resilience, and that provided me with an insight into the psychological as well as the physical aspects of sport. Sport is a microcosm of life, and you need to have balance and fulfilment in order to succeed."

Alice has worked as a high-school teacher, a fitness manager and then a personal trainer in Sardinia, all the time bringing her personable, naturally positive manner to the training process. "I met thousands of people from all over the world and all walks of life," she says. "What I found is that everyone quickly felt an improvement mentally as well as physically after exercise. As a teacher, I was also seeing a lack of awareness from an early age that exercise and well-being is beneficial. I have since strived to address that."

One of Alice's clients, a Harley Street psychologist, asked if she could refer some of her own clients to Alice for training, and Alice soon had her own independent business. "It made me think about making exercise a mental therapy," she explains. "Mental health is not a 'condition' – it's something we all have, and everyone can benefit from looking after it."

HumbleFit was launched in 2014 with two core strands: private clients, including referrals from doctors and psychologists; and corporate sessions, with a focus on employee well-being and occupational health. Alice and her team work with adolescent clients, as adolescence is a time when habits are formed, as well as adults, in a combination of client-based areas, private gyms and open spaces.

"Every package we offer is bespoke and tailored to the individual," she says. "It's about finding the right therapist and trainer. We take into consideration each client's specific needs and goals. Every trainer creates a programme with both the client's mental and physical well-being in mind. The effects that I see happen very quickly. Clients have identified improved energy levels, confidence and mental resilience."

HumbleFit's Corporate Wellbeing programmes also showcase the company's exceptional scope. Not many providers are able to provide a package that includes everything from the organisation of the programme to a variety of services including personal training, massage, Pilates, yoga, and life and wellness coaching. HumbleFit also offers "Energise 10" sessions, a ten-minute "blast" that gets people's attention momentarily away from their desks.

"It improves employees' focus, energy and productivity," says Alice. "We work with firms of different sizes, and address employee wellbeing from many angles. This personal touch fits in with any organisation's ethos."

Whether addressing individual health or team goals, HumbleFit delivers the all-round range and contemporary expertise to help everyone achieve their personal best.

— www.humblefit.com

REST ASSURED

Leverton & Sons

VOCATION IS A significant word when describing the work of independent funeral directors Leverton & Sons. "You may only be connected with a family for a couple of weeks, but in that time you occupy a very privileged position," says company director Andrew Leverton. "It is an intense but brief customer relationship. Many of our staff see their work as a service to the community."

The company now has six branches across North London. "We don't exclude anyone, we treat everyone the same," says Andrew. "We are also privileged to be the funeral directors to the Royal Family." Levertons provided funeral services for Diana, Princess of Wales, as well as Baroness Thatcher.

The firm's own history is a remarkable one. It was established in 1789 by John Leverton in the days when carpenters "undertook" to make coffins in addition to their main work. He built a family business, which endures and has presided at the funerals of, among others, George Orwell and Sir Henry Royce. "That was in 1933 and we collected Sir Henry in our new Rolls-Royce hearse," says Andrew. Whether a state funeral or a modest family ceremony, the principles remain the same. "You have to make time for people and always be there for a phone call, day or night," says Andrew. "The client must never feel worried."

Levertons always strives to ensure that the funeral director who first makes contact with a client takes them through every planning stage. "They are there in person, right up to the funeral, to make sure all goes smoothly," says Andrew. The company provides its clients with as much information as possible regarding the style and format of funeral available to them, and arranges religious and non-religious funerals, woodland burials, willow coffins and horse hearses. It even pioneered the UK's first all-electric hearse. "Our tailored funeral plans help clients convey their preferences," says Andrew, "so the primary decisions are made. This releases any burden on the family."

Through eight generations, Levertons has operated with compassion and meticulous planning. Whether a vocation is learned or inherited, it has achieved the perfect balance of continuity and adaptability in the service of its customers. — www.levertons.co.uk

INDEX

ST JAMES'S HOUSE

About the publisher

THE YEAR 2017 heralds two important anniversaries for the RREC. First and foremost, it marks the Club's 60th anniversary; however, it is also the 10th anniversary of the Club's partnership with its official publisher and events company, St James's House.

"We first partnered with the RREC to celebrate its 50th anniversary in 2007," says Richard Freed, Director of St James's House. "The Club was seeking a publisher to produce an official commemorative album. We had produced similar books for the Royal Navy and other distinguished organisations, and we were a good cultural fit for the Club. We had plenty of experience in helping prestigious organisations communicate about their heritage, values and work, and we understood the Club's needs."

Over the following 10 years, St James's House and the RREC have collaborated on a series of major publications and events, including a 90th birthday party for the Duke of Edinburgh at Windsor Castle, a high-profile exhibition of luxury brands at the Saatchi Gallery and a highly successful yearbook series.

"The yearbook series is our flagship RREC project," says Richard. "Our initial brief had two main objectives. Firstly, we had to develop an annual coffee-table book to showcase the Club and its work, as well as the Rolls-Royce and Bentley brands. Secondly, we needed to create a tailored lifestyle publication for Club members."

The result was the now world-renowned series of collectible, high-quality publications celebrating the Club's rich heritage and showcasing the cream of luxury lifestyle brands. Over the years, the scope of this project has broadened to encompass exhibitions, films, launch events, digital content and publicity campaigns.

A Legacy of Luxury is the latest title in this series. "St James's House has been the official publisher for several major anniversaries," says Richard. "These include the CBI's 50th anniversary, the 750th anniversary of Parliament and The Queen's 90th Birthday Celebration at Windsor Castle. The Club's 60th anniversary sees us continue in this vein of celebrating landmark occasions, and we are very pleased to be launching this important book in the regal grandeur of Kensington Palace."

— www.stjamess.org

CREDITS

PUBLISHER

St James's House
(Regal Press Limited)
298 Regents Park Road
London
N3 2SZ
+44 (0)20 8371 4000
publishing@stjamess.org
www.stjamess.org

Richard Freed, **Director**
richard.freed@stjamess.org

Stephen Mitchell, **Head of Editorial**
stephen.mitchell@stjamess.org

Anna Danby, **Head of Creative**
anna.danby@stjamess.org

Images

Feadship (p.359), Getty, Alain Hamon (p.331),
Emile Holba (pp.198/9), Mike Jones – Waterline
Media (pp.392/3), Alex Peake (p.358), Rolls-Royce
Motor Cars Ltd, The Seeger Collection. Other images
are the copyright of individual organisations.

All information in this book is verified to the best
of the authors' and publisher's ability. However, Regal
Press Limited does not accept responsibility for any loss
arising from reliance on it. Where opinion is expressed,
it is that of the author or profiled organisation and does
not necessarily coincide with the editorial views of the
publisher. The publishers have made all reasonable
efforts to trace the copyright owners of the images
reproduced herein, and to provide an appropriate
acknowledgement in the book.

The inclusion of sponsor organisations in this
publication does not constitute an endorsement,
implied or otherwise, by the publisher or the Rolls-
Royce Enthusiasts' Club. Any readers wishing to
use the services of these organisations should take
up independent references in the normal manner.

ISBN: 978-1-906670-44-3

Printed by CPI Colour. This book has been printed
on BVS Silk by Scheufelen Paper. The paper has been
independently certified according to the rules of the
Forest Stewardship Council (FSC).

RREC CREDITS

RREC CONTENT

Jackie Robotham,
Publications Development Manager

Lindsay Robotham,
Publications Director

Rodney Lewis,
Publications and Production Consultant

Colin Hughes,
Presentation Consultant and Club Photographer

Gerard le Clerc,
International Correspondent for Publications

Editorial Team
David Towers, Christina Wild, Luca Hepburn

Publications Assistants
Sharon Carnell, Susie Swierczek, Mick Wetton,
Barbara Green, Emma Thomas

Contributors
Andrew Ball (Rolls-Royce Motor Cars Limited),
Lt Col Eric Barrass, Davide Bassoli, Stephanie-Rose
Bastock (Bentley Motors Limited), Roy Brooks,
John Fasal, Tony Flood, Isobel Haes, Philip Hall,
Colin Hughes, Eliot Levin, Jackie Robotham, David
Towers, Malcolm Tucker, Johan Vanden Bergh

Images
Bentley Motors Limited, Thomas Dinsdale
(RREC Photographer), Getty, Colin Hughes (RREC
Photographer), The Real Car Company Ltd, Rolls-
Royce Motor Cars Limited, Klaus-Josef Roßfeldt, the
RREC, Ruthless Images, Sir Henry Royce Memorial
Foundation, Rob Streeter. Other images are the
copyright of individual contributors or RREC members

The Rolls-Royce trademarks are trademarks of
Rolls-Royce Motor Cars Ltd and/or Rolls-Royce
PLC and are used under license.

Sources
*The Rolls-Royce Armoured Car: Its Substance and its
Place in History*. A Festschrift in memory of Lt Col Eric
Barrass and Mrs Grace Barrass. Historical Series
No. 48, edited by Eliot Levin

RREC HEADQUARTERS

Johan Vanden Bergh, Chairman
Ian Hick, Deputy Chairman
Barry Gallafent, Business Development Manager
Ailsa Plain, Events Manager
Lisa Alderson, Membership Secretary
Sharron Bland, Records Administrator
Vicky Bland, Club Shop
Philip Hall, Librarian
Sandra Harris, Office services
Linda Kerns, Receptionist/Administrator

RREC Board

Gerwald Anderle, Martin Carnell, Antony Channing,
Richard Fenner, Allan Fogg, Steve Lovatt, Lindsay
Robotham, Allan Rosetzsky

Rolls-Royce Enthusiasts' Club
The Hunt House, High Street
Paulerspury, Northamptonshire
NN12 7NA

Phone: +44 (0)1327 811788
Fax: +44 (0)1327 811797
Club Shop: +44 (0)1327 811489
admin@rrec.org.uk
www.rrec.org.uk